Between Stalin and Hitler

Little has been written on the history of the Second World War on the experience of collaboration and resistance of the Baltic States. The struggle between Nazism and communism was at its sharpest in Latvia, where Latvians were fighting in the Latvian SS Legion as well as in the Latvian Division of the Red Army, hence making it a civil war. Covering the horrors that took place in Latvia from the beginning of the Second World War until 1947, this book focuses on the heart of the twentieth century: Stalinist industrialisation, collectivisation and political annihilation; Nazi expansionism and genocide; with in addition local nationalism, local nationalist rivalries and local anti-Semitism. The author traces the developments in one particular region of Latvia, Daugavpils. There, the dilemma Hitler or Stalin, the ideological struggle of fascism or communism, was more acute than anywhere else in Europe since the population was actively involved in establishing both.

Geoffrey Swain graduated from the University of Sussex and studied for his PhD at the London School of Economics under the guidance of Professor Leonard Schapiro; his doctorate was published as *Russian Social Democracy and the Legal Labour Movement, 1906–14* (Macmillan, 1983). After working at University College, Cardiff and the Monitoring Service of the BBC, he settled at the then Bristol Polytechnic, today the University of the West of England, in 1984. He is now Professor of European History at the University of the West of England. His publications include *Eastern Europe since 1945* (with Nigel Swain, Palgrave Macmillan, 1993, 1998, 2003), *The Origins of the Russian Civil War* (Longman, 1996) and *Russia's Civil War* (Tempus, 2000). It was while working on the Russian Civil War, and the role played in it by Latvian riflemen units, that he first became interested in Latvian history.

Between Stalin and Hitler

Class war and race war
on the Dvina, 1940–46

Geoffrey Swain

RoutledgeCurzon
Taylor & Francis Group

LONDON AND NEW YORK

First published 2004 by
RoutledgeCurzon
2 Park Square, Milton Park, Abingdon, Oxon, OX14 4RN

Simultaneously published in the USA and Canada
by RoutledgeCurzon
270 Madison Ave, New York, NY 10016

RoutledgeCurzon is an imprint of the Taylor & Francis Group

© 2004 Geoffrey Swain

Typeset in Times by
Taylor & Francis Books Ltd

Printed and bound in Great Britain by
Antony Rowe Ltd, Chippenham, Wiltshire

British Library Cataloguing in Publication Data
A catalogue record for this book is available from the British Library

Library of Congress Cataloging in Publication Data
A catalog record for this title has been requested

ISBN 0–415–33193–5

To the resilient people of Daugavpils

Contents

Preface

This book is about the history during the Second World War of a small part of eastern Latvia along the northern bank of the river Dvina. Its subject is the city of Daugavpils and its surrounding countryside, the southern part of the region known as Latgale. Its wartime history of occupation by the Red Army, the German Army and the Red Army for a second time is both fascinating and horrific, but this book will have failed if all the reader gains is an understanding of the dramas faced by a small town in a country of which we know little. The purpose of this book is not just to chronicle genocide, deportation and civil war, but to see if a detailed case study can say something of interest about the nature of the two totalitarianisms which dominated the twentieth century. Daugavpils experienced both fascism and communism during the short period considered by this book, and a comparison of the city's rival administrations reveals both the self-destructive essence of fascism and the reasons for communism's surprising longevity.

It says a lot about Daugavpils in the middle years of the twentieth century that its history can be written by someone with only a very limited command of the Latvian language. Most of the documents used for this study were written in Russian and German, the languages of the occupying powers. By and large, these documents were located in Riga, but as well as frequent visits to Latvia's capital, and of course to Daugavpils itself, writing this book involved using archives in Berlin, London and Moscow. Academic globetrotting on such a scale involves incurring a number of debts, both financial and intellectual, and it is a pleasure to be able to acknowledge them.

The idea of writing a study of the Daugavpils during the years of the Second World War came to me not long after I first visited the town in 1995. However, it only became a real enterprise in 1999 when the Leverhulme Trust awarded me a grant to study 'Collaboration and Resistance in Daugavpils, Eastern Latvia'. This generous award enabled me to pay several visits to Latvia, and to employ a research assistant. Other visits to Riga and Daugavpils were supported by the British Academy, while the Moscow archives were made accessible with a grant from the Nuffield Foundation. The research trip to Berlin was supported by the History School of the University of the West of England. Finally, the Arts and Humanities

Research Board supported my study leave in 2002–3 which enabled *Between Stalin and Hitler: Class War and Race War on the Dvina, 1940–46* to be written up. To all these organisations, thanks.

My greatest personal debt is to Dima Olehnovičs. A graduate student at Daugavpils University, he was at first my paid Leverhulme research assistant, but soon became a friend, colleague and Daugavpils Man Friday, researching for me long after the Leverhulme money ceased. Without his help, the project would never have got off the ground. His greatest single contribution was to compile a translated digest of the Latvian language wartime press, but he also summarised the Russian language war-time press and collected invaluable material from the Moscow archives when he visited them. His wife Ilze deserves a special thanks for translating the frequent emails I was too lazy to write in Russian.

The support of Professor Iréna Saleniece has been of incalculable importance in this project. As head of the History Department at Daugavpils University when it began, she was keen to offer the department's co-operation, and the annual conference of the Humanities Faculty became a sounding board for me to present material as it emerged. She made helpful criticisms of the manuscript and discussions with her, and indeed her colleagues, have been invaluable in the evolution of my ideas. As important, however, was Professor Saleniece's hospitality, and that of her mother and late father. Each trip to Daugavpils became something to look forward to, and produced memories to treasure.

Two other Daugavpils residents have played an important part in this book, in different ways. Professor Iosif Šteiman unwittingly sparked my interest in war-time Daugavpils. I asked myself, if I had been a young Jewish student in 1940 Daugavpils, would I have supported the communists as he had done, and found myself answering 'probably'. He also helped enormously by agreeing to answer many questions and sharing with me the first manuscript version of his memoirs of those years, significantly fuller in certain respects than the later published version. Sergei Kuznetsov proved another great source of local knowledge. His publishing and historical journalism, which he always shared generously, have helped lighten some dark corners.

Although the staff at all the archives I visited proved extremely helpful, a special thanks is due to those running the reading room at the Latvian State Archive. They got used to my garbled language and hectic visits, producing the documents I needed far quicker than the rules allowed for.

Here in England, I must thank two people. My colleague at the University of the West of England, Dr Raingard Esser, gave freely of her time in helping with translations from German, and Matthew Kott, then a graduate student at Oxford, shared his detailed knowledge of contemporary Latvian history and historiography, as well as his language skills, shielding me from embarrassing errors and misconceptions. The errors which remain are my responsibility alone.

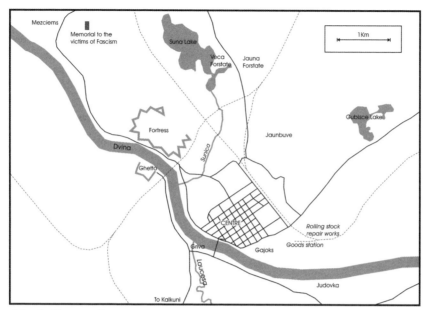

Map 1 Daugavpils

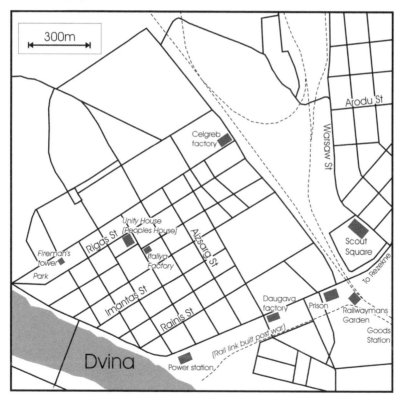

Map 2 Daugavpils centre

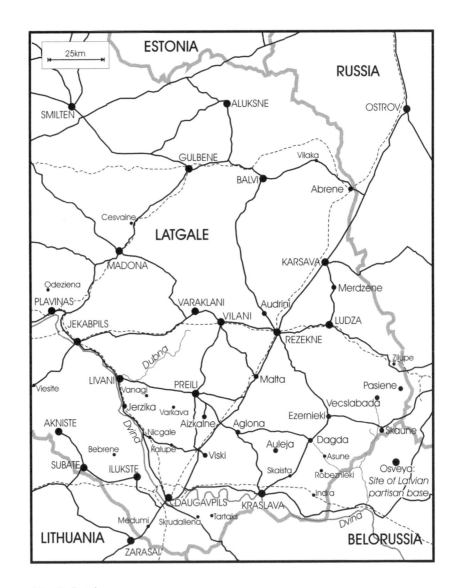

Map 3 Latvia

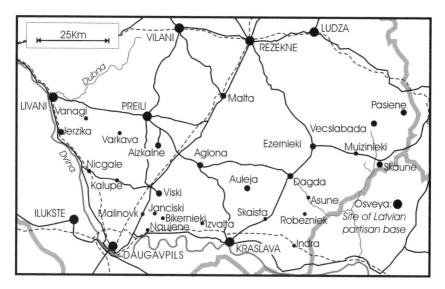

Map 4 Latvia close up

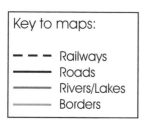

Key to maps:

- - - Railways
——— Roads
——— Rivers/Lakes
——— Borders

1 Introducing bourgeois Daugavpils

In summer 1936 two twelve-year-old boys left the volleyball court of the second Latvian primary school in Daugavpils; their names were Iosif Šteiman and Freds Blūzmanis. Despite the camaraderie of the sports field and happy memories of singing Latvian folk songs, these two boys were to have very different fates.[1] Iosif was the son of a left-wing teacher who had been dismissed from his job two years earlier for his membership of a Jewish teachers' union. Although Iosif was happy in his Latvian school, as he grew older he became interested in politics, more aware of the unequal treatment of the nationalities in 1930s Latvia, and began to associate with those linked to the communist-led Latvian League of Working Youth. By the time the Red Army occupied Latvia in June 1940, Iosif was committed to the communist cause and went on to become an active supporter of the Soviet regime. Freds was the son of a café owner on the main street in Daugavpils, Rainis Street. His father, Roberts Blūzmanis, had fascist sympathies, but until June 1941 kept his ideas to himself. When the Nazi occupation of Daugavpils began, he was among the first to come forward. His active involvement in the massacre of Jews was such that even the German authorities decided he should be put under arrest.

In summer 1942 two boys in their late teens were sitting sunbathing on the banks of the river Dvina near Daugavpils. One turned to the other and said: 'you are really no different from any other guy.' The speaker, recorded simply as Otto, was a young German corporal from the Sudetenland, glad that military service for him meant nothing more terrifying than painting a building occupied by the *Luftwaffe*. The teenager who was 'really not so different' was Shaike Iwensky, a Jew from the small Lithuanian settlement of Jonava, near Kaunas, who had fled to Daugavpils as the German Army advanced in June 1941, only to be captured and interned in the ghetto; he was helping to paint the *Luftwaffe* building, because in the language of the time, he was a 'skilled Jew'. Shaike, or Sidney as he became known in an American afterlife, was one of a handful of Jews who survived the Daugavpils ghetto. The fate of Otto has remained unknown.[2]

This book is about the ideological struggle between communism and fascism, which dominated the middle years of the twentieth century and destroyed such human moments as a game of volleyball or a sunbathe on the river bank. It is a case study of the town of Daugavpils and the surrounding region, to the north of the river Dvina in eastern Latvia. It is an area where the ideological struggle between fascism and communism produced almost unimaginable horrors. In the year of Soviet rule, 17 June 1940 to 22 June 1941, Daugavpils experienced all the economic and political pressures which Soviet Russia had taken two decades to digest. Then, on 14 June 1941, on Stalin's orders, the communist authorities in Daugavpils transported to Siberia a thousand citizens of Daugavpils and the surrounding towns and villages; all were deemed to be remnants of the old bourgeois social order whose reliability was under question in the event of a German attack. That attack came and in July and August 1941, and again in November 1941 and May 1942, implementing Hitler's call for a war of extermination against 'Jewish Bolshevism', at least 13,000 Jews were killed in Daugavpils and a further 7,000 in Latgale as a whole; according to the 1935 census, 11,106 Jews lived in Daugavpils. Then, in actions which took place in May 1942 and August 1943, 11,500 members of the Russian community of the Daugavpils region were deported to Germany.

The targeting of the Russian population for deportation was as much an initiative of the Latvian collaborationist administration as its Nazi overseers. It prompted counter-measures. Members of the Latvian Communist Party, smuggled across the front line from Soviet territory, where they had fled before the Nazi advance, found the families of Russian deportees the most willing to resist, joining Soviet partisan units in operations against the Latvian security units formed by the Nazis. By summer 1943 Soviet partisans were active in the forests and marshes, fighting what was effectively a civil war against German-sponsored Latvian forces. By spring 1944 the Soviet partisans had broadened their appeal from the Russian population to large sections of the Latvian population, anxious to avoid conscription to what was by then a clearly doomed collaborationist army. Yet German retreat did not end this civil war. The return of the Red Army in July 1944 prompted Latvian nationalists to launch their own guerrilla war against the new communist authorities. The forests and marshes, once the home of Soviet partisans, now provided bases for nationalist partisans, whose assaults on the symbols of communist rule were as brutal as those of the Soviet partisans on Nazi rule. Thus the civil war which started in 1943 only ended in 1946.[3]

Deportations, genocide, years of civil strife – why was it that a community based in a historic town amongst beautiful rolling countryside should have visited on it every extreme of the twentieth century in the course of just six years? As Marxists used to say, this was not accidental. There were good reasons related to international and domestic politics which explain why the global struggle between fascism and communism was particularly acute on the river Dvina.

International diplomacy and the Baltic States

Towards the end of the 1930s Soviet diplomacy took an increasing
in the Baltic States. This was quite understandable. Hitler had made cl
ability to use the existence of minority German populations to exten
boundaries of his Third Reich. In March 1938 he had annexed Austria, ،nen
in September 1938 it had been the turn of the Sudetenland. In March 1939
the Czech lands fell, and over summer 1939 the campaign against Danzig
and Poland began. It was quite obvious that, if Hitler got his way in Poland,
he could then raise the 'plight' of the German communities in the Baltic
area to obtain territory ever nearer Leningrad and the cradle of the communist revolution. It was for this reason that, when the Soviet Union discussed
with Britain and France in spring 1939 the possibility of joint action in the
event of future German aggression, the question of the Baltic States kept
surfacing. The protracted negotiations between Britain, France and the
Soviet Union reached one of their many crisis points at the end of June 1939
when Moscow cited the refusal of Britain and France to include the Baltic
States in any future security arrangement as proof that they were not interested in an agreement based on equality.

In this row the British point was that the Baltic States did not want to be
guaranteed by the Soviet Union. The Soviet point was that the interest of
world peace required that certain states had to be guaranteed whether they
liked it or not. In the end, the British backed down on this key matter and
accepted that any guarantee concerning the Baltic States could be covered
by a secret protocol, a protocol which would allow the deployment of Soviet
forces to the Baltic States to prevent German aggression. The talks between
Britain, France and the Soviet Union to guarantee Europe against German
aggression did not break down because of the issue of deploying the Red
Army in the Baltic States without the agreement of the governments of the
Baltic States, but because of the refusal of the British and French to open
serious military talks with the Soviet side. It was this which prompted Stalin
to explore the German hint of early August 1939 that there was no problem
'from the Baltic to the Black Sea' which could not be resolved. When the
Soviet–German Non-Aggression Pact was signed on 23 August 1939, its
secret protocol gave Stalin what he wanted, and what the British too had
been prepared to give him: the Baltic as his sphere of influence.[4]

Hitler did not abandon the Baltic Germans. Having made the Baltic
States a Soviet sphere the Baltic Germans were no longer a potential fifth
column for expansion into the Baltic area, but potential hostages, when
Hitler staged his long-planned assault on Stalin's Soviet Union. So on 6
October 1939 he made a speech in the Reichstag urging the Baltic Germans
to return to the homeland where they could be resettled in newly occupied
Poland. In the case of Latvia, an agreement was signed on 30 October 1939
and most of the Latvian Germans had left the land of their birth by 15
December. A trickle of departures continued until May 1940, by which time

53,000 people had left. After the Soviet occupation of Latvia in June 1940 the remaining 11,000 Germans were forcibly transferred to their homeland between January and March 1941.

Hitler's rapid victory over Poland in September 1939 prompted Stalin to clarify what was meant by a sphere of influence. First he agreed with Hitler that Lithuania should be included in the August deal, and then explained to the governments of the three Baltic States that they had no choice but to accept non-aggression pacts with the Soviet Union which guaranteed the Red Army bases in their countries. These arrangements were signed and sealed in Latvia's case on 5 October 1939 under an agreement whereby 30,000 Red Army troops were stationed in the country. Stalin stood by his promise not to intervene in the internal affairs of the Baltic States until France's rapid collapse in May 1940. With Hitler free to turn eastwards, diplomatic incidents were duly staged between the Soviet Union and all three Baltic States to prove that the existing governments there were incapable of living up to the commitments made in the non-aggression pacts with the Soviet Union; the Soviet Union therefore claimed the right to deploy unlimited forces in each country and form governments more sympathetic to the Soviet Union. On 17 June the Red Army marched into Latvia and three days later a People's Government was formed.

Inter-war Latvia

If international diplomacy explained why both Hitler and Stalin had an interest in the Baltic States in 1939–40, domestic reasons within Latvia explained why that interest should have prompted so many horrors in Daugavpils. However, to understand what happened in Daugavpils, it is first necessary to clarify the situation in Latvia as a whole. When the Soviet Union intervened in Latvian politics on 17 June 1940 it maintained it was doing so to establish a People's Government more willing to act in co-operation with the Soviet government than its predecessor. What was the nature of the Latvian government overthrown in this way?

Like many of the new states formed from the collapse of the Russian, Austro-Hungarian and Turkish Empires at the end of the First World War, Latvia's first years of independence were dramatic. The First World War ended on 11 November 1918 and at once nationalist politicians in Latvia made contact with the victorious British. Although the defeated German forces remained in Latvia under the terms of the Armistice to maintain order, nationalist politicians in Riga felt confident enough to declare Latvia an independent state on 18 November 1918, something the Germans recognised a week later. They were emboldened to act in this way because a Royal Navy ship sailed into Riga bay to fly the flag and ensure that the German forces knew where they stood. However, again under the terms of the Armistice, the German forces withdrew at the end of December 1918 and as they left pro-Soviet armed units marched into the country from Russia in January 1919.

These pro-Soviet forces were the so-called Latvian Riflemen. During the First World War, when the Eastern Front had stabilised across what is today Latvia, the Russian Tsar decided that the formation of specifically Latvian units might stiffen the resolve of his army to retreat no further. To a degree the tactic worked. The Latvian Riflemen fought determinedly over Christmas 1916 to hold a German offensive in check, but with the overthrow of the Tsar and the revolutionary chaos of 1917 they eventually retreated, surrendering Riga in August 1917. However, when Lenin's revolutionary government held elections to the Constituent Assembly in November 1917, the Latvian Riflemen still controlled parts of northern Latvia, and in those areas the election brought victory to the Latvian Bolsheviks, who declared that Latvia would be part of a new Soviet federation with Russia. This state was never established, because history moved on. Before any sort of Soviet federation could be formed, Lenin had been forced by the Germans to sign the Treaty of Brest Litovsk in March 1918, and under that treaty the whole of Latvia was occupied by the Germans. The Latvian Bolsheviks and the Latvian Riflemen retreated to Russia for the duration of the German occupation, but when they returned in January 1919 they denounced the nationalists' 18 November declaration of independence as null and void and insisted that they had a mandate to reconstitute the Soviet federation of 1917, planned but never implemented.

This ushered in the five-month rule of the Latvian Soviet Republic. The ruling Latvian Bolsheviks quickly alienated the popular support they had once had by forcing through an agrarian policy which antagonised almost every Latvian peasant. Arguing dogmatically that Marx had condemned peasant agriculture as petty bourgeois, instead of introducing a land reform which gave land to individual peasants, the Latvian Bolsheviks forced peasants to join a small number of large socially owned farms, surrendering to these farms all their livestock and property. When peasants resisted, terror began. It was a black episode in Latvia's history, saddling the Latvian Bolsheviks with a reputation both for terror and antipathy towards peasant farmers; it also set Latvia on the road to a short but very bloody civil war. By May 1919 the Latvian Bolsheviks had been driven from Riga, but they retained control of parts of Latgale, eastern Latvia, including the Daugavpils area, until the end of 1919. In spring 1920 Lenin decided that the survival of Soviet Russia was more important than the fate of the Latvian Bolsheviks, and negotiations began between Soviet Russia and the Latvian nationalists which resulted in a treaty being signed by the two states on 1 August 1920.

Internationally recognised, the new Latvian state held a constituent assembly in May 1920, adopted a constitution in February 1922 and elected its first parliament in October of that year. In many ways this was a model democracy. The constitution granted clear rights to the German, Jewish and Russian minorities, and gave executive powers to parliament rather than the president. It was not dissimilar to the constitution of Weimar Germany, and, like that constitution, had weaknesses as well as strengths for it produced a plethora of small parties and operated in a political culture of hostility to the social democrats. In parliamentary Latvia the Communist Party was banned; it continued to hanker after the formation of a Soviet federation with Bolshevik Russia and thus questioned the legitimacy of the existing state. The Latvian Social Democratic Party, the biggest single party for most of the parliamentary period, was seen by many on the right to be little better than the Communist Party; it shared the same origins and its programme of social spending and co-operation with Soviet Russia seemed to many like betrayal. An important role in cultivating this nationalist hostility to the political left was played by the *aizsarg* organisation. This paramilitary local defence force had its origins in Latvia's short civil war, but continued to be state funded after the war was over as a sort of volunteer Home Guard. Latvian governments, therefore, tended to be anti-social democrat alliances of a wide-range of disparate parties led by the Peasant Union, the second biggest party; the Social Democrats only led a coalition government from December 1926 to January 1928. Parliamentary Latvia, like Weimar Germany, was politically unstable.

Hitler's assumption of power in Germany in January 1933 and the over-throw of democracy in Austria in February 1934 set a new yardstick of authoritarian rule in central Europe. Kārlis Ulmanis, the leader of the Peasant Union and one of those who had declared Latvia's independence in November 1918, decided to mimic the new trend. Appointed prime minister in March 1934, he proposed to parliament a law which would have greatly strengthened the powers of the president, allowing him to dissolve parliament. When parliament rejected this proposal, he carried out a coup on 15–16 May 1934 with the support of the paramilitary nationalist *aizsarg* organisation. His authoritarian rule lasted until the formation of the People's Government in June 1940. The Ulmanis regime is hard to cate-gorise. He suspended the 1922 constitution, closed parliament and arrested all those deputies he felt would protest. He banned all political parties, including his own. He banned all independent trade unions. He encouraged state involvement in industry through a sort of corporate state which had 'chambers' for the various branches of the economy and professions, and an officially sanctioned trade union organisation. He encouraged the notion of 'Latvia for the Latvians', interfering in the ownership of some firms owned by members of Latvia's national minorities. And yet he was not anti-semitic. One of his friends was Mordecai Dubin, the former leader of the Jewish reli-gious party Agudat Israel. The motivating force of his politics was hostility to the left. Some 2,000 social democrats were arrested during the coup and 400 of them detained for as long as a year.

And the left continued to oppose him. The left wing of the banned Social Democratic Party immediately formed a new underground Socialist Worker Peasant Party of Latvia and in November 1936, in line with the popular-front strategy of the Communist International, this party and the Latvian

Communist Party agreed a strategy of joint co-operation in the struggle to restore democracy. The first fruits of this was the merging of the youth wings of the parties to form the Latvian League of Working Youth, but in practice the Latvian Communist Party was very unenthusiastic about co-operating with its socialist allies, so much so that the Communist International declared it infested with Trotskyism and instigated a purge so vigorous that the party almost collapsed; the purge of those party members living in the Soviet Union resulted in death and exile for many formally prominent figures. The outbreak of the Second World War complicated the prospects for co-operation between the illegal socialist and communist organisations. To some socialists it seemed that the Nazi–Soviet Pact had discredited the anti-fascist credentials of the Communist Party, but by spring 1940 the communists had reassured the socialists of their determination to resist Hitler and in March 1940 the socialists signalled their willingness to forge closer relations with the communists when they resolved to break off contacts with the Socialist International and called for the merger of socialists and communists into a new united workers' party.

Such co-operation was vital. The economic consequences of the Second World War were having an impact on the Latvian economy which suggested a revival in labour unrest might be possible. Ulmanis's *dirigiste* policies, and the recovery of the world economy, had virtually eliminated unemployment by the end of the 1930s; but the dislocation in trade which followed the outbreak of fighting had forced many employers to introduce short-time working. In this situation the communists had had some success in re-establishing factory cells in autumn 1939 and spring 1940. The communists and socialists co-ordinated their plans for May Day 1940, and at the end of April there were anti-Ulmanis street demonstrations. The regime's response, the arrest of over 300 alleged communists, made clear that the left would have been quite incapable of over-throwing Ulmanis without the intervention of the Red Army.

Daugavpils: the town on the Dvina

Daugavpils is situated on the river Dvina, the Russian name for the river which the Germans call the Düna and the Latvians call the Daugava. Two things make the city worthy of study in its own right. First, Daugavpils itself, and the Latgale region as a whole, are extremely mixed ethnically. According to the 1935 census, Jews made up 29.9 per cent of the population of Latgale and 24.6 per cent of the population of Daugavpils. Latvians comprised only 33.5 per cent of the population of Daugavpils, with Russians making up 18 per cent and Poles and Belorussians the rest.[5] Second, there is its social composition. It is a major industrial city, second only to Riga, with a large working-class population. It is situated at the heart of Latgale, Latvia's poorest agricultural region. It was therefore excellent breeding ground for the Latvian Communist Party, which saw itself as the natural party of the industrial working class and poor peasantry.

Daugavpils was founded as Dünaburg in 1275 by German crusading knights based in Riga. It was initially situated on a bluff overlooking the river Dvina, a perfect position from which to defend the crusaders' hinterland, but not a good site for the more peaceful business of trade. By the end of the sixteenth century the heirs of the German crusader knights no longer had political control so far up the Dvina valley and the town had been incorporated into the kingdom of Poland, becoming the administrative centre of the province of Inflantia and a centre of trade along the river Dvina. As such it made sense to move the town ten miles down river to a less hilly position. Daugavpils remained part of Poland until 1772 when, under the first partition of Poland, Inflantia, or Latgale as it came to be called, was incorporated into the Russian Empire of Catherine the Great. Until 1778 Daugavpils headed its own short-lived Daugavpils Province, but from then until the 1917 Revolution Daugavpils was first part of the Polotsk Province of the Russian Empire and after 1802 part of Vitebsk Province.

During the Napoleonic Wars, the strategic importance of Daugavpils prompted Catherine's successors to construct a huge fortress there. Started in 1811, it was not finally deemed to be complete until 1833 when Tsar Nicholas I attended the official opening. However, what really brought prosperity to the town were the railways, which equally focused on Daugavpils because of its strategic position. Daugavpils was the place where the Petersburg to Warsaw railway crossed the line linking Riga, with its ports and industrial processing, to the coal and steel reserves of south-east Russia. Daugavpils became the Swindon of the Russian Empire, a centre for railway construction and repair. The railway network attracted other industries, in particular textiles. At the height of this end-of-the-century boom, in 1893, the town was renamed Dvinsk. As the city grew, the settlement of Grīva, on the southern side of the river, gradually became less of a separate town in a separate region and more of a suburb of the city, although it remained administratively separate.

During the First World War the town suffered terribly. In 1914 the population had stood at 112,837, but the German advance meant that much of its industry and population were evacuated eastwards, and many people never returned to a city which had become part of independent Latvia. Renamed Daugavpils, the city on the Daugava, in 1920 the population gradually stabilised at approximately 30,000 and, as the decade progressed, grew; by 1935 there were 45,160 inhabitants, including 4,168 soldiers of the Latvian Army stationed in the fortress.[6] Ulmanis visited Daugavpils shortly after his coup, in August 1934, and decided that a physical symbol was needed to unite the town's diverse ethnic groups around the principle of Latvia for the Latvians. He agreed that the Daugavpils Latvian Society, to which most local worthies of Latvian ethnicity belonged, should construct a massive new public edifice. It would be built on Market Square, which would be renamed Unity Square, and the edifice, once completed, was named Unity House. Under Ulmanis there were no elected local officials, only government appointees, and the government-appointed Daugavpils city elder duly sold the Daugavpils Latvian Society the necessary land for the purely nominal sum of ten lats, the lat being the Latvian currency. The Daugavpils Latvian Society then launched a public appeal and raised the 10,000 lats needed to construct a classic example of 1930s monumentalist architecture which contained a library, a theatre, a swimming pool, a public bath, a restaurant and a club for the *aizsargs*.[7] Unity House opened in 1938.

The ethnic picture

The fact that by the sixteenth century Daugavpils and Latgale had moved from the control of the heirs of the crusader knights to become part of Poland had two dramatic consequences. First, Daugavpils experienced the Reformation and Counter-Reformation in a distinctive manner. At that time the Grīva side of the river had been part of the Dukedom of Kurland, where Protestant landowners had grown rich on the lands sequestrated from the church. However, Daugavpils itself and the province of Inflantia, Latgale, became a centre of Catholicism. In the heart of Daugavpils stood a Jesuit college which was only moved from the city when construction work began on the fortress. While other Latvians became Lutheran Protestants, Latgale Latvians became fervent Catholics, many making an annual pilgrimage to the Marian shrine at Aglona. This had an impact on the political life of the region. While the Protestant Church took little interest in politics, the Catholic Church was extremely active. Although the name of the party it created changed three times during Latvia's time as a parliamentary republic, the Catholics of Latgale were given clear instructions which way they should vote.[8]

Second, being part of Poland brought Daugavpils and Latgale a large Russian population. This paradox had its origins in a long-running theological dispute within the Russian Orthodox Church which ended in schism in 1667. In the 1650s the leader of the Russian Orthodox Church, Patriarch Nikon, had introduced a series of reforms into the liturgy. To believers, some of these had a deep significance, such as the decision that the sign of the cross had to be made with three not two fingers. However, behind these outward symbols, there was a political motive to the reforms, that of strengthening the power and authority of the patriarchate, the central church authorities, whose members started to destroy icons and other religious symbols deemed to be contrary to the reforms. Nikon's policies sparked an understandable reaction, led by Archpriest Avvakum. His supporters were both radical and reactionary. They were intensely conservative in that they rejected all the reforms to the liturgy, but equally extremely radical in that they rejected the authority of the patriarch, arguing that authority came only from Christ who could communicate directly with His people. When these Old Believers were expelled from the Orthodox Church in 1667, they formed their own communities which rejected all hierarchy and allowed communities to appoint their own priests. Soon there were open rebellions, followed by severe repressions, as Old Believer peasants became involved in unrest more akin to rural anarchism than religious observance.[9] To escape from repression, many Old Believers fled. At first some settled in the Dukedom of Kurland, on the Grīva side of the river Dvina, but eventually more settled in Poland, or more precisely throughout its Inflantia province, Latgale, the region lying closest to Russia.

By the time Catherine the Great incorporated Latgale into the Russian Empire the persecution of the Old Believers had abated. Indeed, Catherine offered Old Believers a compromise: they could keep their separate liturgy so long as they acknowledged the hierarchy of the established church. How many accepted this offer is not known, but the Old Believer communities of Latgale incorporated into the Russian Empire by Catherine were left in peace. By 1935 the Old Believer community in Daugavpils comprised 11 per cent of the population.[10] However, incorporation into the Russian Empire brought a new wave of Russian immigration to Daugavpils, both as administrators and, once the railways came, industrial workers. This meant the establishment of new Russian Orthodox communities, to which a small number of Latvians converted. In Latgale there were 90,700 Orthodox and 78,600 Old Believers in 1935.[11]

Jews began to settle in Latgale in the early seventeenth century when a series of pogroms elsewhere in Poland prompted families to move to the fringes of the kingdom. By the beginning of the eighteenth century Daugavpils had a recognisable community of Jewish traders, innkeepers, craftsmen and estate managers. The traders and craftsmen were welcomed by the local population, but innkeepers and particularly estate managers were often seen as oppressors and exploiters. By 1772 and the First Partition of Poland there were under 5,000 Jews in Latgale. From 1794 to 1804 the Tsarist government defined a Pale of Settlement where Jews were allowed to live, and Latgale, unlike the rest of Latvia, was part of the Pale. Although a tiny number of Latgale Jews entered government service and a similar number took up farming, the vast majority were classified as merchants or petty-bourgeois craftsmen. As Daugavpils grew, so did its Jewish population. If in 1847 there were nearly 3,000 Jews, by 1897 there were over 30,000. In 1865 they formed 38.6 per cent of the population and by 1913 49.3 per cent.[12] However, during the First World War Jews left Daugavpils in vast numbers. This was partly the result of Tsarist policies which questioned the loyalty of the Jewish population and expelled them from frontline zones. In 1920 the Jewish population of Daugavpils stood at 11,000 rising to 12,000 by 1925.[13]

How did these diverse communities get along once Latvia had become an independent state? Certainly not all Russians welcomed the formation of an independent Latvian state, but those with such reservations tended to adopt a wait-and-see approach. No Russians took part in Latvia's declaration of independence, but many fought against Latvia's Soviet regime and went on to support the work of the constituent assembly. Nevertheless, only 13 per cent of Daugavpils's Russian population could speak Latvian, suggesting a sense of discomfort with the new regime. Russian turn out in elections was low, and among the rural population illiteracy was as high as 66.9 per cent, with the numbers speaking Latvian even lower than in Daugavpils. Those Russians who did participate in political life tended to vote along confessional lines, with the result that the plethora of parties diluted Russian representation. Meletii Kalistratov, an Old Believer with decidedly leftist views, was the most colourful figure to emerge from the two Russian communities of Daugavpils; he was elected to all four parliaments.[14]

The Jews participated enthusiastically in the political process, but class alliances had a similar impact to that of confessional differences among the Russian communities. The pro-labour Bund was linked to the Latvian Social Democratic Party and favoured the development of Yiddish; the various Zionist groups favoured the use of Hebrew and this dispute, which concentrated on schooling, weakened the impact of the Jewish vote on political life. Despite their involvement in both national and local politics, many Jews felt there existed something akin to a glass ceiling which kept them apart from full participation in the life of the country. Anti-semitism was non-aggressive, but there. Jews could not become army officers nor take up state jobs, including jobs on the railways, a particular issue in Daugavpils; informal restrictions existed in certain faculties of the University of Latvia. In 1925 there were only 21 Jewish civil servants, two Jewish postal workers and one Jewish policeman. And, when Ulmanis began to bring 'alien' firms under Latvian control, this often meant buying out Jewish owners.[15]

And yet, despite the fact that many Russians felt alienated from the Latvian state and that many Jews felt it discriminated against them, Daugavpils experienced little in the way of ethnic tension in the 1930s. Trade and industry tended to be the preserve of the Jews and Russians, while the state administrators tended to be Latvians and to a lesser extent Poles. Right-wing groups operated amongst the national minorities as well as the Latvian population. Polish nationals existed, as well as Zionists and 'White Guard' Russians, but by and large there was little trouble. Iosif Šteiman recalled few fights between youngsters of different ethnic groups, but equally that there was little intermarriage. There were cases where Russian men married Latvian women, as in the case of Ivan Muzykantik, a future Soviet partisan, but when a Latvian army officer married a Jewish woman there was scandal as the officer's parents pressurised him, in the end successfully, to instigate divorce proceedings.[16] Daugavpils was not on the edge of an explosion of ethnic violence at the end of the 1930s, but there were plenty of issues which those people committed to the policies of ethnic violence could exploit.

The social picture

The social position of Daugavpils also gave plenty of opportunities to those politicians committed to the idea of transforming society. The whole of Latgale was distinctly less developed than the rest of Latvia. In 1925 only 44 per cent of the population could read and half of the children aged 8–14 did not attend school. The agricultural reform of the 1920s unfolded far more slowly in Latgale than in the rest of the country and in a way that discriminated against the region, issues regularly taken up in the parliament by one of Latgale's most prominent Catholic deputies Francis Trasuns. The result was that land holdings in Latgale were far smaller than in the rest of the country: in Latgale 62 per cent of the population lived on holdings of under ten hectares, whereas in the rest of the country the figure was 22 per cent. This produced rural overpopulation: at the start of the 1930s in Latgale there were 50 inhabitants per 100 hectares compared to 28 in the rest of the country.[17] Few Latgale peasants supported Ulmanis's Peasant Union, seen by them as representing only well-to-do farmers.[18]

Inter-war Daugavpils was not the thriving city it had been at the turn of the century. In 1912 there were 2,210 industrial and commercial enterprises, including 100 big enough to be termed factories. As well as the railway repair yards there were factories producing leather goods, cigarettes, matches and chocolates.[19] Many of these closed after the First World War, including the factories producing leather goods and cigarettes, but the city did gain two important textile plants, the *Daugava* and *Italia*, and the rolling-stock repair works continued to operate, if at a reduced scale. By 1938 there were 17 large factories employing in all 1,663 workers and 80 smaller plants employing another 2,498. Until the Ulmanis coup this proletariat was organised into a number of trade unions linked to the Social Democratic Party, and from 1935 an officially sponsored Daugavpils Workers' Trade Union continued to operate. The combination of this working class and the surrounding poor peasantry enabled the Latgale Region of the Latvian Communist Party to become second only in size to the Riga party organisation, representing in 1930 40 per cent of the total membership.[20]

When the Red Army entered Latvia on 17 June 1940 the communists in Daugavpils had been reduced to a tiny rump. However, a decade earlier they had played a noticeable role in the life of the city. In January 1928 Latvia's only Social Democrat- led government collapsed. A couple of months later its successor decided to regain control of public expenditure by closing down some of the job-creation schemes launched by the Social Democrats. One of these concerned Daugavpils, and the government's action prompted a widespread labour protest. In preparations for the national elections due in 1928, the communists had established a front organisation known as the Independent Socialist Party; its leading figure in Daugavpils was Leonid Ershov, who used the job-creation protest to win a majority of the working-class vote for the Independent Socialist Party in the local elections on 11–12 August. Success bred success, and on 22 August the communists organised a protest strike involving a quarter of the Daugavpils workforce to condemn government proposals to limit unemployment benefit. In the national elections on 6–7 October Ershov was elected to one of the Latgale seats in parliament, joining the communist worker–peasant fraction.

There was more unrest in 1929. Some of those who participated in the demonstration of 22 August 1928 had been arrested, and their trial took place on 25 May 1929. They were condemned to terms of imprisonment ranging from three months to seven years, and a furious crowd mobbed the court room and then followed the condemned to Daugavpils prison, situated near the centre of the city, where they held another demonstration which was dispersed by the army. There was more unrest later in the year. The Latvian state had inherited the social-insurance laws adopted by revolutionary Russia in 1917. These meant that social-insurance funds were administered by committees elected by the workforce. Over the summer of 1929 the government tried to reform the system to ensure that employers too were represented on these committees. A one-day protest strike on 18 October forced the government to back down, temporarily. This was a turning point in the fate of the Latvian Communist Party. Like every other communist party it was loyal to the rulings of the Communist International Executive. As the decisions of the Sixth Congress of the Communist International Executive began to be implemented, Daugavpils communists were instructed to denounce the Social Democrats with as much ferocity as the 'bourgeois' government which was steadily undermining the workers' rights. When Ershov addressed 800 striking workers on 18 October he denounced the Social Democrats for not turning the one-day strike into a general strike and sang a peon of praise for the Soviet Union. This assault on the Social Democrats led the Latvian Communist Party further and further from contact with the working class and deeper and deeper into the morass of sectarian introspection.[21]

Nevertheless, the unrest at the end of the 1920s brought to the fore labour leaders who would still be active in 1940. One of those elected to the city council in 1928 was Nikolai Yukhno. His younger brother Mikhail Yukhno quickly joined him as a party organiser taking an active part in some of the spring 1929 demonstrations, only to be arrested in 1930. Further spells in prison followed, but in 1937 it fell to Mikhail to reconstruct the party in Daugavpils after Moscow's decision to purge it of 'Trotskyites'. He later recalled that it had been quite a task to persuade those comrades who had enjoyed seeing communist action as little more than shouting abuse at Social Democrats that the popular-front tactic was aimed at re-establishing the party's links with the working class. To counter such resistance, in 1938 he brought back into the heart of the party those who had cut their political teeth in 1928, like the boiler-maker Kazimir Lazdovskii, who had been active on the city council with Nikolai Yukhno and Ershov. When Mikhail

Yukhno was arrested in 1939, his place was taken by the local Jewish activist Faifish Fridman, who continued Yukhno's policies. The less sectarian leadership chalked up some successes in the first few months of 1940. In March the Latgale Regional Conference was held in Daugavpils, and later the same month one branch of the Latvian League of Working Youth in Daugavpils voted to affiliate to the Communist International, even though there were several active socialists in the branch.[22] Without the help of the Red Army, the communists in Daugavpils would not have emerged from the underground, but they could count on popular memory of labour unrest when it came to looking for working-class support, even if the communists had done much to squander that support during the sectarian years.

The Red Army arrives

On 17 June 1940 the Red Army occupied Latvia and the social transformation of Daugavpils began. This was no spontaneous revolution – contemporaries never claimed it was[23] – but the changes which occurred were nonetheless revolutionary.

Although there had been Red Army units based in parts of Latvia since the mutual assistance treaty of 5 October 1939, it was the coastal regions which were affected. No troops were based in Daugavpils, and, ironically, when the Red Army arrived in the city it came from bases to the west, not the east. In Daugavpils on 17 June there was none of the violence which characterised the events of that day in Riga, where two workers were killed and 29 injured in clashes between the police and pro-Soviet demonstrators. There was no violence and a crowd, numbering no more than 300, some no doubt out of sheer curiosity, responded to the communist appeal and waved as the Red Army arrived from the Grīva side of the river Dvina, crossed the bridge into the city and passed along the embankment out to a temporary base at Stropi in the forests to the north of the city.

The Latgale organisation of the Latvian Communist Party was in a poor state to respond to the new situation, despite its partial revival in early 1940. As it emerged from underground in June 1940 there were only twenty Latgale communists firmly linked to the Central Committee. Not surprisingly they had had their work cut out just to organise a welcome for the Red Army.[24] Over the night of 16–17 June, at the underground print works at 65 Arodu Street in the Daugavpils industrial suburb of Jaunbūve, party activists were working on what would be the last illegal issue of their newspaper *Latgal'skaya Pravda*. Then, at 5.00 a.m. there was a knock on the door and the young communist activist Meier Deich burst in with the news that the Red Army was on its way; he had with him the text of a leaflet which he had been instructed was to be printed there and then. Thereafter, at hourly intervals batches of the leaflet were to be distributed around the town. This leaflet, issued in the name of the Latgale Regional Committee, explained that the deployment of the Red Army was taking place under the terms of the Latvian–Soviet Mutual Assistance Treaty and that it would create favourable conditions for the overthrow of the hated Ulmanis fascist clique. Citizens were called on to welcome the Red Army and join in the active struggle against fascism, bringing that struggle to a successful conclusion.[25]

The Red Army was greeted with some enthusiasm by parts of the Russian and Jewish communities. Some among the Russian population even looked forward to the social upheaval its presence would bring. One recalled more than 60 years after the event: 'we were very pleased [to see the Red Army come], we no longer had to work for the boss, nor did our children; we were pleased.' Asked if there were any Russians who did not welcome the Red Army, the reply came: 'No I do not know anyone ... for we were all the same, we were poor.'[26] As to the Jews, those few who survived recalled that they welcomed the Red Army. Although young left-wing intellectuals took the lead, ordinary Jews also welcomed the Red Army.[27] In Viļāni Jewish youths forcibly prevented members of the local *aizsargs* from firing at the Red Army tanks as the entered the town. [28]

The police carefully observed the demonstration welcoming the Red Army, took photographs of some of the leading participants, and the following day several arrests were made, prompting some communist activists to flee to the forest,[29] for throughout Daugavpils there were widespread arrests of known communists.[30] There were other acts of revenge on 18 June; the 8th company of the 11th regiment of the Latvian Army patrolled the streets of Daugavpils and beat up a dozen or so sympathisers of the new order.[31] Such incidents were not untypical. On the day the Red Army arrived in Daugavpils some of the inhabitants of the small settlement of Prekulevka, on the Grīva side of the river, had welcomed the troops by painting red symbols on their houses. On the 18th a lorry load of soldiers and policemen, led by the Grīva police commander, arrived and beat up the inhabitants of those houses with red symbols including women and children; when they returned the following day they found the whole adult population had fled to the woods.[32] Members of the Jewish community feared an old-fashioned pogrom and closed their shops in anticipation.[33] In the surrounding countryside there were similar clashes.

In the village of Višķi Jānis Skromanis, a railway worker and one of the few Latvians in the underground communist party, joined other communist activists in a clash with local *aizsargs* on 17 June. At first they disarmed them, but on the 18th *aizsarg* reinforcements were sent out from Daugavpils; they first broke up a peasant meeting being organised in Biķernieki and then moved on to arrest Skromanis and the other Višķi communists, transferring them to Daugavpils prison. At Grāveri, between Aglona and Krāslava, a meeting to mark the 'liberation' ended in violence. Participants were beaten up by two cavalry squadrons called out to keep order, who then called on the support of 40 armed *aizsarsi* from Daugavpils who took over from the troops and occupied the administration offices, placing a machine gun on the balcony outside.[34] Further afield Dominiks Kaupužs, a long-term underground party activist, who had spent four years training in the Soviet Union and four years in a Latvian prison, recalled that his comrades had been unable to contact the party leadership and so had been forced to act on their own. During the night of 16–17 June before the Red Army was fully deployed, they had begun to disarm *aizsargs* in Kārsava parish. However, on the 18th, the activists found themselves confronted by officers from the 8th and 9th companies of the Rēzekne infantry regiment which had been reinforced by squads of police and intelligence officers from Rēzekne; the activists were able to hide the confiscated weapons before 24 of them were arrested and transferred to Rēzekne prison.[35] Those communists not arrested began to seek guidance from Red Army commanders since the party leadership were still firmly behind bars.[36]

Such police actions did not take account of the new political situation in the country. Under Soviet pressure President Ulmanis was forced to resign and the new People's Government was formed of left-leaning intellectuals. This government included two local Latgale representatives: Minister of Justice Juris Paberžs had served in that and other ministerial posts during Latvia's parliamentary years and was currently deputy president of the Daugavpils district court, while Vikentii Latkovskii, a teacher and possible Soviet intelligence operative from Dagda, was made Deputy Minister of the Interior.[37] The formation of the People's Government, which was completed on 20 June but announced on the 21st, was followed by a massive demonstration in Daugavpils, as in Riga and throughout the country, to mark the release of communist activists from prison. Thus on the evening of 21 June a large crowd, bigger than that which welcomed the Red Army, gathered outside Daugavpils prison to meet the 50 released prisoners, the most prominent of whom was Mikhail Yukhno. The crowd then marched to Unity House and on to Scout Square where they staged a rally.[38] Soviet revolution had come to Daugavpils.

2 Daugavpils during the terrible year

The year of Soviet rule in Latvia, from the arrival of the Red Army on 17 June 1940 until the start of Hitler's Operation Barbarossa on 22 June 1941, was a time of near permanent revolution in Daugavpils. Known by nationalists and Nazis as 'the terrible year', it began with popular demonstrations in support of the new order and ended with the mass deportation of representatives of the old order. In the first couple of weeks after the formation of the People's Government, Daugavpils experienced a wave of street demonstrations and meetings as the Ulmanis order was overthrown and new workers' committees were established. As soon as the communists emerged from prison, they were engaged in street clashes to disarm the *aizsargs*, that symbol of the old order. They consciously strove to appear internationalist rather than nationalist, and there was much loose talk of 'soviets' as workers' and soldiers' committees were established. This display of popular initiative did not last long. As soon as Stalin's electoral timetable was set and the process of Latvia's incorporation into the Soviet Union began, the era of street politics passed. Communists were no longer expected to dream about communism but to implement communism. Their task was no longer to be part of the worldwide struggle of communism against fascism, but to persuade a sceptical populace of the benefits of incorporation into the Soviet Union, even if that meant relying on the anti-Latvian sentiment of some Russian workers.

Autumn 1940 saw the start of wave after wave of nationalisations, each as hastily implemented and poorly thought-out as the last. As a once efficient economy crumbled, and shortages became widespread, the party launched a campaign reminiscent of Mao's Cultural Revolution in China, seeking to overthrow all that the traditional elites held dear. The Catholic Church was subjected to repression and its priests humiliated and deprived of their livelihood. At the same time, the party started to restore memorials to the Red Army soldiers who had died in the civil war of 1919. The story of that civil war was turned on its head, with the *aizsargs* becoming the enemy and the pro-communist Latvian riflemen the heroes. In a similar spirit, a campaign was launched to re-house workers in the homes of 'the bourgeoisie', while the party clashed repeatedly with teachers over their alleged failure to imbue children with the communist spirit.

Formal incorporation into the Soviet Union meant full participation in the Soviet economy, its five-year plans and its preparations for war. In industry this meant a productivity drive in the form of 'Stakhanovism', something which backfired and actually produced a collapse in morale among the workers' guard and the threat of labour unrest. In agriculture the task of the five-year plan was to prepare for collectivisation. From early in 1941 moves were undertaken to establish machine tractor stations and horse-hiring bases, the paraphernalia of Soviet agriculture, while from spring 1941 Latgale was chosen to pioneer the first collective farms, moves which coincided with a confrontation between the party and the 'kulaks' over the best time to sow. Collectivisation was only stopped when it was overtaken by the more urgent priority of deporting to Siberia all those associated with the old regime who might be expected to co-operate with the Germans in the event of an attack by Hitler. The scale of the deportations were scarcely justified by the few incidents of nationalist unrest that spring.

In Daugavpils city and district 1,000 people were deported to Siberia. Those worst affected as a percentage of the population were Jewish businessmen and traders, but since the most obvious targets were the better-known pillars of the old regime, the deportations appeared to be anti-Latvian in purpose; in rural areas it was often predominantly Latvians who were affected. This impression was reinforced by the ethnic composition of the local communists. It was impossible to hide the fact that the majority of party activists stemmed from Latvia's minority communities of Russians and Jews. This had been the case before 1940 and was only reinforced during 'the terrible year', despite attempts to address the problem. The deportations of 14 June 1941 were followed one week later by the attack Stalin feared, and served to encourage collaboration rather than prevent it.

Revolution through occupation

With the communists released from prison and under clear instructions to bring the struggle against fascism to a successful conclusion, it was inevitable that clashes with the *aizsargs* would take place. Soviet representatives in Riga wrote to the Soviet Commissar for Foreign Affairs Molotov on 22 June asking for permission to disarm the *aizsargs* to avoid unnecessary clashes,[1] and a corresponding decree was published by the government on 23 June giving the *aizsargs* three days to surrender their arms to the police, who would then transfer them to the army. With this decree to back them up, communist activists organised groups to enforce the disarmament. In Grīva on 23 June the local party leader, an underground activist since 1929, led a group of 30 men to disarm the *aizsargs* on the spot; however, despite threats, and the brandishing by one worker of an old gun, the *aizsargs* stood firm and agreed only that they would hand over their weapons within the government's three-day deadline.[2] On 24 June things were more organised. Recruitment to a 'workers' militia' had begun in Daugavpils and one of the first units of this as yet unarmed force set off to disarm the local *aizsargs*. As more volunteers joined, the unit became a crowd of over 100 which surrounded the Daugavpils *aizsarg* regimental building. One *aizsarg* leader fired a shot, killing one militia member and escaping; the others surrendered 20 rifles and 22 revolvers.[3] After a mass meeting at the Railway Workshops on 25 June a crowd marched to the headquarters of the special railway *aizsarg* regiment: they occupied the building and transferred the arms they found to the army.[4]

During this three-day period, marches and demonstrations in Daugavpils were virtually continuous. On 23 June the communists organised a huge rally in Scout Square. Speeches were made in Russian, Latvian, Yiddish and Polish in an attempt to reflect the full ethnic diversity of the city. Formally the purpose of the meeting was to endorse the demands that the now legal communist party was putting to the People's Government, but it was in fact a display of strength. After singing the Internationale, the crowd formed disciplined ranks and marched to all the symbols of the old order. On Warsaw Street they occupied the offices of the Ulmanis trade-union organisation; on Imantas Street they occupied the Handicraft Trades Association building; at the corner of Aizsarg Street and Valdemar Street they occupied the offices of the 'fascist' Jewish Trumpeldor Association. In a similar move, on 25 June massed ranks of railway workers drove the leader of the Ulmanis railway workers' union out of his office and occupied the cinema and other cultural facilities retained for its members. They then moved off to hold another meeting, where, from nowhere, large red banners had appeared.[5]

In the surrounding countryside similar meetings and demonstrations took place, but the communists did not always retain the initiative. Uncontested meetings took place in Biķernieki, Viški and Naujene; while in Preiļi a group of 'revolutionary workers' marched into the deserted county administration offices and occupied them.[6] However, not far away a violent clash almost occurred. In Līvāni a crowd of supporters of the new regime gathered to lay a wreath at the memorial to those who died during the 1905 Revolution; armed police and *aizsargs* gathered outside the town offices preparing to disperse them and a violent clash was only prevented when Red Army units were summoned from nearby Krustpils.[7]

Deprived of clear orders from the Central Committee and intoxicated by both the success of their street politics and by their own ultra-left tradition, the Latgale regional committee twice used the slogan 'a Soviet Latvia', repeating it on 23 and 24 June. It was precisely at this time that the leaders of the Latgale regional committee were in Riga in urgent consultation with the Central Committee and on their return the slogan 'Soviet Latvia' was dropped. However, this did not stop much loose talk of the formation of soviets even after the references to soviets in Daugavpils had been criticised by the Riga communist press on 27 June.[8] When discussing how to organise the class struggle, Daugavpils communists were true to the sectarian traditions of the 1930s. On 26 June 1940 *Latgalskaya Pravda* argued that the instrument for disarming the *aizsargs* should be newly formed 'soviets'; on the Russian model of 1917 'soviets of workers', peasants' and soldiers' deputies' should be formed.[9] The next issue carried the editorial 'the soviets and the government', arguing that it was the task of newly formed soviets to ensure that the government carried out its promises.[10] The first legal meeting of the Daugavpils city communist party organisation held on 26 June saw no reason to question this radical line.[11] It was left to Roberts Neilands, the head of the Latgale regional committee, who arrived in the city on 8 July to bring the Daugavpils communists to heel. He told a meeting of the Daugavpils city party organisation that talk of soviets must stop. In a broad swipe at too much 'leftism' he called on the party not to simply 'write off' entire social groups as enemies; even in the officer corps there were progressive officers.[12]

Whether future soviets or not, the primary task of the tiny Daugavpils communist party in the last days of June was to establish factory committees in every enterprise in the city. Mikhail Yukhno, the leader of the Daugavpils city communist organisation as it emerged from underground, recalled later that it was with great difficulty that the local communists managed to find sufficient personnel to ensure that every factory committee election was attended by a party representative.[13] By 27 June workers at the large *Italia* textile works and other factories throughout the city were electing 'workers' committees'.[14] These addressed both long-held grievances and the requirements of the new regime. At the first full meeting of the factory committee at the *Italia* textile factory it was agreed to re-instate a worker sacked under the Ulmanis regulations, to reduce the working day of factory watchmen from 12 to 8 hours and to pay in full those workers who had taken time off to meet the Red Army and who had worked to establish the new factory committees. Almost as an after-thought it stressed the need for labour discipline.[15]

At the same time soldiers' committees began to be formed at the fortress garrison. The first big meeting of 70 soldiers was reported on 28 June. It too mixed long-held grievances about national discrimination within the armed forces with current demands. The meeting agreed to remove 'fascist elements' from the army; to end anti-communist and anti-soviet agitation; to make it possible for members of all nationalities to be promoted to positions of command; to improve the quality of food; and to give soldiers identical leave entitlement no matter what their nationality.[16] A week later the process of establishing soldiers' committees had been completed.[17] The campaign to establish workers' and soldiers' committees was greatly helped by the appearance of the communist newspaper *Latgal'skaya Pravda* which began to be published regularly on 26 June. It proudly explained how the arrival of the Red Army had completely transformed the situation in the country: the old 'fascist' regime of Ulmanis had been 'blown away like dust'; but, the communists warned, the new government was still opposed by reactionary forces like the *aizsargs* whose disarmament was not complete; only the presence of the Red Army in the background allowed the newly formed and as yet unarmed workers' militia to confront reaction.[18]

During the first week in July the constant campaign of meetings moved on from establishing workers and other committees to preparing for elections to a new parliament, which Moscow instructed on 4 July should take place in just ten days time. On 7 July the first big election rally took place in Daugavpils, opened by Yukhno and attended by garrison soldiers alongside the civilian population.[19] The candidates were carefully chosen to reflect ethnic diversity and a degree of gender balance: Alfons Noviks, Stanislavs Čemis, Bronislawa Yukhno (Mikhail's wife) and Faifish Fridman.[20] The message the party hoped to get across was revealed in guidelines for election agitators published in *Latgalskaya Pravda* on 10 July. These addressed the most sensitive of issues: nationality. Agitators were reminded that poor Latvians had suffered under Ulmanis just as much as members of the national minorities, and that many representatives of the local Latvian intelligentsia and business groups feared that after the elections they would be sacked and replaced by 'Russians, Jews and Communists'.[21]

These were very understandable and prescient fears. As work for the elections got under way, so the nature of the social upheaval in Daugavpils changed. For two weeks after 17 June there had been a time of upheaval, chaos, popular initiative and even popular struggle. This was not a revolution, but nor was it simply the power of the Red Army, although only the arrival of the Red Army allowed popular initiative to develop in the way it did. Once the ten days of preparations for the mid-July elections began with the creation of a fictitious Bloc of Working People things changed, something reflected in the local press. Quite suddenly *Latgal'skaya Pravda* became the sort of paper that could have been read anywhere in the Soviet Union. During the election campaign order began to be imposed on upheaval. As early as 28 June it was decided that alongside the spontaneously formed workers' militia there would be an auxiliary police force, numbering at first just 45.[22] A few days later the workers' militia was formalised into a workers' guard, which required sponsorship from the Communist Party before workers could join it.[23] On 8 July the *aizsargs* were formally dissolved and their arms transferred to members of the auxiliary police.[24] Alongside order there was cynicism: all participants recalled spiralling inflation as the old order broke down and the government made the calculated decision to award a 20 per cent pay increase across the board just before the elections.[25] In Daugavpils the wage rise for workers at the *Italia* textile plant was given widespread press coverage on 12 July.[26]

The elections to the new parliament took place on 14–15 July. As during the parliamentary years, there were to be 100 deputies, 27 from Latgale. However, under the terms imposed on the People's Government by the Soviet leadership, only candidates from the Bloc of Working People could stand, 52 of whom were communists, including all the central committee secretaries, with the rest being representatives of either the trade unions or the communist-sponsored organisations like the Latvian League of Working Youth.[27] Voting was by residence passport, and contemporaries recalled many dark hints about what would happen to those whose passports did not contain a stamp to show they had voted. Those wanting to vote against the Bloc of Working People had to enter a polling booth and strike out the names on the list; those voting for were not required to enter a booth.[28] In many cases voting was a collective act: workers marched to the polling booths carrying red banners and singing revolutionary songs; soldiers were marched to them by their officers. For the halt and the lame there was even a mobile polling booth which toured the hospitals.[29] Despite the pressure to vote, not all did. The election results revealed a far higher percentage of spoilt ballots in rural areas like Preiļi and Dagda than in Daugavpils itself.[30] And, although the press described scenes like that in a village where a veteran of the 1919 Red Army marched the whole village to the polling booth behind red banners, a police report revealed that in Kalupe, at an election meeting just prior to polling, a certain Anton Malakovskii had torn down the red flag flying over the soviet offices in Kalupe and replaced it with a Latvian national flag; he was placed under arrest.[31]

Once the elections were over, the pace of political change quickened still further as the campaign got under way to turn Latvia into a Soviet Republic. Party activists, who had always wanted to work to this end, and who had been criticised for openly campaigning for it prior to the elections, were saddened to discover the fact that implementing this long-held ambition seemed to deprive the communists of the little popular support they had. Reviewing their first six months in power they noted how they had been able to win over many people to active participation in the election campaign, but they were unable to hold on to the support of such people subsequently.[32] If communists found this fall in support incomprehensible, to a non-communist it was scarcely surprising. The overthrow of Ulmanis, the restoration of civil freedoms, the promise of equality for the national minorities and the idea of a People's Government were all concepts which many groups within Daugavpils society could embrace. The notion that such gains could be guaranteed, rather than vitiated, through incorporation into the Soviet Union of Stalin was an act of faith peculiar to the communists. Conviction pushed them forward.

On 19 July, Daugavpils textile workers, allegedly quite spontaneously, wrote to *Latgalskaya Pravda* asking that Latvia should be allowed to adhere to the Soviet Union.[33] The following day resolutions calling for adherence to the Soviet Union were passed at a meeting of workers' representatives from 18 factories.[34] When the new parliament held its first meeting on 21 July it agreed to accede to such demands; it would both restore soviet power in Latvia which had lapsed in 1919 and apply to join the Soviet Union, sending a delegation to Moscow with this request on 30 July. Moscow's announcement on 5 August that Latvia would become a Soviet Socialist Republic was followed by a demonstration and mass meeting in Daugavpils on 6 August, which heard reports by Yukhno, Neilands and other leading communists.[35] The claim that 20,000 people took part in the demonstration was supposed to stress the new unity of party and people.[36]

The renaming of Daugavpils's streets a few days later was no doubt supposed to signify the permanent nature of the new order, as was the reception given to the Soviet President of Latvia at Daugavpils station on his return journey from Moscow to Riga.[37] The transformation of the workers' militia of June and July into a properly organised Workers' Guard of three detachments during the course of August and early September gave the same message.[38] A final turning point was reached on 31 August at a meeting of former political prisoners at the concert hall of Unity House, now renamed People's House. The 'Meeting with Former Political Prisoners' was the last occasion on which local communists acted as the soldiers of the Commmunist International they had once been, rather than as the Soviet apparatchiks they would become. Dominiks Kaupužs gave a wide-ranging speech, describing the terror and abuse suffered by communists at the hands of the Latvian police; Solomon Murin gave a colourful account of how he had been condemned to death, but then pardoned in 1934; but the high spot of the evening was the speech by Benjamin Kur. Kur was a local Jew whose conviction that European fascism should be opposed had led to many hardships. After leaving the Jewish Gymnasium in Riga, he had worked for the young communists and communist party as an underground activists, before spending 1930–4 in prison. On his release he had been called up for military service, but fled to Czechoslovakia in 1935 and from there to Spain in 1937.[39] In Spain he fought with the International Brigade in Catalonia and in 1939 was interned in a French camp. He escaped to Britain, and from there made his way back to Latvia. He would soon have to relate this romantic past to a pen-pushing job as part of the Daugavpils propaganda machine, drafting reports on the non-fulfilment of plans for socialist competition. The enthusiastic applause which greeted his speech on 31 August marked a dividing line between the dream of communism and its reality.[40]

Just what that reality could mean was spelled out in the main story in *Latgal'skaya Pravda* a couple of days after the 6 August meeting had pronounced the unity of party and people. The paper warned that the enemy's main weapon was to play on national divisions, and to do so by mobilising 'the most backward workers'. In many places, the report went on, at meetings people are prevented from using the Latvian language; people shout 'you used to be in charge, but now we are'. This inevitably made many among the Latvian population think that Soviet power was something alien, imposed, something which needed to be struggled against. Very often the most trivial thing could spark national tension, the report concluded.[41] But, deprived of the broadly democratic forces that had supported the party before the elections, there was little alternative for the party than to court such 'backward workers' if they wanted any popular support. Just how widespread the perception was that incorporation into the Soviet Union meant a Russian take-over became clear from the fact that parents had started to move their children from Polish and Latvian schools to Russian ones.[42]

Socialist construction

The change from revolutionary upheaval to socialist construction was signified by changes in the administration of the Daugavpils region. As Yukhno later made clear, until 15 September the city party organisation had scarcely existed in a formal sense,[43] overlapping in reality with the Latgale regional committee. However, on 15 September the Latgale regional committee was wound up and in its place clearly separated city and district party organisations were established for Daugavpils. Since the Daugavpils city party organisation had always existed as a separate entity, albeit sharing personnel with the Latgale regional committee, this meant little change. However, below the regional level there had been five area party organisations in the countryside and these were now abolished and the party organised according to the local government districts; below the district there were to be parish party organisations.

These changes, along with the state monopoly on press distribution imposed on 2 October, were needed so that the party could get to grips with its programme for economic and social changes, without facing carping criticism. The first big socialist upheaval was land reform. On 23 July plans for the reform were announced in *Latgal'skaya Pravda* and it was enacted on 29 July. The reality of the reform was rather modest, having a limited impact on land tenure; of the 17,721 people requesting land under the scheme in Daugavpils district only 3,623 in the end received land.[44] Also on 29 July legislation was drawn up to nationalise the banks and major enterprises: in Daugavpils this meant fourteen plants, including the *Italia* and *Daugava* textile factories; in Rēzekne, the second city of Latgale, four works were affected and in the towns of Ludza and Krustpils, as well as in Kalkūne, essentially a suburb of Daugavpils, one each.[45] To ensure state control of these enterprises each was assigned a 'commissar' sent from the city party organisation.[46] The popular response to such rapid and ill-prepared change was predictable. On 22 July the Soviet- appointed president issued a public statement entitled 'Unnecessary Panic': he denounced rumour mongers, stressed that supplies of all basic commodities were good and called on people to stop buying up goods as if there were no tomorrow; those hoarding supplies would have their property confiscated.[47] In subsequent days the Daugavpils auxiliary police began to detain those individuals and representatives of firms believed to be hoarding goods.[48]

The nationalisation campaign blundered forward. One of the Daugavpils firms on the list was the Flax Processing Works owned by M. Feigel'son. This employed 100 workers working two shifts. Initially the workers' committee took a hostile approach to Feigel'son, accusing him of sabotage by stopping purchases of raw flax in August. In another populist move the local branch of the new communist-inspired Daugavpils General Workers' Union awarded Feigel'son workers a 10 per cent pay rise since the plant was now 'owned by the workers'. However, when it came to hiring a director for the plant they now 'owned', the workers nominated Feigel'son, and accepted his explanation that the decision not to buy raw flax, far from being an act of sabotage, simply reflected the desperate need to carry out urgent repairs to equipment. Agreement was readily reached: the factory would work in August until the old flax was used up, and then carry out the repairs in September. Feigel'son would act as director at least until 1 October when new flax was purchased.[49]

Not all employers were as ready as Feigel'son to cooperate with the new authorities. Since the clear ambition of the Communist Party was to bring Latvia into line with every other Soviet Republic, more nationalisations were likely, as were moves to collectivise agriculture. Bending with the wind seemed the only way forward. So a group of Daugavpils manufacturers and traders bought up 77 hectares of land, won the agreement of a group of landless peasants and established their own collective farm, planting a story in the independent paper *Daugavas Věstnesis* that this was an initiative of the Communist Party. The scheme was uncovered and the land allocated to the state land fund.[50] In the last week in August *Latgal'skaya Pravda* claimed that attempts to salt away money by setting up such false collectives had become almost commonplace.[51] The land reform and persistent rumours of collectivisation persuaded some better-off peasants in Biķernieki to kill their cattle and dispose of their property before it could be confiscated.[52]

Thunderous editorials about the wrongdoing of speculators[53] could not hide the fact that social and economic change at this pace risked chaos. In retrospect, Yukhno conceded that the party had simply been unable to keep on top of the changes demanded of it. Having appointed commissars to oversee nationalised industries, the work of these commissars was never inspected because the party had already moved on to its next task.[54] At the end of September trading concerns were made the target of the next big wave of nationalisations, although rumours had been circulating for some time, which had prompted traders to try and hide or sell off their goods. The decree of 28 September nationalised 74 trading establishments in Daugavpils district and sixty in the city itself. The popular response was identical to that during the first wave of nationalisations. On 3 October *Latgal'skaya Pravda* carried the headline 'Panic is Out of Place', which attacked those engaged in hording: in language worthy of George Orwell's *1984* it explained that price rises under socialism were not a sign of shortage, as they were under capitalism; rents had been frozen, wages had been increased and current price rises were merely adjustments to the new nationalised conditions. It was the former owners of nationalised trading concerns who were spreading rumours of shortages.[55] Among the nationalised firms were such long-established local institutions as Bacon Export and Averbukh Brothers.[56]

It was no wonder *Latgal'skaya Pravda* had to return to the question of hoarding and rumour mongering on 16 October: its editorial linked the two, by accusing the former owners of nationalised property of deliberately spreading rumours about a possible war which would lead to the overthrow of soviet power and the restoration of their property.[57] Although the authorities tried to blame the dubious trading practices of cobblers for the shortage of shoes in Krāslava, the allocation of blame did not address the fundamental issue of shortage.[58] It was characteristic of the speed and lack of planning involved in this stage of the nationalisations that it was mid-November before any plans were announced for the private trading concern to be replaced by a new 'Trust for Supply and Distribution' which would serve a network of co-operative shops.[59] Yet before the new trading system had even begun to bed down, there was another economic upheaval. In a special Monday issue on 25 November (there was usually no edition on a Monday, to give print workers a free Sunday), *Latgal'skaya Pravda* explained how the lat and rouble were being brought into line: wages would go up and prices would go up, but all would benefit because in the Soviet Union there was no unemployment, medical care and education were free, there were good pensions and there had been a land reform; Latvia was all the better for not being a small, isolated country in a world at war. In the New Year the party was instructed to push ahead with the social control of trade. Moves in this direction began to take serious shape at the end of January when the Central Committee sent out instructions for all soviet executives to establish commissions charged with bringing under social ownership the myriad private handicraft enterprises.[60] Between 1 February and 15 March the leaderships of all agricultural credit societies, co-operatives and similar organisations were all re-elected to ensure communist control.[61]

Economic merger with the Soviet Union also meant the completion of political merger. In the aftermath of the July elections the authorities had already moved against potential sources of opposition, in particular the nationalist-oriented student societies and the Zionist societies and organisations.[62] Not long afterwards the Latvian League of Working Youth was replaced by the Communist Youth League (komsomol), to bring it into line with the rest of the Soviet Union. At the end of November moves began to align local government with that operating in the rest of the Soviet Union. Initially the Soviet authorities established a temporary administrative apparatus by appointing their own people within the Ulmanis system of appointed elders. The new, appointed soviets were introduced in November, but were usually headed by the same people. Thus Bernards Škapars, who had been appointed Daugavpils elder, became chairman of the new Daugavpils soviet executive.[63] These changes were necessitated by the fact that it was announced on 13 November that Latvia would take part in the USSR Supreme Soviet elections. These elections presented the communists with their first opportunity to meet the people on whose behalf they claimed to rule and whom they had dragged with so little enthusiasm into the Soviet Union. For Soviet elections, while being a travesty of the electoral process, were taken extremely seriously by Stalin. There might be no choice of candidates, but party organisations were expected to drive everybody to the polling booth. As Kur told a party meeting on 29 November, the party was expected to establish electoral commissions whose twin tasks were to draw up an electoral register and then ensure 100 per cent turn-out.[64] Daugavpils was divided into 24 electoral districts, with seven members of an electoral commission responsible for each district.[65]

Preparations for the elections brought significant changes in the leadership of the Daugavpils city party organisation, which became public at its December plenum on 8 December 1940. Even before that plenum, it was clear that Yukhno's job had effectively been taken over by Fedors Treimans. Treimans was an ethnic Latvian from Moscow who spoke no Latvian but was felt to have a good administrative record. At the start of the meeting he was given the bland title 'a worker of the Daugavpils city committee' but by the end of the meeting he had been appointed first secretary;[66] an acolyte stressed how much the work of the city committee had improved recently since Treimans's arrival.[67] Yukhno was sent to a sanatorium for a rest cure and on his return was appointed to head the party committee in the Daugavpils rolling-stock repair works. The party still represented no one other than itself: 38 per cent of its members worked in the security services, 33 per cent in the local administration, 11 per cent within the party apparatus and only 18 per cent in factories; the only factory party cell as such was in the rolling-stock repair works.[68]

The electoral campaign itself revealed the difficulty party members had in adapting to soviet electoral methods. On 17 December Kur criticised the unwillingness of agitators to persevere when home-owners refused to allow them into their flats.[69] Agitators also had to be reminded that invitations to attend meetings could not just be dropped through letter-boxes: electors had to be confronted in person and the importance of attending explained to them.[70] The campaign in Daugavpils city involved more than 80 electoral circles organising over 100 meetings with electors[71] and one of the local candidates, Antons Luriņš, a member of the district party organisation, pressing the flesh and explaining how he had started working for the underground when employed as a courier for the Daugavpils Land Bank.[72] The second candidate was Jānis Smagars, a worker in the rolling-stock repair works. Many electors may have been keen to know why the third candidate they were supposed to vote for was Vladimir Derevyanskii who had no connection with Latvia whatsoever, other than to have overseen the arrival of the Red Army and to be Moscow's representative on the Central Committee of the Latvian Communist Party. When the election results were published on 14 January 1941 they showed a 99.5 per cent turn-out in Daugavpils city and 99.1 per cent in Daugavpils district.[73]

Most communists seemed happy to take such fairy stories at face value. However, when the district party held a plenum on 7 December, Donats Bolužs, a delegate from Krāslava, a Latvian and a party member since January 1938, spoke his mind. At one level he was just infuriated by the abolition in the September re-organisation of the old Krāslava area party organisation; now, with parish organisations in such places as Izvalta and Skaista, he felt everything had gone to the dogs; but this was systematic of a deeper malaise. 'Everywhere there is no one but Russians enflaming national hatred. ... everywhere the party exaggerates; it exaggerates the number of 'Lenin corners', it exaggerates reports on agricultural work. The district committee does not check things, it rules by reports alone. We elected a people's judge and members of electoral commissions. Are they any good? No! We put forward people with a criminal past, the people were against them, but we chose them nonetheless. In Skaista parish 25 people attended a meeting, but the report states 100.'[74] Such plain speaking was not welcomed by the district party committee, but it reflected the true state of affairs.

Cultural revolution

When Yukhno had addressed the plenum of the Daugavpils city committee on 8 December part of his speech was devoted to the activities of class enemies and the party's uncertain approach to them. He estimated there were 1,600 former *aizsargs* active in the town, along with other questionable characters who were all engaged in wrecking. This situation was not helped by the sorry state of the new police militia; recently two militiamen had killed each other when inappropriately using firearms.[75] Yukhno did not single out any group other than the former *aizsargs* for consideration, but undoubtedly the Roman Catholic Church caused the party its greatest concerns. In country regions especially the Catholic Church had encouraged believers not to take part in those demonstrations in support of the new regime which were such a feature of late June and early July. In Izvalta the local Catholic priest used a funeral oration at the start of July to call on believers not to take part in communist-sponsored demonstrations. Even the communist press had to admit that some people had fallen under the influence of these 'dark elements' and were refusing to join demonstrations or elect committees; some even attacked the homes of those who did take part in the demonstrations. In Viški someone had pulled down all the red flags, and the local police preferred to take no action.[76] On 11 August the communist press took great pleasure in 'discovering' that the monks from the monastery at the great Marian pilgrimage church in Aglona had been moving valuables from the monastery for safe keeping among the local population.[77]

As the land reform moved from rhetoric to reality in September 1940, the future of the land owned by parish priests became an enormous issue. By definition, the priests did not work the land themselves, and therefore, since the land was to go to those who worked it, the priests' land was subject to confiscation; but many priests and their communities used every means they could to resist. In Izvalta, for example, the priest had acted as *de facto* chairman of the long-established local agricultural co-operative and members of that co-operative supported his campaign to be excluded from expropriation.[78] Later a crowd mobbed a visit by the district elder, prompting the press to accuse the Catholic priesthood of 'organising an army of old men and old women to defend the priests' nests'.[79] Then in Skaista over 200 people gathered at the church on 24 September to support the demand of the local priest that he retain some land; his supporters had been out collecting signatures on a petition, and, allegedly, spreading rumours that the soviet authorities intended to close the church. The press made clear that petitions of this sort would not be allowed.[80]

This was an issue where the party refused to back down. Its ultra-left instincts made clear that the Catholic Church was one of the mainstays of reaction in Europe, and its power had to be publicly broken. The party therefore engaged in what can only be called combative symbolism. Thus the land belonging to the Aglona parish priest was not only confiscated but turned into a model Soviet farm.[81] In an even more deliberate attempt to snub the Church, the party took control of the building next to the church in Pasiene where the priest had once lived and turned it into a communist reading room where the local group of the atheist society held its meetings on anti-religious themes.[82] This sort of activity meant that in the countryside the activities of communist activists were on a par with Mao's Red Guards in communist China. Not only the Church suffered but other cherished symbols of the past. In Preiļi local activists seized control of the estate surrounding the local agricultural college and opened it to the public as a park, denouncing the way that in the past the estate had only been accessible to the college director and 'his *aizsarg* friends'.[83]

Memorials to those who had died in Latvia's short but bloody civil war offered a similar challenge to traditional values, now condemned as *aizsarg* values. Young communists in Biķernieki took the lead in a campaign which was to last several months. On 11 September they organised an event to commemorate the death in 1919 of a Red Army man taking part in Latvia's civil war. A crowd of '2,000' was reported to have gathered, while wreaths were laid at the restored grave and appropriately revolutionary speeches made by the local komsomol leader to the predominantly young crowd.[84] A fortnight later similar events were staged in Naujene, Viški and Ludza,[85] while on 29 September the graves of those who fell at Izvalta were restored,[86] as were those at Vecie Stropi just outside Daugavpils.[87] At the beginning of October in Tartaks the grave of a Red Army man killed in 1919 which had been 'moved by *aizsargs* in 1938' was re-established.[88]

In the version of history favoured both in the parliamentary republic and under the authoritarian rule of Ulmanis, the Red Army men who died in Latgale in autumn 1919 were fighting a rearguard action to prevent the formation of an independent Latvian Republic. They represented all that was bad and anti-national. In the communist tradition they were true inter-nationalists, Latvians who put the survival of Soviet Russia, the first workers' state in history, above their own national interests. The civil war memorials campaign was thus deliberately provocative and confrontational, aimed at shattering the icons of 'bourgeois' Latvia.

Rhetorical confrontation with the 'bourgeoisie' was also seen in the party's housing policy. On 12 September 1940 the authorities launched a campaign to improve workers' housing. That day the editorial in *Latgal'skaya Pravda* waxed lyrical about the luxurious flats owned by the rich, while the poor lived in damp cellars. The message was repeated a fort-night later.[89] Although in the mean time grandiose but vague plans had been drawn up to build new schools, hospitals and apartment blocks in Daugavpils,[90] the only way to re-house people was to expropriate the flats of the rich; the property of those owning more than 220 square metres of living space was nationalised at the end of October.[91] However, it was only in early February 1941 that *Latgal'skaya Pravda* could announce that workers had begun to be re-housed, vacating their 'damp cellars' and occupying the former apartments of the rich. In an act of educative social justice, Kazimir Kozlovskii, who had worked for many years at the *Celgreb* factory, had left a tumble-down wreck of a house in Grīva to be re-housed, with his wife and seven children, in the flat once owned by the *Celgreb* factory owner.[92] Despite this propaganda coup, the city committee admitted on 20 February that the re-housing scheme was progressing unsatisfactorily,[93] since the orig-inal plan had been to move at least 100 families in February alone.[94]

Schools were the other great area for a clash between the party and traditional Latvian culture. The long-term plans of the authorities were clear: to produce new cadres of teachers prepared 'to work in the spirit of socialism'. To this end they closed down the Daugavpils Teachers' Institute completely and decided to concentrate their efforts on Rézekne; there the existing Teachers' Institute would be restructured as a State Pedagogical Institute modelled on those of the Soviet Union, where teaching would be in Russian and the course would last for four years. All the Daugavpils students would be transferred to Rézekne. As to the building of the Daugavpils Teachers' Institute, it would be handed over to a new state Jewish school in a reorganisation of education in Daugavpils which would also see a new Russian school.[95]

The problem with these grandiose plans was the drastic shortage of teachers. Despite re-appointing many of those social democrat teachers dismissed in 1934,[96] a shortage remained. As a result the director of the Handicraft School in Daugavpils, sacked as a 'fascist', had no difficulty getting a job as the director of Riga Handicraft School.[97] Teachers could therefore simply refuse to co-operate with the new authorities, a stance adopted by many. When a meeting of teachers was arranged in Līvāni in mid-October, many teachers refused to attend and those who did made clear that they objected 'to their peace and quiet being disturbed'.[98] On the other hand, teachers were quite happy to take part in campaigns of which they approved, like that against illiteracy launched with great fanfare on 24 November 1940.[99] At the end of November a school in Krustpils was criticised for not establishing a wall newspaper, while another refused to take part in the official campaign to celebrate 30 years since the death of the Russian novelist Tolstoy.[100]

To try and get a firmer grip over what happened in schools, the communists began a 'leadership' campaign. This would have two prongs: first, parent committees would be set up to influence the teaching programme; and second, links would be established between factories and trade-union organisations.[101] The first seven links between factories and schools were announced on 29 November,[102] with more joining the process over subsequent months.[103] It was soon discovered that parents could not always be relied on to follow party policy. Grants were issued in one school to help children from poor backgrounds; but the parents insisted on sharing the money out amongst all their children and the authorities had to intervene to put things 'right'.[104] The Daugavpils city plenum of 8 December heard bitter words about the state of affairs in schools, including the refusal to sing the Soviet anthem and continued teaching of religious studies.[105]

The clash between the teachers and the communist authorities came to a head on 3 January 1941. A conference of teachers in Daugavpils city and district revealed that, while there was general satisfaction with the expansion of education provision, the greater part of teachers were unhappy at the attempt to develop the komsomol movement in secondary schools and establish a pioneer movement among primary- school children; they were also unwilling to take part in communist-inspired 'community work'. When three days later teachers from the whole Latgale region gathered in Daugavpils, the same issue came up: communist organisers and teachers were at loggerheads. Teachers insisted that communist organisers had no pedagogic training and no right to interfere in the education process. School directors insisted that since they were responsible for the running of the school, they had to be allowed to attend all meetings, even communist party meetings if they affected the school. They were not impressed to be told that even if the school director were a party member he could only attend a party meeting on schools policy by invitation. Such bitter clashes were having an impact on the work of the schools: pass rates in certain classes were at worryingly low levels, sometimes as low as 50 per cent. Teachers put such failure rates down to the fact that children were constantly out of school on some 'community work' organised by the komsomol.[106] Despite increasing pressure, some school directors continued to insist on teaching Bible study,[107] while in Krāslava secondary-school teachers refused to take part in the planned socialist competition in honour of Red Army Day.[108] Teachers' success in resisting the growth of the pioneer movement can be seen from the fact that in mid-February 1941 only 14 per cent of pupils at schools in Daugavpils district were pioneers.[109]

In April 1941 the party decided that the way forward was to call in all school directors individually and discuss with them the importance of teaching such topics as the history of the Bolshevik Party and the Stalin Constitution.[110] By April a sort of armed truce had settled on relations between the authorities and the teaching community. Poor examination results gave both sides a common interest. Surveys showed that in Daugavpils city 23.2 per cent of students were failing to achieve satisfactory grades. In its editorial *Latgal'skaya Pravda* blamed school directors, attacking the director of the 1st Latvian School by name where truancy rates were as high as 20–30 per cent, something the director allegedly put up with since the pupils had become so disruptive that their absence was better than there presence. However, the paper followed this with a much more conciliatory article which pointed out how difficult the academic year had been with so many new initiatives and how, by and large, the broad mass of teachers had done what was expected of them. It conceded that many of the problems had been caused by the lack of suitable teaching materials and urged teachers to identify clearly where students were failing – most frequently in their second language, be it Latvian or Russian – and arrange extra teaching support. Students in danger of failing would be excused 'community work' in order to undertake extra tuition.[111]

Yet broadsides against individual teachers continued: in Aglona secondary school one of the teachers allegedly taught 'capitalist morality', while the director of Izvalta secondary school refused to accept the Soviet view that in the 1905 Revolution Father Gapon had been a police agent and not a popular hero.[112] When a conference of teachers from Daugavpils schools was held on 27 April the authorities were apoplectic with fury that many schools had observed Easter. Teachers were still avoiding 'community work' and those teaching the Stalin Constitution only ever stressed the rights it gave, not the duties it imposed.[113] Finally as the school exams of 20 May approached, the authorities rather grudgingly accepted that schools were putting on extra classes to ensure the majority of pupils successfully completed the year.[114] To improve its work in schools, the party looked to teachers in its own ranks or those of the komsomol. Iosif Šteiman was allocated a job teaching the new subject of social studies at the commercial college, despite being scarcely 18 years old himself. In May 1941, as the city committee prepared a report on the situation in schools, a new name appeared on the list of those instructed to help draft it: Šteiman, now a member of the komsomol,[115] was brought in despite his youth to help implement the war against the old-guard teachers.

A five-year plan in five months

At the start of the New Year Stalin anticipated that war with Nazi Germany was little more than 12 months away. Latvia was expected to make an immediate economic contribution to the Soviet economy. The leader of the

Latvian Communist Party, Jānis Kalnbērziņš, returned from the XVIII Conference of the Soviet Communist Party in February 1941 with clear guidelines. Soviet Latvia should start making a positive contribution to the Soviet economy in terms of tax returns and expanded production.

The first sign of this change was a circular issued towards the end of February by the Central Committee in Riga which made clear to Daugavpils and all city and district committees that Moscow deemed Latvia to be behind with all its contributions to the USSR State Bank. Less than half of the income expected from the turnover trade of co-operative societies had come in; less than 20 per cent of the expected revenue from income tax; and less than a third of the income expected from rents. Insurance contributions were only 40 per cent of the anticipated target, and instead of money coming into the state's coffers in the form of individual investments in state savings accounts, nearly three million roubles had been withdrawn by individuals. However difficult Latvians were finding it to adapt to the Soviet economy and have confidence in it, the clear message of this circular was that, from Moscow's perspective, things were not happening anywhere like quickly enough.[116]

In March the press began to turn its attention to creaking aspects of the industrial sector in Daugavpils, which, far from expanding production seemed to be retrenching. What was proposed were Stalin's preferred cure-alls for difficulties with the five-year plan, one-man management and 'Stakhanovite' socialist competition. The press produced a series of exposés of scandals prompted by two meetings, that of the city party organisation on 5 March 1941, which passed a resolution on 'serious failings in industry and transport',[117] and that held on 6 March of factory directors and representatives of local party committees, which discussed ways of strengthening 'one-man management'.[118] The rolling-stock repair yards, once the pride and joy of the Daugavpils proletariat, were portrayed as being shoddy and incompetent. Wagons taken in for repair would be returned in such a poor state that within days they were back in the yard for further repair work; so-called 'urgent' repairs could take up to a month to complete. The catalogue of problems relating to poor productivity continued.[119] The city's main construction enterprise only fulfilled 40 per cent of its plan in the first three months of 1941,[120] while at the motor-transport base, things were worse; drivers got drunk and the bus-repair programme was so far behind schedule that only 30 per cent of buses were in service, meaning buses were always full and many workers had to walk to and from work, arriving late at both ends of the day.[121] Things on the railways were scarcely better. In May only 60 per cent of trains were arriving on time; on 9 May the Daugavpils station-master simply forgot about the night train to Rēzekne which eventually left over two hours' late.[122]

As a delegate told the meeting of the Daugavpils city party organisation on 8 December 1940, we allowed factory committees to be elected and then we did not tell them what they should do.[123] At all the major factories there was no serious attempt to control costs, and little in the way of labour discipline. The problem was a lack of clarity between the powers of the factory committee and the director: at the *Italia* factory, once held up as an example of good practice, the factory committee spent hours debating petty points of detail, allowing the director no initiative whatsoever.[124] Directors had to be given the power to manage and discipline their workforce – this was the clear message after Stalin's XVIII Party Conference. Yet, as the press made clear at the end of March 1941, factory directors alone could not be trusted: at the *Daugava* textile works, the director had told the factory committee that its job was simply to put up a wall newspaper and leave the director in peace; it was not the business of the committee if repairs to machinery were going slowly. However, the party was now very clear that such things as the speed of repairs had to be its concern if productivity were to improve in the build up to war. The director had to manage, but under the guidance of the party committee in the factory rather than the factory committee – that was the goal to which the party was now directing its efforts.[125] In the course of March a total of 1,578 'conversations' were held with workers in the 20 largest Daugavpils factories about the meaning of the decisions taken at the XVII Party Conference and the need to expand productivity.[126]

The party's preferred method of increasing productivity was to encourage socialist competition among workers to meet the high production targets once achieved by the Donbas coal miner Aleksei Stakhanov. At a meeting of the Daugavpils city party organisation on 12 April 1941 it was decided to try to make Stakhanovite methods more popular.[127] However, workers showed little enthusiasm. The Stakhanov School held on 9–10 April was attended by only 20 people, 16 of whom were already Stakhanovites.[128] As more and more plants were transferred to piece-work,[129] fines were introduced for infringements of labour discipline.[130] Yet in many branches of industry little improved: in a workshop producing electronic brushes for dynamos the April plan was only 65 per cent fulfilled and, in the same plant, seven men took 22 'sickies' and faced no punishment.[131] Workers showed no interest in Stakhanovism because by spring 1941 any enthusiasm they had once had for 'their' government had evaporated.

This fall in morale also affected the workers' guard. On 5 February 1941 the Daugavpils city committee discussed the situation that had evolved over the last couple of months and decided that the workers' guard was on the point of collapse. No political work was being undertaken since the commander, a certain comrade Reshetov, showed no interest in such work. Worse than that, members of the workers' guard met simply to get drunk, and it was not unknown for them to sell their weapons in order to raise cash for these binges. Concerned that in these circumstances all sorts of unreliable people might join the guard, it was decided to sack Reshetov and appoint a new commander, comrade Pupel', who was instructed to purge the membership. At the same time the factory principle of organisation would be abandoned and the workers' guard formed according to the district in which workers lived. At the same time it was decided that arms training would be supervised by the police chief.[132] The workers' guard was wound up nationally on 15 May 1941.[133]

The new regime of increased labour discipline and higher productivity imposed after the XVIII Party Conference inevitably ran the risk of exploding into labour discontent and strike action. At about this time the city party first secretary Treimans was sent an anonymous letter by 'an honest and committed worker'. This stated that the new obsession with labour discipline was courting disaster. The author was clear: a change of both line and leadership was essential 'if you do not want thousands of people to become enemies of Soviet power and people to live under constant fear of prison with the best people being arrested.'[134]

It was not only industry which was supposed to expand after Stalin's XVIII Party Conference – agricultural output was to grow as well. For this to happen the new farmers who had been allocated land under the land reform, and the bulk of those who had not been allocated land but simply remained small farmers, needed access to agricultural machinery and horses. The party's policy was to establish a network of machine-tractor stations, linked to satellite horse-hiring bases. The first task for the district party, then, was to identify farms in each parish suitable for expropriation and transformation into machine-tractor stations.

The farms chosen for expropriation reflected the prejudices of the communist administrators. The owners all belonged to 'enemy' catagories: Jezup Czszibovski was described as an active Polish nationalist; Vilhelms Mucinieks was not a farmer at all, but a lawyer, living in Daugavpils; Iosif Lučik was an associate of *aizsargs*; Antons Kudinš was 'the greatest kulak in the area'; Filip Vasiliev 'drank with *aizsargs*'; Petr Rubin had been an active member of the Peasant Union, the party led by Ulmanis; Vasilii Korelov was the son of an *aizsarg*; Jānis Locs came from a landlord family and had deserted from the Red Army in 1918; Antons Bodans's son had been arrested by the security services for *aizsarg* activity; Ksaverii Zarekovskii was not only an *aizsarg*, but also a 'Polish fascist' and 'Polish spy'; Stanislavs Ivbuļs had once been Minister of Transport representing the Catholic Party in parliament; Pavel Melnikov was not a farmer but a Riga builder with land and houses in Daugavpils and the surrounding countryside; Stanislav Petrovskii had a brother arrested for *aizsarg* activity; Jazeps Dyura had represented the Catholic Party in parliament; Jānis Klimanis had two sons who were *aizsargs*; Justins Volonts was the brother of Ulmanis's one-time Minister of Welfare; and Nataliya Temer was a Baltic German who had returned to Germany on 25 February 1941. Initially on the list was Sebastians Paberžs, the brother of Juris Paberžs, Minister of Justice in the People's Government of June 1940, but he was excluded from it as the communists extended their hold on power. Although he was a suitable candidate for expropriation in many ways – he was an absentee landlord, a former leading member of the Progressive Party and director of the

Daugavpils Savings Bank Society, in which capacity he refused to allow his workers to take part in communist propaganda campaigns – it was decided it would not be politic to include him because of his brother's status.[135]

To equip the horse-hiring bases it was party policy to impose compulsory purchase orders on those families who possessed horses. Peasants were paid 800–1,500 roubles if they were providing a horse for a horse-hiring station. However, it was a temptation to take advantage of those peasants who appeared to be in debt to the Agricultural Bank, for the animals could then be seized without payment to recover the debt allegedly owed. Such measures were widespread: in Viški, the chairman of the local soviet comrade Danilov seized the horse of Iosif Daukše for the local horse-hiring base in lieu of an alleged debt, and somehow managed to extract a bribe of 300 roubles on top of that. This case was seen as so unjust that it was reported to Derevyanskii, the representative of the Soviet Communist Party in Riga, who ensured that the horse was returned.[136]

The authorities' plans for agriculture became abundantly clear on 19 April when decrees were issued concerning the compulsory delivery to the state of wheat, meat, milk, wool and potatoes. The press asserted that these delivery quotas were modest and warned that only 'enemies' would believe rumours to the contrary.[137] In the following week meetings were organised throughout the region to acquaint peasants with these regulations and attempt to justify them. Reading between the lines of the press it is clear the decrees were not well received: communist speakers were forced to acknowledge that 'enemies' would see the quotas as exploitation and try to prevent deliveries being made. Even in Aizkalne, where the local party activist A. Sudiks was supposed to have established a good rapport with the peasants, the picture of the meeting held to discuss quotas shows a room of glum faces.[138] Nor was this the end of the demands made on the peasantry. Scarcely a month later, on 17 May, the authorities announced a new agricultural tax. Although described as modest and just, the detailed tables printed in the press suggested this was far from the case; to escape the tax a peasant had to have an annual income of less than 1,200 roubles. However, income was not real income but arbitrary potential income: so, the possession of a cow was said to give an income of 280 roubles, the possession of a pig 160, of a horse 200 and of a bull 150; similarly each hectare of plough-land was assumed to give an income of 300 roubles, of kitchen garden 380 and of meadow 120.[139]

As the spring sowing approached the party found itself at increased loggerheads with those peasants it called 'kulaks'. As the campaign to try and complete the sowing got going, the authorities found themselves in a dilemma. The weather was unusually wet. Kulaks advised delaying the sowing; agronomists advised delaying the sowing; but the party had set a target of completing the sowing by 25 May and that target had to be met. And so the press launched a campaign against those machine-tractor stations which listened to those who urged delay. Although on 8 May the press carried a story praising the Aglona machine-tractor station for being one of the first to start ploughing,[140] a few days later it became clear this was mere propaganda. The same machine-tractor station was then criticised both for the small amount of land ploughed and because thus far the only ploughing had been done by horses and the tractors had never gone into the fields, presumably for fear of sticking in the mud.[141] The Preiļi machine-tractor station, with its eight caterpillar tractors and seven wheeled tractors, was also criticised for delaying ploughing until there was a break in the weather.[142] On 15 May there was a meeting of district-party activists to assess the situation. It decided that the machine tractor stations should work around the clock to meet the 25 May deadline, and that any acts of deliberate vandalism against tractors or other agricultural machines should result in arrest.[143]

Yet in many areas these decisions were simply ignored. As the deadline of 25 May approached, the press found more and more examples of both party activists and their own agronomists following the 'kulak' line that sowing should be delayed until the end of the wet spell. Kulaks made a great show of not sowing,[144] and in Biķernieki the party activists went along with them.[145] Meanwhile the agronomist at the Aglona machine-tractor station was again pilloried for refusing to allow his tractors to operate at night.[146] Although the 25 May target was not met, by the end of the month the target had been met in Latgale everywhere except Rēzekne, which was 86 per cent complete, and Daugavpils, which was 96 per cent complete.[147]

The decrees on the compulsory delivery quotas made clear that those who joined collective farms would be freed from some of the compulsory deliveries.[148] The regulations for the 17 May tax regime also made clear that members of collective farms could benefit from a 20 per cent reduction in tax.[149] These were the first public acknowledgements that collective farms were on the way. Back in August 1940 the press had been at pains to point out that rumours about collectivisation were being circulated by enemies such as kulaks.[150] This was not entirely true. Young communists in Biķierniki had claimed to detect signs that poor peasants there wanted to form collective farms and for a short while *Latgal'skaya Pravda* seemed to support them.[151] Officially, however, collective farms were not on the agenda until after Stalin's XVIII Party Conference. Then, after the February Central Committee Plenum in Riga, which debated the decisions of the XVIII Party Conference, the Daugavpils district party decided to start a mass collectivisation campaign.[152] As a general meeting of the district party organisation was told on 9 March, this would not be a campaign for full-blown collectivisation overnight, but a gradual campaign to popularise the most basic form of collective farm, always referred to by the acronym TOZ.[153]

Towards the end of March there were some oblique public hints that collectivisation might not be far off. Writing on the moves to set up machine-tractor stations and the agreements signed through them on which land to plough with tractors, I. Bobrok, the secretary of the Daugavpils district komsomol wondered in the press if the next logical step would not be to establish a TOZ where land, but not livestock, was owned and worked collectively.[154] Peasants were quick to catch on: at the end of March a purely fictitious 'Central Land Committee', composed of peasants opposed to collectivisation, put around a circular stating that peasant meetings were to be held at which peasants would be given the choice to 'join the collective or lose your land'.[155] No such meetings were planned, but the party was pressing ahead. On 17 April 1941 the press reported the formation of Latgale's first TOZ: six families in Aizkalne had agreed to farm their land in common, keeping back a hectare of land for each family's kitchen garden; all houses, barns, equipment and animals remained privately owned.[156] The formation of a second TOZ was reported three days later.[157]

The district committee endorsed the decision to establish these first two TOZ collective farms on 26 April.[158] By the end of April *Latgal'skaya Pravda* had taken up the cause of generalising on the Aizkalne experience. Under the headline 'Let us head this initiative of the working peasants', it called on all party workers to explain to peasants how best to go about establishing a TOZ. Sudnik, the party organiser in Aizkalne, was praised for the initiative he had taken, but warned that he should not do everything himself but involve more people.[159] Although a further TOZ was reported in Skaista on 11 April,[160] the Daugavpils district committee was worried it was running before it could walk and wrote to the Central Committee for guidance. In particular it was unsure what a TOZ collective farm contract should look like and sent a draft from one of the Aizkalne farms for consideration.[161] Despite these reservations, the collectivisation campaign continued throughout May. The press praised the achievements of new TOZ established near Aglona,[162] Naujene and Indra[163] in the course of the sowing campaign. At the end of the month the press stressed that it was the TOZ that had over-fulfilled their sowing plans.[164]

On this basis, the collectivisation campaign entered a new phase. At Naujene in Daugavpils district a model collective farm, suitably named Iskra, was established on 14 June, bringing together 16 families.[165] On 16 June the national communist daily *Cīņa* published the Collective Farm Statute adopted in the rest of the Soviet Union in 1935.[166] On 23 June the Iskra TOZ was again feted by the press since here it was agreed that, as in the model statute, individual families would retain private plots of only 0.5 hectares.[167] When the Central Committee met in Riga on 19–20 June its original intention was to launch a full-scale collectivisation campaign, as documents drafted for that meeting made clear. A briefing paper on progress with the formation of TOZ collective farms noted that by May several were in the process of formation in Latgale, although in one early experiment near Rēzekne poor preparation had meant that of the 23 families at first interested 20 subsequently dropped out.[168] This example was included to stress the need for careful preparatory work, not as a reason to call off the campaign. Among these Central Committee papers were a draft model statute dated 14 May and a pro-forma version where only the name of the collective farm needed to be filled in. There were also notes for agitators including a draft speech entitled 'Let us head this initiative of the working peasantry', echoing the line already taken by *Latgal'skaya Pravda*, which praised the developments in Aizkalne, explained how kulaks were constantly giving a false idea of what the statutes should be, and then went on to describe the workings of a model TOZ.[169] A nationwide campaign was clearly in the offing.

Terror

The abandoning of the collectivisation campaign was prompted by Stalin's decision to deport to Siberia unreliable elements from the Baltic States and other border regions. At this time Stalin was concerned lest the war with Germany he hoped to postpone until 1942 might break out earlier. On 5 May 1941 he made an impromptu comment during a Kremlin graduation ceremony for military cadets which suggested that he wanted military preparations intensified; within ten days he had endorsed a new war plan. There was, therefore, a certain logic to bringing forward plans, which had already been discussed in principle, for removing from border regions those people who might be likely to co-operate with an advancing German Army. When Stalin spoke on 5 May he had not seen his security chief Lavrentii Beria for ten days; he held meetings with him on both 7 and 9 May.[170] On 14 May Stalin took the decision to deport nine categories of people living in those territories annexed since the signing of the Nazi–Soviet Pact, namely the three Baltic States, Western Ukraine, Western Belorussia and Moldavia. The deportations would take place a month later on 14 June. The categories were: 1) members of counter-revolutionary organisations and their families; 2) leading staff of former gendarmes, police and prison personnel, plus those other officers on which there was compromising material; 3) former landlords and traders worth 150 thousand lats; former factory owners worth 200 thousand lats and former leading civil servants of the bourgeois government; 4) former officers on whom there was compromising material; 5) the families of those condemned to death for counter-revolution; 6) people repatriated from Germany on whom there was compromising material; 7) those refugees from Poland who had not obtained Soviet citizenship; 8) criminal elements who continued their illegal activity; 9) and police-registered prostitutes, who continued in their profession. Notes made clear that compromising material meant activity engaged in prior to the incorporation into the Soviet Union and/or connection with foreign intelligence services.

In the country as a whole 14,194 people were deported from Latvia, some arrested and some administratively deported, usually the families of those arrested. A total of 4,065 men and 137 women were arrested and 9,992 people administratively deported. Of those arrested, 3,318 were Latvians, 559 were Jews and 26 were Russian with 76 falling into the category of 'others'. Of the administratively exiled there were 8,100 Latvians, 1,212 Jews, 519 Russians, 10 Germans and 151 others. In straightforward percentage terms, the Latvians were most affected: over 80 per cent of the victims were Latvian, while Latvians comprised 75 per cent of the population according to the 1935 census. However, the same census put the Jewish population at just under 5 per cent, whereas nearly 12 per cent of those deported were Jews; thus in percentage terms per head of population, the Jews suffered more than any other nationality. By profession those arrested on 14 June included 616 traders, 306 policemen, 29 prison personnel, 166 army officers, seven former parliamentary deputies, six diplomats, 31 judges, 71 teachers, 24 doctors, seven clergymen, 15 students, 39 forest workers, 1,345 farmers, 44 village elders and 13 village secretaries; 1,789 of those arrested had been *aizsargs*. The age profile fitted the target group: most were aged 30 to 50, active members of the old order.[171] The logistics of the operation were horrific. In all 661 railway wagons were used, 24 in Daugavpils, 11 in Rézekne and three each in nearby Kráslava, Indra, Līvāni and Nīcgale.[172] Four trains passed through Daugavpils station loaded with deportees from all over the country.[173] As the stationmaster waved one of these trains through he little realised his own daughter, a student in Riga, was among those being deported and could see her father from a crack in the side of the goods wagon.[174]

These national statistics could hide major local variations. From Daugavpils district, including the city itself, 1,007 people were exiled, 500 men and 507 women; 624 came from the city and the rest from the districts. By nationality there were 572 Latvians, 209 Jews, 157 Russians, four Germans and 65 others. With 20 per cent of those exiled Jews, Daugavpils was above the national average, and an unscientific survey of Rēzekne put the figure of Jews deported at nearer one third.[175] Yet in many rural parts of Daugavpils district, the targets were almost exclusively Latvian. In Preiļi town all 16 of those detained had Latvian names, and it was the same for the ten detained in Preiļi parish. In Līvāni town all but one of the 25 detained had Latvian names as did all of the 43 detained in Līvāni parish. In Aizkalne all ten of those deported had Latvian names, as did the seven deported from in Naujene. It was the same in Aglona, where all of the 23 deported had Latvian names, as did all but one of the 52 taken from Kalupe. In rural areas Russians did not escape arrest entirely: in Indra there were many Russian names among the 41 people affected, while in Biķernieki four of those arrested were Russian; but the statistics give the clear impression that the targets were the old administration and its *aizsarg* supporters.[176] Although drafted on class lines, the deportation guidelines impacted on ethnicity and in many rural parts of Latgale seemed anti-Latvian in content.

The deportations in Daugavpils took place in the following way. Local communist leaders were briefed about the operation five days beforehand and instructed to establish a five-person planning team involving the city or district secretary and representatives from the security services.[177] These teams were to identify local targets, in line with the guide figures issued to them from on high.[178] The next stage was to identify a team of 204 people, made up from party and komsomol members and the non-party sympathisers. Then an élite group of 32 party members and candidate party members was identified which would be sent to rural areas of Daugavpils district. At 7.00 in the evening of 13 June the team was called to a meeting and told of the need to purge the town of counter-revolutionary elements; it was then given detailed instructions as to how the operation should be carried out. According to Treimans's report on the affair, dated 17 June, the decision was welcomed and there were no cases of 'cowardice' or of people giving 'excuses' as to why they could not take part. Sensing the real reason for the operation, the party activists filled in the gap between the end of the briefing meeting and the start of the operation with a detailed discussion of the international situation. This discussion could have gone on for some time because to help with the operation the city was allocated 100 students from the Leningrad Militia School, but they only arrived at 2 in the morning of the 14th. This meant the operation began very late: instead of starting at midnight as planned, it began at five in the morning and continued until eight at night.

In the city things went smoothly and Treimans could report that there was no active or even passive resistance. However, there was some resistance in the countryside. In Kalupe parish there was an incident of armed opposition. A former policeman and *aizsarg* Jānis Babris persuaded his brother to open the door and pose as him, while he dived back into the house and grabbed a pistol. He then opened fire on the two men sent to detain him, killing militia-man Sluts and lightly wounding candidate party member Ozans. Babris then grabbed Sluts's gun, jumped on his bicycle and disappeared. Otherwise the operation went smoothly, and the 24 wagons used for transportation were properly supplied with food and left as planned at 2 a.m. on 16 June. Once the trains had departed, officials set to work on an audit of confiscated valuables.[179] Treimans felt his men had performed well and that workers understood why the deportations had taken place. He did not challenge the popular explanation that 'war will start soon and that is why the enemies needed to be exiled'. Among the more prominent men detained, whose families were also deported, were the former mayor Andrejs Švirksts and the former merchants Iosifs Feigelsons and Solomons Nirenburgs.

The case of these two businessmen highlighted the arbitrary nature of this operation. Nirenburgs owned a small paint shop and lived in a modest house; but the value of his paint stock meant his turnover was over 150,000 lats. To meet the guide figures issued from Moscow, there was little interest in exploring the true circumstances of those targeted. Feigelson had once been wealthy, but at the time of his arrest he owned nothing and was simply in charge of three delivery bicycles used to transport *Laima* chocolates.[180]

Feigelson had employed Faifish Fridman, second secretary of the city party organisation, and was on good terms with him,[181] but targets were targets. Yet the combination of central control figures and local targeting could enable some people to escape arrest. The arrest of seven former parliamentary deputies did not mean that all deputies were arrested. Despite his past as a prominent parliamentary deputy Miletii Kalistratov, the leader of the Old Believer community in Daugavpils, escaped arrest on 14 June. However, when the Nazi invasion started on 22 June he was one of a further 71 'enemies' detained and summarily executed in Daugavpils prison.[182]

Although Stalin's decision to deport his 'enemies' was prompted by the evolving international situation, there had been a marked increase in anti-Soviet activity as spring turned to summer. Before 14 June 1941 in Latvia as a whole 77 men and two women had been arrested for political crimes, 59 Latvians, eight Russians and seven Jews.[183] Of the local figures arrested prior to 14 June 1941 Professor Feils, the director of the Daugavpils People's Conservatory, and Edgar Chernyaevskii, a pupil at the commercial college and one of the town's best basketball players, stood out.[184] The first arrests took place in the autumn. Between 18 October and 17 November the security services arrested ten participants in a nationalist group based in No. 1 Secondary School in Daugavpils, including its leader Haralds Muižnieks, aged 19; all those arrested were roughly the same age and all were Latvian.[185] Then at the end of January 1941 the Catholic Priest Anton Lopatenko was sentenced to 18 months prison for 'hooliganism', although it is clear from the charge sheet that his actual crime was to mobilise opinion against the regime.[186] Shortly afterwards, in the early part of 1941, the security services penetrated the Daugavpils branch of a student organisation known as KOLA and arrested its leaders in March–April.[187] Meanwhile on 18 March the Daugavpils security chief Iosif Barkovskii, a former building worker of Polish ethnicity, informed Treimans that the man who ran the post office, a Russian named Zaichikov, had anti-Soviet views and had a policy of employing only those with similar views, such as the Latvians Kārlis Žagate and Voldemars Ceriņš.[188]

In April 1941 things took a potentially more dramatic turn. Between 17 and 23 April there were three fires in Daugavpils which all seemed to have been cases of politically motivated arson. The first building to suffer was a dacha used as a convalescent home for Red Army invalids; the second damaged one of the city's non-graduating secondary schools; and the third, which inflicted serious damage, was an attack on the building used by the party's city committee. In the first and the third cases people died in the fires. Investigation had made clear that ant-Soviet groups were involved, but no arrests had been made. The investigators argued that Treimans had resolved to hush the matter up rather than confronting an obvious nationalist challenge head on.[189] The militia was even less able to do much about constant acts of petty sabotage, like when it was discovered in early May that the car belonging to the Dvina river port authority had sand in its radiator and water in its petrol tank[190]

When the spring sowing campaign got under way, the authorities decided to arrest their most vociferous opponents among the peasantry. On 30 May 1941 *Latgal'skaya Pravda* reported that K. Tropiņš had been arrested for sabotage and sentenced to two years in prison and ten years of exile from Latvia; his crime was to refuse to sow his land. On 14 June 1941 the same paper reported that Antons Laizāns, a former lawyer who owned 30 hectares of land, had made no effort to sow his land by the deadline of 25 May; his defence that he was prepared to sow, but only when the weather permitted, was rejected and he was sentenced to one year in prison, the confiscation of his property and loss of civil rights for five years.[191] There was some unease that these arrested kulaks became martyrs: in a report sent to Riga at the end of May it was noted that kulaks were using their court appearances to make 'provocative' speeches.[192] Yet none of these incidents was serious enough to merit the deportations that followed.

The Anti-Latvian party

What was the party like that was prepared to deport its fellow citizens? Although Treimans and others had been drafted in from the Soviet Union to help the stretched local Communist Party, those who ran Daugavpils in 1940–1 were still by and large veterans of the local underground struggle: in June 1941 37 per cent of the members of the Daugavpils city party had a background in the pre-war underground, with the rest split between new members and Russian incomers.[193] In 1940–1 the total number of Russian incomers for the country as a whole was about 1,000, and by and large these people were not allocated to the NKVD, where the Latvian Communist Party concentrated its own members,[194] but to servicing other commissariats. Pre-war communists took the lead in Daugavpils and by arguing that Soviet democracy was a higher form of democracy than western democracy, and by stressing that Latvia needed to move on from the Ruritanian utopia of Ulmanis, they could defend both adhesion to the Soviet Union and the economic rigours imposed after Stalin's XVIII Party Conference. Complicity in the deportations changed that. The deportations were a cynical, and completely ineffective, move by Stalin to improve the defences of the Soviet Union. Loyal communists in Daugavpils could not disobey an order from Stalin, but it deprived them of any lingering popular support.

The administration of Daugavpils in 1940–1 was the antithesis of 'Latvia for the Latvians'. During the first rather chaotic fortnight of Soviet rule, the local communists found it hard to find a Latvian orator for their mass meetings. They frequently used Osvalds Štāls, who had never been a major figure in the underground; he taught physics in the commercial college and would shortly become its director.[195] Of the 168 people assigned to the Daugavpils city electoral commission in December 1940, arguably the city communists' most loyal supporters, 40 had clearly Latvian names, ten had clearly Jewish names, while the remaining names were

Slavonic.[196] Preparing for the Supreme Soviet elections had forced both the city and district party organisations to hold plenary meetings, that of the district party being held on 7 December and that of the city party on 8 December.[197] Both meetings revealed how relatively small the party membership was, how under-represented Latvians were in the new political system and how insecure the party felt.

The meeting of the Daugavpils district party organisation on 7 December was attended by 55 members, 18 candidate members and 17 delegates from the Red Army. The nine-member presidium included two Red Army men and only one Latvian.[198] The national mix of the district committee itself was better: Arnolds Zandmans had been appointed first secretary on 1 December at a meeting which confirmed Iosif Selitskii as second secretary;[199] other members endorsed on the 7th included Iosif Barkovskii, Isaak Borok and Antons Luriņš. As to the membership at large: of the full members, there were 32 Russians, 16 Latvians, 10 Jews and 2 Poles; while for the candidate members the figures were 49, 19, 4 and 1 respectively. The komsomol had 129 full members on 1 October 1940 and 116 candidates; by ethnicity it was 40 per cent Russian, 25 per cent Latvian, 21 per cent Jewish and 14 per cent Belorussian. The 'non-party sympathisers' comprised 434 groups with 4,200 members.[200] Among those reporting to the district committee was L. Avdyukevich, listed then as the director of an industrial concern.[201] The meeting of the city party organisation the following day gave even less representation to the Latvian community. Only one local Latvian sat on the new city committee: its members were Mikhail Yukhno, Pavel Leibch, Aleksandr Tarasov, Abzal Miftakhov, Girsh Efun, Fedor Treimans, Ignatii Yakhimovich, Ilya Gandler and Faifish Fridman. The revision commission comprised Solomon Shal'man, Solomon Murin and Astafii Yankovskii.[202] Of the 51 members of the city party organisation, 18 were Jews, 12 were Russians, 12 were Latvians and 9 were Poles; of the 42 candidate members 15 were Russians, 10 were Jews, 10 were Poles, 4 were Latvians and 3 were Lithuanians.[203] The first secretary, Yukhno, was Russian and the second secretary was a Jew, Faifish Fridman.

Six months later, the situation was no different. On 6 June 1941 the district party admitted 32 new members: there were seven Latvians, 18 Russians, two Belorussions, three Jews, one Pole and one Latgalean.[204] A review of the city party that same month suggested Latvians made up only 13 per cent of the party's underground core.[205] The party could display sensitivity in the national question: in April 1941 it decided to reallocate two of its party organisers; the man assigned to Rudzāti, a Latvian area, knew no Latvian and so was swapped with the Latvian speaker Cveks, who had originally been assigned to Naujene.[206] Nevertheless, it was difficult to counter the view that Bolshevik rule looked like a Russian take-over.

It was equally clear that there were grounds for talk of a Jewish take-over. The Daugavpils communists did not trumpet their Jewishness. In the July 1940 election campaign the party was keen to win the support of the Jewish vote and the press was quick to denounce acts of anti-Semitism: on 29 June 1940 *Latgal'sksaya Pravda* reported under the heading 'Our Enemies' how a Latvian reserve officer had been abusing the new People's Government and venting his anger on Jewish soldiers,[207] while on 3 July 1940 the same paper reported that junior and uncommissioned officers were still assaulting 'Russians and Jews'. However, once on the eve of the elections the Jewish community had called on all its members to vote for the Bloc of Working People, there was little special pleading for the Jewish cause, except to support a campaign launched in the autumn to develop a Jewish theatre in the city.[208] Yet, deliberately or inadvertently, the policies pursued by the local Bolsheviks could be portrayed as pro-Jewish and a deliberate snub to Latvian sensibilities. The decision to close Daugavpils Teachers' Institute, whose director was Valerija Seile, a pillar of the Latvian educational establishment, and to use the building for a Jewish school was fraught with symbolism.

If most of the city committee elected in December 1940 were Russian, one third of its members were Jews. The only Latvians were the Moscow Latvian Treimans and the local head of the city komsomol organisation Pavel Leibch.[209] After Yukhno's dismissal, the most prominent local communist was second secretary Faifish Fridman, who was also one of the city's Latvian Supreme Soviet deputies. Contemporaries recall him as the most dynamic figure in the leadership. The organiser of the city party committee, Grigorii Efun, and the popular Spanish Civil War veteran Benjamin Kur, who ran the agitation department, were both Jewish. Solomon Shal'man was a prominent member of the criminal police and Solomon Murin a prominent member of the security police, both Jews. The prison supervisor Aron Gandler and his brother Ilya, who ran the state bank, were Jews, as was the head of the district komsomol Isaak Borok.[210] These were very visible positions. In some of the rural parishes, Jews very clearly dominated the new order. Thus in Preiļi the mayor was Reuben Arsh, his deputy Mikhail Kogan and the chairman of the censorship committee Yerachmich Kolov.[211] For those who believed in a Judeo-Bolshevik conspiracy, there seemed plenty of evidence.

On one issue, however, the communist party adopted a stance akin to that of Latvian nationalists. It dealt firmly with a vociferous minority within the party which deviated towards nationalism on the question of the Latgale language and culture. On 3 August 1940 *Latgal'skaya Pravda* reported the appearance of the new Latgale-language paper *Latgolas Taisneiba*, but at the same time criticised the line it took. The editorial had referred to 'the Latgale people as a whole' ignoring the correct Marxist-Leninist approach which recognised the existence of Latgale kulaks who could have no common stance with the poor peasants of Latgale; the second issue of the paper was force do issue a correction. Two months later, on 1 October 1940, *Latgal'skaya Pravda* criticised those intellectuals 'mostly from Riga' who tried to create a Latgale separatist movement. Nevertheless, there were still problems closer to Daugavpils and on 11 January 1941 the Daugavpils district committee debated the situation concerning *Latgolas Taisneiba*. It concluded that right from the start the paper had made mistakes about nationality policy, thereafter its editorial board had behaved improperly by using the paper to criticise the district committee without getting prior permission; it had also issued slogans while knowing that only the party's Central Committee had this power. Then, in the run-up to the elections on 12 January 1941, confusion between editors and printers had resulted in the paper appearing to suggest that those who took part in the elections were enemies of the people. The editor, Dominiks Kaupužs, no longer a hero of the underground, was held to be responsible and was sacked; he had once been expelled from the underground party for his Trotskyist comments on the national question.[212]

The party itself recognised that it had lost popular support after Stalin's dictated elections of July 1940. It had been forced to rely increasingly on the bigoted views of 'backward', mostly Russian workers. By March 1941 those 'backward' workers in the workers' guard were found to do little other than get drunk. By June the distortions to the economy imposed at Stalin's XVIII Party Conference meant that these workers could not even be guaranteed their beer. On 12 June the Daugavpils city committee discussed a report which addressed the shortage of beer, especially where it was most needed, in the parks and places of popular entertainment. Workers' wives were probably more concerned at the shortage of summer shoes, especially children's shoes, and summer clothes generally, which the report also revealed.[213] Even before the deportations revealed the terror inherent in the Stalinist system, it was clear that Soviet socialism in Daugavpils was not working.

3   Genocide

On 22 June 1941 the Nazi invasion of the Soviet Union began. As the German Army advanced on Daugavpils, the Communist Party leadership organised a chaotic evacuation plan which enabled the leading party cadres to escape, but left many junior soviet officials behind; an uncertain number of Jewish families were also able to escape, but the majority did not. As the German Army and the Red Army fought for control, popular militias emerged on both sides. The workers' guard was hastily re-established and tried to defend the town, while in the countryside nationalist partisan groups were formed by those who had escaped deportation on 14 June. The greatest success of the workers' militia was not on the battlefield, but in implementing a scorched earth policy for Daugavpils, which saw much of the city set on fire in the immediate aftermath of its occupation.

As soon as the Nazis had control of the city, their war against 'Jewish-Bolshevism' began. Attacks on the Jews were piecemeal at first, and it was only men of working age who were imprisoned; by August a ghetto had been established on the Grīva side of the river Dvina where all Jews were detained. Systematic killings began on 9 July when those detained in the prison were executed in the nearby Railwaymen's Garden. From 29 July the preferred execution site was the nearby resort of Mežciems where throughout August Jews were shot in a series of mass actions. Many of those killed at this time were Jews brought from other parts of Latgale, but large numbers of Jews were also killed in villages and towns throughout the region. Although these killings were ordered by the Nazis and were initially carried out by Germans, local police volunteers soon became involved, some showing great enthusiasm for the task. For some this was because of membership of the anti-Semitic Pérkonkrusts party, for others it reflected inarticulate notions of resentment coupled with greed. Those involved in the killings had the pickings of Jewish property, as well as copious supplies of alcohol.

By the end of August 1941 the non-Jewish communities were adapting to the new order. Rationing and restrictions were met with sullen acceptance. On his appointment on 1 September, the Daugavpils Gebietskommissar Friedrich Schwung tried to push forward a normal civilian agenda. He

encouraged the development of People's Aid, one of the few new organisations which did not fall under the ban on political associations introduced
on 20 September, and set about trying to implement the anticipated land
reform. But, despite the dehumanising brutality of normal life in the ghetto,
the SS wanted more victims. After the exhumation of 'victims of
Bolshevism', press hysteria paved the way for the annihilation on 7–9
November of all Jews except specialist workers and the families of doctors.
Those Jews still alive at the end of 1941 had either survived because their
labour brought financial benefit to the administrators of the city, or because
local people had hidden them.

Red retreat

The radio broadcast announcing the Nazi attack of 22 June 1941 was
reported in the local press the following day. Thereafter the press gave no
clue as to how the war was developing and the civilian population was
quite unprepared for the speed of the German advance. Even those
working in the Daugavpils fortress, where units of the Red Army were
deployed, did not realise how rapidly the Nazi Army was approaching.[1]
That things were going badly only became clear when *Latgal'skaya Pravda*
did not appear on 25 June and refugees began to arrive from Lithuania.[2]
The first Nazi planes began to bomb the city on 26 June, flying low and
targeting political as well as strategic targets: thus one of the first buildings to suffer was the headquarters of the security services near People's
House.[3] The party leadership, however, knew the true state of affairs and
implemented its plan for evacuation.

The evacuation was largely the work of Astafii Yankovskii, an underground veteran, who was one of the last communists to leave the city on the
morning of 26 June.[4] The first secretary of the Daugavpils city party organisation Treimans, who had been imposed by Moscow to improve the local
administration, was one of the first to flee.[5] Three categories were eligible
for evacuation: communists, policemen and Jews. The majority of party and
komsomol officials were successfully evacuated, but the vast majority of
Jews were left behind.[6] A report compiled during the war made clear that all
the leading party and soviet personnel had escaped, with the exception of
two deputy ministers and a few deputies to the Supreme Soviet. Lower down
the hierarchy things had not gone so smoothly: 700 rank-and-file party
members had been left behind, from a total membership of 2,557 and only
half of the parish soviet chairmen escaped; at the bottom of the hierarchy
the figures were just 20–30 per cent.[7] At the height of the evacuation there
were ten trains trying to leave Daugavpils goods station.[8] A witness to the
scene at the goods station embarkation point spoke of 'military and civilians
all shoving and pushing to get on board any train available ... there were still
Soviet security men among them. Whenever word of a train passed around,
everyone surged toward it, kicking, elbowing, anything to inch forward.'[9]

The mass evacuation of the civilian population began only once the party leaders had left. However, since the goods station was being constantly bombed on the 26th, many preferred to escape on foot and a column of refugees set off towards Krāslava.[10] The last train to leave the city did not make it, but was stopped by the German Army outside the city and those on board ordered to return.[11] Many Jews decided not to flee. Older members of the Jewish community remembered the German occupation during the First World War when the Jews had come to no harm and the German administration had even appointed a Jew as mayor; they refused to believe that times had changed.[12] The behaviour of the Soviet press during the time of the Nazi–Soviet Pact encouraged such naivety: there had been no criticism of Nazi Germany's anti-Semitism, the details of the horrors of the Warsaw ghetto only being published in *Pravda* on 26 June 1941.[13]

Not everyone fled without putting up a fight. Mikhail Yukhno, the veteran of the underground and former first secretary, rallied the railway workers he now represented to form a new workers' guard; workers' guard units were established at the track and points workshop, the rolling-stock repair yards and the station. Among the volunteers was another underground veteran Kazimir Lazdovskii.[14] To obtain arms, a lorry was sent to Riga, but by the time it returned it was clear that the Red Army was retreating and there was little enthusiasm for a fight. Although the majority of the weapons brought from Riga were handed to the security services, the most disciplined of the workers' guard units did fight, and retreated together with the Red Army,[15] a retreat which began on the night of 25–26 June.[16]

To capture the road bridge across the Dvina between Grīva and Daugavpils the Germans parachuted in a team dressed in Red Army uniforms. This sowed confusion and meant that the city's major defensive line was breached from the outset.[17] The German Army entered the city at 3.00 p.m. on the 26th and met a determined but futile rear-guard action around the post office where the fighting was heavy.[18] The other area of fierce last-minute resistance was on the edge of the suburb of Jaunbūve, by Gubišces lake.[19] Such resistance overcome, the German Army began pulling down placards and portraits of Stalin.[20]

Once it became clear that the city had fallen to the Germans, the remnants of the workers' guard set about implementing a scorched-earth policy, destroying what industry they could. Vladislav Voevodskii, who commanded the workers' guard at the track and points workshop, organised a demolition crew which set fire to the works and virtually destroyed it. Voevodskii and his associates hid from the Germans, but were arrested on 12 August.[21] The extent of this scorched-earth policy makes clear that far more people than Voevodskii were involved. A German report of 16 July noted that only a small part of the city had been destroyed in the battle, but 'the larger part of the city burnt down' as a result of arson, leaving the electrical works burnt out and the water-supply system crippled but operative.[22] Another report of 31 July spoke of the 'greater part of the town' being destroyed by fires 'started by Jews'.[23]

On 6 August the German-sponsored Latvian-language newspaper reported that of the 1,923 buildings destroyed in the fighting, 1,912 had been deliberately destroyed 'as the Jews fled the city'.[24] This was almost certainly an exaggeration, which underplayed the extent of earlier bomb damage, but it became fixed in the German official record. The figure of 1,912 buildings deliberately burned down was repeated when the anniversary of capture of Daugavpils was celebrated in June 1942. The German version of events was that the town was basically whole when the first German soldiers entered the city on the afternoon of 26 June and that the fires began during the night of 26–27th.[25] An independent eyewitness confirmed these dates. Entering the city on the night of 26–27 June she recalled: 'the city of Daugavpils was on fire and the entire horizon seemed to be ablaze; I thought it looked like a painting, a painting of a city in flames.'[26] The fighting in Latgale had been fiercer than anywhere else in Latvia; in Riga only 115 houses had been destroyed in the capture of the city.[27]

The great majority of the inhabitants had fled the city as the German Army took control, leaving only 8,000 inhabitants in the first days of the new order.[28] Their situation was desperate. On 27 June eyewitnesses reported looting in the city,[29] followed by a German order that all those looting would be shot; all the co-operative shops were then closed down and only bread shops allowed to open.[30] Despite the threat of summary execution the looting continued, especially on Riga Street in the heart of the city which had mostly been spared serious damage other than broken windows through which people now carried away anything they could.[31]

Outside the city, there were places where groups of spontaneously formed Latvian nationalist partisans helped the German advance. In Bebrene, across the river Dvina from Daugavpils in Ilūkste district, no sooner had the Soviet authorities left than former *aizsargs* dug up hidden weapons and formed a 'self-defence force'.[32] They were mostly people who had escaped deportation on 14 June by being outwardly loyal – one had served on a trade-union committee – and now came together to establish a brigade which seized trophy weapons and arrested local Jews and communists;[33] formed on 28 June the Bebrene brigade included among those it arrested a young woman teacher at the local school deemed to be pro-Soviet whom they handed over to the Germans.[34] There were other clashes nearby. To the east of Bebrene, near Dviete, a group of unarmed Latvian nationalists attacked the local communist headquarters and seized their weapons, suffering one dead and five wounded in the process.[35] In Rubeņi two brigades were formed by associates of those deported on 14 June,[36] while there were also incidents near Aknīste.[37] On the Daugavpils side of the Dvina, in Vārkava, near Preiļi, there were several wounded and one fatality among a group of nationalist partisans claimed in the German sponsored press to be 300 strong;[38] this group included activists in nearby Kalupe and Aizkalne. One of those almost certainly involved in this group was the Līvāni journalist Edvards Zundans. He had worked on the local paper

Daugavas vēstnesis until soviet power forced him to take a minor administrative post in Preiļi.[39] He fled on 14 June and hid in the forest, where he joined others who had fled from Preiļi for the same reason.[40] Similar groups were formed in Viški[41] and Krāslava.[42]

The activity of these nationalist partisans was mostly recorded in the German- occupation press, which had an interest in exaggerating the impact of these groups. However, other evidence has corroborated the claims. At the end of the war, Otomar Oškalns, the second secretary of the Jēkabpils district communist party, described how he and Milda Birkenfelde, the first secretary of the Jēkabpils district communist party, had escaped at the time of the German advance. He noted how 'everywhere' they and their companions faced 'bandit' attacks as they moved from an initial hiding place between Nereta and Viesite towards Kārsava and the Russian border. This journey took them close to Bebrene, Līvāni and Preiļi.[43] The activity of nationalist partisans in Līvāni and Preiļi should come as no surprise, given the way the deportations in both places had affected the Latvian population exclusively.

Executions

Order was re-imposed in Daugavpils from 28 June 1941 when the Latvian Auxiliary Police was established. With German help this rapidly grew into a force of 240 men.[44] The new local administration was appointed three days later on 1 July.[45] The man put in charge was a former captain in the Latvian Army, Ed. Pētersons. He was the first head of the city's Auxiliary Police and initially he also headed the civil administration until mid-July,[46] when he transferred authority for the police to Roberts Blūzmanis, retaining for himself the post of city elder. Blūzmanis, who until then had owned a café on Rainis Street,[47] then appointed the heads of the six police prefectures – A. Sakārnis, Ž Strazdiņš, R Keipans, R Ērglis, Kr. Burgelis and H Krūmiņš[48] – and took as his deputy Osvalds Štāls, the director of the commercial college who had appeared to be such a prominent supporter of the Soviet regime.[49] As to the rank-and-file members of the auxiliary police, witnesses noted how they strode around with their rifles and green armbands, some 'wearing long hidden *aizsarg* uniforms'.[50] The administration appointed by the Germans to run Daugavpils was very much a Latvian administration. On 24 July the names of 100 top officials were published; less than 10 per cent of those names were Slavonic.[51] V. Priselkov, the man appointed agronomist for the Daugavpils region, was one of the few exceptions.[52]

Even before the city administration was fully established, Pētersons turned his attention to 'the Jewish problem'. On Sunday 29 June a poster appeared throughout the city in German, Russian and Latvian ordering all Jewish males aged under 60 to report to the market place. There, from the thousands present, including numerous refugees from Lithuania, work gangs of the youngest and fittest were selected. Under the direction of

German soldiers and Latvians wearing the armbands of the auxiliary police, the gangs were put to work burying the bodies of soldiers and civilians killed in the fighting.[53] At the end of their day's work the members of these gangs were taken to the prison, where they rejoined those Jewish men not selected for forced labour who had been taken straight from the market square to the prison. While the fit men in the work gangs had been clearing the city, the old men in the prison had been forced at gun point to jump like frogs and perform all sorts of ridiculous gestures as some sort of bizarre entertainment for their guards.[54] At some point during the day a car drew up at the prison, an SS officer got out and shouted at those in the courtyard: 'Jews, your time has come; soon you will be shot.'[55]

However, the city authorities were at first uncertain how to act. Jewish women, children and the men over sixty were subject to harassment and sporadic attacks for the first ten days. They were discriminated against in that they had to form a separate bread queue to that of the 'Christians', but they were not systematically harmed; those women who turned up with their men folk in the market square on 29 July were told to return home.[56] That does not mean there were no assaults on Jewish families at this time. One survivor recalled that Latvian policemen frequently broke into Jewish houses, taking property and killing those who got in their way.[57] Jewish shops were ransacked and some Jews were forced out of their homes, especially if they were in central locations.[58] Another survivor recalled the constant German threats at this time – despite being a woman she was used for forced labour, and one day she returned to find her home confiscated.[59] Yet such actions were not systematic. Other families were left untouched.[60]

The truth was that, as yet, no clear decision had been taken on what to do with the Jews. According to a German report at this time the prison population comprised 1,125 Jews, 32 political prisoners, 85 Russian workers and two 'criminal women'.[61] Although initially guarded by German soldiers, in subsequent days that task was increasingly transferred to the Latvian auxiliary police.[62] On 30 June a mock execution was staged of some of those accused by the Germans of setting fire to the city; but the prisoners were returned to their cells. For the next week a pattern set in. From 1 July the young and fit were selected for work duty, burying dead horses or unloading food, cement and other supplies; the older men remained in prison. All that changed with the arrival of SS Obersturmbannführer Dr Erich Ehrlinger and his Einsatzkommando 1b; he brought a deadly purpose to the solving of the 'Jewish Question'. Although some units of Einsatskommando 1b had arrived in Daugavpils on 26 June, it was not until 5 or 6 July that its main force arrived in the city; Ehrlinger himself probably arriving on the 6th.[63] The SS was under orders to encourage the local population to 'liberate themselves' and make it appear that they were taking the initiative in annihilating the Jews, ensuring that Nazi control of this operations was hidden from view.[64]

What perturbed Ehrlinger was that leading Latvians 'behaved passively towards the Jews'; it took the arrival of Einsatskommando 1b to persuade Pētersons's men to drive the Jews from their homes. As inhabitants began to return, many Latvians had put themselves forward to help restore the city and seemed positively disposed to the German authorities, Ehrlinger reported, but they seemed to have forgotten that half the population of Daugavpils had been Jews who 'ruled the city absolutely'.[65] Ehrlinger was not the only Nazi to note that their Latvian collaborators had to be prodded to action. In an overview of Latvia as a whole a report stressed that, given the Bolshevik atrocities, the Latvians should have engaged in spontaneous pogroms; but in fact local forces by themselves had liquidated only 'a few thousand' Jews. It had therefore been necessary to set up special teams, with the help of selected members of the Latvian auxiliary police, 'mostly the relatives' of those who suffered under Bolsheviks, to undertake wide-scale purging operations.[66]

Under Ehrlinger's guidance the killings began. On 8 July one of the Jewish prison work gangs was given the task of digging trenches in the Railwaymen's Garden, adjacent to the prison yard. On 9 July the executions began. Working methodically through the three floors of the prison from the ground floor upwards, the Jewish men were marched to the basement, where they handed over their remaining possessions, and then into the prison yard where they formed groups of 20. They then joined the vast coiling serpent of a queue which led from the courtyard, through an iron gate and out into the Railwaymen's Garden where the execution ditches had been prepared. A survivor recalled: 'I could see above us, on the embankment, German soldiers and their sweethearts looking down on the scene below as if we were in an amphitheatre ... The blue sky was almost clear, with only here and there a wisp of cloud ... I was struck by how quiet everyone was. There was no crying or wailing or hysteria. Just stillness. Stillness, shots and groups moving ahead.' He recalled how, when the execution site was reached, four were executed at a time by shots in the head at close range. It was, he felt, unlikely that the same executioners operated all day, but by the end of the day it was Latvian auxiliary policemen who pulled the triggers, to the command of an SS officer. In the end it became clear the Nazis had miscalculated; there was simply not enough room in the trenches for all the prison inmates. The last 200 prisoners were returned to their cells and a Jewish work gang sent to dig an additional trench for a cart-load of unburied bodies. Curious townspeople watched as this gruesome task was completed.[67] Reporting on progress on 11 or 12 July, Ehrlinger stated that to date 1,150 Jews had been killed.[68]

Ehrlinger also seemed to have plans for how to cope with the Jews not detained in prison. Immediately after the first prison massacre, the authorities requisitioned all Jewish homes, allegedly to re-house those who had lost their houses in the 'Jewish' fires'.[69] Thousands of women, children and men over 60, both Jews from Latvia and the many refugees from Lithuania, were herded into the Gajok synagogue. The Jews were told that the synagogue would be blown up and they would be burned to death. Cameras were in place to film the proceedings for the Berlin newsreels. For some reason, perhaps the danger of fire spreading, it was decided not to go ahead. On 11 July those detained in the synagogue were taken to the now empty prison. Here their remaining valuables were confiscated in the prison courtyard, before being locked in their cells.[70]

On 13 July Ehrlinger handed over to Obersturmbannführer Joachim Hamann, who began to prepare methodically for the next stage of the killings, which would end with his departure on 22 August when a further 9,012 Jews would be dead.[71] Over the next few days, the male Jewish prisoners were categorised according to work capacity and those identified as 'specialists' allowed to organise themselves into work teams; they were given a white card which prevented them and their families from being executed. However, with political prisoners and POWs arriving all the time, the prison was soon full again. On Sunday 16th there was another massacre of 'non-specialist' male prisoners which was followed on the 17th with the execution of women. Although the vast majority were Jews, this time those executed included some arrested for political crimes and some POWs. As before, they assembled in the prison courtyard before being executed in the Railwaymen's Garden. An observer noted that while most went heroically to their death, some broke down and pleaded for their lives with the Latvian auxiliary police who stood guard. On this occasion machine guns were reportedly used for the executions.[72] Executions then continued regularly until the end of July in five batches, as the Nazis worked methodically through the 'non-specialist' Jews brought to Daugavpils from towns as far afield as Kārsava and Balvi.[73] Those Jews living in the suburb of Gajok could hear the executioners' shots.[74]

By the end of the month the prison contained about 300 family members of 'specialist Jews',[75] while many of the specialist Jews themselves were engaged in forced labour to transform the Grīva bastion, part of the fortress complex situated on the Grīva side of the Dvina, into a Jewish ghetto; for easy access they constructed a wooden bridge next to the partially destroyed railway bridge. The Daugavpils ghetto was ready for occupation on 25 July, and by the 26th was full to overflowing.[76] By 29 July there were approximately 6,000 Jews crammed into the ghetto, including not only the 300 family members of the 'specialist Jews' transferred there from the prison under armed guard,[77] but Jews from the surrounding countryside[78] and those Daugavpils Jews who escaped detention in the prison.[79] The Nazi solution to this overcrowding was to resume the killing. On 29 July ghetto inhabitants were told they could move to a new camp being constructed seven kilometres away. They crossed the river and headed downstream to Mežciems, a wooded area by the river on the outskirts of town where there had once been a spa resort and where the better-off still had weekend cottages. Here the Jews were surrounded and executed. On 1 August non-

Daugavpils Jews, from such places as Dagda, Krāslava, Viški and Indra, were told they were being marched back home, but met the same fate.[80]

The first issue of the Latvian language newspaper *Daugavpils latviešu avīze* came out on 15 July, and that enabled the new authorities to justify their actions. The first page of its very first issue brought out the twin propaganda obsessions which would haunt Daugavpils for the next five years. The message was that the communists and the Jews had set out to destroy the Latvian land and its culture and had begun to implement that plan with the June deportations to Siberia. To emphasise the point, the same issue reported that excavations at Daugavpils prison on 13 July had revealed the bodies of those killed by the *Cheka*.[81] The paper did not report that local Jews were forced to carry out this exhumation and wash the bodies, before being attacked and killed by the onlooking crowd.[82] A fortnight later the paper brought out the other propaganda weapon at its disposal, collectivisation. With some justification it stressed that the German invasion had saved the country from full-scale collectivisation; the first collective farms, at the initiative of Russian rather than Latvian peasants, had already been set up.[83]

The ghetto was impossibly overcrowded; at its peak 14,000 Jews were crammed into it.[84] *Daugavpils latviešu avīze* gave a warning of what was to follow. On 5 August it carried a picture of war-devastated Daugavpils with the legend 'destroyed by the Jews'; the next day there was an aerial picture of damage to the suburbs; and that was the day the killings resumed. On 6 and again on 18 and 19 August the Nazis began the annihilation of all those Jews who did not have the certificate issued to 'specialist Jews' and their families. On each occasion, the ghetto inhabitants were lined up in the courtyard, on one occasion standing for hours in steady rain, and selected for life or death at Mežciems. As with the July killings, survivors recalled that these executions were prompted by the arrival of 'a German official', presumably Hamann.[85] The ghetto commandant Eduards Zaube received police chief Blūzmanis at the ghetto on 7–8 August.[86] Those who participated in these massacres put the number of 'actions' slightly higher than those who survived them. According to one participant, between 8 and 25 August there were five actions, with approximately 800 being killed on each occasion;[87] another participant recalled six 'actions' from the end of July to the end of August.[88] On 17 August 2,000 Jews were killed.[89] Escape was virtually impossible. One 14-year-old boy escaped by running and hiding in the forest.[90] Two 16-year-olds were saved at the graveside when their mother convinced a guard that their father was German; the mother was executed.[91] Such cases were extremely rare.

In some provincial towns the Jews were not brought to Daugavpils but were killed locally, and sometimes some Jews were killed locally in an initial outburst, before others were transferred to Daugavpils. In Rēzekne the Jewish community of 3,342 made up a quarter of the population in 1935. The German Army took the town on 3 July and on the 4th all Jews were ordered to the town square; 1,400 assembled as instructed, and a random ten were shot. Two large-scale actions took place on 9 and 15 July, when mostly men were killed; women and children were killed in August as each town district was cleared of its Jewish population. In nearby Viļāni and Malta the killings took place on 4 July.[92] In Preiļi half the town's population was destroyed over the course of a weekend. Latvian auxiliary police units arrived on 26 July and on the 27th forced 900 Jews into the synagogue; later that day 400 of them were taken away and executed, with the other 500 being killed on the 28th. On both occasions the Jews were told they were being transferred to another town. On 8 August those Jews who had survived the earlier massacre were killed.[93] In Līvāni, where the 1,000 Jews registered on the 1935 census made up 20 per cent of the population, the killings took place locally in early July. In Varakļāni, where the 952 Jews represented 57.3 per cent of the population, the killings did not take place until 4 August when 500 were killed. In Viļaka the killings took place on 11 August.[94]

Krāslava had a population of 1,444 Jews according to the 1935 census, or 34 per cent of the population. After the German Army arrived there were some random killings, but the vast majority of the local Jews, approximately 1,000 of them, were assembled in the synagogue towards the end of July, and then ordered to march to Daugavpils; two small groups were shot *en route* because they were felt to be old and were holding up the convoy.[95] In Ludza between 800 and 900 Jews were initially detained in a ghetto established in the town. Then on 17 August 'a special Latvian team' killed 830 of them. The survivors were moved to Daugavpils in October, with some being shot *en route*; all but a few specialists died there in November.[96] In Višķi, where 423 Jews had represented 56 per cent of the population, the Jews were initially detained in a temporary prison in the fire station. Most men were then shot locally, with the women and elderly being transferred to Daugavpils; again, those deemed unfit for the journey were shot *en route*. In Aglona 80 Jews were killed, not only members of the 57 strong local community but those brought in from the surrounding countryside.[97]

Although the killing of Jews ended for a while after the middle of August, other killings continued. The Nazis imposed their policy of 'euthanasia' against the allegedly mentally enfeebled. On 4 August the Daugavpils Psychiatric Hospital was closed down and its patients transferred to Aglona School. There, on 28 August, SS troops arrived, surrounded the building and announced that the patients were designated for physical destruction. In groups of 20 they were taken to the nearby forest and shot; 445 in total, of all nationalities – Russians, Jews, Latvians and Poles. Further 'actions' were ordered on 29 January 1942, when 368 were killed; on 14 April 1942, when 243 were killed; and finally on 22 October 1942 when 98 were killed.[98] 'Euthanasia' was not the only policy of Nazi eugenics brought to Daugavpils to strengthen the Aryan race. On 11 November 1941 the Reichskommissar Ostland, Hinrich Lohse, issued instructions that the sterilization programme should begin at once in the hospitals in Daugavpils, Rēzekne and Ludza. In Daugavpils the programme would be implemented by Dr Vilis Zaķitis, formally a prominent member of the Daugavpils Latvian Society.[99]

Executioners

The question of Latvian participation in these horrific events has caused much debate among historians. Members of the Latvian auxiliary police were clearly ready to brutalise and mistreat the Jews, but it took guidance from the Nazis before they embarked on genocide. Ehrlinger found Blūzmanis and Pētersons quite willing to introduce discriminatory measures against the Jews, but he had taken the initiative in stage-managing the execution of the Jews in the Railwaymen's Garden. Latvians played second fiddle, but some did so with great enthusiasm. As time went on, the involvement of Latvians grew. A survivor stressed that at the time of the Railwaymen's Garden killings most Latvian guards undertook support tasks such as guarding those who were digging the pits, although some Latvians were involved even in these killings.[100] Once the Hamann killings began in August on such a mass scale the close co-operation of the Latvian auxiliary police was essential. Arvīds Sakarnis, Chief of the First Police District, reported that there was no lack of volunteers for 'this unpleasant task ... [which] was carried out without hatred and shame, the men understanding that it would help all Christian civilization'.[101] Survivors were in no doubt that some of the participants in the execution squads wore Latvian Army uniform.[102]

Those Latvians who so quickly adapted to genocide did so because anti-Semitism was not simply a feature of Nazi propaganda, but an obsession shared by those Latvians who co-operated most closely with the German authorities, the Pērkonkrusts. Back in November 1933, when the Latvian parliament voted to lift the parliamentary immunity of its communist deputies and allow their arrest, the communist press declared that fascism in Latvia was on the march. The only issue at stake, the communists claimed, was which fascist group would take the lead: would it be the soft fascism of the reactionary Ulmanis or would it be the strident fascism of the paramilitary Pērkonkrusts. The communists, rightly, predicted that Ulmanis would be backed by the 'bourgeois parties',[103] but the Pērkonkrusts organisation did not disappear. Its slogan 'a Latvian Latvia'[104] was not so different from the 'Latvia for the Latvians' proclaimed by Ulmanis and both Ulmanis and the Pērkonkrusts idealised peasant Latvia and feared industrialisation. Unlike Ulmanis, the Pērkonkrusts wanted a corporate state modelled on that of Mussolini, rather than Ulmanis's rather pragmatic authoritarianism, and, unlike Ulmanis, the Pērkonkrusts were virulent anti-Semites. The party was banned by parliament in March 1934, under pressure from the Social Democrats, and several of its leaders were arrested.[105] After his coup of May 1934 Ulmanis was prepared to work with the Pērkonkrusts and even offered their leader Gustavs Celmiņš the post of ambassador in Paris. Celmiņš, possibly seeing this as an attempt to sideline him, refused to co-operate. Ulmanis then arrested Celmiņš and 100 lesser figures. Between 1934–8 some 800 members of the party were detained and a further 2,000 lost their jobs.[106]

The party had been based on Latvia's intellectual elite. Although it claimed a membership of 12,000, in reality there were 6,000 ready to don its paramilitary uniform of dark grey shirt, beret and trousers tucked into knee boots. It was small but well educated and above all young. Nearly half of its central committee were under 30 and nearly two-thirds either civil servants or students.[107] In 1933 its supporters had won control of the student council at Latvia University in Riga[108] and it had many members among the Lettonia student fraternity.[109] The Pērkonkrusts continued to campaign against Ulmanis, retaining an underground organisation until 1937 and engaging in acts of terrorism and disruption.[110] Although its membership was small, its ring of sympathisers was considerable. In the same way, while its active membership tended to be tied to Riga, any grad-uate of the University of Latvia, especially one who had joined the Lettonia student society, could be a sympathiser. In Daugavpils, Wilhelms Mucinieks, the lawyer whose land was expropriated early in 1941 for a machine-tractor station, was described as being 'closely associated to the Pērkonkrusts' but not actually a member. The active membership was small and hardly felt.[111]

Celmiņš favoured international solidarity among the far right. He was released from prison in 1937[112] and while in exile in Italy he made contact with Romanian fascists,[113] and when the Soviet Union invaded Finland in 1939 he joined the international brigade formed by pro-fascist groups.[114] Pērkonkrusts journalists used Ulmanis's refusal to take sides in the Finno-Soviet War, made necessary by the Mutual Assistance Treaty with the Soviet Union, to question his commitment to the struggle against Bolshevism.[115] After the Finnish defeat in March 1940 Celmiņš went to Germany, and it was the Pērkonkrusts who in summer strove to foster the closest possible links with the new German authorities. When on 4 July the Riga-based national newspaper *Tēvija* called on 'nationally thinking Latvians to take an active part in cleansing our country' it was members of the Pērkonkrusts who were appealed to first, followed by students, officers and *aizsargs*.

Although the leading party intellectuals went into journalism, many put their anti-Semitism into practice. The Pērkonkrusts movement was still strongest in Riga and there a Jewish student who survived the war recalled how, when he was rounded up by the green-armbanded auxiliary police in early July 1941, those who detained, questioned, tortured and degraded him along with other young Jews greeted each other with the party salutation and sang Pērkonkrusts songs. They made no bones of the fact that they were legalised Pērkonkrust members now out to get 'their pound of flesh' from the Jews. Many had avoided persecution when Ulmanis was in power by joining the *aizsargs* as a cover, and some seem even to have taken this a step further in 1940 by feigning, like Štāls in Daugavpils, to become committed Soviet activists.[116]

The most notorious former Pērkonkrusts, Victors Arājs, who headed one of the killing commandos active in Daugavpils and the surrounding districts, had been in the party when he started his student career in 1932 studying law. An aspirant to Latvia's elite rather than a member of it, he had to work to make ends meet; he joined the police reserve and as a result had to leave the party. There is a certain irony in the fact that he only completed his degree in 1941, when the Soviet regime was encouraging graduates from humble backgrounds; since Soviet degrees were not recognised by the Nazis, he only finally graduated in 1944.[117] With his Soviet diploma he specialised in taking up the cause of those peasants deprived of their property for refusing to obey the new communist decrees on agriculture. Arājs was not alone in putting the anti-Semitic views of the Pērkonkrusts into the most brutal reality. Mārtiņš Vagulāns was another former Pērkonkrusts student who ended up running a killing commando.[118] These men targeted former army officers and *aizsargs* for recruitment to the killing squads.

After the war survivors mentioned the names of some of those actively involved in the Daugavpils executions. They were 'former *aizsarg* Špak, cavalry lieutenant Kupcis, the teacher Linde, the scout leader Sovers, the policemen Karaļūns, Lisovskii and Bulavskii and the former officer Krauklis'.[119] Some of those involved were captured by the Soviet authorities in 1944. None confessed to carrying out the killings, but several told how they were engaged in digging and covering the burial pits, and they were therefore present when the killings took place. According to these interrogations the killings were carried out on the orders of the Germans, under the supervision of a team of German officers that was regularly changed,[120] but this supervisory team operated with the active collaboration of volunteers from the Latvian auxiliary police.[121] These volunteers were primarily former *aizsargs* and former officers in the Latvian Army.[122] The executioners on the 'action' of 29 July were Germans, but they used the day to indoctrinate the Latvian volunteers, making speeches about settling scores with the Jews who had used Soviet power to make themselves the bosses and subjugate the Latvian people.[123]

In the subsequent executions in August it was teams of five Latvian policemen who oversaw the victims undress, teams of 15 Latvian policemen who escorted the now naked prisoners to the burial pits and teams of ten Latvian policemen who carried out the executions.[124] There were two teams of ten executioners: their victims knelt looking into the grave and were then shot in the head from a distance of two to three metres; after each execution the policemen would hand their weapon to a member of the other team.[125] The protocol was that the executioners were brought from outside the region and had no contact with the other groups involved in the executions. Thus, after the pits were dug the team was ordered 400 metres back and put under police guard; after the shooting, the team was ordered back to scatter lime over the bodies and fill in the pits.[126] Similarly those who dug the pits, who were local, had no contact with those who dealt with the confiscated Jewish property, the third group involved.[127] All were warned not to talk about what they had witnessed.[128]

The reality was rather different: the policeman Savitskii not only helped organise the gravedigging team, but guarded those about to be shot, as did the cousin of one of the gravediggers; and some of the policemen involved in marching the Jews to the execution site also carried out the killing.[129] After the shootings were over the police were allowed the pick of the confiscated property, before the gravediggers had their turn; only then was it taken away by those responsible for its safe-keeping.[130] The gravedigger Ivan Lisovkii, a Pole, confessed that his rewards amounted to the pick of the shoes and clothing, in which he sometimes found valuables like watches, earrings, rings, cigarette holders, even on one occasion 1,000 roubles in cash. none of this he surrendered to the authorities; indeed, Lisovskii acted as a fence, taking clothes from Savitskii among others and selling them later in both Daugavpils and Riga, or exchanging them for moonshine vodka. Pilfering became such a problem that on at least one occasion Blūzmanis came to the execution site and collected up all the valuables himself.[131]

The auxiliary police paid for the execution pits to be dug and covered,[132] and oversaw the recruitment of gravediggers. These were simply local volunteers, or those whom the police felt they could put pressure on.[133] Thus Lisovskii, the leader of one of the gravedigging teams used at Mežciems, was recruited by the Latvian auxiliary police to prepare the mass grave for the first Mežciems execution on 29 July and was recalled the following day to fill it in.[134] He was then summoned to the police HQ and agreed to Savitskii's suggestion that he act as a team leader of 40 men on future occasions.[135] When he recruited people to his team, like the Russian Kuz'ma Beinarovich, he mixed the material promise of rich pickings with ideological blandishments about the time to put an end to living under the Jewish yoke.[136]

All accounts of the mass killings, whether written by survivors or perpetrators, commented that those concerned with the killings needed to be fortified with alcohol. Those recruited by Savitskii recall he was often drunk, usually in the company of Lisovskii;[137] the gravediggers always fortified themselves with 'spirt' (industrial alcohol) before starting work.[138] The executioners too needed vodka before the killings began and this was topped up during the killings.[139] When it was all over, the gravediggers would celebrate with another drinking bout, paid for from the 30 roubles they received for every 'action'.[140] Alcoholic fortification was needed because of the horrific nature of the work.

Arrested after the war, Lisovskii recalled at his interrogation being horrified when he was first called on to descend into the graves and inspect the corpses; his whole team had shared his horror, but they accepted the need for it.[141] Lisovskii stressed that, despite the personal profit he made from the killings, he did what he did because he supported the German new order, considered that the Germans had liberated the country from the yoke of Jewish-Bolshevism, and that it was time to deal with the Jews and communists once and for all. He took part in the killings as part of a great political mission. Although he agreed to his interrogator's suggestion that the Jews had never harmed him personally, he insisted he hated the Jews and wanted to be one of the first in the German new order.[142] Another gravedigger, Antons Vilcāns, stated that he took part because he hated the Jews, although he too accepted that they had never harmed him personally. The involvement of the police helped overcome any doubts he had about whether his actions were just.[143]

The police under Blūzmanis's leadership were certainly involved. His actions were so extreme that he was eventually arrested by the German authorities, spending two months in Daugavpils prison in autumn 1941. On 21 August the Daugavpils Field Commander had ordered he serve a sentence of six months' imprisonment on the grounds that, while he had not done so maliciously, he had seriously mishandled affairs while carrying out his duties. As Daugavpils Gebietskommissar Friedrich Schwung later explained in a letter to Riga, what this rather vague charge actually meant was this: 'in the last days of July, he had been over-enthusiastic during the summary shooting of Jews.' Schwung, who helped to get Blūzmanis an early release by paying a fine on his behalf, stressed that this behaviour towards the Jews showed that Blūzmanis was positive about the Nazi cause. On his release, Schwung brought him back into the heart of the city's administration.[144]

Judenrein Daugavpils

Once the Jews had been imprisoned in the ghetto, the re-established Latvian language press announced the area 'free of Jews'. This status was accorded to Daugavpils on 30 July and Grīva on 31 July. Readers were told that the era was over when, in Daugavpils, 75 per cent of trade, 80 per cent of industry, 90 per cent of workshops and 70 per cent of rented apartment owners had been in the hands of Jews.[145] Citizens could now concentrate on reconstructing normal life. By the end of July the 'self- administration' had restored water supplies and the telephone system was back in action.[146] By early August the postal service was back in operation;[147] measures were being taken to restore the library, burnt down during the occupation with the loss of 41,000 books;[148] and supplies of basic foodstuffs like cabbage and potatoes were said to be good.[149] Ration cards were issued on 30 July after a series of military decrees fixing basic purchase prices,[150] followed by decrees fixing retail prices.[151] The previous day the Reichsmark had been introduced as the new currency, alongside the rouble at a fixed exchange rate of 1 mark for 10 roubles.[152] By 13 August the population was said to be

22,372[153] and by September it had reached 25,202.[154] By the middle of August the new taxation system had been drawn up and the *Italia*, *Daugava* and *Celgreb* works and other major factories had resumed production.[155] By the end of August an Agricultural Credit Society had been established and the law courts re-established on a pre-Soviet basis.[156]

At the same time a whole series of measures were introduced to supervise the population. From the start of August house owners were made responsible for everybody living in their premises,[157] and citizens were banned from moving house without permission;[158] any new arrivals in the city had to register with the police within 24 hours.[159] From 12 August rural authorities were told to keep records of anyone coming into their area, making sure that all incomers registered within three weeks.[160] From 11 August the Labour Exchange started operating and all those capable of work had to register. Priority in work allocation would go to German firms and the needs of agriculture;[161] those who did not register would lose their ration cards.[162] In the same spirit, rural authorities were to carry out a census of all animals and make an inventory of all agricultural stores.[163] In the second half of August a series of decrees made clear that all forms of motorised transport were expropriated and appropriate permission was needed to use them; this included not only abandoned Red Army lorries but also the tractors attached to the former machine-tractor stations.[164] Finally, decrees made clear that all arms, including hunting rifles, had to be surrendered; this applied to the auxiliary police as well as the civilian population and one auxiliary police volunteer was court-martialled for refusing to surrender his old Soviet rifle.[165]

The public at large showed little enthusiasm for the new regime. On 3 August the official German-sponsored newspaper *Daugavpils latviešu avīze* carried a front-page photograph of the German Army being met by Latvian crowds waving the red-white-red Latvian flag. This was the launch pad for a month-long campaign to persuade people to put their signatures to a public letter to the Latvian community in the USA supporting the view that the Latvian people had been saved from Soviet atrocities by the intervention of the German Army; this was before Pearl Harbour and America's entry into the war. Almost every day for the first half of the month there were stories of the growing number of signatures collected and how the campaign was developing in rural areas; the names of some of the more prominent signatories were given. Yet despite the fuss, the paper found it difficult to work up enthusiasm for this campaign. Only on one occasion did it publish the actual number of signatories received, which at 2,492 was fairly modest.[166] Indeed, the paper itself was struggling to get established, relying on a small number of volunteers to carry out its distribution.[167]

If the press were to be believed, many of the restrictions so hurriedly imposed were ignored. The fact that the ban on 'cannibalising' abandoned German and Soviet cars was routinely ignored suggests as certain rebelliousness.[168] Despite the hysterical anti-Semitic campaign which continued throughout August, a cab driver was found regularly transporting Jews to and from the ghetto as late as 20 August.[169] Early in September the authorities found it necessary to re-issue the rules on how to behave towards Jews.[170] It was the same with POWs. Latvian POWs from the Red Army were well treated, being given jobs in the city hospital,[171] but Russian POWs were to be held in camps and left to survive as best they could. To enforce this, the authorities issued a decree banning all contact with Russian POWs; passing them food parcels was specifically banned, as were simple conversations.[172] Yet many citizens, both Russian and Latvian, were punished for smuggling food into the camp.[173] The press had to remind the population once again on 2 October that the supply food to Jews was forbidden and would be punished by a fine; the same article repeated that Russian POWs were subject to the same ban.[174] On 7 September those who had not come forward for work were given 'a last instruction' to report to the Labour Exchange; the original instruction had called on them to present themselves within three days.[175] Clearly the initial instruction had been widely ignored, although the delay was partly caused by the Labour Exchange's hunt for permanent offices.[176]

On 1 September 1941 Daugavpils was transferred from military to civilian authority, although a curfew continued to be imposed, operating between 10 p.m. and 5 a.m.[177] The Gebietskommissar appointed to administer the new Dünaburg Region, which included not only the old Daugavpils district but Abrene, Rēzekne and Ludza districts as well, was Friedrich Schwung. Schwung, it was explained, had been brought up in the area of Germany bordering on France and therefore understood the problems of border areas. His deputy was at first Herman Riecken, who ran the region for the first week of September until Schwung arrived, before taking up a new post.[178] Schwung's adjutant was Egon Rauch, a Baltic German who had studied at Latvia University before starting a military career based in Daugavpils, a career cut short when the Baltic Germans were repatriated.[179] By the end of August the other major civilian appointments were in place. Pētersons remained the Daugavpils city elder and his district counterpart was Jānis Kamaldnieks. Kamaldnieks had served in the Liepaja Infantry Regiment, seen its incorporation into the Red Army and then deserted from it in early July 1941, becoming one of the first to volunteer for the auxiliary police.[180] As a sort of normality returned, the schools reopened on 22 October, the Eden cinema reopened on 19 October[181] and the theatre reopened on 27 November.[182]

Rather late in the day the Communist Party and its associated organisations were banned on 20 September. This same decree made clear that no new political parties would be allowed, and it would seem that the real target of the ban was not so much the Communist Party as the Pērkonkrusts. Even those who had rallied so quickly to the German call had reason to wonder if they had made the right choice. The Germans were putting strict limits on Latvian nationalism. Back on 19 July deputy police chief Štāls informed members of the auxiliary police that their armbands, their only official uniform at this stage, could not be in the red-white-red national colours; only green was acceptable.[183] On 20 August it was made clear that the Latvian auxiliary police had no authority over those carrying German passes, and would be shot if they tried to restrict the movements of people carrying these passes.[184] This was apparently because the Pērkonkrusts had started to take it upon themselves to make arrests without consulting the German security police.[185] The Blūzmanis case probably accentuated the need to reign in overenthusiastic Latvians. So, when in September the ban was placed on political parties, the German authorities saw no reason to exempt the Pērkonkrusts.[186] Under the decree non-political associations had two weeks to register with the Gebietskommissar; he alone could decide whether any meetings could be held.[187]

The decree allowing for the registration of non-political associations encouraged Latvians to establish an association which would ultimately bear the name People's Aid. The first preparatory moves in Daugavpils were reported on 8 October and the formation of the Daugavpils section of People's Aid was announced on 5 November.[188] Ten days later Daugavpils People's Aid held a grand inaugural meeting on 16 November and announced that its initial budget, formed from voluntary donations, amounted to 3,213 Reichsmarks. Pētersons, the city elder, was made nominal head of the organisation and its other key figures were named as deputy chief M. Svieśés and secretary E. Zēbergs.[189] The original task the organisation set itself was to help the victims of Bolshevism, in particular the families of those deported. Gradually, however, it would acquire a broader social agenda.

The major economic development affecting Schwung and his team was the abolition of the Soviet land reform. Those peasants who would benefit from the reform were clearly keen for this to happen, since on 12 August the press had to make clear that, until further instructions were given, landhold-ings would remain unchanged.[190] It was over a month later, on 22 September, that the press explained how the 'new farmers' established by the Soviet land reform would be deprived of their land. The justification given for this change was economic efficiency: those given land by the Soviets had proved unable to make good use of it, whereas those who had lost the land were traditional, efficient peasant proprietors, who had farmed the family patrimony for centuries. All the land reallocated by the Bolsheviks would be confiscated, and where the original owners could not be found the land would be held by a special commissar.[191] The farmers who benefited from these changes were told that they had the right to POW labour to help farm it,[192] for since 11 September Latvian, Lithuanian, Estonian and Ukrainian Red Army POWs had been released from camps for agricultural labour.[193]

At the start of October 1941, Schwung went on what can only be described as an extended progress through his Latgale region. He took a week to visit every one of the parishes over which he held jurisdiction. On the tour he met the new administrators elders who were being put in place to run the parishes, and presumably he discussed with them how best to plan the implementation of the proposed agricultural changes.[194] His tour was followed by a series of decrees relating to the compulsory delivery of potatoes and the requisitioning of carts and lorries.[195] The implementation of the land reform was delayed until the New Year so as not to complicate the process of bringing in the harvest.

Agricultural products were needed to match supplies with the ration cards. In September, with the rationing system now firmly established, there were the first signs of black marketeering and the authorities started to issue warnings that goods could only be sold at published prices,[196] a message which had to be repeated a fortnight later when shortages meant new higher prices were introduced and the rationing scheme revised.[197] It was clear that some of this black marketeering was in goods confiscated from Jews by the likes of Lisovskii. Since former Jewish property was officially state property, those trading in these goods were threatened with the death penalty,[198] although when two members of the auxiliary police were charged with this in the first half of September they were sentenced to only two months in prison.[199] Their cases were perhaps discussed when Schwung held talks with Pētersons on 11 September.[200] Be that as it may, the authorities were determined to get control of all confiscated Jewish property. On 1 October 1941 *Daugavas vēstnesis* issued an instruction that all property taken from the Jews had to be handed in to the city authorities; the deadline for this was extended more than once until it was set at 30 November.[201]

As to life in the ghetto, there was for a while a sort of terrible normality there too. The ghetto was run by a council of elders, jointly nominated by the German and Latvian authorities.[202] The head of the council was Mikhail Movshenson, whose father had been the German-appointed mayor of Daugavpils during the German occupation of 1918. The Council ran a hospital and an orphanage, as well as organising worship for the religious Jews.[203] It was also in charge of food supply, as well as overseeing law and order through its ghetto police. In theory, the ghetto was funded through the earnings of its 'specialist Jews', who worked outside the ghetto; many of them were in fact housed outside the ghetto, so that they could be close to their place of work.[204] And throughout September and October there was plenty of work restoring damaged buildings or collecting timber.[205] The daily ration of 135 grams of bread and a bowl of cabbage soup meant that only the fittest survived.[206] By October its population numbered 2,175 inhabitants.[207] There was nothing resembling ordinary family life, since men and women were segregated and only allowed to congregate in the courtyard during daylight hours. It was administered by Eduards Zaube, a Latvian official appointed by the city administration. He had been a white-collar official in Ulmanis's day, but was reduced to working in the railway depot by the Soviet authorities.

According to the testimony of a guard who served there from 8 to 25 August 1941, there was no abuse in the ghetto, although he conceded that the inhabitants lived in terror.[208] Ghetto residents told a different story. They recalled how ghetto commandant Zaube and senior police officials liked to select attractive Jewish women and rape them, before having them killed. Such rapes sometimes took place in public, even in front of the parents of the girl concerned. According to one source the sister of a local Daugavpils doctor, Dr Goldman, was raped in this way and tried to persuade her brother to help her commit suicide, such was her shame. Suicide in the ghetto was not uncommon.[209] For those who infringed the rules, there was only one punishment: death. Survivors recalled how the 18-year-old Mariya Schneider was shot after she tried to pass herself off as a Christian.[210] On the orders of the Gestapo, a Jewish woman was hung in the ghetto courtyard by fellow Jews and the execution filmed because she had allegedly stolen from a Latvian woman.[211] The local Gestapo leader personally put the noose around the neck of a young women discovered in town allegedly not wearing the yellow star, while another woman was shot for allegedly trying to smuggle a piece of bread into the ghetto.[212]

The killing resumes

The terrible normality of ghetto life was not to continue for long. A report issued as early as 7 August claimed that only one thousand Jews were actually needed in terms of the economic well-being of the city. Their employment, it was hoped, could be organised through the joint offices of the ghetto council of elders and the city administration.[213] That meant that the other inhabitants of the ghetto were deemed unnecessary, which in the climate of 1941 could mean only one thing. The press immediately began to turn to issues which might justify a further assault on the Jews. From July to the start of September *Daugavpils latviešu avīze* had been publishing articles about Bolshevik crimes. It published the stories of people held in Soviet prisons,[214] estimated the number of those deported on 14 June on the basis of an analysis of the Daugvapils prison archive[215] and gave a gruesome account of the torture methods used in Daugavpils prison, which no doubt did involve sleep deprivation and electric shocks.[216] Then, starting on 14 September, the paper began a series of four reports on the workings of the *Cheka* (the Soviet secret police). These mixed fact with fantasy, but had a clear purpose: to cement the link between Bolshevik terror and the Jews. The details on the *Cheka*'s *modus operandi* – late night knocks on the door, the use of false confessions by associates, the bugging of telephones, as well as the routine use of torture – would be familiar to any student of Stalinism, but the newspaper always added that the *Chekists* were nearly always Jews, occasionally Russians and never Latvians.[217]

On 18 September, the paper reported that the exhumation of the bodies of the victims of Stalinism was about to begin. Already, back on 16 July, the

Nazis had ordered imprisoned Jews[218] to start excavation work near the prison and there they had discovered 33 graves of victims of Bolshevism.[219] These graves were now reopened in order to recover the bodies and on 20 September the paper reported, with pictures, the horrors that had been found. It also provided a list of the names of all those held in the prison just before the German Army captured the city. Later the press published the names of 480 people, about 90 per cent of them having Latvian names, who were transferred from Daugavpils prison to the depths of Russia as the German Army approached.[220] A further article on 25 September, written by a former prison inmate, was at pains to link leading local communists like Yukhno and other local 'idlers', who might retain some residual popularity among the inhabitants of Daugavpils, to the Jews who had run the prison.

This press hysteria, which continued when on 1 October the new title *Daugavas vēstnesis* replaced *Daugavpils latviešu avīze*, prepared the way for the next action against the Jews, to take place, symbolically, on the anniversary of the Bolshevik Revolution. This action took place on the orders of Obersturmbannführer Günter Tabbert, who used the Arājs commando to carry out the killings, although Arājs himself was not present.[221] Once again the press hinted at what was to happen. On 6 November *Daugavas vēstnesis* blamed 'the yid Gandler' for the *Cheka* horrors discovered in the prison; Aron Gandler had indeed been responsible for overseeing the prison. Then on 7 November, as the action began, the paper carried two pictures of Daugavpils in flames during the fighting for the city, repeating the legend 'burned by the Jews'. To rub the point home, another article in the same paper alleged that on the eve of the German invasion 'Dagda Jews' had taken the first moves to establish a collective farm in that parish.

Practical preparations for the action had begun early in November. The ghetto authorities recalled all the existing white work permits and started to issue new red ones; these went only to the Jewish 'specialists', not to members of their family,[222] although an exception was made for the families of doctors.[223] On 5 November the authorities demanded that all remaining valuables such as rings and watches be surrendered, threatening to hang three hundred people in retribution if the order was disobeyed. The Jews were told that this 'contribution' was to pay for a new ghetto which was being constructed in the city and to which the Jews would soon be moved. Some believed this story, others did not and made preparations to commit suicide. Realising that their time was up, Dr Knochs and his family took poison and collapsed dead to the floor just as they were ordered to join the group selected for execution.[224] In fact the action got off to a false start. One survivor recalled that on 7 November, late in the day, the inmates were all assembled, made to wait for what seemed like hours, and then sent away again.[225]

The action began in earnest at dawn on 8 November and continued on the 9th. Nineteen people were found hiding in the ghetto and were summarily shot in the courtyard.[226] At Mežciems one youth escaped, but on the 9th police found him hiding in a nearby dacha and shot him on the spot.[227] After three days of killing, when a minimum of 1,134 people died at the Mežciems execution site,[228] the ghetto was empty, but for one block for specialists in the far corner from the entrance gate.[229] The number of Jews left in the possession of red cards was about 950. One report put the figure at 935,[230] while a survivor estimated one thousand.[231] A report issued at the end of January put the number of ghetto inhabitants at 950 and described them as good specialists, essential to maintain the economy.[232] Another report issued at about this time referred to 429 male and 528 female Jewish specialists.[233] However, not all specialists survived. On 8 November a 'specialist carpenter' was stopped by the police. His name was Fridman, and the police thought they had found Faifish Fridman; he was taken to the prison and executed.[234]

Immediately after the November action, Tabbert wrote to Schwung explaining that, despite the execution on that occasion of 1,134 Jews, some still remained, linked to business organisations. He expressed the clear hope that this would simply be a temporary measure, and he clearly anticipated that there would be more killings in December, as would be the case in Riga. However, Daugavpils was excused a December action, having made the case that the Jewish specialists were essential to the survival of the economy.[235] It was not so much that the Jews were able to perform tasks that no other workers could, but that the income derived from Jewish labour became an important part of the Daugavpils city budget. In March 1942 the sale of goods left by executed Jews made up the biggest single source of income for the city administration, twice as much as the sum derived from fines; just under a quarter of the city's apparent wealth came from this source, which was rapidly disappearing as more and more goods were sold.[236] Jewish labour, unlike Jewish property, did not disappear. Jews were not paid for their labour, but the enterprises which used their labour were charged 15 Reichsmark per month by the city administration. Over a six- week period in summer 1943, just before the scheme ended, the hiring of Jewish labour brought the Daugavpils city administration 44,322 Reichsmarks, more than enough to cover two months expenditure on schools.[237]

How many people survived the final anti-Jewish action of 1941 is impossible to say, but three of those who escaped death at this time later wrote down their experiences. A young woman known only by her surname Fridman, from a Daugavpils family which had been on good terms with its Latvian neighbours, managed to take advantage of the delayed start to the action on 7 November. Chance played a crucial role. A complete stranger, a woman who worked at the hospital and who had therefore been issued with a specialist's red permit, had given her pass to a friend on the morning of the 7th before she left for work. Convinced that something was about to happen, she told her friend that if an action began, she should say that she had missed work that morning because she was sick and then show the pass and ask to be allowed to leave the ghetto and attend work because she was feeling better. The friend tried to do this, but a guard refused to let her leave the ghetto because she did not know the password for that day. Miraculously the red permit had not been confiscated, so she offered it to Fridman to see if her luck might be better.

Fridman could not learn the password without being informed of it by the ghetto commandant; but if she went to the commandant, it would be discovered she had borrowed someone else's red permit. She decided she might get away with it if she could pretend to have come straight from the commandant's office. So she showed the red permit to gain access to the commandant's second-floor office, hung around for a suitable length of time and then left the office, telling the courtyard guards she had the commandant's permission to leave. This worked with the guards who had seen her enter and leave the commandant's building, but it did not work for the perimeter guard. She explained to him that she worked at the hospital, but had returned to the ghetto from work because she was worried about her elderly mother; she now intended to return to the hospital and work for the rest of the day. The guard asked who she worked with at the hospital, but since Fridman knew many people who worked there, she could answer. Then, when asked the password she burst into tears, and said she had had such a terrible day, and now had such a bad headache, that she could not remember it. 'The guard looked me over from head to toe. I was shaking. He looked around. No one had seen. "Well, off you go and God be with you." '[238]

The second person to escape the November executions was 17-year-old Shaike Iwensky, who had left his home in Lithuania on 23 June. Separated from his parents on the 24th, he and his brother decided on the 25th that they would find safety in Daugavpils, protected as it was by its massive fortress. They arrived on the morning of 26 June, crossing the bridge into the centre of the city.[239] Unfortunately Shaike boarded the last of the evacuation trains, which was stopped by the German Army, and so he returned to Daugavpils, lived rough for a few days, and then joined the other Jews in Market Square on 29 June. As a young, fit man he was among those used in the work gangs clearing the city of dead bodies. He should have died in Daugavpils prison on 9 July, but managed to hide and remain in hiding until the prison filled up with those originally destined to be burnt alive in the synagogue. He then claimed to be a specialist carpenter, which gave him specialist status for a while; the Germans soon discovered he was no carpenter but certified him as a painter instead. By October his regular employment was over and he had lost his white permit. As soon as the white permits were exchanged for red ones he decided to go into hiding and made a den in a loft space. From his hiding place he heard how 'the Latvians surged into the rooms, reeking of liquor and waving clubs'.[240] Back on 19 August Shaike had saved the life of a girl he scarcely knew by claiming her as his wife, the wife of a 'specialist painter'; on this occasion he could do nothing for her.[241]

The third person to escape in November 1941 was Semyon Shpungin, then only 12 years old. His family was in that part of the ghetto liquidated on 9 November. Somehow he got separated from his family as the order was given to line up. When the subsequent order came for the families of doctors to step forward, he knew that he had no choice but to do just that. He then looked round, spotted his family dentist, moved towards her and pretended he was her son; this ruse succeeded even though Semyon was the son of the well-known owner of a photographic studio on Rainis Street.[242]

The genocide in Daugavpils was a very public affair. The first killings at the Railwaymen's Garden took place in the heart of the city. As the main road to Rēzekne rises from the flood embankment to cross the railway bridge it is indeed possible to look down at this execution site almost like looking down on an amphitheatre. Mežciems, which became the preferred execution site, was no distance from the city centre, and a spot where many people went to relax at weekends. Transporting Jews to this area could not have gone unnoticed. The genocide was carried out on the orders of the Nazis, but in the name of the local inhabitants' justified wish to throw off the Jewish yoke and exact revenge for the deportations, the planned collectivisation of agriculture and the burning of the city as the German liberators arrived.

There were those citizens of Daugavpils and the surrounding area who not only failed to share this blood lust against the Jews, but actively sought to thwart it. Pauls Krūmiņš headed the violin section of the Latgale People's Conservatory and often performed with his young pupil Cecilia Gradis. Like other Jews, Cecilia and her sister had been driven to the synagogue in July 1941, but escaped and managed to pose as Latvians. Krūmiņš then hid the girls and got them false papers. He was later arrested and imprisoned for obtaining official documents by deception, but the girls got away and survived. In Biķernieki, in Daugavpils district, the Old Believer Kalistratii Grigoriev hid a Jewish vet and his wife in a barn. Fetinya Ostratova, a pensioner from Grīva, hid a young woman she had known since childhood, along with the woman's husband. Petrunella Vilmanis hid the girl for whom she had once been a nursemaid, secreting her in a house in the Jaunbūve district of the city. In Līksna district, just outside Daugavpils, Ignats Matuļs, a farmer, hid a pharmacist and his wife in a specially constructed pit.[243] In all, details of 69 cases have survived where Jews were saved by the local population of Latgale. In Līvāni and Aglona deacons of the Catholic Church were involved and suffered terms of imprisonment as a result.[244]

Even after the annihilation of the Jews, Daugavpils remained an ethnically mixed city; a survey of the registered inhabitants carried out on 27 September 1941 revealed 7,674 Russians, 7,584 Poles, 7,244 Latvians, 176 Belorussians, 171 Lithuanians, 119 Germans, 17 Estonians and 63 others.[245] Yet this diversity was not reflected in the make-up of the new administration, nor in the make-up of its active citizenry: when the schools reopened in October only 10 per cent of the teachers were Russian[246] and the Polish school was closed down; those involved in People's Aid, particularly in the rural parishes, were overwhelmingly Latvian by nationality.[247] If the 'terrible year' of Soviet rule had seen the Russians take revenge on the Latvians, the tables had now been turned and there were those close to the new adminis- tration who argued that making Daugavpils *Judenrein* (free of Jews) was only the start of the process to make Daugavpils suitably Latvian. Savitskii, the policeman so actively involved in the August killings at Mežciems, was one such person. To a Russian whom he pressurised to dig the burial pits he said: 'dig faster, soon there will be space for you Russians here too.'[248]

4   Dünaburg under Schwung

Friedrich Schwung remained Gebietskommissar for Daugavpils, or Dünaburg as the Germans referred to it, until 19 August 1942. During his tenure of office the German administration gradually distanced itself from those Latvians who had first come forward to support them. Their agenda for an ethnically pure Latgale hampered the smooth administration of the region. There was a logic to targeting the Russian community in Latgale, once the 'Jewish Question' had been resolved. It was among Russians that there were the first signs of resistance to the regime established by the Nazis. When Moscow did not fall to the German Army in November 1941, there were some, particularly in the Russian Old Believer communities, who thought it worth while to help Red Army men who were trapped far behind the front line and constantly on the run. The Nazis stamped out this form of resistance with merciless executions of guilty and innocent alike. Apparently secure as 1942 began, the Daugavpils authorities faced the misery of a typhus epidemic and unremitting economic shortages. This misery, combined with the Red Army's spring counter-offensive, prompted a second wave of rather fitful resistance and the formation of the first loosely organised partisan groups.

However, the German authorities were less concerned about these first partisan formations than the ambitions of their own newly established General Directorate which was to administer Latvia. Its formation encouraged the old elites to dream of a revived Latvian independence, and such nationalist ambitions bordered on what the Germans considered to be 'national chauvinism'. In Daugavpils such nationalist ambitions focused on plans to revive the Daugavpils Latvian Society, which the communists had closed down. Schwung first welcomed the restoration of the Latvian Society, and then decided to close it down. He soon began to resent what he saw as interference in the administration of Daugavpils from what he termed the Latvian intelligentsia, believing he was being manoeuvred into advancing an anti-Russian agenda. And that is precisely what happened in May 1942 with the plans to deport large sections of the Old Believer population, a campaign that ended in chaos in Daugavpils when Latvians were targeted alongside Russians.

This May action, and the flagging economy, gave an important stimulus to the resistance movement, and convinced Schwung that the time had come to look beyond the Latvian elite and engage the support of local religious communities, in particular the Orthodox Russians. He distanced himself from events marking the anniversary of the Bolshevik deportations of 14 June, and turned instead to the Church leaders. Just at the moment when this policy was being adopted, Schwung was dismissed for corruption. It took his successor Heinrich Riecken a while to find his feet, but by the time Latvia's leaders visited Daugavpils in mid-October 1942 for a ceremony to install the district elders, Riecken had found his catch-phrase: Latgale was no longer Latvia's stepdaughter, but a proper daughter. All its various communities had to be embraced.

Audriņi

It was ethnic Russians who were the first to display opposition to the new regime. Indeed, once it had become clear that Moscow would not fall, the Nazi administration found itself dealing with a steady rumbling of discontent which it resolved to stamp out in the most brutal fashion possible. The Latvian communists tried to organise resistance to Nazi rule from shortly after their rather ignominious retreat to the Soviet heartland. These attempts were almost entirely unsuccessful. In August 1941 four small groups, comprising 26 men in all, were sent across the front to establish bases near Abrene, Cēsis, Jelgava and Daugavpils. Contact with them was lost at once.[1] It was no better in October when Vilhelms Laiviņš was sent on his first mission to establish a partisan base. His group was parachuted to Latvia on 9 October, but failed to rendezvous with the other groups sent in at the same time. When he tried to establish links with the local population, he was turned away. Up against 'constant *aizsarg* patrols', Laiviņš and his men escaped encirclement and decided to return across the front line back to Soviet Russia after less than a fortnight.[2] The verdict of the Germans on these early efforts was dismissive. A report on what was called partisan activity from 1 October to 31 December 1941 recorded the arrival of eight such groups, each comprising eight to ten members. Of these, three had been caught and all their members executed; in four cases half the group members had been caught and executed, while the other half had fled; only one group had survived, but appeared to have dissolved itself. The Germans concluded that these groups were made up of mostly young communists who simply wanted to return home.[3]

This was not entirely fair. Pavel Leibch, the head of the Daugavpils komsomol, was one of the earliest to return. He crossed back as early as 2 July 1941, contacted an aunt in Daugavpils and then worked on a farm near Bebrene, before moving to Riga on 6 September. There he took a job in a factory, began to organise a communist cell, and was arrested on 4 June 1942 after a Daugavpils policeman visiting Riga had recognised him. He was last seen alive in Riga prison in August 1942.[4] Parachuted partisans did not always surrender without a fight. On 10 November three such partisans clashed with armed Latvian units near Abrene. One was killed in the initial clash and the other two were trapped in their camp and shot.[5] Ten days later, near Rēzekne, another group of parachuted partisans fought a gun battle with Latvian units in which one policeman was killed and two wounded; they were only cleared from the forest a month later when German SS forces were brought into action.[6]

Organised, communist-led opposition made little progress, but there were other types of opposition. Most significant was the refusal of significant sections of the Russian Old Believer community to recognise the new authorities. The SS were convinced the Russian Old Believers were a bedrock of support for the communists. An Einsatzkommando report of 18 July 1941 stated: 'The Old Believers always had a strong communist orientation and, with the Jews, were the leading elements in the communist party. A part of the Old Believers, especially the young generation, organised themselves into gangs after the arrival of the Germans, and communists lead these gangs.'[7] This assessment, while a wild exaggeration, seemed to be confirmed by the events which took place in the Old Believer village of Audriņi, near Rēzekne. The announcement by the security police commander in *Daugavas vēstnesis* on 6 January 1942 summed things up: for three months the inhabitants of Audriņi had hidden five Red Army men, provided them with arms and helped their anti-state activity in every way; in the struggle against these elements Latvian policemen had been shot.[8]

In the action to seize these Red Army men, which began on 18 December 1941, the police discovered a house with a cellar and a secret access tunnel; but the Red Army men escaped, killing the 25-year-old Latvian policeman Alfons Ludboržs as they did so; the son of the owner of the house where they had been hiding fled with them. At once 35 local police set off in pursuit, joined on the 19th by 80 more. On 21 December, at midday, the Red Army men seemed to be cornered on a hill top in the forest; but they used automatic and semi-automatic fire to defend themselves and three Latvian auxiliaries were killed: Antons Mugus, Viktors Gleists and Andris Purmals, all aged from 25 to 35.[9] The Red Army men escaped again. Then on 30 December their luck changed. They broke into an isolated farmhouse not far from Viļāni and held up the family of Ivan Tikhanov. Mrs Tikhanova feigned the need to use the privy, slipped off the farm and called the police in Viļāni. In the final shoot-out, the Red Army men died as the farm was set on fire.[10] The revenge of the authorities was horrific. On the orders of Schwung, issued on 22 December, all the inhabitants of Audriņi were arrested. The village itself was burned to the ground on 2 January, while the 235 inhabitants were all shot on 3 January, 30 men in public in Rēzekne market square.[11]

Although by far the worst incident of its kind, what happened at Audriņi was not unique. A few days later it was reported that 47 villagers from Morduki, a village near Ludza, had been arrested and shot for protecting

Red Army men; just as at Audriņi, Latvian policemen had died in the attempt to arrest them.[12] Other German reports cited an incident near Viļani on 31 December 1941 where six Red Army men were arrested after a clash with locals, and a week later near Rēzekne there was a report that locals had helped Russian POWs escape from a labour assignment.[13] At the end of 1941 the German authorities were convinced there was a communist cell in Daugavpils and were worried that Polish nationalists in the city were putting out leaflets calling for joint Polish–Russian resistance to the occupier. This coincided with an increase in propaganda leaflet drops from Soviet airplanes.[14] In November 1941 the communist cell led by a certain Nina Demidova had been uncovered in Daugavpils: she was hiding an escaped POW and attacked the police who tried to detain her with a knife.[15]

Although on 12 December 1941 Schwung could report that the area was fully under his control, the only source of unrest coming from some elements of the Polish population,[16] on 9 January 1942 a security report expressed concern at the amount of enemy propaganda circulating in Latgale and noted that in recent weeks there had been a revival in activity, not only by some Polish agitators but by the communists as well; the stability of November and the first half of December had begun to crumble. This was put down to the counter-offensive launched by the Red Army and the German Army's 'withdrawal of advance units to already prepared winter positions'. There were rumours of some sort of communist action over Christmas and talk that the Red Army would soon return; as a result there had been several displays of communist activity in Daugavpils district, the report stated.[17]

On 16 January 1942 Schwung issued an instruction published in German, Latvian, Russian and Polish which stated that, despite all the warnings, 'recently in Latgale in many places' there had been occasions when German orders had been ignored and 'criminal' moves made against the local authorities. Schwung then referred both to the Audriņi and Morduki incidents and stressed that, whatever a person's nationality or social standing, orders had to be obeyed and disobedience would be severely punished.[18] Despite this, at the end of March five Soviet sailors were discovered by a Latvian forester, who was rewarded with 500 marks,[19] while in May a certain Fotii Anisimov brought to the authorities a surviving member of a group of partisans that had been dropped by parachute in November and who had been hidden by Anisimov and other villagers in Vecā Zelenovka and Janciški, both near Višķi. For surrendering the partisan Anisimov was granted a pardon, but his former comrades Ivan Titov and Osip Grigorev, who had helped conceal the partisan, were hanged in public. The Daugavpils Field Commander made clear in the press that he had set a deadline of 25 May: any person, like Anisimov, who had given help to such 'saboteurs' but turned them in before 25 May would not be punished, but after that date, any support for saboteurs would merit the death penalty. Those who helped catch them would be rewarded.[20]

Disease and shortages

Life in Daugavpils was difficult in the winter and spring of 1942. At the start of the year the security services reported that transport failures meant that the supply of basic provisions to Daugavpils was still very poor. Worst of all was the supply of soap, which had been unavailable since the start of the German occupation in June.[21] This inevitably impacted on the city's health, for the winter of 1941–2 was dominated by an outbreak of typhus. On 28 November the Daugavpils district elder Kamaldnieks issued a decree noting that in some of the parishes around Daugavpils there had been cases of typhus and typhoid. The city's inhabitants were instructed to call a doctor if they developed a temperature and, if either disease were detected, they should then put their household into quarantine, placing a notice of infection on the door. As a further precaution, all events involving guests, including weddings, christenings and funerals, were banned.[22] These measures did not prevent typhus spreading. The ghetto was affected on 3 December 1941[23] and the disease became particularly virulent in the POW camp inside Daugavpils fortress.

The POW camp, for most of its existence known as Stalag 340, was first based in the former powder stores of Daugavpils Fortress and then, in winter 1942–3, moved to a specially constructed complex erected on the fortress esplanade. There were also separate sections at the old depot at Daugavpils station and elsewhere in the city. Later witnesses stated that the POWs 'looked like scarecrows'[24] and survived either on food given illegally by the local population[25] or cannibalism,[26] even though anyone found to have engaged in cannabalism was shot.[27] The POWs were certainly not fit enough to survive a typhus outbreak.

Soon more rigorous restrictions on movement had to be imposed. On 6 December 1941 it was reported in the press that access to Daugavpils from the provinces was closed and the bridge across the Dvina from Grīva barred; inevitably this also meant the closure of Daugavpils market.[28] On 10 January 1942 it was announced that both Daugavpils and Grīva were to be hermetically sealed and passes would be needed to move between them. This decree added that the ban on the market would in future be rigidly enforced and alternative food-supply bases would be established in its place. The frozen river Dvina would be patrolled and anyone trying to cross on the ice would be shot on sight. These warnings were repeated in the press for the next few days.[29] Although by mid-February the bridge between Grīva and Daugavpils could be crossed by those with special permission,[30] the list of restrictions on movement was extended. By 10 February all schools and churches had been closed and all assemblies banned: at that time there were 52 people suffering from the disease in Daugavpils city and 152 in Daugavpils district; and, despite the best efforts to isolate sufferers, one case had been reported in Abrene. It was not until 8 March that *Daugavas vēstnesis* could report that the epidemic was declining.[31] In his report of 19

March to his superior Generalkommissar Otto Drechsler in Riga, Schwung noted that the measures to control the epidemic had been difficult to impose and that people had increasingly started to circumvent them. Since the situation was improving, he explained that he had decided to reopen the churches on 14 March, since Lent had already begun. Priests and pastors would be responsible for ensuring that no two members of their congregation were ever closer to each other than 18 inches.[32]

The typhus epidemic was a major diversion from Schwung's main agenda item, land reform. If the land reform could increase agricultural production, then supplies could improve and the rationing system could be eased. A grand meeting of parish elders was organised to discuss agricultural and other matters in mid-February.[33] This quickly agreed about such issues as milk delivery quotas, but found it more difficult to address the twin issues of abandoned land and the implementation of the land reform. On abandoned land, it was agreed that local elders should have the power to allocate land abandoned by Soviet sympathisers to those peasants who lived nearby, but that this land could be neither bought nor sold. The implementation of the land reform caused more discussion. In total 480 of the 'new farms' established by the Bolsheviks were to be restored to their former owners. However, there was one case in Līvāni where the Soviet 'new' farmer, who had been allocated former church land, had built new buildings and invested a lot in his farm. True to the spirit of efficiency and respect for good husbandry, which was supposed to be the basis of the reform in contrast to Bolshevik ideological preconceptions, this 'new' farmer was allowed to keep his land. The meeting was presided over by Kamaldnieks, and was followed by a banquet addressed by Schwung.[34]

However, until a new harvest, belt tightening was the order of the day. Apart from the restrictions imposed to cope with the typhus epidemic, Nazi administration involved continuing restrictions on personal life. On 27 January 1942 Pētersons, the city elder, published details of more revisions to the rationing system[35] and on 30 January 1942 Schwung ordered that all convertible currency and valuables had to be surrendered to the authorities,[36] and, in a clarification of the situation regarding confiscated Jewish property, Pētersons demanded on 10 February that all cows taken from Jews, even those bought after 17 June 1940, were the property of the authorities.[37] February also saw the introduction of a standardised rent policy, yet further tinkering with the ration system,[38] and the replacement of the Soviet income-tax law of 5 April 1941. In its place the Nazis introduced a progressive income tax which, on paper at least, made fairly low demands on those earning under 250 Reichsmark per month, the average income being about 180 Reichsmark.[39] On 4 February Schwung used the pages of *Daugavas vēstnesis* to issue a stern warning about what would happen to those peasants who failed to fulfil their delivery obligations to the new regime.[40]

In such a climate of restrictions the black market inevitably thrived, particularly around the railway station. There were regular reports in

February 1942 of those arrested for 'speculation' being fined,[41] and these reports continued throughout March and April.[42] As a sort of normality returned to the city, an accommodation crisis developed. Daugavpils was a regional administrative centre, and new jobs attracted new inhabitants; the work of the hospital was also expanded, and the influx of new medical personnel also put pressure on the housing stock.[43] An analysis of ration cards published at this time suggested that the population of the city in early March had risen to 25,741.[44]

As well as such obligations, the inhabitants of Daugavpils and the whole Latgale region were encouraged to take part in voluntary campaigns. The campaign to supply the German Army with warm winter clothing was well under way by February, with local leaders like Pētersons making an appeal in the press.[45] On 10 February 1942 Schwung announced that from October to the close of the campaign on 8 February 1,247 Reichsmarks had been collected, 42 shirts and ten pairs of socks.[46] This suggested that the citizens of Daugavpils and its environs had been both unable and unwilling to give very much, for it was a tiny amount from a population of over 30,000. The collection of metal which was to be smelted down for guns was suspended during the typhus outbreak, but resumed in March.[47]

Reporting to Riga on 20 April Schwung painted a depressing picture of the city. The fact that it was full of soldiers caused resentment even among the Latvian population, for their presence meant added restrictions and few benefits. On top of these restrictions nothing was being done to rebuild the burnt out city. It would be necessary, he stated, to restore apartment blocks even if only partially because the current living conditions meant the danger of infectious diseases in Daugavpils was particularly acute. This danger was

Figure 1 Schwung 2 – Gebietskommisar Friedrich Schwung addresses a crowd from the steps of Unity House

all the greater 'because of the bad weather and the many thousands of shot Jews and dead Bolsheviks scattered around the vicinity of the town'.[48] Security reports for May suggest things were no better then. There were long queues for all goods, with vegetables in particularly poor supply. There was hardly any cooking oil, and milk supply 'had not improved'.[49] A second report that month added flour and fire-wood to the list of items in short supply, noted that even potatoes were difficult to obtain and stated that it had been impossible to acquire salt for some time.[50] The press report on 15 May that no more shops would be allowed to open in Daugavpils since the present number matched current needs fooled no one.[51]

Resistance

Deprivation did not of itself lead to resistance, but other political factors helped turn some of those disgruntled with endless shortages into active opponents of the regime. The actions taken by the German authorities early in 1942 suggested that the possibility of resistance was being taken seriously. Towards the end of January the authorities introduced regulations to register all typewriters and duplicators.[52] On 25 February the press published a 'Notification' from the head of the Daugavpils Branch of the Security Police SS Obersturmführer Hugo Tabbert, that it had been ascertained that many inhabitants of Latgale were hiding communist and Marxist literature, and even symbols and photographs of the Soviet regime; these were to be handed into police stations by 15 March 1942 or 'firm measures' would be taken.[53] When he reported to Riga on 19 March Schwung was concerned at the recent success of propaganda 'distributed by Poles and Bolsheviks'. The banning of church attendance during the typhus epidemic had enabled them to argue that the Germans, unlike the Bolsheviks, had closed down the churches. The ban on church attendance was proving particularly unpopular with the Catholic population, Schwung stressed.[54] The concern of the German authorities was shared by the Latvian collaborationist administration. On 11 February 1942 the press reported a radio broadcast by the General Director of Latvia's 'Self-Administration', General Oskars Dankers, in which he referred to the propaganda emanating from the 'Latvian Government in Moscow', which he stressed was composed of 'Jews and representatives of other nationalities' who had no right to speak in the name of the Latvian people.[55]

What gave heart to those willing to resist was the offensive early in 1942 by the Red Army, an offensive which initially was quite successful. As the Red Army advanced westwards, the exiled leadership of the Latvian Communist Party was asked to develop a sustained partisan operation so that the retreating German Army could be harried from the rear. At its Central Committee meeting on 1 March 1942 plans were commissioned to form 'several partisan detachments',[56] and by the end of the month an Operative Group had been set up specifically to develop partisan warfare.[57]

At the same time hundreds of thousands of leaflets were prepared to coincide with the offensive[58] and radio broadcasts regularly called for partisan action to begin.[59]

This propaganda barrage had an impact. Communist sympathisers recorded how rumours that Pskov had fallen to the Red Army had prompted some members of the Latvian police to start packing their bags.[60] Schwung was informed in mid-March that communist leaflets were 'having a great impact',[61] and in his own report to Riga a few days later he referred to the worrying success of 'zealous' communist propaganda which had 'caused some depression'. The poor economic situation and transport problems meant that ration cards could not always be honoured and meeting the ration, he argued, was a political barometer; improved transport and more deliveries would be the key element to combating enemy propaganda.[62] Schwung described the period from mid-March to mid-April as one of great communist activity, particularly near Rēzekne where many communist leaflets had been found, producing a sense of great insecurity. His April report also noted that the popular mood was such in some parts of Latgale that it was difficult to find suitable people to come forward as village elders.[63] The communist leaflets, which supposedly were in line with a political programme drawn up by representatives of the Latvian people in Moscow on 1 March 1942, all called for the expansion of partisan struggle.[64]

Some people in Daugavpils, almost exclusively Russians, responded at once to the call to arms emanating from Moscow. During summer 1941 the Latvian police had been ordered to cast its net widely and detain not only suspected communist sympathisers but any Russian male who had come to Latvia after 17 June 1940; their family members could be left at liberty.[65] By mid-December this blanket detention was felt to have served its purpose. On 20 December the newspaper *Rēzekne ziņas* reported that, after the completion of a verification process of their political status, a number of prisoners had been released from Rēzekne prison. Among those released under this scheme was Evmenii Maksimov, one of those who, like Pavel Leibch, had been sent behind enemy lines almost as soon as the Red Army left Latvia. He had been among a group of communists sent back into Latvia on 3 July, the day after Pavel Leibch.

Maksimov had been instructed with 18 others to go to the Daugavpils, Jēkabpils and Nereta areas to re-establish a communist network; his target was Daugavpils. *En route* he stayed with friends near Rēzekne, where he was arrested on 10 August and put in prison. He was released on 24 December, since there was no clear evidence against him, and transferred to a labour gang in the Daugavpils railway workshops where he made contact with a group of underground communists led by Kazimir Lazdovskii, who in 1928 had served as a communist on Daugavpils city council and who in June 1941 had joined the hastily formed Daugavpils workers' guard. The other prominent member of the group was Elena Titova, the wife of a Soviet officer evacuated in June 1941, who had been unable to flee herself because she was so heavily pregnant. They, and a small group of comrades, mostly Russians, listened to Soviet radio and engaged in petty acts of sabotage, like putting sand in petrol tanks and disabling steam engines. In February 1942 they put out a few leaflets, and made contact with a Soviet intelligence officer who had been dropped by parachute and was hiding just to the north of Daugavpils, on the river Dvina at Līksna.

Their plan was to provide information about the deployment of German troops by using the good offices of a Latvian member of their group, Marija Zeile, who was a nurse who worked for the head of the city's sanitary department, a German who spoke good Russian since he had been a POW in the 1914–18 war. However, after one meeting with the intelligence officer in an abandoned villa at Mežciems, contact was lost. In March they learnt that the melting snow had revealed a cache of weapons in a local cemetery, sufficient arms for ten men. Partisan activity was now possible. On 26 March at 6.30 in the evening Maksimov and his group set fire to an army store at Daugavpils goods station, in a fire that burnt for several days.[66] Sabotage on this scale could not be ignored, and *Daugavas vēstnesis* published an appeal by the head of the Daugavpils Department of the Security Police, SS Obersturmführer Tabbert, for help in catching 'a young man in a reddy-brown overcoat' seen near the scene.[67] Maksimov then went into hiding. On 29 April he formed a small group of partisans based near Višķi. However, they at once clashed with the police, losing four of their members. Those who survived retreated for a while to Daugavpils and then transferred operations further east to the Rundēni area; Maksimov survived there until autumn 1942.[68] Lazdovskii and Titova continued with their underground work.

Another early attempt at partisan warfare in Daugavpils was the work of Milentii Nikiforov. He had been a metal worker in Daugavpils until 1936, when he had moved to Riga. There he had supported the new Soviet regime, becoming an instructor on a soviet executive. When the Germans invaded, he decided to slip back to his native village of Jaunsaliena, between Skrudaliena and Daugavpils, and from there to an isolated farmhouse. Gradually he assembled a group of like-minded comrades who met in the farmhouse to listen to Moscow radio; they also assembled a cache of weapons from those found abandoned in the area. Having listened to one of the broadcasts in which the former Soviet Latvian Prime Minister Vilis Lācis called for the development of partisan warfare, Nikiforov and twenty or so associates formed a small group of partisans. Their first act was to destroy a bridge on the river Dubna, a tributary of the Dvina. They then retreated to the area known as the Russian Marsh east of Jersika and there they formed a base, from which they engaged in sabotage of the Daugavpils–Riga railway, attacking it between Jersika and Līvāni. They were tracked down by the police at the end of May and caught in an ambush. Nikiforov was killed but other members of his group survived until October.[69]

These were small-scale operations by scattered groups and those who joined them had no other contact with Moscow than listening to the radio. German reports at this time noted clashes with groups of partisans in Aglona, Kapiņi and Biža, resulting in the arrest of 160 people, both partisans and partisan supporters.[70] Soviet reports recorded that another small partisan group had been formed in Daugavpils led by Pavels Pizāns,[71] as well as two other groups, one near Rēzekne and the other in an unspecified area of Daugavpils district. The Central Committee also believed there were several other groups which had acquired arms and were simply waiting for the right moment to act.[72] However, as the Red Army's counter-attack stalled and the German Army advanced towards Stalingrad, the prospects for partisan operations meant that not all communist sympathisers thought the time was right to take to the forests. After the security hiccoughs of the early spring, collaborationist Daugavpils entered its halcyon days.

Disappointed Latvian ambitions

It was in the rather uncertain climate of February 1942 that the mass campaign began to recruit volunteers for a Latvian armed force to fight 'Bolshevism'. The press had reported the formation of the first Latvian military, rather than police, units at the end of October 1941, when the Pērkonkrusts leader Gustavs Celmiņš, described as 'the leader of the Latvian national socialist movement', was pictured meeting General Oskars Dankers, the man designated to become Latvia's General Director.[73] These units were formed from the original volunteers to the auxiliary police, who at the end of August 1941 had been re-christened the Ordnungspolizei. The new units were given the name Schutzmannschaften in November 1941 and they sent their first men to the eastern front in early December. When, in January 1942, the Germans asked Dankers's 'self-administration' to provide more recruits, it was given permission to appeal for volunteers and to handle the recruitment. After a meeting between Dankers and other leading collaborationist politicians, his deputy for matters concerning internal security, Lieutenant-Colonel Voldemārs Veiss, made a radio-broadcast appeal entitled 'We are going into struggle for Latvia and a new Europe' which called for volunteers, especially from the former Latvian Army, to join the restructured Latvian military formations.[74] The appeal for volunteers was published on 16 February.[75]

Even before these central moves were taken in Riga, the local press was giving coverage to what were portrayed as local initiatives. Thus, on 2 February, a small group of former Pērkonkrusts members in Krāslava, who claimed to have first taken up arms against the Bolsheviks in June 1941, banded together and volunteered to go to the front.[76] On 12 February SS Obergruppenführer General Friedrich Jeckeln appealed to inhabitants of Latgale on the pages of *Daugavas vēstnesis* for more volunteers to join the police service and defend the well-being of the Latvian people; details of salary, leave entitlements and family benefits were published the following day.[77] Once the official announcement had been made in February, the first volunteers from Daugavpils came forward: they were a former senior lieutenant in the Zemgale artillery division and a railway worker. The headline in *Daugavas vēstnesis* made clear what the paper felt was the political purpose of this armed force. The actions of such men, it stressed, would decide whether 'Latvians were to be just a group of people with a common language or something more'. The recruitment campaign during the second half of February appealed to Latvian emotions. Reporting recruitment in Višķi and Kalupe, *Daugavas vēstnesis* noted how two brothers had signed up to seek revenge for those in their family who had been deported by the Bolsheviks. The paper took the same line and reminded the inhabitants of Daugavpils that there were local victims of Bolshevism to avenge, although its claim of 4,000 victims was an exaggeration on the true figure of 1,000.[78] As the campaign developed the district elder gave details of how to register at police stations and special temporary posts at Pustina, Višķi and Kalupe. Those registering were reminded they needed a statement on their political reliability from the parish elder.[79]

Recruitment was also encouraged by the formation of local volunteers' committees. The Daugavpils volunteers' committee was established on 25 February and was led by the district elder's assistant Aloizijs Budže, with Valerija Seile, the former head of the Daugavpils Teachers' Institute, as his deputy; they were joined by Pētersons, Blūzmanis and Zundans, the editor of *Daugavas vēstnesis*.[80] This group organised two big appeals in the paper on 1 and 5 March, both signed by Budže, and the second listing all 14 members of the volunteers' committee.[81] By 7 March 1942 five hundred had volunteered and four battalions had been assembled, two based in Riga, one in Liepāja and the other in Krāslava.[82] By mid-March the focus of the campaign moved to Daugavpils district and beyond; the press reported volunteers signing up in Līvāni and Dagda, and a volunteers' committee being established in Rēzekne.[83] In his report for April Schwung noted that nine teachers from Daugavpils district were among the volunteers.[84] The campaign in *Daugavas vēstnesis* reached a peak on 24–25 March, with letters from the new volunteers supplementing other stories.[85] As the press campaign ended its purpose was summed up by Celmiņš, who had been made the head of propaganda for the volunteers' committee: the headline in *Daugavas vēstnesis* made clear that each volunteer 'was struggling for his people, his land and his national culture'.[86] It was not as simple as that.

The campaign to recruit Latvian volunteers in the fight against Bolshevism coincided with moves by the Daugavpils Latvian Society to resume its activities under the terms of the 20 September 1941 decree which permitted activity by non-political associations. In Ulmanis's day the Latvian Society had brought together the great and the good of Daugavpils to develop Latvian culture. The society had been the main instigator behind the construction of Unity House; it had sponsored the commercial college;

and, because of this close association with leading members of the Daugavpils political establishment, the Bolsheviks had closed the society down for propagating nationalism. At the time of its closure it had 1,604 members. On 20 December 1941 the surviving members of the society applied to Schwung for permission to resume their work. They took great pains to stress that the society was a victim of Bolshevism, since eight of its leading members had been arrested by the Bolsheviks, including the former mayor, the former police chief, the former inspector of schools and the former director of the railway administration. Those petitioning Schwung continued to be the cream of Daugavpils society. The chairman of the society was Konstantins Ozoliņš, president of the regional court, and among its leading members were the Latgale language scholar and member of the city administration Francis Zeps, as well as such active supporters of the new regime as assistant police prefect and director of the commercial college Osvalds Štāls and Vilis Zaķītis, the director of Hospital No. 1 who had been made responsible for implementing the sterilisation campaign.[87] Schwung agreed in writing on 28 December 1941 that the society could resume its public activities.[88]

After a couple of months of preparation, *Daugavas vēstnesis* made the re-launch of the society its main story on 1 March 1942, stressing that the society's task was to work for national and cultural improvement. The paper listed the luminaries who were involved and a few days later printed a brief history of the society, going over its role in the construction of Unity House and reminding readers of the arrest of its former chairman, the former mayor Andrejs Švirksts. The paper promised that the first event organised by the society would be a concert planned for 14 March.[89] However, that concert was never reported in the paper and on 11 April 1942 Schwung decided to postpone the renewal of activities. As a consequence the society went into a state of limbo. At the moment of its suspension it had assembled 161 new members.[90]

Although no explanation for the suspension of the Daugavpils Latvian Society has survived in the archives, it was clear at this time that Schwung was growing tired of what he saw as the pretensions of the Latvian intellectual elite; the Pērkonkrusts party of Celmiņš was based around graduates of Latvia University. On an individual basis Schwung was prepared to praise the legal work of Ozoliņš, as he did in a report of mid-March 1942,[91] but he was not convinced about the assumed Latvian superiority over the other inhabitants of Latgale. In a report to Riga written in early November 1941, Schwung stressed that 34 per cent of Latgale's inhabitants were Russians: they carried out orders more cheerfully and more industriously than the Latvians, and as far as he could tell, were as racially and politically aware as the Latvians.[92] By mid-March 1942 Schwung was worried about the growing political activity of the Latvian intelligentsia. His report to Riga on 19 March talked of the growing danger that the Latvian intelligentsia was beginning to pull together and act politically, but this was happening in a way which avoided the emergence of a single leader and which therefore made it difficult to decapitate. By comparison, he went on, the Russian population was 'easily guided'.

Schwung saw himself as acting to calm excesses, for 'the Latvian element still try to treat the Russians as inferior in order to press for one of their own political aims, to play the Russian population off against the German authorities'. According to Schwung, 'it was not true, as commonly assumed that the Russian population is infected by Bolshevism'. There were the incidents of parachutists being protected, but the moment the front line moved forwards such incidents would cease. Having praised the Russians, as members of a border community which always suffered during periods of regime change, he took a side-swipe at the Latvians who were 'characterised by informers'.[93] In this report Schwung charged that 'the Latvians start to forget that we have given them freedom'. The Latvian intelligentsia were 'trying to change direction and saw the German administration as unnecessary'. In particular it infuriated him that orders made by himself as Gebietskommissar were circumvented by appealing to the Latvian General Directorate. The General Directorate would then approach the Generalkommissar in Riga who would, wittingly or unwittingly, overrule Schwung. It was extremely awkward to be faced by a piece of paper from Riga when challenging the behaviour of local administrators, Schwung reported.[94]

Schwung had indeed found himself in a web of conflicting authorities when it came to appointing city and district elders for Daugavpils. On 19 January 1942 Schwung had rationalised his key local administrators. Blūzmanis replaced Kamaldnieks as Daugavpils district elder, and his new assistant was Aloizijs Budže.[95] Kamaldnieks took on the more honorific post of president of the district court.[96] However, with the formation of the General Directorate, all such appointments had to be reconfirmed or new appointments made with the agreement of the General Directorate. When Schwung and the other Gebietskommissare for Latvia were summoned to Riga on 6–7 March 1942, the appointment of Latvian officials was the second item on the agenda.[97] A fortnight after his return to Daugavpils, Schwung found himself having to explain to Riga why General Dankers had accused him of exceeding his powers by appointing Budže the new district elder for Daugavpils. Schwung explained that he had done nothing of the sort, but had inherited a situation where Blūzmanis, the official district elder, and Kamaldnieks were effectively carrying out the tasks of the district elder's post in what he called a 'personal union'. Since both men were more suited to the policing aspects of the job than political administration, Schwung had appointed Budže as Blūzmanis's assistant. However, the formal position remained that Blūzmanis was district elder until a new nomination could be agreed with the General Directorate.

Nonetheless, Schwung made clear that Budže would be his choice for district elder when the time came because of his great political experience;

Schwung described him as his 'best colleague'.[98] Budže had a local back-ground, having worked as a teacher in Krāslava from 1922–6 and then briefly as a civil servant in Rēzekne. However, he had then been elected to parliament for the Latgale Peasant Democrats, becoming Deputy Minister of Internal Affairs in 1929–31. This parliamentary background meant that he was not close to those who ran the General Directorate, but he had suffered under Soviet rule. From 1934–9 he had worked in the Daugavpils finance department, and had then retired, but his past involvement in poli-tics was known to the Bolsheviks. His brother was arrested in August 1940 and his wife was deported on 14 June 1941; he was on the list to be deported, but he was not at home when the police arrived. Subsequently he fled to the forests and then took an active role in the new pro-German administration, becoming chairman of the Volunteers' Committee and People's Aid.[99] In the end Schwung got his way and Budže was appointed.

When, at the end of March, the General Directorate suggested that a former Latvian Army officer might be a suitable candidate to replace Pētersons as Daugavpils city elder, Schwung was appalled at the idea. He exploded: 'it is quite impossible to appoint another Latvian officer, indeed a senior Latvian officer ... the political structure in this region does not permit the appointment of former Latvian officers. I have being trying hard to elim-inate these very elements, who in an instant start to advance their right-wing political programme.' Schwung was quite happy to see Pētersons moved to a police role, but favoured the appointment as city elder of someone with local knowledge; he had in mind the former mayor of Grīva.[100]

That some of the Daugavpils administrators were working to a nation-alist agenda which was verging on the anti-German became clear the following month. Schwung informed Riga in May that even 'his best colleague' the Daugavpils district elder Budže had been in contact with an underground nationalist group while visiting the General Directorate in Riga. Schwung believed the centre of this organisation was somewhere in the General Directorate itself, but what was certain was that, since Budže's visit to a General Directorate meeting, a flood of anti-German leaflets had reached Daugavpils from an organisation bearing the name 'The Trumpeter of Tālava'.[101] Budže apparently sent this material on, for in July parish elders were all sent a nationalist proclamation which made clear that, if the Bolsheviks were the greatest enemy, the 'Vons' seemed incapable of saving the Latvian people from the Bolshevik threat.[102] As early as January 1942 some in the German security services were worried that their Latvian collab-orators had become obsessed with the issue of nationality.[103]

The attitude of the Daugavpils collaborationist authorities to their Russian neighbours and even local Latgale speakers was disdainful. In July 1941 *Daugavpils latviešu avīze* had criticised non-existent communist attempts to encourage Latgale separatism and stressed that the inhabitants of Latgale and the rest of Latvia were one and the same.[104] As to the Russians, those villages with large Russian populations 'hindered national life', the paper asserted, although gradually many Russians were seeing sense; thus in places like Biķernieki where the Soviet regime had initially been welcomed, the inhabitants had quickly realised their mistake and 'nationally thinking people' had come forward.[105] As well as condescension there was prejudice, as revealed in a newspaper story of August 1941. This told how a Latvian woman had gone into a shop and spoken to the shop assistant, only to find the shop assistant curse her in Russian and carry on chewing on a gherkin.[106] Such prejudices were given more articulate formulation in an article published in *Daugavas vēstnesis* in early February 1942. K. Stašulāns argued that the Latgale Latvians had lived for so long on the country's border, mixed up with the Slav population, that this had greatly changed their mentality; they were not necessarily 'bad', but less practical than the inhabitants of Vidzeme and Kurzeme and more prone to mysticism and dreaming, traits which in wartime should really be shed.[107]

The German authorities could not afford to be so dismissive. The first issue of the Russian-language weekly *Dvinskii vestnik* appeared on Saturday 7 February 1942. In that first issue the Latvian editor Alberts Zembergs explained, again inaccurately, that the Bolsheviks had tried to encourage Latgale separatism and found some people ready 'to sell their blood and conscience' in return for material advantage; such people had been removed. Latgale's true situation, the paper argued, had been noted when Schwung arrived in the region: 'I was told, and I can now see it with my own eyes, that you are honest and hard-working people, and I am horrified at the thought that you were robbed and cheated by the Bolsheviks and dirty Jews for a whole year.'[108] On 24 January *Daugavas vēstnesis*, the later article by Stašulāns not withstanding, published an article describing favourably the work on Latgale culture carried out at the start of the century by Francis Trasuns.[109] Later in February *Rēzeknes ziņas* announced its intention of starting a series of articles about the Latgale language and on 11 March it published an appeal for volunteers written in Latgalean.[110] The promised series of articles included the scholarly 'The Peculiarities of the Mores and Customs of Latgale Latvians' by Valerija Seile.[111] At the end of March the same paper reported how the Old Believer community in Ciskādi, just to the west of Rēzekne, had donated its church bell to the war effort.[112]

Settling scores

During the Jewish massacres, the policeman Savitskii had talked of turning on the Russians once the Jews were out of the way. The SS were convinced that the Old Believers were a bedrock of support for the communists. Schwung, on the other hand, felt that his local Latvian collaborators were intriguing to press forward their own political aims, one of which was to 'play the Russian population off against the German authorities'. In May 1942 these contradictory pressures came to a head. The German and the Latvian security services seized the opportunity to live out their racial prejudices.

It was said in certain Latvian circles that it was wrong to expect people to volunteer to fight Bolshevism when there were still Jews alive in Daugavpils.[113] Whatever the motivation on 1 May 1942 the Arājs commando was used to reduce the size of the ghetto by half and effectively liquidated it. Of the 935 specialist Jews still alive, only 450 survived, 200 billeted in the city and 250 remaining in the ghetto;[114] the killed were those too sick, too young or too old to work, along with the whole ghetto administration, its policemen and its governing committee. Some thirty people, including children, were killed in the ghetto itself when they refused to get on the lorries sent to transport them.[115] For some reason they were then taken first to the prison and from there to the killing ground at Mežciems. Two who survived stated that the scene in the ghetto was hellish: 'the Latvian auxiliaries went wild ... [and] threw old and sick people through second floor windows, shot those who refused to leave their rooms, and killed some of the very small children by cracking their heads against the concrete walls of the building.'[116] Even before May, those Jews who had lost the capacity to work were quietly executed, as happened to two sick Jews on 4 March.[117] In all at least 13,000 Jews had been executed in Daugavpils since the German Army arrived, with a further 7,000 in the rest of Latgale.[118]

No sooner had the ghetto been liquidated than the security forces turned their attention to the Russian population. In May 8,000 people, the vast majority of them Russians, were deported to Germany to work as forced labourers. This affair was complicated by the fact that two parallel campaigns were under way in Latgale in spring 1942, one to recruit labour for Kurzeme and other parts of Latvia where there was a shortage of agricultural labour, and the other to recruit labour for work in Germany. Latgale was perceived to have high rural underemployment and a labour surplus, yet the Kurzeme campaign went badly from the start. In his May report to Riga Schwung noted that 'the moment for this recruitment is particularly unfortunate in the light of the political situation' and that no one wanted to leave their own patch of land to work on that of others. Nevertheless, village elders had been mobilised and an effort would be made.[119] On 31 May *Daugavas vēstnesis* published an article entitled 'Not Servants, but Heroes of Labour' which sang the praises of those agricultural workers being sent from Latgale to Kurzeme. The previous day *Dvinskii vestnik* carried an article 'Not Landless Labourers, but Fighters', which was similar in tone. But none of this worked and in his June report to Riga Schwung decided to challenge the figures on which the campaign was based, stressing that the population of Latgale had in fact fallen under the Bolsheviks so that there was no longer a labour shortage. He then argued that a Latgale harvest brought in by willing workers was likely to yield as much if not more than a Kurzeme harvest brought in by forced labour from Latgale.[120]

The second campaign, that for volunteers to work in the Reich, had always had priority. This campaign began on 8 January 1942 with a big editorial in *Daugavas vēstnesis* calling on all men born in the years 1920–2 to volunteer; an accompanying article stressed the honour of being called for such service. More press appeals followed on 13 and 15 January, while on the 29th the category of those eligible was extended to youngsters born between 1918 and 1925.[121] In early March 1942 the press published more information about voluntary work in German, the wages on offer and the possibility of sending those wages home.[122] On 24 March much press coverage was given to the departure of the first labour volunteers from Daugavpils; Schwung saw them off at the station.[123] The reality did not match the propaganda fuss. Schwung had real doubts as to whether the campaign would work. In his report to Riga of 19 March he expressed his reservations. At this stage he was still willing to concede that Latgale was an area of Latvia with some surplus labour, but the initial target figure of 40,000 volunteers was extremely high. He would carry out his duty and begin recruitment and an associated propaganda campaign, he stated, but he warned that although a start could probably be made 'without serious unrest and large protests', disruption of the administration was possible, as were negative political consequences.[124] A month later in his report of 20 April, Schwung noted that the campaign was facing great difficulties, partly because of people's memories of the Bolsheviks' forced deportations a year earlier. He was ready to tour Latgale in person, he said, in an effort to raise more recruits, but careful propaganda would be needed in Russian-speaking areas. He stressed that the basis for recruitment had to be voluntary, with force being used only in exceptional circumstances.[125]

The press campaign resumed in mid-May with stories of the happy life enjoyed by the first volunteers. *Daugavas vēstnesis* published what purported to be a letter from Visvaldis Dzenis, an inhabitant of Grīva, who had volunteered to work in Germany. He had gone to the assembly point in Jelgava, and from there taken a train to a resort near the Friesian Islands, where they were based in a holiday camp, four Germans and four Latvians to a room. They had quickly learned the language, worked and studied hard; in short, life in Germany was great.[126] A few days later a certain B. Binca, from Varakļāni, wrote about how sad the one hundred volunteers from that town would be to leave after their marvellous time in Schwerin. The work was easy, the cinema great fun: 'do not believe any tales about things here being bad.'[127] These letters were fabrications. On 20 May Schwung sent Riga a copy of a real letter sent from Germany which had been intercepted because it painted such a negative picture of life in Reich work-camps.[128]

As recruitment targets failed to be met, things changed dramatically. Schwung's call for the voluntary principle to be honoured simply did not result in sufficient recruits; in his own words it ended in 'shipwreck'.[129] The situation was discussed in Riga on 2 May. Here Schwung again expressed his reservations and argued that there should be a delay until the authorities could begin to close down the small industrial concerns not needed for the war effort, thus providing a ready pool of workers who might be willing to move to Germany.[130] This rational, but long-term, solution was rejected and instead it was decided to use force. On 4 May a police action was launched to bring in the required labour. Ignoring the propaganda myth of cheerful Latvian youth joining their Aryan German brothers and sisters, the police decided to target exclusively non-Aryan Russian Old Believers and the Poles, their political enemies. In this way the chief object of acquiring labour could be combined with the removal of politically unreliable elements.[131] The police team had originally been given the task of seizing 24,000 volunteers, but unilaterally decided to reduce that number to 8,000. Its members were to comb Latgale and bring the Old Believers and Poles to collection points in Ludza and Daugavpils.[132]

The theory was that village elders and religious leaders would take part in the process by identifying suitable candidates; force would only be used if no volunteers came forward. Things went relatively smoothly in Daugavpils district and neighbouring Ludza district, and little police presence was needed; the German police detachments had no need of the thirty strong Latvian Schutsmannschaft units designated to act as back-up. Nevertheless, some officials expressed concern. The leader of the Daugavpils 'A' Schutzmannschaft was worried that not enough care was being taken, and that abrasive behaviour was proving counter-productive.[133] The head of the security service in Daugavpils made the same point on 11 May: the 'purges' were unsettling the 'Poles and Russians', most of whom expected to be exiled or put in a camp.[134] Schwung reported his suspicions that many Latvians were hoping to gain personal advantage through acquiring the property of those deported.[135]

It was in Rēzekne district that things got completely out of hand. There a shortage of staff at village elder level meant that the preliminary registration of those to be conscripted had not taken place. So the German police leader assembled a force of 165 Latvian Schutsmannschaft soldiers and surrounded whole villages at night, causing terrified inhabitants to flee to surrounding forests and marshlands. Some of those who fled seized weapons, including automatic rifles and hand grenades, and armed clashes followed between them and the pursuing police. These clashes continued for some time, and most of the Poles and Old Believers not caught up in the fighting had fled to other districts,[136] despite a travel ban on such movements.[137] In the worst incident those who had taken to the forest effectively became partisans since they tried to free some of those already conscripted by opening fire on a transport of labour conscripts, hitting an SS man in the back. Two Old Believers were hanged on the spot as a reprisal. According to Schwung, writing on 20 May, this affair had 'created unnecessary martyrs' and produced such unrest that the only really secure way forward was to consider deporting the whole Old Believer population.[138]

As Schwung later tried to explain to his masters in Riga, the Russians saw Russians as Russians, without distinguishing clearly between Old Believers and Orthodox believers. This had enabled Bolshevik propagandists to spread the rumour like wildfire that all Russians were being deported to the

Reich. What made things worse was the behaviour of the Latvian police brought in from Riga who, despite being told that the action was aimed at Old Believers, failed to make this distinction and simply used the slogan 'the Russians are to be banned and shot'. Schwung added that there had been a number of unpleasant occurrences during the action, which had brought in a daily flood of complaints. He had concluded that most of these complaints had turned out to be exaggerated, but commented: 'Latvian policemen almost all have a bit of sadism in their blood.'[139]

By 27 May 1942, 4,300 people had been detained and sent in four convoys to Germany; a further convoy of 2,000 was ready to leave Daugavpils on 31 May. This left 1,700 to be recruited before the anticipated end of the action on 6 June. Daugavpils itself was the only area where 'recruitment' had not yet taken place and the action began there on 3 June.[140] With only three days to go, there was no time to register Old Believers and Poles. No account was taken of nationality and the way the action was carried out alienated the entire population. As a detailed denunciation of the events showed, written with barely controlled anger on 4 June, the action became a simple 'hunt for people': a lorry would simply turn up at a crossroads, snatch squads would grab who ever was closest and load them on to the lorry at gun point, and then the lorry would head off to the assembly camps. 'These activities were so brutal that the methods used can certainly be compared to the methods of the *Cheka*', the denunciation concluded. In the village of Križi, situated to the north of Stropi lake, and in the Vecā Forštate suburb those detained were Old Believers and Poles, but in the rest of the city the assault was random and involved Latvians as well.

The denunciation written on 4 June cited 13 incidents. The first took place at the market and involved the gratuitous violence of a special squad of armed men in civilian clothes wearing SS armbands, who had been brought to Daugavpils from Riga. They simply grabbed people from the shops near the market, and 80 per cent of their victims were Latvian. One woman, kneeling and pleading that her children had been left unattended at home, was kicked to the ground. In the second incident two drunken men, carrying guns and wearing SS armbands, broke into the house of a police officer and tried to arrest him, even though he showed them his police identification. The third incident involved this same drunken group breaking into a flat, and then leaving it unsearched, breaking the windows simply for pleasure. The fourth incident again concerned the market, where a member of the snatch squad fired in the air, giving his comrades the pretext to point their guns at those they were tormenting on the grounds that they had come under attack. In the fifth incident two plumbers working for the Waffen SS were detained and had great difficulty establishing their true identity. By the afternoon of 3 June some sections of the local security services had decided that enough was enough, and the sixth incident involved an attempt by the local police to detain one of the snatch squads, but it was tipped off and escaped. The seventh incident involved the arbitrary arrest of women queuing for milk at the central dairy; no regard was taken of nationality and one heavily pregnant woman gave birth while the arrests were under way. The eighth and ninth incidents were similar: the arbitrary arrest of those working for the Waffen SS and other workers in essential industries.[141]

The tenth incident described in this long denunciation was not so much a single event as a constant stream of complaints which came in during the day. As became clear from an official investigation undertaken on the 5th the action had begun at 4.00 in the morning of 3 June, without informing the local police. Deputy police director Štāls learnt what was happening in the market at about 9.00 a.m. and was involved in attempts to try and find out exactly what was going on, demanding to see SS chief Tabbert and visiting the market himself to ascertain the facts. Despite discussions with Tabbert held in the afternoon of the 3rd and an apparent promise to call the action off, in some parts of the city the action had resumed in the evening.[142] This was the eleventh incident. Some snatch squads were even waiting at various cross roads on the morning of the 4th. The twelfth incident was the complaint was that those arrested were detained in the same camp in Daugavpils fortress as people awaiting transportation for agricultural labour in Kurzeme; this was interpreted as a blatant attempt by Tabbert to reach the 8,000 target by mixing together those who had volunteered to work in Kurzeme with those who were being forced to work in Germany. The final thirteenth incident took place on 4 June when at a meeting of those involved and affected, no institution would own up to ordering the action; Tabbert volunteered only that he had participated in it.[143]

With a startling degree of insensitivity, on 4 June *Daugavas vēstnesis* published a story about Latvian girls working in Germany, the beauty of the countryside and the joy of hard labour.[144] However, the investigation undertaken on 5 June concluded that the impact of the day on the Latvian population had been enormous: what was the point of Latvians coming forward as volunteers in the war against Bolshevism when innocent civilians could be rounded up at whim by the German police?[145] On 10 June the head of the security service in the Daugavpils third precinct stressed that the whole affair had been a self-inflicted wound, since the successes of the German Army on the battlefield as it advanced on Stalingrad had recently reduced communist propaganda. In the aftermath of the deportations he assessed the mood as suddenly very perturbed, since so many people caught up in the affair had simply been arrested on their way to work. Wives had to wait for ages to find out news of their husbands, rushing from office to office, while enterprise managers had to trace crucial workers and arrange for their release. Most popular criticism was focused on the Latvian policemen who were not locals and who had been drafted in by the SS to carry out the street arrests; universally they were seen as drunk and rude.[146] Writing in the middle of June, Schwung stressed that the whole episode had been a gift for Bolshevik propaganda, which had become stronger as a result. In this report he also expressed his delight that talk of recruiting more agricultural labour for Kurzeme had been dropped.[147] The May deportations had been a political disaster, but the SS could report with pride on 10 June that the target of 8,000 'volunteers' had been met.[148]

The partisans

Although a few partisan groups had been formed in March and April 1942, it was the 'hunt' for Old Believers and Poles at the end of May which really stimulated the development of the partisan movement. It was at this time that Aleksandrs Groms, who had established a komsomol cell in Šķaune and Pasiene, decided that he and his supporters had no alternative other than to become partisans, taking to the surrounding countryside.[149] His group did not stay in Latvia for long. Partisan groups had been operating nearby in Belorussia for some time and were already well established. Seeking respite, Groms crossed the border. Then, on the night of 12–13 June 1942, Groms, aided by his Belorussian allies, launched the most audacious partisan attack yet: 150 men seized control of Šķaune, cut the telephone lines and occupied the town offices for 24 hours, before successfully escaping.[150] Schwung had been complaining since May of an alarming increase in partisan activity,[151] and security reports made clear that most of this activity was the work of Belorussian partisans crossing the lightly defended border.[152] By his report of 18 July 1942 Schwung was referring to the 'heightened' partisan problem: he recorded the capture of two partisan groups, one operating near Ludza and the other near Daugavpils, but the escape of a third;[153] security reports for late July talked of 400 partisans based across the border at Osveya and linked them to recent sabotage operations near Rēzekne, Ludza, Daugavpils and Abrene.[154] Latvian partisan units from Latgale were becoming part of a broader partisan problem for the occupation authorities.

Ever since March 1942 the communists' Central Committee had been planning to send a force of trained partisans into Latvia to co-ordinate the activity of those groups like that of Groms which had been formed spontaneously. More than 200 men were trained and ready by the end of April, but there had been problems obtaining arms and other supplies from the commanders of the Red Army's North West Front.[155] In the end it was only on 6 July 1942 that the 'For a Soviet Latvia' Regiment set off. It was commanded by Laiviņš, whose experience of work behind the lines in October 1941 had been so disheartening, and the regimental commissar was Otomārs Oškalns, former second secretary of the Jēkabpils district party committee, whose evacuation from Latvia had been so peppered by conflicts with nationalist partisans. Marching as three brigades with 16 horses there was little attempt to hide its purpose. The original plan of constructing an airfield and supply zone near Pskov had to be abandoned, and just as the regiment reached the Latvian border disaster struck. The partisans had divided into small units to cross the frontier. Then, on the evening of 16 July, the leading group was surrounded, and in a bitter fight one of its leaders was killed, another wounded and Oškalns separated from the commanding group. He tried again to cross the frontier a few days later, but failed. By the end of July most of the regiment had crossed the front line and returned to their base but, in the general confusion, one group led by Voldemārs Ezernieks succeeded in crossing the border and established itself to the north of Balvi near the Gulbene–Abrene railway.[156] The German report on this disastrous adventure was not complementary: at the first clash with the security forces the partisans had 'lost their heads and slipped on their hands'. Even Ezernieks was successfully tracked 'to the forests between Alūksne and Balvi', although he was never captured.[157]

Just before the 'For a Soviet Latvia' Regiment fiasco began, the communists had received a report, which suggested there might be a better way of co-ordinating partisan activity. On 24 June 1942 the Central Staff of the Partisan Movement in Moscow received a report from Belorussia stating that a group of forty Latvians had turned up in Osveya who included among them Imants Sudmalis, the former Secretary of the Jelgava district party committee and member of the Central Committee.[158] When in August 1942 the party decided to send four smaller bands of partisans into Latvia, the presence of Latvians in Osveya and the renewed contact with Sudmalis made it sensible that one of these bands should travel to Osveya. The man chosen to lead the Osveya mission and establish there a base for operations in the Daugavpils area was Ivan Baranovskii, a native of Daugavpils; he had worked in a local factory until the establishment of the Soviet regime, when he had emerged first as the chairman of a factory committee and then as a recruit to the NKVD. He arrived near Osveya at the end of September and while in action inside Latvia in October, he and his men maintained regular radio contact with the Central Staff of the Partisan Movement, the first Latvian partisans to be in regular contact with Moscow. Increased partisan activity was made possible not simply by the establishment of radio contact with Moscow, but by a change of mood within Latgale itself. An intelligence report of October 1942 noted that while peasants would still always inform the authorities about the presence of outsiders, increasingly they would delay doing so for 24 hours to allow those concerned to move on.[159]

During October Baranovskii's team destroyed a railway bridge near Daugavpils, again with the help of Belorussian partisans.[160] Success like this meant they served as a magnet for others: Varfolomejs Rubulis, who had reached Latvia as part of the 'For a Soviet Latvia' Regiment,[161] brought a small group of partisans he had formed near Rēzekne to join the growing team in Osveya;[162] also in autumn 1942 Evmenii Maksimov moved to join the Belorussian partisans.[163] Thus when the party held a meeting in Moscow on 19 November 1942 to reassess its partisan strategy, Sudmalis, Oškalns and Vilis Samsons, another veteran of the 'For a Soviet Latvia' Regiment, could argue that a Latvian partisan headquarters should be established in Belorussia at once. Sudmalis, Oškalns and Samsons were duly ordered to make their way to Osveya.[164]

By summer 1942 the press had begun to pay attention to the development of partisan activity. On 19 July 1942, in one of its very few references to partisan struggle, the Daugavpils Latvian-language paper *Daugavas vēstnesis* noted that partisans were operating near Rēzekne, that at any moment a shot could ring out from behind a bush, that every effort should be made to defeat the partisans, and that, despite all the warnings, some peasants were supporting them. A short report on 25 July recorded that S. Leigaunieks, a member of the security services, had died in a clash with 'red bands'. Daugavpils's Russian-language press was more outspoken. On 1 August 1942 *Dvinskii vestnik* published a front-page article reminding people that wherever the local population supported the partisans, retribution would follow. There then followed a regular series of bloodcurdling front-page articles about the evils of the partisans. On 12 September 1942 *Dvinskii vestnik* reminded its readers that in the struggle against partisans 'the gallows are to protect the Russian people'; on 26 September the partisans were 'the scourge of the peasantry', surviving only by unleashing a reign of terror against them; on 24 October *Dvinskii vestnik* posed the question in its leading article 'Bandit or Hero?'; and on 5 December *Dvinskii vestnik* had a front-page story of how partisans had burnt down the churches in the villages of Dubrovska, near Sebezh on the Russian side of the border near Zilupe, and Chaika near the Latvian town of Indra.

Summertime blues

Apart from references to the partisans in the press, the inhabitants of Daugavpils itself were unaffected by the unfolding unrest in the countryside. Daily life remained extremely difficult. A major source of this was the stagnating economy. In March the Reichskommissar in Riga decided to close the *Daugava* and *Italia* textile factories. Schwung protested, but he had to concede that the factories would not be able to reopen soon since the type of thread they needed was not available.[165] The flax factory went down to 50 per cent production in July because of similar delivery problems; indeed such problems were affecting the whole of Daugavpils industry.[166] In May 1942 the occupation authorities announced that the staff of the Daugavpils city administration was being cut to save money.[167] The only bright spot in the economy was privatisation, though this was still very limited. At the end of March the privatisation of five small establishments had been announced. These were mostly radio repair shops and hairdressing salons. In April the intention of privatising the O. Racens furniture factory which employed 22 workers was announced.[168] However, it was the end of July before the Racens plant and four others were privatised, although it was promised that ten more were in the pipeline.[169] Racens no doubt used his influence as president of the handicraft association to ensure his factory was one of the first on the list.[170] Measures continued to control the workforce. In early June workers began to be issued with work books,[171] and in mid-August it was stated that the courts would be used against those who violated labour discipline.[172] This was balanced by appointments to officially sanctioned labour organisations. Jānis Bauers, editorial secretary of *Daugavas vēstnesis* and a former teacher was elected chairman of the United Trade Union of Latgale, and Imants Sveilis appointed to head its 'Strength through Joy' section.[173]

Continuing economic shortages meant that the struggle against the black market never ended. In July there was nothing in the shops other than the goods on ration.[174] On 1 August inhabitants were encouraged to collect berries and mushrooms and preserve them for winter, but warned that they could only be sold via delivery points and those people ignoring this would be punished.[175] Early in August the fines for speculation were increased and it was announced that the worst forms of it would attract the death penalty.[176] Yet the black market was so widespread that by summer 1942 even surviving Jewish seamstresses in the Daugavpils fortress were selling remodelled clothes; by the end of the year they had a steady trade in seal-skin coats.[177] By the autumn the authorities felt they needed a clearer grip on the size of the city's population if they were ever to get on top of its provisioning. Temporary documents had been issued in May for six months and by October the process of a full re-registration of passports was under way.[178] But it was goods that were in short supply, rather than there being an excess of people. In fact, by the summer of 1942 the housing shortage was said to be small, despite the fact that the city administration had never seriously addressed it.[179] In October inhabitants were reminded that the flats of Jews could only be occupied with the permission of the city housing inspectorate.[180]

Like the Bolsheviks a year before, the Nazi administration was desperate to have a successful sowing campaign leading to a bountiful harvest. In mid-April Blūzmanis hosted a big meeting of agronomists to prepare for the spring sowing and to encourage the production of flax.[181] A few days later Schwung announced the formation of a credit bank to encourage agricultural investment.[182] On 3 May Schwung placed an appeal in *Daugavas vēstnesis*, printed in German, Latvian and Russian, calling for every furrow to be sown. It was time to mend equipment, to share out draft animals amongst less well-off villagers, and to clear the fields of stones. In another echo of Bolshevism, Schwung stressed that those who ignored this order were committing sabotage; the optimum time for sowing should be discussed with the local agronomist, he concluded.[183] As if to underline the regime's positive support for the region's agricultural development, the local press gave prominent coverage to the presence of local leaders at the first graduation ceremony for the Višķi agricultural college.[184]

At the same time it was reported that teams of schoolchildren were being sent into the countryside to help with summer work in the fields.[185] The start of the process was delayed by talks between the education department on the director of labour, but by the middle of June 650 children were reportedly involved in the scheme.[186] Over the summer agricultural labourers were expected to work an 11-hour day, seven days a week,[187] the only exception to this being those who had volunteered for the anti-Bolshevik struggle;[188] under the terms of their contract, they were allowed to return from duty for essential agricultural work.[189] As *Daugavas vēstnesis* reminded its readers on 12 June in the article 'Legal Norms of the War Economy', agricultural production was not the personal concern of the peasant but an affair of the state. At the end of June Schwung issued another appeal for peasants to hand over supplies in order to help the soldiers at the front.[190]

As harvest time approached *Daugavas vēstnesis* stressed that gathering the harvest was a duty, it was a matter of returning a debt to the liberators.[191] On 23 August Schwung appealed to all citizens to devote a day's labour to bringing in the harvest, and P. Ducmanis, head of the official sports organisation in Latgale, called on all sportsmen to offer their help with the harvest.[192] On 27 August Kamaldnieks called on all policemen to take on the task of bringing in the harvest for those families whose members had died in the struggle against Bolshevism, while the Daugavpils Gymnasium delayed the start of its term till the end of September so that pupils could continue their agricultural work.[193] In the end, the start of the academic year in all schools was postponed until 12 October because of the need to bring in the harvest.[194]

And there were still volunteers to be found to work in Germany. The terrible events of May 1942 did not mean that the issue of voluntary labour in Germany had disappeared. Letters from Visvaldis Dzenis, the supposedly contented young worker in Germany, became a regular feature of *Daugavas vēstnesis* in the summer.[195] On 5 August the recruitment campaign for the next batch of volunteers began in earnest. Recruits would register from 15 to 31 August at the offices of the Gebietskommissar in Daugavpils and the district elders' offices in Rēzekne, Ludza and Abrene. After registration they would be asked to assemble in October, and by the end of that month they would be starting work in Germany.[196] During the registration period, meetings were held,[197] the names of the first five volunteers, all Latvians, were given due publicity,[198] and the campaign was extended to the Russian-language press.[199] However, there was little press coverage when the volunteers assembled on 12 October and left for Riga and the onward journey to Germany.[200] This time force was not used and the families of those sent duly received the small monthly allowances of 20–40 Reichsmarks to which they were entitled.[201]

Schwung's initiative

The violence associated with the May events had done nothing to improve relations between Schwung and his Latvian administration. This latent hostility became clear as the People's Aid organisation gradually expanded its brief. In mid-February *Daugavas vēstnesis* published a report on the initial work of the Daugavpils branch of People's Aid. Its purpose was to help liquidate the consequences of the Bolshevik occupation and its main task was to allocate benefits to those families which had lost breadwinners during the year of Soviet rule and the new war against Bolshevism; there had been a total of 453 requests to receive the modest benefit of 70 marks per month. Other help it offered was to find work for people, establishing a carpenters' workshop and a sewing workshop. Its funds still came mostly from donations, but often on a more organised basis than had been the case at first; teachers at the Daugavpils First Secondary School donated part of their salary each month.[202] The Pērkonkrusts activist Adolfs Šilde was the organisation's general secretary, an appointment reported on 8 March,[203] and the Latgale chairwoman was Valerija Seile.[204] Despite the dominant position of Latvians among its leaders, the Germans made clear that the organisation was to help all the inhabitants of Latvia without distinction of nationality.[205]

From the very start, People's Aid interpreted its brief broadly, since in the view of the organisation's leaders all Latvians were to an extent victims of Bolshevism. The organisation always expressed its concern for the welfare of children, plans were drawn up to establish a children's camp at Mežciems,[206] but it was equally at pains to involve children in its work, aware of the potential propaganda value this could have; on 29 April Šilde made a radio broadcast which was addressed to school children.[207] The organisation's activities soon went beyond conventional welfare. On 1 April it was reported that the organisation's central office in Riga had allocated Daugavpils district 60,000 marks to be used to help poor farmers; this could mean a grant of 100–150 marks per family.[208] As the type of work it was involved in expanded, its committee became more organised. When Pētersons the city elder was re-appointed chairman of the Daugavpils branch at a meeting on 12 April, it was resolved that the local branch had not been active enough.[209] Ten days later it hosted a big fund-raising event.[210] Fundraising remained a core activity and in the autumn there were regular calls in the Latvian press for donations to support the work of People's Aid;[211] towards the end of October it was reported that schoolchildren had collected over 4,000 marks.[212]

Tension developed between Schwung and People's Aid over how to mark the anniversary of the deportations of 14 June. In the first week of May the graves of victims were tidied, on one occasion by children from primary school number 1. In Viški trees were planted for every village inhabitant who was repressed.[213] Then on 21 May it was announced that a series of commemorative events sponsored by People's Aid would take place on 14 June in honour of the city's 745 deportees.[214] The first hint of trouble came at the start of June when it was made clear that any event to mark the anniversary should be strictly religious in nature.[215] People's Aid was allowed to organise a concert at Unity House and this was addressed by Gustavs Celmiņš, as leader of the Latvian volunteers's committee.[216] However, the concert was not attended by the German authorities, and it was Schwung's Baltic German adjutant Egon Rauch who attended the church service not Schwung himself. Rauch's speech on this occasion was bland, mentioning the common commitment of Germans and Latvians to the struggle against Bolshevism. At the church, Celmiņš spoke passionately about the 121 people he claimed had died during the Red Army's occupation in 1940 and he linked their sacrifice to that of the 85 volunteers who had died so far on the eastern front. The press coverage of this speech on 16 June included a photograph of Celmiņš.[217]

Clearly, People's Aid was becoming a vehicle for what the Germans condemned as Latvian national chauvinism. Schwung found he did have time two weeks later to make a speech at the celebrations to mark the anniversary of Latvia's liberation by the Nazis,[218] and in the course of July moves were made in Riga to prevent things going any further. By the end of that month the former Pērkonkrusts members of People's Aid found themselves out of favour. Šilde had been effectively side-lined and Bruno Pavasars appointed the new head of People's Aid.[219] At the end of October Pavasars was called in by the Germans and told to keep an eye on both Šilde and Celmiņš; the later had produced four publicity posters for People's Aid which the authorities felt were anti-German in spirit. Pavasars agreed that Celmiņš had overstepped the mark, but stressed that he had had a long talk with Šilde who had assured him of his loyalty.[220]

By summer 1942 Schwung was finding his Latvian collaborators even more tiresome than he had done in the spring. In his June report to Riga he again suggested that the Latvians were trying to get the Germans to do for them what the Latvians had failed to do during twenty years of independence; they wanted to get rid of the Russians 'behind the cloak of the Germans'. He stressed that, in this 'German political aims are not at one with the Latvians ... The Russian component, that has lived here for generations, is racially equal to the Latgaleans ... it is even possible to say that the Russian peasant farms more intensively and economically than his Latvian counterpart; observations and visits have proved this to me.'[221] The establishment of the Latvian self-administration had prompted the intelligentsia to promote the idea of a free Latvia, flooding administrative offices with leaflets, while those working in district offices on the ground were simply not up to the task and still needed constant guidance: 'the worst situation here is the usual informers, which is inbred apparently in the Latvians; where one sees white the other sees red, and vice versa.'[222]

In his June report Schwung told Riga that he was looking for a new way forward 'to stablilise the situation' after the May and June deportation. He had decided to approach the churches and win their support since 'in an area of population with strong confessional identity it is both necessary and right to use the Church for essential tasks'. An illustration of the fervour of the Catholic community can be seen from the fact that in mid-August 30,000 pilgrims visited the shrine of the Virgin in Aglona.[223] To win some of these hearts and minds Schwung called a meeting of representatives of all four

Figure 2 Unity House during the Nazi occupation

major confessions and all had attended, giving the impression that they were 'on our side ... and willing to support the measure that we have to undertake from the pulpit'.[224] In public this change of tactic was manifested by a short press appeal, dated 14 July, for church bells to be smelted down in the war effort. Alongside the signatures of representatives of the Catholic and Protestant churches frequented by Latvians, came the Orthodox and Old Believer churches of the Russians; the Orthodox respondent was L. Ladinskii, described as 'representative of the Latgale Orthodox parishes'.[225]

The dismissal of Schwung

Doubts about the competence of Schwung began to emerge in March 1942. In the middle of the month he submitted to Riga a budget statement for Daugavpils which he conceded gave insufficient detail; he requested that an experienced bookkeeper be sent to Daugavpils to help track expenditure. The following month the amount itemised as the city's reserves was dramatically recalculated.[226] The General Directorate, already critical of Schwung because it was believed he had appointed Budže district elder of Daugavpils without its endorsement, quickly seized on these failings. Writing to Generalkommissar Drechsler it reported that it had sent an inspector to Daugavpils who had returned horrified at the state of the accounts, stressing that the budget was incomprehensible and bore no relation to the real figures.[227] Schwung dismissed this as part of a campaign against him by the 'Latvian officers' he so despised, but Drechsler took the issue seriously. On 5

June an official from the Generalkommissar's finance department reported on his visit to Schwung in Daugavpils on the first and second of that month.

The first day, he said, had been particularly difficult, since Schwung adopted the attitude that no one had the right to interrogate him over such matters. By the second day the inspector was less interested in the budget than the level of food supplies in the city and the fact that the rationing system in operation appeared to be out of line with that outlined in instructions sent from Riga. This was in contrast to the opulence of Schwung's own lifestyle. The inspector expressed grave concern that Schwung and his immediate colleagues had established a residence in one of the best Mežciems villas, where they had installed a housekeeper and four maids. With guests and hangers on, this meant that twenty people usually gathered in the evening, consuming quantities of meat well beyond what was appropriate, particularly when the Gebietskommissar had recently ordered the introduction of meat-free days, insisting that even salami at breakfast time was impossible. The inspector concluded that Schwung and his entourage had let things slide and were no longer taking good care of their district.[228]

Further enquiries revealed Schwung's possession of a small private armoury, as well as a large number of furs; there was also the suspicion that he had benefited from the mysterious disappearance of 77 leather flying-jackets.[229] Schwung attended the gathering of Gebietskomissars held in Riga on 15 August, but again did not impress. The meeting decided that the formal appointment of all district elders should be concluded by 1 September, but Schwung pressed for an extension until October, which meant postponing the visit Drechsler hoped to pay to the region.[230] Clearly it was felt at this point that enough was enough and on 19 August 1942 it was decided to dismiss Schwung on the grounds that he was not up to the tasks expected of him. At this stage the doubts about his probity were not pursued, and Drechsler even intimated that he would soon be offered a new posting.[231]

Schwung packed up his belongings and returned home to Kassel. However, he left behind eight trunks to be forwarded to him at a later date. On 24 September these trunks were opened by investigators, who found an extraordinary quantity of luxury items concealed in them. There were 11 bottles of spirits, five bottles of Benedictine, 500 cigarettes, various weapons and trophies and, at a time when the typhus outbreak was still fresh in people's minds, 60 bars of soap and 15 blocks of toilet soap. Two of the trunks also contained property confiscated from the Jews, including many fur coats and 516 silver spoons. The total value of the eight trunks was estimated at 3,700 Reichsmarks. A month later a bill came in from the Rēzekne brewery which the authorities at first refused to pay, until they were persuaded that if it were not paid, Drechsler's October visit to the town could be compromised. Eventually four trunks were returned to Schwung, containing those goods which the investigators deemed were his personal possessions.[232]

After Schwung's dismissal there was a lengthy campaign to get him to repay the sum he was deemed to owe Daugavpils. He eventually accepted that he owed 2,985 Reichsmarks, but always maintained that he had known nothing of the 77 flying jackets. However, a hearing in January 1943 decided that he was responsible for these jackets and demanded a further 1,145 Reichsmarks; it was at this hearing that he was formally stripped of the title Gebietskommissar. In April 1943 he handed over 2,000 Reichsmarks and in May 1943 Daugavpils was reimbursed the missing 2,985 Reichsmarks. Although Schwung received several more demands for the outstanding money, even offering that it could be paid by instalments, he never accepted the extra liability. On 3 April 1944 he handed over a further 99.35 Reichsmarks, but to underline the point that this cleared him out, on 5 April 1944 he made a further final payment of 4 pfennigs, leaving him with a debt calculated at 1,230.16 Reichsmarks. On 8 June 1944 the last attempt to extract this money from him was returned to sender; Schwung had been sent to the front, presumably the eastern front.[233]

Schwung was replaced by Herman Riecken, who had stood in for Schwung in early September 1941. He came from a peasant family and was reported to be one of the earliest converts to National Socialism; his immediately previous appointment was as commissar in the coastal town of Pärnu in southern Estonia. Once Riecken had found his feet, he completed the work of appointing the new city and district elders. Pētersons was removed as Daugavpils city elder and Blūzmanis as Daugavpils district elder; both had been extremely prominent in the assault on the Jews and both represented that first wave of collaborators who were now seen to be a political embarrassment. Blūzmanis was replaced by his deputy Budže and Pētersons by Jānis Niedra, a local boy who had been born in in Balvi parish near Abrene on 21 December 1908 and attended Aglona gymnasium. He left school in 1927, studying first at a Jesuit college in Vienna and then at Latvia University's History Department. An active member of student corporations, he eventually worked as a civil servant in the Agriculture Ministry, the Railway Administration and the State Control Department. In the early 1930s he also did some journalistic work and became an active member of the Latgale Christian Peasant Party. Sacked by the Soviet regime in November 1940, he was reinstated by the Germans.[234] There were other changes. In the SS leadership Tabbert was replaced, and in the local police the responsibilities of Štāls were changed;[235] his role as director of the commercial college continued.[236] Lower down the hierarchy Jānis Eglājs resigned as vice-chairman of the Daugavpils district court and was replaced by Emārs Miķelsons, a Daugavpils legal investigator sacked by the Bolsheviks.[237]

The formal appointment of Niedra and Budže to their new posts brought the Latvian Generalkommissar Otto Drechsler down from Riga for a two-day visit to Daugavpils. on 14–16 October, including whistle-stop visits to Rēzekne, Ludza and Abrene. General Dankers travelled with him, as well as various police leaders. After the appointment ceremony for Niedra and Budže, as well as for district elders in Rēzekne, Ludza and Abrene, a grand meeting was held in Unity House to hear speeches by Drechsler, Dankers, Riecken and Budže. Drechsler suggested to those present that German peasants were suffering in the war more than Latvian peasants; Dankers attacked those who he called 'moaners'; it was left to Riecken to stress the peculiarities of the Latgale region and the importance of working with local communities. Riecken therefore pressed ahead with Schwung's strategy of winning over the Russian community.[238] As he made clear in his speech, Latgale was 'not Latvia's stepdaughter, but a genuine daughter'.[239]

Reflecting this, *Daugavas vēstnesis* began to take an interest in the activities of those it had disdained. On 25 September it reported that a Russian choir was being set up, and three weeks later published an article by Metropilitan Sergius, the spiritual leader of the Russian Orthodox in Latvia.[240] The Russian choir was led by L. Ladinskii who had responded to Schwung's earlier appeal and was now described as 'representative of the Russian population of Latgale'. This position was unrecognised, yet at the same time a certain A. Krel was described as the 'chairman' of the Russian population in Ludza and Rēzekne, when he arranged for those graduating from Russian schools to attend Rēzekne Technical College.[241] Earlier, in late August *Dvinskii vestnik* suddenly turned to an issue that Russians felt deeply about, the treatment of POWs.

In spring 1942 conditions for Russian POWs improved when it was decided that even Russian POWs could be put to economic use. In May the city authorities put several hundred to work restoring the city. This revived the perennial problem of contacts between the prisoners and the civilian population. On 19 May the citizens of Daugavpils were reminded that it was an enemy act to engage in conversation with the POWs and such instances would be punished.[242] Dropping a cigarette for a POW to pick up led to a brutal beating for one Russian worker at the hands of the local Gestapo chief, who took this as a sign that the worker must be a communist who listened to Moscow radio.[243] Yet such incidents clearly continued, with many conversations between POWs and civilians ending with successful escape attempts. On 23 June Schwung issued a reminder, published in German, Latvian and Russian, that anybody supporting runaway POWs would be severely punished, while those who helped track them down would be rewarded.[244] At the start of July readers of *Dvinskii vestnik* were again reminded that there should be no contact with POWs,[245] and in September the justice department ruled that it was illegal to marry a POW.[246]

Yet, suddenly, at the end of August, *Dvinskii vestnik* published a series of articles about those who had surrendered and 'put themselves under the defence of the Germans'; there could be no mercy to those who abused German generosity, it said, but life in the camps was good.[247] In mid-October *Dvinskii vestnik* carried an article entitled 'Volunteers against Stalin' which suggested that the paper's editorial offices had been inundated with

letters from Russian POWs asking to know if they could be allowed to
volunteer to fight the Bolsheviks; letters had also been received from
members of the local Russian community. The paper called their desire for
vengeance justified, and urged people not to write to the paper on this
matter but to contact the relevant authorities.[248]

There was, of course, a good reason for this change of policy. As the
German Army became bogged down at Stalingrad, the tide of the war
began to change. There was a perceptible change of mood in the autumn.
Early in September a Committee of Volunteers was set up to start raising
money for the families of wounded volunteers,[249] while in early October a
recuperation unit for wounded volunteers was set up in the grounds of the
former Daugavpils psychiatric hospital.[250] On 24 September *Daugavas vēstnesis* published an article entitled 'Our Tasks' in which the author called for
hard work and patience, since 'it is not known how long the war will last'. A
week later 'We Will Help Ourselves' took a similar line: the Bolsheviks were
overthrown but the war was continuing and more sacrifices would be called
for.[251] A further sign that the war was not yet won came in October with an
air raid. It was not the first air attack: on 18 April 1942 a lone Soviet plane
had dropped eight bombs on Daugavpils passenger station and the goods
station, doing damage to 75 structures and killing three soldiers.[252] However
the October raid was a full bombing raid, and it had an enormous impact
on those willing to resist. Shaike Iwensky, one of the few surviving specialist
Jews, recalled: 'Last night there was an air raid warning – Russian planes
were in the vicinity! The sirens sounded like music. It was the first time since
the outbreak of the war that this had happened … [It was] an air raid! How
extraordinary. Bombs were dropped right here in Daugavpils.' The raid did
considerable damage to parts of the fortress where Iwensky and the other
surviving Jews were housed.[253]

5   Dünaburg under Riecken

For most of Herman Riecken's tenure of office as Daugavpils Gebiets-kommissar he found himself at the centre of a tripartite conflict that was impossible to resolve. He wanted to take forward Schwung's policy of wooing the Russian population, and thus distancing them from the partisans. The security forces preferred to tackle the partisans head on, and by so doing drove more and more people into their arms. By the time Riecken's mutli-ethnic self-administration was in place in November 1943, the partisan movement was unstoppable.

At the start of 1943, the leaders of the Latvian partisans made a determined effort to establish a secure base at Osveya, across the border in Belorussia. Their initial successes were soon challenged by the 'Winter Magic' anti-partisan drive which, while it held the partisans in check for a while, was such an arbitrary and violent assault on the Russian population of the border area that it ultimately backfired. The logic of 'Winter Magic' contradicted the strategy, advanced first by Schwung and subsequently developed by Riecken, of trying to woo the Russian population of Latgale. Thus in February 1943 there was criticism of the 'national chauvinists' who argued for Slovak-style independence for Latvia. Then in April 1943 the Daugavpils Latvian Society was definitively closed down. At the same time Russians were encouraged to join the specifically Russian Security Battalions, a Russian National Committee was formed and Stalin's deportations of 1941 were recast as an assault on 'Christians' not just Latvians.

This policy almost brought Latgale some stability. By the early summer of 1943 the city had adopted a relatively normal budget, reflecting peacetime priorities like reconstructing flats and offices and making repairs to hospitals and schools. The summer festival of Ligo was celebrated without restriction. Yet, as the summer months passed, the situation worsened. Waves of refugees arrived as the German Army retreated from Stalingrad, and this made the rationing regime more oppressive than ever. Nor did the partisan problem go away. By summer 1943 proper supplies were arriving from Moscow, which put the struggle on a higher plane. The Nazi response highlighted the contradictions of the German administration. A new series of deportations followed in August, which were entirely counter-productive, since they prompted protests from the Russian National Committee and indiscipline within the Russian Security Battalions. Riecken's fury at the way police actions like this wrecked the self-administration policy was shared by the whole civilian administration.

Despite these setbacks, Riecken was determined to push ahead with the self-administration policy. He quashed the final attempt by 'national chauvinists' to re-launch the Daugavpils Latvian Society, and denounced critics of the policy within the security services. Instead of favouring 'national chauvinism', he agreed to the publication of a newspaper in the Latgale dialect. Yet at the same time that the self-administration policy was pushed through, Riecken had to recognise in public the worsening situation at the front. Soon he was appealing for additional support in the struggle against the partisans, for they, following Moscow's orders, had relocated to various bases within Latvia and had extended their operations. By the end of 1943 they had undermined the morale of the Russian Security Battalions and were chipping away at the confidence of the Latvian Legion. In this context Stalin's vague offer that after the war there would be limited autonomy for Latvia within the Soviet Union, an offer apparently agreed with Britain and America, compared favourably with Hitler's refusal to give Latvia any meaningful independence.

Resistance kept in check

Not long after Riecken had welcomed Drechsler to Daugavpils in mid-October 1942, Oškalns and other partisan commanders arrived in Osveya to develop the small groups of Latvian partisans operating from there into something akin to the brigades formed by Soviet partisans in other parts of occupied territory. Moscow had already made its commitment. By the autumn Moscow radio's broadcasts to Latvia had been increasing their output, adding a sixth broadcast from 18 October; each day two of the six broadcasts were devoted to partisan affairs totalling 30 minutes per day.[1] There had also been an increase in the number of leaflets air-dropped into Latvia.[2] Oškalns and Laiviņš arrived in Osveya during the first week of December;[3] they were joined a fortnight later by Samsons and Sudmalis.[4] The Germans were soon aware of these changes. A security report dated 6 February 1943 proved remarkably informed: it noted that an 80-strong group of Latvian partisans had been established near Osveya at the end of December, led by Oškalns with Laiviņš and Samsons his closest advisors; they joined the existing 30–40 men led by Baranovskii and Rubulis. The arrival of Oškalns and Laiviņš prompted others who had fled across the border to gather in Osveya, in particular the band led by Groms. Oškalns's first action had been to blow up a train on 28 December, the German report concluded.[5]

Establishing a partisan base was not easy; building winter quarters took 15 men the best part of a month. Oškalns quickly learnt that the rule of partisan warfare was self-supply. The Belorussian partisans informed him that food and other supplies for the Latvians would have to come from within Latvia, not from Belorussia, although they were quite prepared to help in carrying out the necessary raids.[6] And supplies were certainly a problem: two partisans captured by the Germans in January 1943 complained that they had had nothing to eat but potatoes.[7] So on 11–12 January 1943 a joint raid was launched on the small town of Vecslabada. Some 200 carts were used to bring back supplies from the 40 inhabitants who were robbed. Some 600 Reichsmarks were seized from the town offices, along with 500 litres of vodka and 400 pairs of shoes.[8] However, of most use were the 700 kilos of wool that was seized; this was painstakingly reworked into snow-boots (*valenki*). Acquiring food, clothes and shoes meant taking them from the peasants. In his first report to Moscow, Oškalns stressed that this had gone well. They had tried to target only collaborators – Baranovskii recalled that his intelligence men had special lists of former *aizsargi*[9] – and usually peasants understood and 'often helped load carts'. Buildings were never set on fire on purpose, although during fire-fights this could not always be avoided.[10]

Such expropriations followed class rather than national principles: on 15 September 1942 a group of seven to eight partisans raided a farm at Silajāņi, north-east of Preiļi; the village elder and the secretary who reported the attack were Latvian, but the farm was owned by a Russian, J. Firsov, deemed rich enough to hand over clothes and shoes.[11]

Self-supply also meant acquiring weapons. Here the Latvian partisans were at a disadvantage. Ever since spring 1942 the Belorussian partisans had regularly raided Latvia to replenish their weapon supply. Now the Latvians had to look for weapons where the Belorussians had already scooped the pool. This was a real problem for Oškalns, since he could not run the risk of forming large numbers of unarmed partisans. His first report shows great frustration that in February 1943 new partisan volunteers began to arrive, but he had no arms to give them. 'New partisans arrived. In a short time we could have formed many detachments, but we had no arms.'[12] What was even more frustrating was that before any arms could be collected the Germans launched their 'Winter Magic' anti-partisan drive.

Having monitored Oškalns's arrival, and the success of the Vecslabada operation, which was the culmination of raids throughout November and December and was quickly followed by a raid on Robežnieki,[13] the Nazi authorities were determined to stamp on the Latvian partisans before their movement took hold. 'Winter Magic' began in mid-February and lasted until 31 March 1943. It was undertaken in three stages, but reports have only survived for the second and third stages. In the clashes between the partisans and the nine Latvian Schutzmannschaft Battalions sent against them, the casualties among the Latvian units were 21 dead, 12 seriously wounded and 49 lightly wounded. As to the partisans, 132 were killed and 21 taken prisoner; a further 2,548 partisans and partisan helpers were executed and 3,951 people deported whose links with the partisans could not be clearly established.[14]

One of the partisans claimed that 26 villages had been burnt to the ground and the population either burnt with the buildings or shot.[15] This was no exaggeration. In the aftermath of the campaign Reichskommissar Ostland Hinrich Lohse received so many complaints that he asked Drechsler to investigate what had taken place.

The aim of the anti-partisan drive was to establish a barrier along the old Latvian–Russian border which would prevent partisans crossing into Latvia. On the Latvian side special regulations regarding the curfew and registration of visitors were introduced,[16] but on the Russian side it was decided to create an artificial no man's land. The campaign was led by SS General Jeckeln, and the plan was to create a 40-kilometre swathe of desert, apart from a five-kilometre stretch along the Rēzekne–Moscow railway line which would remain under Army control. All males living in the area were invited to leave, and many did so. Villages in the zone were then occupied and partisan supporters shot; since the male population had been invited to leave, this meant killing all the remaining males aged 16–50. Old men not deemed fit enough to join the forced march of deportation were also shot. The surviving women and children were then taken to a filtration camp; those who failed to keep pace were shot as stragglers. From the filtration camp most were sent to Salaspils concentration camp near Riga, from where the women were sent to work in Germany and the children under 16 found homes in Latvian families. The cleared villages were burnt to the ground.

As Drechsler's report made clear, the campaign was not only brutal, but arbitrary. Families living in villages within five kilometres of the railway zone were untouched and became a refuge for those in neighbouring villages. Worst of all, those men who had left the zone voluntarily did so on the understanding that their families would not be deported. They would therefore turn up to collect their families from the filtration camp, sometimes with scarce motor transport provided by the civilian authorities, only to find that their families had already set off for Salaspils and were lost to them. It was, Drechsler concluded, 'negative' in its propaganda impact. Nor had it worked militarily. Soon the numbers of Latvians fleeing to the partisans across the border had increased and the partisans were stronger than ever.[17] In a letter the following month Drechsler stressed that, because the villages destroyed were on Russian territory, the campaign had had nothing to do with him.[18] Nevertheless, it was the Latvian General Directorate which had to find homes for the evacuated children, although its officials noted that, since these were Russian children not Latvian children, and since there were 1,000 of them, it would not be necessary to exercise the usual level of care in finding homes; the older children were suitable for work on the land.[19]

Undeniably, 'Winter Magic' set back the development of the partisan movement in the very short term. German security reports showed no partisan activity in the vicinity of Daugavpils in April 1943, although in the same month there were still 23 partisan actions in Ludza.[20] Yet on 9 April

1943 the press office in Riga authorised an increase in the *Daugavas vēstnesis* print-run from 15,000 copies to 18,000 copies because of the need to counter Bolshevik propaganda in the 'partisan threatened region of Latgale'.[21] By May and June Oškalns felt the situation had recovered. He reported that 'Winter Magic' had driven the partisans 'pretty far' from the Latvian border; but June saw the partisans active again, and plagued only by the shortage of arms, which still prevented large-scale recruitment.[22] Too much time was spent hunting for weapons and too many partisans remained unarmed – this was the message repeatedly transmitted from Osveya to Moscow.[23] The fact that Dominiks Kaupužs, the former disgraced editor of *Latgolas Taisneiba* who was sent to the Abrene area at the same time as Baranovskii was sent to Osveya, succeeded in organising a partisan group of 70 men in March–April 1943 lends credence to the notion that there was a ready supply of recruits.[24]

It was perfectly logical therefore that, even at the height of the 'Winter Magic' anti-partisan drive, in March 1943, the Latvian partisans should inform Moscow that they had formed themselves into a Latvian Partisan Brigade, broken down into three detachments. This decision was taken on the advice of a Central Committee Operative Group, which arrived in Osveya on 21 January 1943. The Operative Group included among its members Milda Birkenfelde, the former first secretary of the Jēkabpils district committee who had retreated to Soviet territory in July 1941 in the company of Oškalns, clashing with nationalist partisans all the way.[25]

Within Daugavpils there was clear evidence of a growing mood of resistance by spring 1943. The group formed around Lazdovskii and Titova continued to operate, and even expanded to link up with an underground cell in Stropi, which dared to raid a small arms store. A komsomol group led by Nikolai Shkrabo also began its activity at this time.[26] Between 21 December 1942 and 21 January 1943, 95 people were arrested in Daugavpils for 'communism and Marxism'.[27] A police report for March 1943 showed that more people were arrested for 'Marxism' in Daugavpils than anywhere else in the country; the figure was 68 as opposed to only 42 in Riga. The same report noted four acts of sabotage.[28] Resistance was not confined to Daugavpils itself; in spring 1943 communists were again active in Preiļi and such places as Višķi, Aglona, Silajāņi and Dagda.[29]

Thoughts of resistance had even reached those few surviving Jews, now carrying out various jobs in the fortress. Some Jewish women and the teenager Semyon Shpungin were working for Heerunterkunftsverwaltung 322 repairing the uniforms of dead and wounded soldiers, and just occasionally grenades and other weapons turned up in the bundles they handled. These could be accumulated and other clothes could be traded. By March 1943 Shaike Iwensky, who worked as a painter in Herresbaudienstelle 100, and was the boyfriend of one of the girls who repaired uniforms, had acquired a Soviet Nagan pistol and his comrades two automatic pistols plus several grenades, although they had no ammunition. They had heard rumours of partisans operating in Belorussia, and began to plan how they might reach them.[30] For fully 18 months these Jews had lived an almost normal life, working with free Daugavpils citizens and living in a mini-ghetto inside the fortress, a hostel with double bunk beds and no guards. News of partisan actions encouraged three girls – Sonya Prezma, Sarra Ziv and Sonya Levina – to join some Russian POWs quartered in the same building in an escape bid in June 1943. They were abandoned by their less than gallant Russian comrades once outside the city. The girls returned to the fortress and were shot.[31] Despite moves to separate the POWs from the Jews, a group of POWs and Jews, including Shaike Iwensky, escaped on 10 September taking with them the arms they had secreted. They returned to the outskirts of Daugavpils a few days later in an unsuccessful attempt to bring out more POWs and Jews.

As they left the city, Iwens and his comrades noted that their guides were experienced and seemed to have made the journey several times before.[32] In fact an escape network to the Belorussian partisans was quite well established and separate from the Lazdovskii underground network. Yulii Sokolovskii, a former Daugavpils postal worker, who had joined the komosomol as a youth when evacuated to Omsk in the First World War, acted as the link figure. Blank passes would be obtained from cleaners working in the fortress and used to get the POWs past the guards; then couriers took them to the 'Antonov' Belorussian partisans based near Braslava.[33]

Not all the partisans were as far away as Belorussia. On 22 March 1943 a police unit searching for escaped POWs on the outskirts of Daugavpils was attacked by a group of partisans; in the short exchange of fire one partisan was killed but the four others escaped.[34] In this exchange, two of the policemen were killed and a police clampdown followed. The surviving members of Lazdovskii's organisation had no choice but to flee. Titova followed the escape route to the Belorussian partisans, while Lazdovskii tried to organise a partisan group hiding near Medumi, south of Daugavpils; he and his men were discovered, arrested and later shot.[35]

Despite these setbacks, the Central Committee's Operative Group, which had based itself at the partisan headquarters in Osveya, was keen to develop contacts with Daugavpils. It brought to Osveya any partisan of Latvian origin fighting with the Belorussian partisans so that it could learn as much as possible about any underground communist groups that had been formed. In this way Titova moved to Osveya, giving the Osveya partisans an entrée into Daugavpils. On the basis of her information Alberts Prostaks was sent by the partisans to re-establish an underground network. This soon claimed to have 70 members and it certainly exchanged propaganda materials for medical supplies and intelligence information so badly needed by the partisans. However, the network was penetrated by the police in June 1943, and Prostaks and Titova were arrested with 50 others.[36] The break of the link with the Osveja partisans did not bring underground activity to a complete halt. In place of the Lazdovskii–Titova network two komsomol organisations developed, run by Ivan Muzykantik and Nikolai Shkrabo; by the autumn both would establish links with the Latvian partisans[37] and eventually join them, but over summer 1943 and into the autumn they had more or less secure links with the Braslava partisans, via the POW escape route.[38]

Nationalist aspirations checked

Since the beginning of November 1941 those selected by the Nazis to run Latvia had been lobbying for a greater degree of independence. Twice that month the Generalkommissar in Riga was sent a request from General Director designate Dankers that Latvia should be given a similar degree of autonomy to Slovakia. On 2 December 1941 the Generalkommissar formally rejected the idea. However, the General Directorate did not abandon the notion and it was revived at the start of 1943. Defeat at Stalingrad made it imperative to expand the German Army and on 24 January 1943 Himmler won Hitler's support for the idea of mobilising recruits to a Latvian SS Legion; apparently he had been impressed by the contribution made by the Latvian volunteers on the Leningrad front. In this context Dankers and his General Directorate tried to argue that, unless there were political changes along 'Slovak' lines, it would be impossible to recruit to the legion. This piece of blackmail almost worked. On 8 February Hitler was presented with a plan for Latvian autonomy, but he refused to sign it. The Latvian Legion would be formed, but it could not be traded for an autonomous Latvia.[39] Hitler's permission for the formation of a Latvian Legion was made public on 10 February 1943,[40] and the Legion was officially inaugurated on 27 February,[41] although the nationality of the command staff, Latvian or German, was only agreed in mid-March.[42]

The political speculation at this time about a possible 'Slovak' solution for Latvia had a dramatic impact in Daugavpils. The editor of *Daugavas vēstnesis* approached Riecken's press office on the evening of Saturday 20 February to ask for permission to publish a special Sunday issue of the paper to cover the proclamation of Latvian independence. Permission was refused. The editor made a second phone call, but when this was again refused, the issue was dropped. The press office were clear: this was 'a typical Latvian move to make political capital by engaging in tendentious reporting; *Daugavas vēstnesis*, which had the status of being Riecken's official journal, could not become a mouth piece for national chauvinism'. Riecken's attitude was more relaxed, for, as he later recalled, there were all sorts of rumours circulating at this time and these rumours had a certain basis in fact, since negotiations were underway in Berlin and some 'German officers created the impression that such steps could be expected'. News of the Berlin talks had been telephoned to Riga and the Riga editor of *Daugavas vēstnesis* had tipped off Daugavpils.[43]

Riecken's press officer thought it politic at this time to write a political assessment of the editor of *Daugavas vēstnesis*, which was far from flattering and concluded by suggesting he was not suitable for the editor's post. The original editor of *Daugavas vēstnesis* had been Eduards Zundans, but he had fallen seriously ill in February 1943 and had been replaced by Paul Duzmanis. Duzmanis came from an aristocratic Daugavpils family, and, after taking a law degree, he became a sports journalist; during the Soviet administration in 1940–1 he had been prevented from writing and was transferred to his paper's archive department. He joined *Daugavas vēstnesis* on 20 October 1941. Ducmanis was assessed as 'a leading crass national-Latvian intellectual', who was dismissive of the local Latgale peasant population and its culture and constantly stressed the need to complete the assimilation of Latgaleans into Latvia; he had, it was said, a Great Latvian mission. Ducmanis belonged to the Daugavpils Latvian elite, 'a small group of administrators and intellectuals who with some one hundred people are a tiny minority within the 30,000 population of Daugavpils'. This small intellectual circle followed the lead of 'certain circles in Riga', and was constantly opposed by the small Latgale elite.[44]

By spring 1943 the Nazis were increasingly concerned at the behaviour of Latvian nationalists. A security police report for March 1943 noted a worrying rise in Latvian nationalism,[45] and it was no doubt for this reason that in April 1943 the authorities finally decided to close the Daugavpils Latvian Society. The society had been left in a sort of limbo since the suspension of its activities in April 1942. The authorities had ruled on 1 July 1942 that the aims of the society contradicted the 20 September 1941 ban on political associations, but made no definitive ruling about its future. Nothing happened for over six months until, apparently out of the blue, the decision was made by Riecken to close it on 19 April 1943. The very next day the society appealed above the head of Riecken to Dankers and the General Director in Riga, re-telling its role as the cultural epicentre of the city since its first registration on 7 May 1938.[46]

The only public organisation permitted to operate freely remained People's Aid. This took on an increased role as the provider of social services. The press portrayed the work of People's Aid in Stiernienes muiža parish, in the far north of Riecken's domain, as typical. There the parish elder and parish secretary took the initiative in developing a busy local branch of People's Aid. Families suffering as a result of the war, or needing support in general, were helped with collections from the local community of both money and goods in kind; some made contributions through monthly deductions from their salaries.[47] People's Aid continued to be associated with help for peasant farming, its members collaborating closely with the various agricultural societies.[48] People's Aid was also actively involved in health care. At the end of April 1943 *Daugavas vēstnesis* called for health centres to be set up in Daugavpils, Ludza and Ilūkste under the auspices of People's Aid.[49] At the same time district elder Budže called on all parish elders to support a 'cleanliness week and family day', with the support of People's Aid; the schools and agricultural societies should also join in to improve the quality of life in the region.[50] By autumn 1943 People's Aid had established a health directorate,[51] which concentrated on monitoring the health of school children and organised maternity classes for women.[52] Funding still came from voluntary donations. In October 1943 the citizens of Daugavpils collected 7,327 Reichsmark in one day of special appeal,[53] a total topped at the start of November when 10,997 Reichsmark were collected;[54] these collections were part of a special event to mark two years since the work of People's Aid had started.[55]

Wooing the Russians

At the same time as frustrating the political ambitions of the Latvian elite, the authorities continued to strengthen their overtures to the Russians. Building on the links established by Schwung in July 1942, the Russian Orthodox priest Leonid Ladinskii, 'the representative of the Russian population of Latgale', was given a more permanent role. Ladinskii had been born in Pskov in 1895, the son of a priest, and had trained in Pskov seminary and then Petersburg Theological Academy, before abandoning his studies to fight on the White side in the Russian civil war. After the Bolshevik victory, he moved to Latvia and worked in the forestry industry for a while before resuming his religious training and becoming a priest at the Alexander Nevsky Cathedral in Daugavpils.[56] By December 1942 he was heading a campaign to collect Christmas presents for those of Russian nationality who had volunteered to fight Bolshevism. At this time his organisation extended throughout Latgale, with contact names in Daugavpils, Rēzekne, and Abrene. As part of the same campaign Ladinskii arranged a concert later in December[57] and visited a number of Russian schools in January, the Orthodox Christmas falling a fortnight after western Christmas; Niedra, the Daugavpils city elder, provided a truck to help with the collection.[58]

This was part of a conscious Nazi policy of frustrating the perceived ambitions of the Latvian administration the Nazis had themselves appointed. A police report on the situation in January 1943 revealed continuing tension between the Latvian and Russian communities. Indeed, if anything, the situation was getting worse: 'the aim of the Latvians is to exclude Russians from industry and to discriminate against them politically, basing this assault on the perception that the Russian community collectively co-operated with the Bolsheviks', the report stated. To prevent the Russians assuming that their woes were the result of German policies, the Generalkommissar 'has wanted to develop a form of Russian representation for some time, but until now no plan has been developed; however, the construction of Russian representation must be undertaken in the near future or the Russians will feel that it is not only the Latvians but the

Germans as well who see then as second class humans'. Appropriate leaders from the Russian community had to be found for propaganda and educational work, the report concluded.[59]

It would take nine months for real progress to be made on this issue, but a number of steps in this direction were quickly taken. Early in 1943 a census was due to be carried out and the census material was translated into Russian for Russian speakers.[60] In March in the Russian village of Malinovka, the Orthodox church was restored; it had been set on fire during the Bolshevik retreat in summer 1941.[61] On 27 March *Dvinskii vestnik* announced that, as of 21 March, its editorial board would be composed of Russians and not Latvians. Early in April, when Rieken toured the region addressing a series of meetings on agriculture, he spoke in Russian in Naujene and other places where this seemed appropriate.[62]

It was as part of this process of wooing the population that a new impetus was given to the privatisation of the economy. On 6 March the press repeated the announcement that property nationalised by the Bolsheviks would be returned,[63] and on 10 April gave details of some of the first enterprises to be privatised and their new owners.[64] A police report for March revealed how this stage of privatisation was having a particularly strong impact on the Russian population where some communities were almost exclusively Russian: the relation between privatised Latvian and Russian factories in the Latgale area was roughly 60:40.[65] By July the process had been completed in Daugavpils, where 58 small state enterprises had been sold to new owners and 28 workshops once owned by Jews had been rented out.[66] A prominent Russian, A. Balabkin, served as a director of the city's trade department.[67]

At the end of January 1943 there was an even more striking change in the attitude towards Russians. It was announced that Russian POWs could after all volunteer to serve in the struggle against Bolshevism; up until then only Ukrainian and other non-Russian POWs had been able to volunteer. This change was said to be in recognition of their good behaviour, and a response to many thousands of letters, which had been received in previous months by the editors of *Dvinskii vestnik*. In reality the Germans had decided to support the formation of a Russian Liberation Army under the leadership of General A. A. Vlasov, who after his capture by the Germans had volunteered to form an army from Russian POWs willing to fight to overthrow Stalin. *Dvinskii vestnik* supported Vlasov's campaign by republishing an appeal for volunteers published by the newspaper of the Vlasov movement, *Dobrovolets*, as well as by publishing an article about the achievements of those who had volunteered thus far.[68] Vlasov was allowed to make a direct appeal to the Russians of Latgale on 20 March. Under the title 'The Defender of Moscow Declares War on Bolshevism' he called for a war against Stalin, a war for a new Russia. German and Russian interests coincided, he argued, so that a war against Stalin was actually a war for the Russian people.[69]

In a subtle use of terminology, *Dvinskii vestnik* called on Russians to volunteer for the 'Latviiskii' not the 'Latyshskii' Legion.[70] This choice of words reinforced the point that the Latvian Legion was open to all inhabitants of Latvia, not simply ethnic Latvians. However, voluntary recruitment did not meet expectations and so conscription was introduced.[71] On 7 April parish elders in areas with a Russian population were ordered to prepare lists of those eligible for service in these units, and to complete the task by 2 May. Sergius, the head of the Russian Orthodox Church, informed his clergy that they had no choice but to co-operate in this process.[72] The public campaign was announced at the end of May when Russians from Latgale were called on to volunteer to join the Russian Security Battalions (RSB), where they would be able to fight Bolshevism under the Russian flag.[73] Such calls continued in the Russian-language press throughout June, when recruitment really took off.[74]

The RSB were put under the command of General Garin, a close associate of Vlasov, who called on the Russians of Latgale to join him. Recruitment took place in Ludza and Riga as well as Daugavpils, but the centre for recruitment and training was in Daugavpils.[75] The official founding of the battalion was marked on 1 August when the troops were blessed by the Orthodox priest Savva Trubitsyn.[76] Three weeks later it was spuriously announced that so many volunteers had come forward that a regiment would be formed, rather than a battalion, and, to staff it, an appeal went out to any former Russian officers to come forward and bring their experience and leadership to the struggle against Judeo-communism.[77] More appeals for volunteers followed, along with articles giving an idealised account of live in the new units.[78] The formal oath-swearing ceremony to the German command was reported on 29 September.[79] First to be formed were the 314th, based in Daugavpils; the 315th, based in Bolderāja; and the 283rd, based near Sebezh,[80] which was sometimes called the 'Latgale Battalion' and was frequently used in anti-partisan operations.[81] By spring 1944 the 326th, 327th and 328th had been formed and were operating near Sebezh.[82] Early in 1944 the strength of the Daugavpils based 314th was put at 650 officers and men.[83] In what might be seen as a parallel operation, Russian women were encouraged to volunteer as nurses; their first training course ended in March 1944.[84]

Since both Latvians and Russians were being mobilised to fight Bolshevism, the Nazi administration had firm grounds on which to expect the Latvian authorities to treat them equally. Towards the end of April 1943 Budže issued an appeal to the population, both Latvian and Russian:

> At this time when at the front the existence or extinction of a new, cultured Europe is being decided, when the heroic German people is firmly repulsing the assault of Jewish-Bolshevism, there has to be unity in the rear; everyone has to rally into serried ranks to support the front, without distinction between nationality or religious confession, and

without enmity, which only harms every good initiative and all friendly collaboration. Only in common work to help the front will the gap which has developed in some places between the Latvian and Russian populations disappear ... With these words I call for unity, but above all I turn to the Russian intelligentsia, to Russian public activists and to all intelligent youngsters in both the city and the district. Only you, the soul of the Russian population of Daugavpils district can destroy the dissension which now exists between Latvians and Russians. ... Inhabitants of Daugavpils district, remember your recent past, when the red terror raged. All of us, Latvians and Russians, cowered under its knout then ...Only in common friendship can there be success in the struggle against the red filth.[85]

Shortly afterwards, on 25 May, a meeting took place in Riga to improve collaboration between the Russian community and People's Aid. The meeting was called by Vladimir Aleksandrovich Presnyakov, appointed the plenipotentiary for Russian affairs by the General Directorate's welfare department earlier that month, and was also attended by Georgii Alekseev, a representative of industry; Professor I. D. Grimm, the representative of Metropoitan Sergius; and Notar Batshchukov, a representative of the intelligentsia. The meeting recommended establishing a Russian section of People's Aid, but the choice of the leader of this new section caused some controversy. Presnyakov proposed Ivan Dmitrevich Fridrich, a graduate of Daugavpils Teachers' Institute and the head teacher of a primary school near Abrene; he had been active in the Latvian Red Cross before 1940, spoke Latvian fluently as well as Russian, and was, in Presnyakov's view, right thinking. However, Presnyakov advanced Fridrich's name without consulting Alekseev, Grimm and Batshchukov, who immediately protested, suggesting in Fridrich's place the Riga-based Leonid Alekseev; Fridrich, they stressed, was a provincial who knew no German. The row continued until 16 June when Pavasars, the head of People's Aid, was brought in to arbitrate; and he came down in favour of Andreev, who unlike the Latgale teacher, spoke German.[86]

At the end of May a Russian National Committee was set up in Daugavpils. Ladinskii was its dominant figure, but he was joined by A. Balabkin, of the city's trade department and several others. They elected as an honorary committee member P. Mel'nikov, the former chairman of the Russian National Society in Daugavpils.[87] Soon there developed around this group a very clear 'Russian specific' propaganda line, verging on the notion of confronting 'Jewish' Bolshevism with 'National Bolshevism'. An early sign of this came alongside press reports which no longer sought to hide the extent of the Nazi defeat at Stalingrad. In mid-February *Dvinskii vestnik* published a story about Lenin's famous testament, in which he criticised all his likely successors but made plain that Stalin should be removed from the post of General Secretary because of the power he had accumulated and his inability to use it wisely. The title of this article was 'Stalin should be replaced'.[88] Vlasov's appeal of mid-March took up the same national theme.

When in 1943 it came to the commemoration of the June 1941 deportations, *Dvinskii vestnik* took up the point made by Budže in April and stressed that it was the town's 'Christian' population which had been deported,[89] countering the message of the previous year that this had been an assault on the Latvian population; there was, of course, no acknowledgement of the large number of Jews who had been deported. Another sign of the times was the recognition given to the fact that there was a long tradition of specifically Russian anti-Semitism. *Dvinskii vestnik* noted how the former Tsarist minister V. V. Shulgin had been influenced by Hitler's *Mein Kampf*, although in fact Shulgin had first appreciated the mobilising powers of anti-Semitism earlier than this when he put them to horrific use during the Russian civil war. Russian anti-Semitism had suffered in the past from not being aggressive enough, the article suggested, but this was no longer the case – the Russians had overcome their instinctively charitable attitudes.[90] In another appeal to conservative Russian sentiment, *Dvinskii vestnik* commemorated the assassination of the Imperial Royal family later in July.[91]

Assessing the work of 'the Russian representation' during 1943, *Dvinskii vestnik* said much had been done to improve the living conditions of the Russian population both in the town and the district, as well as to improve relations between the population and the authorities. As a result there had been far fewer complaints from Russian peasants. Much had also been done to pay the school fees of the poorer students and to employ more Russian teachers.[92] Examples of this were Presnyakov's lobbying in August 1943 for the establishment of a Russian primary school in Rēzekne, a campaign which the General Directorate were not keen to support,[93] and the decision in mid-July that 'representatives of the Russian people' would be able to enrol as students at Rēzekne Teachers' Institute.[94]

An uncertain summer

In many ways the summer of 1943 was the most normal of the German occupation. In June and July Riecken decided to put back the curfew to midnight, and lifted it completely on the night of 23–24 June, Līgo, the time of the summer solstice and a traditional Latvian holiday. As planned, Riecken re-imposed the 10 p.m. curfew on 28 August.[95] When the city authorities drew up their accounts for the financial year 1942–3, they outlined construction plans for the financial year 1943–4. These mostly related to work on schools and hospitals, where a number of repairs and improvements were itemised. Other projects included a new filter plant at the water works, with repairs to reservoirs and distribution pipes, as well as a programme of bridge and road repairs.[96] Over summer 1943 a lot of restoration work was done on Daugavpils schools.[97] A year later, the accounts for 1943–4 showed that little else had been achieved. Expenditure on repairs had been dramatically less than planned, and two-thirds of the money available for construction projects had been used to build air-raid shelters. Real spending in 1943–4 was dominated by security, which had risen from 55 per cent of spending in 1942–3 to 82 per cent in 1943–4.[98] This change of priorities evolved over summer 1943.

At the end of March 1943 Hitler had made a widely publicised speech explaining that the crisis on the eastern front had been overcome.[99] By the summer it was clear that this was not true. Reminders about the ban on listening to Soviet radio broadcasts, issued in April,[100] could not hide reality. After Stalingrad, the outcome of the war was no longer certain. The number of Latvian volunteers dying at the front rose all the time. At the end of July 1943 Štāls issued an appeal for all the families of volunteers and legionaries to register with the police prefecture.[101] This was essential so that death benefits could be paid out as appropriate. On 2 September *Daugavas vēstnesis* explained what benefits were available to the families of volunteers killed in the struggle: for three months the widow would receive full pay, followed by a pension of 54 marks. There was also a payment for children of 10.80 marks per child plus an additional 20 marks. Benefits were also available for surviving parents; each parent received a monthly allowance of 150 marks, with reduced benefits for elderly parents.

However, the most dramatic illustration of how the tide of war had changed concerned the arrival of refugees from Russia. On 2 April 1943 Riecken was informed that 60,000 refugees were being removed from Russia as the Red Army advanced. Not all would come to Daugavpils, but 10,000 would be arriving in the city for delousing, before being distributed to camps in Ludza, Rēzekne and Daugavpils itself. The POW camp at Rēzekne, constructed for 20,000 people and currently inhabited by only 8,000, would take the most. Thus between 8–12 April 1943 some 2,000 were billeted in Daugavpils and 6,000 in Rēzekne.[102] It was the start of a steady stream. In order to fund this evacuation work, the Generalkommissar in Riga ordered that the 480,000 Reichsmarks raised to cope with the children deported from the Russian border area as part of the 'Winter Magic' campaign should be used to help Russian refugees in general.[103]

Presnyakov soon began to take an interest in these refugees. After paying a visit to the Rēzekne camp, he denounced not only the sanitary conditions, but the policy of sending children who had become separated from their parents to the Salaspils concentration camp. In June Presnyakov took 500 children from the Rēzekne camp under his own protection, arranging for them to be taken in by local Russian families. This initiative turned into a row: he stressed that he had acted as an individual and that the move had not been connected with his official capacity as an employee of the welfare department of the General Directorate; this explanation did not wash with the authorities, and Presnyakov was told in no uncertain terms that he had exceeded his powers, for as a plenipotentiary he had no right to intervene in what were political matters. Presnyakov was instructed to compile a list of the 500 children and their current whereabouts, while Riecken was reminded that it was the camp commandant, not Presnyakov, who should take any future decisions concerning these children.[104]

By mid-September there were 13,606 Russian evacuees in Rēzekne, apparently the biggest concentration and certainly the most problematic. Fears began to be expressed that the presence of so many Russians was exacerbating tensions between the Latvian and Russian populations.[105] So, when at the end of September it was reported that another batch of refugees was on the way, there was relief that the furthest east they were to be billeted was Jēkabpils; however, one third of these refugees would still be transported via Daugavpils.[106] Conditions in the Rēzekne camp were so bad that, at the start of October, Riecken visited it himself and ordered improvements to the sanitation.[107] A report of December 1943 still spoke of 'poor air' in the barracks, and in January 1944 Riecken tried to get the army to take over its administration.[108] By mid-May 1944, when their removal from Latvia began,[109] there were 11,739 evacuees in Daugavpils, 7,800 in Rēzekne, 5,992 in Ilūkste, 952 in Abrene and 735 in Ludza. The total for Latvia as a whole was 155,624.[110]

It was partly in connection with these population movements and the arrival of Russian refugees in the Daugavpils fortress that the remaining Jews of Daugavpils were rounded up and sent to Mežaparks concentration camp on 28 October 1943. Rumours of a final action against the Jewish survivors had been circulating for some time, and when on 28 October the Jews were ordered to gather in a courtyard outside the building they occupied in the fortress, Dr Grisha Goldman and his sister committed suicide, while Bentsii Shafir killed his family and then flinched from killing himself. Semyon Shpungin saw an open window, jumped through it and fled; when detained on a road outside the city a day later he claimed to be a Russian refugee and was assigned to work on a farm near Kalupe where he survived the war.[111] Some of these horrors were witnessed by Iwensky and the other Jews who had fled with him to the partisans. Their time with the partisans had not been a success. No sooner had they arrived with Antonov's partisan band than a German anti-partisan drive began. Iwensky and his comrades felt abandoned when ordered to break down into small units and fend for themselves. So they returned to the Daugavpils fortress and arrived there on 22 October. Hidden by the mother of Iwensky's girlfriend, they had to witness from their vantage point the final rounding up of the Daugavpils Jews. They caught sight of a column of Jews, 'surrounded by gun-toting Latvians', which then marched off. Later they learnt that their friend David Bleier had also committed suicide. A week later, still in hiding, they learnt that not all the Jews had left the city. A group of twenty Jews in the Herresbaudienstelle had not yet been sent to Mežaparks. However, when Iwensky's girlfriend's sister left hiding and approached the Germans to see if other Jews could be allowed to join this group, she was arrested, although other members of her family were temporarily allocated work by German officers who had shown sympathy to them in the past. By 4 December even these Jews had been rounded up and sent to Mežaparks. Iwensky and two companions, still hiding in their loft space in the fortress, were the only Jews left in Daugavpils. In the end these three youngsters made contact with a German guard who had once had a crush on one of the Jewish girls. He gave shelter to the youngest of them, passing him off as a Russian refugee, and helped Iwensky and his companion flee the city.[112]

By the end of the summer it was clear that the economic situation was getting worse rather than better. The new ration cards introduced in April 1943 had not had the desired impact.[113] Supplies continued to be hard to come by and in August the inhabitants of Daugavpils were informed that henceforth they would be tied to just one shop where their ration cards would be recognised.[114] On 12 October Niedra, the city elder, introduced further restrictions on the opening hours of shops and a fortnight later restricted them still further.[115] In mid-September inhabitants were informed that no newcomers could settle in the city without the written consent of city elder Niedra.[116] A week later they were informed that permission to leave Daugavpils would only be given in exceptional circumstances.[117] On 26 August inhabitants were reminded that tax had to be paid on domestic animals such as hens and pigs; many had failed to do this, but in future this requirement would be rigorously enforced.[118] Throughout August the press carried regular reports throughout August of speculators being fined, sent for forced labour and executed, depending on the severity of the case; there were at least three executions.[119] Misery was compounded when on 9 October Riecken issued an order to prevent any heating being put on in buildings to conserve fuel. He relented a week later.[120]

On 6 August General Director Dankers explained that it had proved necessary to extend the working week to 48 hours. This was because of the continuing need to supply the front, with a labour force diminished by those joining the Legion.[121] Peasants also had to face additional hardships. They were reminded that if they killed one of their own animals, they could not keep all the meat; if a pig was killed 100 kilograms of pork had to be given to the authorities, 20 kilograms of veal from a bullock and 14 kilograms of meat from a lamb.[122] It was rumoured that a peasant could avoid the compulsory surrender of his cow by paying a bribe of 30 bottles of vodka,[123] even though the penalty for the production of moonshine vodka was raised in September to six months in a labour camp.[124] At the same time that these additional burdens were placed on the civilian population, the annual appeal for the supply of warm winter clothing for the troops began on the pages of *Daugavas vēstnesis*.[125] This was followed almost at once by a campaign to provide Latvian volunteers at the front with a 'people's present'; for this purpose 21 collection points were identified in September.[126]

As had been the case in 1942, the harvest was the authorities' overriding concern. In a strange echo of the Soviet authorities' obsession with machine-tractor stations, courses for tractor drivers had been advertised in April.[127] As harvest time approached Riecken called a meeting early in August to discuss preparations for the harvest campaign, which was attended by the Daugavpils district elder Budže and an array of agricultural experts.[128] Once again, everyone was mobilised to bring the harvest in. The theatre was closed so that the staff could help with the harvest,[129] and the start of the school year was again delayed until 18 October so that children could help in the fields.[130] In mid-September Budže made clear that, despite the difficult summer, the harvest simply had to come in; those who delivered on time would be rewarded, and those who delivered late would be punished. Nevertheless, the authorities had to cope with many instances of peasants refusing to work on Sunday, as the Germans had instructed them to do. Some peasants also refused the offer of police or legionary support with harvest work.[131] In an apparent attempt to win peasants over, the authorities offered some flexibility. Peasants were told that if they could not meet their delivery targets for one product, they could negotiate and substitute the delivery of other essential items.[132]

In this climate the old propaganda shibboleths began to lose their appeal. The exhibition 'A Year under the Bolsheviks' was visiting Daugavpils schools at the end of June and in early July. The exhibition stressed that it was the Latvians who had suffered most at the hands of Bolshevik repression. Yet the magic mobilising power of this assertion had begun to wear off. Conjuring up the details of the Bolshevik terror no longer seemed to be working, since people had to be encouraged to attend the exhibition.[133] Nor did references to the Jews seem to help. On 24 July *Daugavas vēstnesis* published an article entitled 'The People's Plague in Daugavpils'. It summarised alleged Jewish control of the Daugavpils economy before 1940 – they owned all three cinemas, 46 of the 53 non-food shops, 12 of the 15 meat shops and 11 of the twelve salami shops – but, the article concluded, it was now necessary 'to remind those who had forgotten' about these alleged facts. It was as if the old certainties had gone. There was just a hint of desperation in the article 'Cry of the Motherland', published in *Daugavas vēstnesis* at the end of July, which stressed there was no alternative to fighting; either the Germans would be victorious or Europe would drown in Bolshevik chaos.[134]

Yet Red Army successes forced Nazi propaganda on to the defensive. At the start of September *Daugavas vēstnesis* warned those 'who flirted with Bolshevism' that Bolshevism brought only starvation, as evidenced by those fleeing areas of Soviet rule.[135] Later in the month the collaborationist press found itself responding to Bolshevik initiatives rather than setting the agenda. On 19 September *Daugavas vēstnesis* responded to an article in *Pravda* which had stressed how the Baltic States had voluntarily joined the Soviet Union and prospered during the year of Soviet rule. Entitled 'The Latvian Sword Gives the Answer', it concluded that Latvians did not want the return of the Bolsheviks.[136] Yet the possibility the Bolsheviks might return could no longer be ignored, as Riecken conceded. During the first week in October he gave a series of speeches on the importance of the harvest and the situation at the front. First he addressed a meeting of village elders organised at Mežciems and then he attended a similar rally near Rēzekne.[137] Thereafter, during the second week in October he received a delegation of peasants. To them he summed up the situation. He reassured them about the position at the front but had to accept that 'certain Bolshevik successes need to be recognised, but they have no decisive significance'. The inhabitants of Latvia could remain calm.[138]

'Sommerreise'

It was not only the situation at the front that was the problem; behind the lines were the partisans. The partisan movement had been set back by the 'Winter Magic' drive of early 1943, but it soon recovered as statistics collected by both sides confirmed. Until January 1943 German reports on partisan activity did not feel the need to record the actions of Latvian partisans separately; thereafter they did. These recorded incidents in February 1943, a complete absence of activity in March when the impact of 'Winter Magic' was greatest, and then regular incidents until the end of June, when the reports stop. If in April there was a partisan incident on average only every other day, by the end of June the average had risen to one a day.[139] That rate of activity continued to be reflected in the reports sent regularly to Moscow by the partisans from August 1943; on average, there was a partisan action every day.[140] The press could not ignore this level of activity. On 1 May 1943 *Dvinskii vestnik* published an address from Dankers calling on citizens to 'give information about parachutist saboteurs'. Six weeks later Riecken wrote in *Dvinskii vestnik* about the danger of supporting the partisans and spreading rumours about them; anyone spreading rumours was 'a Bolshevik agent', he concluded.

Even as 'Winter Magic' unfolded, Oškalns and Laiviņš had debated how best to develop the partisan movement with the leader of the Operative Group sent from Moscow, Kārlis Ozoliņš. Ozoliņš was under clear instructions from the Central Committee that the base for partisan operations should be moved to Latvia; Oškalns and his colleagues said this was impossible, and Ozoliņš bowed to their superior knowledge. However, constant efforts were made to improve links with Latvia. As soon as Samsons had arrived in Osveya, attempts had been made to trace the whereabouts of Ezernieks and his small group of partisans based north of Balvi; but it proved impossible to track Ezernieks down.[141] In March Samsons was informed that his 1st Partisan Detachment was to be moved to Latvia, but the attempt to cross the border in April failed.[142] Explaining the situation, Ozoliņš sent a long report to Moscow in April suggesting that the key to successful operations in Latvia was to break the morale of the Latvian Schutzmannschaft Battalions; that would happen, but it had not happened yet.[143] Coldly the Central Committee replied that the 'primary task' was to transfer operations from Osveya to Latvia. Despite this instruction, when Samsons left Osveya in early May, the new base he established was in Russia, across the border from Zilupe, not in Latvia itself. From this base his men did succeed in contacting Ezernieks, thus adding a new 4th Detachment to the Latvian Partisan Brigade, and a detachment based firmly in Latvia.[144] At meetings held from 21–28 July between Samsons and Milda Birkenfelde, who represented the Central Committee's Operative Group, Samsons agreed to help reinforce Ezernieks's detachment; but there was still no mention of Samsons himself moving to Latvia.[145]

Reporting to Moscow in June 1943 Oškalns could be up-beat. Proper ten-day long training courses for new partisan recruits had been established. There were good links with the communist underground in Daugavpils, Rēzekne, Krāslava, Ludza and even Riga; and new contacts had recently been made with Līvāni, Varakļāni, Viļāni and Plaviņas. Supplies were needed, particularly shoes; these were in such short supply in Latvia that it was politically unwise to expropriate them, he said. As to moving to Latvia, he concluded his report by asserting 'we are constantly researching and studying the possibilities of basing operations in Latvia'.[146] His reward for such hard work was a massive supply operation ordered by Moscow. Between 15 and 29 June Oškalns was sent 106 men, 214 rifles, 172 light automatics, 16 wheeled machine-guns, three mortars, ammunition, radios, paper, a printing press and bandages.[147] By mid-August the Latvian Partisan Brigade could claim a staff of 80, a 1st Detachment of 120, a 2nd Detachment of 90, and a 3rd Detachment of 70.[148] To this should be added Ezernieks's 4th Detachment within Latvia itself, recently reinforced by the transfer to it of the partisan group led by Kaupužs, approximately 50 men more.[149] And more were willing to join: all commanders reported that they were turning away recruits because of the lack of arms;[150] in October 1943 the 1st Detachment claimed it had 150 men ready to join if arms could be provided.[151]

The Nazi response to this revival of the partisan movement so quickly after 'Winter Magic' was to target and deport the families of partisans and those who sympathised with them, including those with relatives who had escaped to the Soviet Union in 1941.[152] This campaign took place in two phases, May–June 1943 and then August–September 1943; the second phase, the larger of the two, was given the code name 'Sommerreise'.[153] On orders from Riga, the first relatively small-scale operation was undertaken by the Daugavpils district police on 11 June in the five villages of Šķaune, Istra, Rundēni, Pasiene and Brigi; in all 224 people were deported in an operation which involved 135 troops.[154] Over the summer parish elders were instructed to compile lists of those suspected of sympathising with the partisans. As Riecken explained to Generalkommissar Drechsler in Riga on 9 July 1943, the plan was to identify those to be deported by establishing commissions made up of representatives of the German, the Latvian and the minority communities.[155] This was a cumbersome process and took time to put in place, so the police decided to act on the basis of their own lists. On the eve of the action Riecken sent a telegram to Drechsler on 19 August arguing that it was essential to ensure that the police lists and the locally produced lists were identical.[156] However, in the event the local lists were often ignored.

According to orders drawn up in Riga on 20 August, and confirmed to Riecken on the 21st, the plan was to arrest and deport 4,000 people linked to the 'bandits' in an action which would start on 25 August. The target figures for the arrests were as follows: 1,400–1,500 for Ludza District, 600 for Abrene District; 1,000 for Daugavpils District; and 800–900 in Rēzekne District. The final figures for those detained in the operation did not quite match the targets. Thus those arrested were in Abrene 649 (191 men, 270 women and 188 children); in Daugavpils 1163 (338 men, 422 women and 403 children); in Ludza 928 (236 men, 413 women and 279 children) and in Rēzekne 544 (193 men, 180 women and 171 children). The total number of people deported was 3,284, 958 men, 1,285 women and 1,041 children. The gap between the planned and actual figures in Rēzekne and Ludza was partly explained by the flight of men, women and children to the partisans.[157] In Ezernieki, three men had offered armed resistance and one of them was shot.[158]

The police made an effort not to repeat some of the mistakes of May 1942 or 'Winter Magic' earlier in 1943. The soldiers were ordered to behave 'correctly', and no alcohol was to be consumed after 9.00 p.m. on 24 August; looting would be punished by death.[159] But the failure to reconcile the police lists with the local lists meant dozens of innocent people were deported. Complaints flooded in. On the very day of the action, parish elders submitted a list of 73 people who had been arrested despite not being on the list and demanded that they be released at once; there were 12 cases like this in Asūne, eight in Dagda and Naujene, and seven in Indra and Krāslava. In Dagda one of those arrested had been the wife of an SS volunteer. The arbitrary nature of the affair was reinforced by the fact that the elders added to their list the names of eight people who should have been arrested but had not; three of these came from Preiļi.[160] By 27 August Budže had carried out a survey of eight parishes which revealed that only in Višķi had the parish elder been properly involved in identifying whom to deport. By the end of the month, the representatives of the Russian population in Rēzekne and Ludza had complained to Riecken, and a week later Presnyakov took up the issue with Drechsler in Riga. He professed not to understand why the Russian population had been targeted, arguing that peasants owning upwards of 20 hectares of land were scarcely likely to be communists. The only explanation, he suggested, was the chauvinist attitudes of the local police. As the weeks passed, the number of names on the list of those wrongly arrested grew from 73 to 160.[161]

The 'Sommerreise' deportations had a dramatic impact on Daugavpils, seriously undermining Riecken's plans for inter-ethnic harmony. In the aftermath of the assault on the families of partisans, there was unrest in the ranks of the Daugavpils-based 314th RSB. According to reports reaching the partisans, in early September the soldiers of this battalion went on strike, refusing to turn out for their assigned construction work for over six hours in protest at the deportations. At the end of September news even got to the partisans that there had been an armed clash in Daugavpils between the RSB and a unit of Latvian legionaries in which 17 Latvians had been killed.[162] Some of the news reaching the partisans was based on rumour rather than fact, but certainly something happened during 'Sommerreise' itself involving the 283rd battalion, since a German report recorded criticism of the officer who tried to order this battalion to play a leading role in the operation.[163]

Equally there was no doubting Riecken's fury at the way 'Sommerreise' undermined his self-administration strategy. He had been promised by an aide to Reichskommissar Ostland Hinrich Lohse that, while he remained Gebietskommissar in Daugavpils, there would be no further deportation operations. When it became clear that deportations would be necessary, Lohse had agreed to Riecken's policy of involving the minority communities in the selection of those to be deported. Thus not only did Riecken feel he had grounds for complaint, but Lohse too wanted to know why their agreed policy had not been implemented.[164] Riecken summed things up in a written report to Riga in December, which picked up on points first made in an earlier report of 26 October. He made clear that he had not agreed to the operation, and in particular to the way it was implemented. The failure to abide by the lists drawn up by parish officials had made things extremely difficult. The basic problem was that in implementing the operation the security services 'fully disregarded my office and the self-administration office'. This, Riecken felt, undermined his authority. Repeating his principled opposition to this type of operation, he stressed that many innocent people had been caught up in it. Things could only improve if there was an executive power able to co-ordinate the work of his office with that of the security police.[165]

Lohse saw things similarly. When in January 1944 he felt he had received a full report on the 'Sommerreise' affair, he wrote to Drechsler informing him that the next time the security police came up with such a plan, Drechsler should contact Lohse, who would raise it with the highest police authorities and try and prevent it.[166] Lohse and Drechsler had already been in communication about the powers of the police. Drechsler wanted to collaborate with a broad range of Latvian nationalist opinion, not 'a few chauvinists', and found the attitude of the police unhelpful. He complained to Lohse in mid-June 1943 that he had 'no influence' over the action of the police in security matters. Mass actions, executions, these were outside his sphere of influence. He felt this situation amounted to a system which laid the ground for 'incessant unsatisfactory altercations' and 'impeded the correct and unified administration' of Latvia.[167] The Reichskommissar, the Generalkommissar and the Gebietskommissar were all agreed that arbitrary police action made their jobs impossible.

Great Latvia versus Latgale Latvia

In the aftermath of 'Sommerreise', Riecken was in no mood for concessions towards those he considered 'national chauvinists'. In autumn 1943 further moves were made by the Latvian elite to reassert its position. Over the summer there had been a determined attempt to revive the *aizsargs* as a popular movement which would support the regime. A Soviet report based on partisan information suggested that such moves began in July[168] and *Daugavas vēstnesis* reported on 1 August that Kamaldnieks, now president of the Daugavpils district court, had indeed called on all former *aizsargs* to register with the purpose of re-establishing the Daugavpils *aizsarg* regiment. The paper called on all patriotic youngsters over 18 to consider joining.[169] However, the Germans did not give their consent. Moves to re-establish the Daugavpils *aizsarg* regiment were still continuing in late October, when Kamaldnieks, who was by now in charge of the operation, predicted that the campaign would spread to surrounding parishes 'as soon as various necessary formalities' were completed.[170] One paper reported that the local *aizsargs* were reformed on 7 November 1943,[171] but this seems to have been a sign of wishful thinking. The 'necessary formalities' dragged on and in February 1944 Kamaldnieks was moved to a new job.[172] The actual re-establishment of the Daugavpils 18th *Aizsarg* Regiment could only be reported on 15 June 1944, a desperate concession by the Germans in the last days of the occupation.[173]

At the same time that the plans to revive the *aizsargs* began to run into the sand, a final attempt was made to re-launch the Daugavpils Latvian Society. In mid-October 1943 *Daugavas vēstnesis* reported that the society would resume its activities very shortly. Making no mention of the decision to close the society, the paper explained away the decision to call off the planned inaugural concert back on 14 March 1942 with a reference to the outbreak of typhus and a vague suggestion that the time had simply not been right. Nor did the paper explain that, after the decision to close the society, there had been an appeal to the General Director. It was simply stated that on 10 June 1943 the General Director's Office for Internal Affairs had agreed to allow the society to resume its activities. Resuming the work of the society over the summer months, when many inhabitants of Daugavpils were in the countryside helping with agricultural work, had not seemed appropriate but with the harvest safely in, the provisional leadership had decided the time was right to organise an inaugural meeting.

Daugavas vēstnesis also explained that recently the provisional leadership had been greatly strengthened since it had been joined by Daugavpils city elder Niedra and Daugavpils district-court president Kamaldnieks. Representatives from such organisations as the Latgale Traders' Association ensured it was the legitimate voice of the local elite. Resuming the programme abandoned 18 months earlier, the society's first big event was to be a concert. This was planned for 6 November in Unity House. As well as planning the concert, the society's temporary leadership also discussed the status of the society's choir which had affiliated itself to the Daugavapils branch of People's Aid during the period of closure; it was felt the choir should now return to the society.[174] Three days later *Daugavas vēstnesis* published an article by a certain R. Mazjānis, who stressed the importance for Latvian culture of the re-establishment of the Daugavpils Latvian Society. Readers, Mazjānis said, had been delighted by the news of the re-opening of an organisation so close to their hearts.[175]

There was no concert in Unity House on 6 November. When the concert did take place ten days later there was none of the anticipated fanfare. A small notice appeared in the press on 16 November to say that the concert would take place that evening in the Music School hall at 52 Aizsarg Street.[176] There was no explanation and no more mention of the Daugavpils Latvian Society in the local press. A security-police report of 12 January 1944 stated that the society had reappeared in October 1943 but was in practice a political party of the Greater Latvia movement. Enquiries were continuing, but examination had revealed that the society's president, Ozoliņš, had failed a political investigation to establish his reliability and the police were investigating the names of some two hundred members of the society, most of whom worked in the office of the Gebietskommissar, the Daugavpils city administration, or as teachers. Included in the list of those being investigated was the Daugavpils district elder Budže,[177] whose political unreliability had already been established in 1942.

Even before the decision to re-launch the society was made public, German security officers had been monitoring events, and in particular the recent line taken by *Daugavas vēstnesis* under the editorship of Duzmanis. On 1 October 1943 the question of Duzmanis's behaviour in February 1943 and the attempt to publish a special issue of the paper to announce Latvia's independence was raised again. Riecken had to explain why he had not taken action earlier.[178] In the autumn the editorial line of *Daugavas vēstnesis* had become both nationalist and strident. When launching the campaign to send a 'people's present' to that Latvian volunteers at the front in September 1943, *Daugavas vēstnesis* said the soldiers were 'fighting for our freedom and independence'.[179] Independence was not a word the Nazis liked to read. At the same time it revived the idea of Latvian hegemony seen in the winter and spring of 1942, before Schwung made his conscious turn towards the Russian community. Thus on 1 October, under the title 'A United House', *Daugavas vēstnesis* published an article by R. Mazjānis which included a vicious attack on the Russians and Poles as the 'ruthless destroyers of our national unity'. This was the same Mazjānis who had stressed the importance to Latvian culture of the Daugavpils Latvian Society. This type of 'national chauvinism' was no longer what the Nazis wanted to encourage. They wanted to support the Latgale Latvian cultural elite and establish a self-administration in Latgale which matched the region's ethnic diversity.

Wooing the Latgale Latvians

Riecken's vision of self-administration was that all the multi-ethnic communities of Latgale should co-operate closely. That meant encouraging local Latgale leaders. The first overt sign of support for a specifically Latgale Latvian elite came with the patronage given to the Latgale song festival. At the start of July preparations for this event were given great prominence in the local press,[180] and the festival itself was attended by Drechsler, who made one of his rare visits from Riga. In his speech about the need to work hard for victory, he put at the top of his list the need to place on one side all disagreements among peoples in the struggle for the common good.[181] This was quickly followed by clear signs of approval for the writings of Francis Trasuns. His work had been referred to occasionally in *Daugavas vēstnesis*, in January 1942 and again in April 1943, for example, but these articles had been general and did not go into the details of his life.[182] In mid-August 1943 *Daugavas vēstnesis* reprinted some of Trasuns's pre-First World War writings on the relationship between Latgale Latvians and Latvians from the rest of the country, articles which stressed their common origins.[183] On 1 October Trasuns was again praised in *Daugavas vēstnesis* for making clear that Latgale would always be part of Latvia.[184]

To say Latgale would always be part of Latvia, was not the same as saying Latgale should be Latvianised. Should the cultural differences be ridiculed or celebrated? Riecken had already made clear that he had tired of the disdain 'Great Latvians' in Daugavpils showed towards 'backward' Latgale Latvians. In November 1943 he took the dramatic step of endorsing the proposal to publish a Latgale-language newspaper and on 3 November the first issue of *Latgolas Bolss* appeared. The editors were keen to remind readers that the Bolsheviks had closed down the Latgale-language press, and stressed that, while there were still those Latvians who thanked God there was no Latgale press, there was no shame in saying Latgale was Latgale. In a short comment Riecken gave his blessing to the appearance of the paper. The paper's direction was given in the article 'One People, One Path' by F. Z (presumably Francis Zeps, the Latgale scholar), which stressed that it was never the inhabitants of Latgale who talked of separatism, only those from elsewhere: Latgale was Latvian but had its dialect, its Catholic religion, its own tradition of song, and a problem of economic backwardness which the new paper would constantly address.[185] Nine months later, as the German-occupation regime was crumbling, the paper's editor, Norberts Treipša, recalled the difficulty the paper's supporters had had in persuading the Nazi authorities that there was no hidden separatist agenda behind the paper.[186] There was no separatism in the scheme for a newspaper, he argued; Latgale would be no more nor less separate than Latvia's other regions of Kurzeme or Vidzeme; he praised the Germans for creating conditions where all could live as free and independent peasants on their own land.[187]

Understandably, the first issue of *Latgolas Bolss* reported in depth the speech made at the end of October when Riecken could at last introduce the long discussed new regulations concerning self-administration which extended this principle to non-Latvian communities. A preamble to the regulations made clear that the origins of these proposals were to be found in the growing participation of the Russian community in the work of People's Aid.[188] Riecken's speech to self-administration workers on 22 October made clear what was a fact of life in Latgale, that the region's population was broken up into many nationalities and that this hindered the emergence of a sense of community since each people had its own views and demands. Riecken stressed that he had worked hard to resolve this issue in a way satisfactory to all, and the result was the following proposal. From October on it was decreed that Russians and Belorussians would be able to take part in the self-administration of Latgale according to their numerical representation within the population, although the dominant nationality would be the Latgale Latvians. Riecken went on:

> I always support the Latgale Latvians because these members of the dominant community here I consider part of the Latvian people as a whole, tied fast to the Latvians of other regions. Yet it must also be recognised that Latgale has its own culture, its own literature and art, that here songs, artistic experimentation and even the language have their own specific value. But this fact I also recognise, that this has never been considered separatism.[189]

The new regulations concerning the Russians and Belorussians were officially announced on 18 November.[190]

For a while Latgale's cultural diversity was celebrated. At the end of November *Daugavas vēstnesis* devoted its back page to a discussion of the latest literary works in the Latgale dialect,[191] while a couple of days later Niedra was reported to have opened an exhibition of fine arts in Daugavpils.[192] At the end of January 1944 *Dvinskii vestnik* urged more Russians to join People's Aid.[193] Other forces, however, remained deeply suspicious of this policy. A police report from the General Directorate's Department for Internal Affairs of 17 March 1944 questioned the wisdom of the self-administration policy. Harking back to the obsession with the pro-Bolshevik sentiments of Old Believers, the report stressed the links this community had with the partisans and implied that almost any Old Believer would be ready to lay mines on the partisans' behalf.

From now on, the Russians shall be participating in self-administration according to their demographic quota. If the Latvians are unhappy with this order, this cannot only be because of traditional racial antagonism; undoubtedly there are more valid reasons for this opposition. It is a particular blow to the Latvians if Latgale district towns such as Abrene and Ludza have Russians mayors. In such cases the parish stamps will fall into the hands of those whose reliability is more than questionable. This will be dangerous because it will cause serious uncertainty as to the reliability of personal identity cards and other official documentation. Therefore, I would seriously recommend rethinking the idea of Russian participation in self-administration and whether it serves German interests.[194]

Attached to this report was a summary of the situation in Ludza, drawn up by the local police. The Ludza police chief estimated that 80 per cent of the Old Believer population supported the partisans. In these circumstances, he stressed, developing self-administration was difficult. The man proposed as parish elder in Rundēni was the Old Believer Palagei Timoshchenko; but it turned out his sister had worked for the NKVD in Ludza and his brother had fled with the Bolsheviks. The assistant parish elder in Pasiene, Vasilii Demchenko, had been a factory committee activist in 1940 and was believed to have been associated with an act of arson in Zilupe. The proposed deputy town elder of Ludza, Petr Oshchtenkov, was a former factory-committee activist believed to be in contact with the partisans. Finally in Kārsava, Boris Silmanovich, another proposed self-administration activist, had once been a leading member of a factory committee.[195]

The work of the Ludza police chief was shown to Riecken, who was dismissive. He insisted that all those people put forward for posts within the self-administration had been thoroughly checked by the security police, while parish elders had checked all those involved in parish administration. 'The proper handling of the appointment procedure,' he insisted, ' means that it will never happen that men will be appointed to parish offices if it is known that they are politically unreliable.' He therefore doubted the motives of the authors of the report and concluded: 'what is written in the report is typical of the fundamental attitude of those Latvians who are opposed to the decree published by the Reichskommissar.'[196] In other words, unreconstructed Latvian policemen would never be prepared to work with the Russians.

Extending the partisan war

Riecken's problem was that the self-administration policy was too little, too late. By the time it was formally introduced in November, the partisan war was entering a new stage as it moved its operational base from Belorussia to Latvia. The 'Sommerreise' deportations had done nothing to reduce partisan activity, but however successful the partisans were by autumn 1943, they were still not being led from Latvia but from the Osveya base in Belorussia. In September 1943 the Central Committee decided something had to be done to force the reluctant commanders of the Latvian Partisan Brigade to relocate to Latvia. Two Central Committee representatives were flown to Osveya for talks, which soon became acrimonious. As Ozoliņš recalled, the Central Committee's chief negotiator insisted that all the partisan detachments be transferred at once to a base in Latvia; the local commanders refused point blank. They insisted they could only operate within Latvia in small groups, and that a single base in Latvia was an impossibility.[197] Indeed, the local commanders spelled out clearly that 'they would not take responsibility for such a move'. The Central Committee representatives stayed for a fortnight and, although the local commanders felt they had won a famous victory, in the end a compromise was reached.[198] The idea of a single brigade-level base in Latvia was abandoned and instead three detachment-level bases were selected for future activity: the forests near Jēkabpils, the forests near Lubāna and the north Latgale region where Ezernieks was already established; the hope was that, once these detachments were securely established, they would grow into brigade size units.[199] When on 16–17 September the Central Committee representatives travelled to communicate these decisions to Samsons, rumours of the row preceded them. Samsons was told how the partisan commanders had virtually been

Figure 3 A group of Soviet partisans

accused of cowardice: they had scouted out the forests near Jēkabpils for a base, but scuttled back to Osveya at the first sign of difficulty, a suggestion which prompted Oškalns to stand up, bang the table and declare that he would go to Jēkabpils himself.[200] The Central Committee representatives returned from Osveya on 27 September 1943.[201]

The transfer of detachments to Latvia was piecemeal. First to move was the 2nd Detachment, which with great difficulty got established in the Lubāna area.[202] Then Oškalns set off, resting at Samsons's base before leaving on 6 October for a rendezvous with the 2nd Detachment near Lubāna;[203] on 20 October he moved towards the Dvina and his ultimate goal of Jēkabpils.[204] Next the 1st Detachment was reorganised into three sub-groups, one operating near Abrene, the second between Viļaka and Balvi, and the third near Kārsava, although over 100 men were retained at the Russian base.[205] Further moves were disrupted by another anti-partisan operation, forcing the 3rd Detachment to abandon its repeated attempts at relocating from Osveya.[206] However, the Lubāna partisans were soon causing the authorities considerable trouble. Towards the end of November a reports noted that the partisans had first appeared there in September, and had subsequently concentrated on collecting supplies from the peasants. Then they began attacking threshing machines and dairies, until 'three-quarters of the district was being terrorised by the bandits'. Milk, butter and other agricultural deliveries were being seriously affected. It was the same near Balvi, where towards the end of November the partisans had seized over twenty cows.[207]

The partisan danger was serious enough to persuade Drechsler that local village leaders needed to be properly armed. On 28 September 1943 he requested that 19 machine pistols, 160 hand grenades and 80 carbines be distributed to parish elders and other local leaders in Latgale. When this request was ignored, Drechsler wrote angrily on 1 November 1943 that 'insecurity in these districts is so great' that pistols simply did not give local representatives enough protection.[208] Throughout October Drechsler had received a series of letters and reports from Riecken complaining at the unacceptable growth in partisan activity. To one of these he attached a description of how, near Šķaune, a whole series of villages had been attacked in one night 'as now happens so often'.[209] In a particularly bad attack of 24 October, on the road from Pasiene to Zilupe Baron Rudolph von Stromberg, a former member of the Baltic German nobility, born in Ilūkste and at one time Ludza District Governor, was killed, while the local police chief was wounded and two of his officers killed.[210] The next day orders were given to prepare for a new drive against the partisans. 'Operation Heinrich' lasted from 2 to 12 November,[211] but was not successful and towards its close two companies of the 283rd Russian Security Battalion were withdrawn from the front line;[212] reports made clear that these redeployments were linked to unspecified infringements of army regulations.[213]

There were other clear signs that what Ozoliņš had predicted would happen was happening by autumn 1943: Latvian security units were beginning to change sides. In October 1943 an air-drop of arms came down twenty kilometres from the partisan base; but two policemen from Madona district and their relatives brought the arms to the partisans.[214] Samsons's detachment had reported in early October that thirty people had recently joined them from the local population, including several deserting from the local garrison; a further 150 were willing to join if the arms could be found to equip them.[215] Laiviņš's reports showed clearly that the steady flow of recruits in October increasingly included members of the Latgale recruited Russian Security Battalions, complete with their weapons.[216] Reports from defecting members of the Latvian Legion at this time suggested that Latvians as well as Russians now had far less stomach for a fight. One defector told his Red Army interrogators 'you'll never catch them since behind every peasant is a partisan',[217] while a second stressed that legionaries were well aware that the Red Army was not far off and that 'in Latgale everyone is waiting for the Red Army to return, because of the taxes, the high prices and the demands of the Germans'. He added that leaflets produced by the partisans were frequently seen attached to telegraph poles.[218]

By early December Riecken was again complaining to Drechsler that 'bandit terror' had resumed.[219] Even while 'Operation Heinrich' was under way, Oškalns and his men moved ever westward; on 4 November his forces were spotted by the Germans near Jaunjelgava and extra guards were put on all Dvina bridges.[220] However, Oškalns stole a boat, slipped across the river and established a camp between Birzgale and Linde.[221]

Possible futures

When the partisans relocated to Latvia in late 1943, the future of Latvia was by no means certain. Reflecting this, and the need to broaden their basis of support, partisan commanders were under clear instructions to open negotiations with nationalist groups whenever possible. Samsons recalled that talks took place with 'liberally minded armed nationalist groups' in Alūksne, Kārsava, Ludza and Cibla, but none made any progress.[222] Apparently referring to the end of 1943, Laiviņš recalled in reminiscences recorded late in 1944:

> We held talks with the nationalists. We met them and held talks. It took place in Valka District. In other districts we just could not make contact. At that time the nationalists were split, breaking up into separate groups. There the Valka HQ had a secretary and he led the talks. We met with them and tried to persuade them to fight.[223]

On 10 November 1943 Oškalns recalled that he too held talks with the nationalists. He met representatives of the *Latvija* underground resistance newspaper, which was based in Riga, at talks held near Birzgale. They began by singing the 'bourgeois' national anthem of Latvia, and Oškalns and his group joined in. But when the talks began, little progress was made. The nationalists urged people to oppose mobilisation to the Latvian Legion, but rather than actively fighting the Germans, they should preserve their strength until help came from Britain and the United States to preserve Latvian independence. Despite such 'anti-Soviet' views, Oškalns kept in contact with these local nationalist activists, but felt he never reached the leading core; this disappointed Oškalns, who recalled late in 1944: 'I would have given anything to make contact with them, but was unable to do so.'[224]

If talks got nowhere, grass-roots level co-operation did. In spring 1944 when Oškalns had moved his base to the river Viesite near Zalvi he found himself undertaking joint action with 'an *aizsarg* nationalist called Komarovskii'. He led a group fighting the Germans and on the night of 15–16 April 1944 he and Oškalns had fought side by side breaking out of an encirclement. Komarovskii had been distributing nationalist leaflets, and these had led Oškalns to him; 'when we made contact with him, he fought splendidly in our ranks'.[225] While still based between Birzgale and Linde, Oškalns had first operated his policy of not opening fire first on fellow Latvians. A group of forty legionaries found themselves surrounded by Oškalns's men, but they did not open fire. As he wrote in his final report, we did not open fire because 'we had earlier warned: we will never be the first to open fire on Latvians'.[226] Confirmation of this policy comes from a witness who recalls how a RSB unit set off into the forest looking for Oškalns with its band playing.[227]

The partisans who made overtures to the 'bourgeois' nationalists acted partly from a desire to open up a dialogue, and partly because the instructions they had received from Moscow did not reflect the most recent diplomatic developments. The foreign ministers of Great Britain and the USA arrived in Moscow for talks with Molotov on 18 October 1943. Those talks concluded on 30 October with an agreed agenda for the Tehran Conference between Stalin, Churchill and Roosevelt. It had been widely assumed, although this was not in fact the case, that the foreign ministers' conference discussed the Soviet Union's post-war borders. That question was left to Tehran. Stalin therefore used his speech of 6 November, marking the anniversary of the Bolshevik revolution, to predict that the Baltic States would soon be liberated. In doing so he was laying down a marker between the Moscow Conference of Foreign Ministers and the Tehran Conference, making clear his territorial ambitions.

The Tehran Conference took place from 28 November until 1 December and spent a great deal of time discussing the future of Poland. The future of the Baltic States was not discussed by all three leaders, but in a private session between Roosevelt and Stalin. Roosevelt explained that he recognised that the Baltic States would remain in the Soviet Union after the war, although for domestic reasons he could not say this publically. Having said this, he urged Stalin to make some sort of 'gesture in favour of the principle of self-determination'.[228] Ten days after the conclusion of the Tehran Conference a big 'anti-fascist meeting of the Latvian people' was stage-managed in Moscow on 12 December in the presence of the members of the exiled Latvian Soviet Government, a clear sign that Stalin intended it should return to power. Greetings from Stalin were read out, and in his address the President of Soviet Latvia Augusts Kirhenšteins stressed that it would not be long before 'the Red Army frees our beautiful Latvia'. Stressing the same patriotic note, the communist leader Jānis Kalnbērziņš called on his 'brothers and sisters' to join in the growing partisan struggle: 'let the Latvian land burn in the fire of partisan war.' His speech was followed by a short comment from a Latvian partisan.[229] Building on the Tehran decisions, Stalin decided to amend the Soviet Constitution to give all Soviet Republics the right to have their own foreign and defence commissariats. These changes to the Soviet Constitution were announced on 1 February 1944 and, in the language of the time, they were frequently referred to as the autonomy decrees.

The press in Latvia followed these developments closely. It was quick to stress that the inhabitants of Latvia knew what Stalin's talk of 'liberation' signified; Latvia had had a year of Bolshevik 'freedom', so it would fight on in support of the German Army.[230] There then followed a series of stage-managed demonstrations and public meetings to protest at Stalin's ambitions, the biggest of which took place in Riga's cathedral square on 13 November. This rally was given extensive coverage both before and after-wards in the Daugavpils press.[231] These protests continued on 18 November, the anniversary of Latvia's independence. In Daugavpils the anniversary became a day of protest at Stalin's ambitions. According to the press, the inhabitants of Daugavpils had an unhesitating determination to fight on to victory.[232] In his speech Niedra stressed that 'from Zilupe to Liepāja there was one Latvian people and one Latvian land, as loved in Latgale as Zemgale and Kurzeme', and he protested at the decisions of the Moscow conference of Allied foreign ministers.[233]

There were those in the German administration who felt that, in this climate, when Stalin seemed to be offering Latvia autonomy, the way forward was to revive the idea of Latvian autonomy or even independence. The Latvians had not been allowed to celebrate 18 November in 1942. In 1943 they were allowed to do so in style. In Riga the city was decked with national flags. There was a march past by the Latvian Legion and a special opera performance. In Daugavpils the event was lower key: children took part in a series of school events and in a demonstration, carrying national flags; in the evening there was a concert.[234] *Daugavas vēstnesis* devoted its front page to a picture of the Latvian flag. Earlier, on 22 October, when he addressed self-administration workers about the plans for Russian and

Belorussian self-administrations, Riecken set out where he stood on the question of autonomy. Alluding to the dangers posed by rumours, by underground leaflets and by communists exploiting national differences, he stated: 'I do not believe that agitation among the Latvians could lead to what happened in Italy with Badoglio; I have a different, a higher opinion of Latvians.'[235] But despite such talk, autonomy was not forthcoming.

The refusal of the Nazi authorities to make even token concessions on the autonomy issue made Stalin appear the more generous of the two dictators. At the suggestion of the western Allies he had made a small concession. The collaborationist press tried to ridicule Stalin's proposals, but in February 1944 inadvertently gave encouragement to the notion that the post-war Soviet Union might be rather different from the dictatorship of the 1930s. The press gave great stress to the fact that 'liberation by the NKVD' would mean a return to the horrors of 'the terrible year'. *Dvinskii vestnik* reminded readers that Stalin had promised the Baltic States 'independence' once before, in 1940; the consequences were all too well known.[236] Nevertheless, Stalin's 'trick' in introducing changes in the status of the Soviet republics was comprehensively discussed and one article dismissed the proposal as giving Soviet Latvia a status equivalent to a 'British Dominion'.[237] To those weary of war, life in a British Dominion might have seemed decidedly attractive.

6 Re-establishing Soviet Daugavpils

In the last months of Nazi rule, the morale of the German administration suffered repeated body blows as draft avoidance and desertion deprived it of the Latvian collaborators on which it had once relied. Without this support the partisans, both pro-Soviet and nationalist, became increasingly successful, while Soviet air raids inflicted increasing damage on the region. Riecken had no choice but to evacuate, as the Red Army and the Soviet-operative group entered Daugavpils. Although the Communist Party had been planning its return for several months, it had had great difficulty finding the cadres it needed, scouring the Soviet Union for those with even the most tenuous connection with Latvia. The result was that in Daugavpils city the new administration was predominantly Russian and showed little continuity with the 1940–1 regime. This was less pronounced in the case of Daugavpils district, but all analyses of key personnel showed clearly the degree of Russian dominance. This caused some bitterness among Latvian communists, and prompted some half-hearted measures to redress the balance, but propaganda about the Latvian nature of the new regime could not hide the fact that even Latvian communists had been excluded from the key security posts they once dominated.

Although Russian dominance would lead to anti-Russian feeling, the peasant population was far from universally hostile to the Russians as the Red Army entered the country. There was sympathy among poorer peasants and even 'better off' peasants were far from hostile. Yet the land reform implemented by the new regime ignored such subtleties. The land reform not only returned to the poor the land confiscated by the Germans but sought to ignite the class-war instincts of the poor peasants by treating the rich and 'better off' peasants as one hostile group. It was resisted by the peasantry, and forced through by the party. Peasants were happy to see the land taken by the Germans restored to the poor, but expropriating both the 'better off' peasants and the rich 'kulaks' proved deeply unpopular. Some party members also had their reservations, but the land-reform proposals came from Stalin himself.

The communists were determined to re-educate the population they took over. Their propaganda stressed two points: first that a humane Soviet society had been torn apart by Nazi brutality in 1941; and second, that this humane Soviet society had been established legitimately in June 1940. In the latter ambition they had little success, but the former was an easier case to argue, so long as attention was deflected from the deportations of June 1941. The approach taken was to stress that those massacred by the Nazis were innocent Soviet citizens, sliding over the fact that the vast majority of victims were Jews, who had been Soviet for less than a year. Practical propaganda, the reconstruction of Daugavpils, was likely to win more recruits than such sophistry. The combination of Soviet air raids and Nazi scorched-earth tactics left the new Daugavpils administration a task of reconstruction for which it was quite unprepared. Initial successes stalled, and it took the intervention of the Central Committee and the dismissal of the Daugavpils first secretary for even limited progress to be made. For all the promises of cultural restoration through a new pedagogical institute and the restored People's House, daily survival depended on a crumbling ration system and the black market.

End game

Early in February 1944 the Red Army crossed into Estonia and the bitter fighting for the future of the Baltic States began. In Latvia many simply wanted to keep their heads down and avoid any involvement in the fighting. The next recruits to the Latvian Legion were due to begin service in February 1944, a year after its formation. The recruitment campaign began in November 1943 when Štāls, now a Police-Major and the Daugavpils Prefect, called on all those born in 1923–4 and who lived within the administrative boundaries of Daugavpils city to start reporting to the recruitment commissions on pain of penalty.[1] At the start of February 1944 the press carried reports about where the recruits needed to report in order to undergo medical checks, and how each parish elder would be required to provide accommodation for the expected 200–300 recruits per parish.[2] Three weeks later the press reported that the work of the first medical checks in the recruitment centres had been incorrectly organised and that these checks would be repeated; those recruits incorrectly rejected as unfit would be recruited after all. An investigation was under way into the criminal activity involved surrounding this affair.[3] Clearly, there had been bribery to avoid the draft on a pretty large scale. Those who could not pay bribes simply did not turn up. In Latgale less than 20 per cent responded to the February 1944 call for conscription.[4] Nor did those recruited necessarily stay in the Legion long. By June 1944 the press was openly referring to cases of desertion, particularly among the Russian population,[5] for by then the desertion rate had reached one in three.[6]

For the committed, things were different. Alongside the Soviet partisans, nationalist partisans were beginning to emerge, as Oškalns had discovered. The Soviet partisans had been in contact with nationalist groups, hoping to negotiate common action with them. Their failure to respond had not mattered too much while the nationalists remained unarmed, but from January 1944 the communists began to show alarm that, as more and more men deserted from the Latvian Legion, not all were joining the communist partisans. Other groups were being formed. These concerns centred on the appearance of nationalist partisan groups operating near Daugavpils and Rēzekne. First mentioned in a report to Moscow on 8 January 1944, by the end of February, the communist partisan leaders were getting seriously worried and expressed concern at the growing number of nationalist partisan groups which were attracting possible recruits away from the communists. The communist partisans stressed that more arms were needed if the communists were to retain hegemony in the anti-German struggle and if young people were not to be lost to 'anti-Soviet elements'. Moscow hastened to ensure the requested supplies were delivered, but this was a problem that would not go away.[7]

However, the Soviet partisans continued to play the dominant role in the anti-Nazi struggle. Their numbers continued to be fuelled by desertions from the Latvian Legion and Russian Security Battalions. A Soviet intelligence report dated 1 January 1944 stated that 74 men had recently deserted from the 314th RSB; 150 from the 283rd; and 50 from the 315th.[8] At the end of February 1944 the hastily formed 317th Latvian Police Battalion disintegrated during its first confrontation with the partisans and 15 men deserted to the partisans. Also at the end of February half the 238th RSB joined the partisans after fleeing the field of battle.[9] By the end of the war half of Oškalns's partisans were former members of the Latvian Legion,[10] and German reports stressed that as many partisans could be heard speaking Latvian as Russian.[11]

The retreat of the German Army and the advance of the Red Army meant that by the end of 1943 the Osveya base was no longer secure and Laiviņš informed Moscow on 23 January 1944 that the base had been evacuated.[12] In this way the original controlling apparatus of the Latvian Partisan Brigade had effectively collapsed. However, on 9 March 1944 Moscow contacted Samsons and asked him to found a new Partisan Brigade.[13] Constructed from the former 1st and 4th Detachments, the 1st Latvian Partisan Brigade was active in the triangle of land between Abrene, Ludza and Rēzekne. In April 1944 the old 2nd Detachment operating near Lubāna became the 2nd Partisan Brigade, and over the summer Oškalns's group was renamed the 3rd Partisan Brigade.[14] In May 1944 these partisans were responsible for 199 incidents recorded by the German security forces. In June the figure was 297; by far the most, 131, occurred near Abrene; then came Madona with 56, Rēzekne with 29, Daugavpils with 24, Ludza with 15 and Jēkabpils with 15.[15] The partisans were more active than ever, but with the disintegration of the Osveya base the centre of gravity of their operations had clearly moved northwards. When the Latvian Staff of the Partisan Movement was dissolved in October 1944 its final report of 5 October 1944 claimed 2,729 armed fighters, 2,293 men in the unarmed reserve and 849 agents carrying out intelligence work – a total of 5,871 partisans.[16]

While the partisans disciplined those of their number who terrorised local villagers,[17] they did not hesitate to take revenge on those they identified as collaborators. In July 1943 the journal of Samsons's 1st Detachment recorded laconically the execution of a village elder as a German spy.[18] The assassination of the deputy head of the Grīva police by Antonov's partisans was another such target,[19] as was the killing by partisans of Foma Samsonov, a former *aizsarg* in a village in Biķierniki parish near Daugavpils, who in November 1941, it was alleged, had executed 12 Red Army POWs.[20] A particularly violent incident concerned the activity of Vasilii Kononov. During 1940–1 Kononov had emerged as komsomol secretary at Ludza Technical College. He was evacuated with the Red Army, volunteered as a partisan in 1942 and became a prominent member of the 1st Partisan Detachment, responsible for inflicting much damage on the Rēzekne–Ludza and Rēzekne–Daugavpils railway lines. In February 1944 his partisan unit was ambushed in Mazie Bati (Malye Baty), a village near Ludza. In revenge, on 27 May 1944, his men returned to the village, dressed as Latvian partisans often were in German uniforms, identified the two households held to be responsible for the ambush, executed the family members and burnt their homesteads. In all nine people were killed, three of them women, one of whom was pregnant. Six of those who died were locked in a barn which was set on fire, while the surrounding partisans cried 'Long Live Stalin!' Those who later investigated the Kononov affair came across other excesses against alleged collaborators in spring 1944, so many in fact that a report was sent to Moscow. Among those executed was a policeman who was actually working as an informant for the Red Army.[21]

Riecken not only had to deal with the partisans – air raids became increasingly frequent during spring 1944. From the end of February 1944 the danger of air raids was being discussed in the press[22] and on 31 March a training day was held in Daugavpils on the central square for how to cope with fire-bombs.[23] The first big air raid in the region was on Rēzekne on 6–7 April when 100 civilians were killed.[24] The raid began at 8.20 in the evening and lasted for a couple of hours. In its aftermath, much of the civilian population fled, fearing that these attacks would continue. They did, with another big raid on 15 April.[25] After two air raids in Daugavpils the authorities there responded with the establishment of safe areas and from 3 May all buildings with cellars were commandeered for shelters.[26] A particularly bad attack took place on 12–13 May which caused much damage but few casualties; because of the damage to shops the rule that inhabitants could only use their assigned shop was lifted.[27] Riecken was in Rēzekne at the time of the April raid, and later reported to Drechsler on it and subsequent raids. Between 6–19 April 73 civilians were killed and 103 wounded and 80 soldiers were killed and 124 wounded. In all 215 homes had been completely destroyed and 303 partly destroyed. No buildings had any glass left, and 95 per cent of the population had fled. An estimated 6,700 bombs had fallen on the town. Riecken therefore proposed that five Germans and nine locals, including the representative of the Russian community, should be awarded medals. To his evident frustration, he found that non-Germans were ineligible for the medals he proposed, and his correspondence on this matter was still ongoing as the Red Army arrived.[28]

Despite these frustrations, and the deep sorrow he felt when his colleague in the regional agricultural department Count George Lambsdorf was killed by partisans on 6 February, Riecken stayed at his post.[29] At the end of May members of certain professions, doctors and skilled craftsmen were allowed to leave Daugavpils,[30] but Riecken remained. In mid-July he appealed to the population not to be alarmed by the news from the front. Workers should arrange for their families to move to the countryside, but should then return to the city and carry on working. This instruction was repeated on 11, 12 and 17 July.[31] However, on 16 July he informed Riga that he was preparing to leave. The evacuation of troops and administrative personnel had already taken place and had gone smoothly, he stated; he remained in the city with just a few officials. Riecken sent a similar report on the 17th and his last communication was with a local military commander on the 18th.[32]

The Red Army returns

Approximately 50,000 people fled Latvia in June 1941 as the German Army advanced.[33] The most politically active of these volunteered to join the 201 Latvian Riflemen Division, which Stalin agreed to establish on 3 August 1941. Although officered with the help of the Red Army, the division was 90 per cent composed of citizens of the Latvian Soviet Republic. This enabled the Latvian Soviet Government-in-Exile to insist the division was Latvian, but like the Soviet administration of 1940–1, the division's composition reflected an ethnically mixed Latvia; 51 per cent were Latvians, 26 per cent were Russians and 17 per cent were Jews. Some 20 per cent of its members were communists. As the division expanded, it was re-named the 43 Guards Latvian Riflemen Division, and as preparations for the re-conquest of Latvia began in 1944 it was transformed once again into the 130 Latvian Corps, comprising 16,000 men. Its men moved to the front line near the Latvian border on 3 July and on 18 July first crossed into Latvian territory, playing an active part in the fight for control of Daugavpils.[34] Among those to join from Daugavpils were Bernards Shkaprs, former chairman of the Daugavpils city soviet, Yuzef Selitskii, secretary of the Daugavpils district committee, and Isaak Borok, secretary of the district komosmol organisation. Less prominent volunteers usually came from the lower levels of the soviet administration or militia and included the young komsomol activist Iosif Šteiman,[35] who had been given responsibility for the oversight of schools on the eve of the German invasion.

From the end of 1943, once Stalin had Roosevelt's assurance about the future of the Baltic States, the Latvian communists began active administrative preparations for their return. Reporting to Moscow at Christmas 1943, Latvian communist leader Jānis Kalnbērziņš noted that the core of a new soviet and party apparatus had been assembled in Moscow, numbering two hundred people. As well as this an operative group of forty key workers for the Latgale area was already stationed close behind the Baltic front, in its 'second echelon', while a special corps of railway workers had been established, along with key security personnel. Kalnbērziņš added that work on identifying city and district committee leaders was beginning, but there was a need for additional personnel; he therefore sought permission to start recruiting not only from inhabitants of inter-war Latvia and those who had come to Latvia during 1940–1, but also from ethnic Latvians who had not seen their homeland since leaving the country during the First World War or during the agricultural colonisation of parts of Siberia at the turn of the century.[36] Permission for this was granted, but recruitment remained slow. By February 1944 the party leadership was concerned that, from the 3,000–3,500 ethnic Latvians living in the Soviet Union, the party's cadre department had contacted only 450 of them.[37] Despite these difficulties, the key personnel for the various commissariats and party committees were established in the course of spring 1944 and work began issuing reports and drafting budgets.[38] A train-load of 2,000 members of the new administration left Moscow shortly before the Red Army crossed the Latvian border on 3 July.[39]

The fighting for Daugavpils was extremely heavy and was preceded by a pitched battle fought near Nīcgale. By 25 July the city was half surrounded by Red Army forces, and on the 27th the operation to take the city began.[40] As the troops entered the city 11 members of the Soviet operative group came with them. Its task was to re-establish a Soviet civilian administration in the city, but its work was initially hampered by the fact that the German Army was still shelling the city from Grīva on the opposite bank of the river.[41] These German forces only retreated on the 28th, when the task of administrative reconstruction began in earnest.

The work of the new Daugavpils city and district administration was complicated in the first weeks of Soviet rule by the fact that Daugavpils was established as the temporary capital of Latvia until the liberation of Riga on 15 October. The Central Committee had originally established itself in Ludza, but resolved on 19 August to move to Daugavpils, a move planned for 27 August.[42] The designation as temporary capital encouraged other quasi-governmental organisations to move there at once: on 20 August the Partisan Staff was allocated offices in Daugavpils on Riga Street,[43] while the Extraordinary Commission into Nazi Atrocities had no sooner been set up on 23 August than it began the transfer to Daugavpils. Most administrative offices moved between 25 August and 1 September.[44] The Central Committee's 5th Plenum was held in the city's Coliseum Cinema on 25–26 August.[45]

Despite the multi-ethnic composition of the Latvian Division, as of the partisan units, finding suitable cadres with a local background proved extremely difficult and often those appointed reflected the reality of whoever was available. The Daugavpils city committee held its first formal meeting on 9 August 1944,[46] although its final composition, and that of the district committee, was not agreed with the Central Committee until 19 August.[47] In selecting members of the new city administration, few concessions were made to the sensibilities of local communist veterans from the underground years. The man appointed first secretary was G. S. Aleksandrov, who had been brought in from administering a Moscow factory. He soon fell out with Faifish Fridman, the most prominent leader of the old city administration to return, who had been reappointed to his old post as second secretary. On Aleksandrov's request, Fridman was quickly transferred to a post as a Central Committee instructor in Riga and by September he was no longer attending city committee meetings. Fridman was replaced by a Russian and the all important post of cadre secretary also went to a Russian. The chairman of the city soviet was I. Breidis, a 'Russian' Latvian who no longer knew a word of Latvian. A small group of Jewish survivors of the pre-war years were brought into positions of secondary importance. Lena Maizel headed the organisation department and the secretary of that department was Berta Gandler; the accounts department was headed by Rakhil Efun, the sister of Faifish Fridman.[48]

Re-establishing the soviet administration allowed a few more local cadres to be used, but the composition of the city soviet caused Moscow placemen like the local cadre secretary a great deal of concern. Česlav Kibiš, the son of a Daugavpils railway worker who had been a komosmol activist in 1940 and then a partisan during the war, was considered an excellent deputy chairman of the city soviet, and Jānis Upitis was felt to be a good choice as head of the industry department. However, many of the other people appointed by Breidis were felt to be unreliable.[49] On 26 March 1945 the city committee called on Breidis to dismiss those seen as not up to the job, including four former shopkeepers and a member of a Russian religious sect. When these calls were ignored, a closed meeting of the party cell within the city soviet was held on 10 April 1945 and the deputy chairman in charge of security was sacked and replaced by a certain A. P. Sinchenko, who had been sent to Daugavpils by the Central Committee.[50] A year later, on 5 March 1946, Breidis was sacked as soviet chairman and replaced by Sinchenko.[51] Sinchenko was not Latvian but came from Khabarovsk on Russia's Pacific Coast.[52]

In the Daugavpils district administration more account was taken of local sensibilities. The key figures at the first meeting on 10 August were Arnolds Zandmans, reappointed first secretary, and cadre secretary L. Avdyukevich, who had headed an industrial concern in Daugavpils in 1940–1 and who had become a commissar in the partisan brigade during the war.[53] By 30 August they had been joined by Mikhail Yukhno, whose underground credentials were impeccable, and by Donats Boluẑs, whose outspoken comments in 1940 had so upset the party leadership.[54] Aleksandr Nikonov replaced Zandmans in the first week of April 1945 when the latter retired on health grounds; Nikonov had been first secretary in Abrene district and was a local Latgale Russian.[55] The district soviet chairman was Antons Luriņš, another veteran of 1941 and a deputy to the Supreme Soviet.

National tensions

Relations between the incoming Russians and the local cadres were often strained. Speaking at the 5th Central Committee Plenum on 25–26 August Milda Birkenfelde, who after her time with the partisans had been reappointed Jékabpils district secretary, openly criticised the incoming Russians: 'there are many people,' she said, 'who waited for us [communists to return], who fought the Germans in some way or another, and they must be found, trusted and included in constructing soviet power; we must work with them; if we rely only on the activists who have come from the Soviet Union, we will achieve nothing.'[56] Party leader Kalnbērziņš took a very different line. He told the 6th Central Committee Plenum in November 1944 that 'the greatest danger today is local nationalism'. Much anti-Russian feeling at this time was directed towards the Red Army and at the 6th Plenum the spokesperson for such nationalist sentiments was Fricis Bergs who in 1943 had travelled with Birkenfelde for her talks with the partisan commander Samsons; Bergs had been instrumental in getting the partisans in the Kaupuẑs group to relocate and join the Ezernieks detachment. For Kalnbērziņš, Bergs, despite his loyal service behind enemy lines, was encouraging the most dangerous form of nationalism by criticising the Red Army, he was encouraging those who simply whispered that 'there are too many Russians' or insisted that meetings should be conducted in Latvian.[57] Kalnbērziņš modified his stance somewhat by December 1944. At a meeting of the Central Committee on 12 December it was accepted that ignorance of the Latvian language could seriously impair contact with the masses and that, therefore, all party organisations, soviet offices and economic enterprises should teach Latvian to those leading officials who did not know the language. Lest this be seen as a concession to local nationalism, however, the very next decision of the Central Committee was to instruct the few party activists who did not know Russian to learn it at once.[58]

By summer 1945 the problems caused by a deficit of Latvian speakers were becoming clear and further moves were taken to encourage the use of Latvian. At the 7th Central Committee Plenum on 13 June 1945 Kalnbērziņš reminded delegates that they could speak in Latvian if they wanted to, and a couple of delegates availed themselves of this opportunity. Yet there were clear limits on what could and could not be said. One delegate took this apparent concession to mean the party could discuss the danger of Russification. The delegate concerned, who was a veteran of the first Soviet Republic, reminded the plenum of a lesson from history for in 1919 discussions had been held about separating Daugavpils from Latvia and assigning it to Russia. This sort of thing happened then, he said, and could happen again because of Russification. The truth was that the bulk of Russian cadres did not want to learn Latvian. Kalnbērziņš was furious at this intervention and the plenum condemned such views as 'bourgeois nationalism'.[59]

However, in mid-July the Central Committee did concede that the time had come to publish a Latgale-language paper, *Latgolas Taisneiba*, 'since a considerable part of the population' do not know Russian.[60] The editor was carefully chosen: Konstantin Vorzhevodov was described as a Latgalean, but he had been born in Krasnoyarsk in Siberia.[61] In a similar balancing act, on 31 July the Central Committee criticised those district soviets which refused to accept reports written in Latvian or Latgalean and insisted that all communication should be in Russian; but it also stressed that it was wrong for officials to insist on replying to letters or complaints in Latvian. Public signs should in future be bilingual, and official correspondence should take place in the language used by the member of the public concerned.[62]

Such decisions did little to change the overall picture of Russian dominance. The population of Daugavpils district was 60 per cent Latvian and 25 per cent Russian.[63] These proportions were not matched by the party. A list of parish communist agitators for February 1945 revealed that 47.4 per cent were Russian; 31.5 per cent were Latvian; and 13.7 per cent Belorussian; most of the remainder were Poles.[64] On 1 May 1945 an inspection by the city's cadre department of the city's key administrative and industrial posts revealed that 140 were occupied by Russians, 36 by Latvians, one by a Lithuanian, 21 by Jews, 23 by Poles, four by Belorussians, four by Ukrainians and one by a Georgian; Latvians, therefore, comprised only 15.6 per cent of those holding key posts.[65]

The Daugavpils district committee, unlike the city committee, did respond to such measures. On 23 April 1945 it criticised the Kalupe party organisation for not working among the Latvian population[66] and on 22 May formally discussed the question of the Latvian language. This meeting resolved that all those officials who did not know the language should learn it. The committee established to implement this decision included in its membership the head of the propaganda department and the security chief M. A. Titov; Latvian-language classes were to be held every Monday between 9 and 10 in the morning.[67] A few days later the district committee organised a plenary meeting to discuss the same issue. Nikonov used his address to state that there were clear moves being made to set Latvians against Russians,[68] and the district representative of the war commissariat was even more candid: 'under the influence of kulak agitation Latvians often call soviet power in Latvia 'Russian' power and in place this leads to the hostility of Latvians towards Russians and vice versa.'[69] Bending the truth a little, at the start of July 1945 *Latgal'skaya Pravda* stressed how, unlike the Germans, the soviet authorities had encouraged the traditional Līgo holiday at the summer solstice.[70] Huge celebrations were also organised on 12 September in connection with the 80th anniversary of the birth of Latvia's national poet Rainis, who had gone to school in Daugavpils.[71]

But propagandising Latvianness was not the same as being Latvian. When a teachers' group was established in September to study Marxism-Leninism, 103 of the 139 students were Russian and only 36, or 25.5 per cent, were Latvian.[72] When the Daugavpils city conference took place on 1–2 December 1945 it was attended by 79 Russians, 21 Latvians, 14 Jews, 4 Belorussians and 12 others; the Latvians represented 16.2 per cent of the total. Among the secretaries of local party organisations 24 were Russian, six were Jews and only four were Latvians.[73] Among the heads of the city's polling divisions there were 48 Russian, 34 Latvians, two Jews, four Poles, three Belorussian and five others, an improvement, but still only 35 per cent Latvian representation.[74] The ratio was not dissimilar when a survey took place in autumn 1946 of members of the Daugavpils-district destroyer battalion: of its members 297 or 48.4 per cent were Russian and 217 or 35.5 per cent Latvian.[75]

Latvians remained excluded from key posts. Meeting on 2–3 November 1945 the Central Committee concluded that in much of the country its July decisions on the Latvian language had been ignored, partly, it conceded, because the long-awaited 'Teach Yourself Latvian' textbook had only recently become available.[76] At the 9th Central Committee Plenum on 12–13 November 1945 the Jēkabpils cadre secretary expressed his frustration at what he saw as the continuing dominance of the security services by Russians. Before the war, he pointed out, there had been many Latvians in the security services. Many of these people still held posts in the Latvian government, but no longer in the field of security, despite the fact that the nationality issue was so sensitive. As a Latvian speaker he was constantly called on by Russian comrades in the security services to translate for those they had arrested, reinforcing the impression that this was not a Latvian administration but a Russian one. The Jēkabpils cadre secretary recognised that, after the purges of 1937–8, some of these Latvian security officials had had to be dismissed, but they were now needed once again if perceptions of Russian occupation were to be countered.[77]

The harvest and land reform

With the cadres that could be found, the returning communists, both incomers and locals, were uncertain as to what awaited them. To supplement the information gleaned from the partisans, Soviet intelligence carried out surveys of the popular mood, and these conveyed mixed messages. A report, circulated to the party leadership on 10 April 1944, stated that in Latgale, unlike in Kurzeme, the Red Army could expect a positive reception: both the Latvian and Russian population had warm memories of the

Red Army in 1940, it stated, remembering especially the politeness of the Red Army soldiers; in addition the majority of the population now supported the partisan movement, something the Germans implicitly recognised. Clearly, there was a strong element of wishful thinking in this assessment, since politeness was·not a trait many people recognised among Red Army men – quite the opposite in fact.[78] Yet the report was honest enough to note that there were people, 'not only Latvians but Russians as well', who were hostile to the Soviet Union and who motivated that hostility with reference to the deportations of June 1941 and Soviet plans to introduce collective farming.[79]

When the Red Army arrived in July 1944 this picture was confirmed. By and large the Red Army was welcomed by the Russian population. 'Our boys have come' was a common reaction among the Russians of Daugavpils district.[80] The attitude of the Latvians was more complex, and the subject of a survey carried out by Soviet military intelligence. At one level the picture was again positive. The initial concern of many Latvians related simply to their immediate safety, and here people were pleasantly surprised. The first military intelligence report related what had happened when the Latvian Corps encountered a group of Latvian civilians who had been hiding in the forest. They sent out a representative, a woman, who tried to establish from a Latvian officer what the attitude of the Red Army would be to the local Latvians. The group wanted to return to their houses, but feared to do so because before the Germans had left they had stressed that the as soon as the Red Army arrived it would 'make short shrift' of the Latvian population. Other Latvians claimed to have been in tears as they hid in the forest for three days because of German talk of certain death when the Red Army came; even a local teacher believed such stories, assuming she would be arrested on the spot.

Once it was clear the Red Army was not bent on taking revenge on the Latvian people as a whole, the picture painted in the military intelligence reports was more worrying. Interviews with three Latvian poor peasants, those expected to be most sympathetic to the Soviet order, hardly exuded enthusiasm: 'We do not mind who is in power, as long as we live well', one said. 'We did not live badly in bourgeois Latvia, and under your government it was all right, perhaps even better, since your government confiscated land from the landowners and priests and gave it to us landless peasants, when before the Russians came we had to pay the priests rent for it. When the Germans came to Latvia, they took the land away again and gave it back to the rich farmers and the priests, and we landless suffered.' Thus far, rather grudging praise, but this was the most positive comment made. The second poor peasant immediately pointed out that Soviet power meant collective farms and a far poorer standard of living. The third poor peasant stated that 'we did not live badly under the Germans, since everybody had his own farm'. He then asked if it were true, as the Germans had said, that the Soviet government would drive them into collective farms.

If such was the view from the poor farmers, who were supposed to be sympathetic to the regime, the attitude of better-off farmers came as no surprise to the military-intelligence officers who were steeped in Bolshevik theories of class analysis. Yet they must have been reassured that the hostility of these peasant farmers was to Soviet agricultural practices, not the Russian people:

> We are not worried by the Germans or the Red Army, although it would be best if Ulmanis came back. We are afraid of collective farms; if they come, Latvian agriculture will collapse and we will all be poor. We recognise that Latvia, as a small state, cannot exist independently. Living on friendly terms with Russia will not be bad, as long as the laws of 1940 are not brought back; that would be bad for Latvians. In 1940 we were deprived of all rights to land; a farmer could only own thirty hectares, which is not very much, and the buying and selling of produce was banned, which meant there was no profit to be made.

The same basic points were made by another better-off peasant. 'We consider Russia our close friend. It is a big country, and apparently a rich one; but we fear collective farms. If they were to exist here, then many things would go to the dogs. In 1940 there was an attempt to set up collective farms in Russian villages, but nothing came of it. It would be better if there were no collective farms.'

Finally, Soviet military intelligence came across a significant section of the Latvian population of Latgale which was still pro-German. One farmer praised the relatively low taxation of the German regime, including the relaxed attitude to non-payment, and boasted that on his own farm he could produce more than any collective farm. The other two pro-German farmers interviewed linked their hostility to Soviet power to the deportations. One stated: 'we do not need the Russians; the Bolsheviks tormented 60,000 Latvians, while the Germans freed us from Bolshevik collective farms.' Another linked his hate of the Red Army with the arrest of his son in 1940: 'the Germans are better than the Russians – Hitler gave us freedom.'[81] As the head of Riga radio reported in May 1945, Nazi propaganda had been particularly effective when it stressed the danger of collective farms and tried to present the exile on 14 June 1941 of 'Ulmanis supporters and specu-lators' as the first stage in a campaign 'to deal with the Latvians'.[82] As the new administration began to establish itself and move from Latglae to win control of such areas as Valmiera and Cēsis, the questions remained the same: would the Latvians be exiled to Siberia; would collective farms be established soon; and what would happen to those who had fought in the Latvian Legion and deserted from it?[83]

The issues raised in the report by Soviet military intelligence should have been analysed carefully by Latvia's communists. The fear of collective farms clearly united all sections of the Latvian peasantry, from the poor peasant to the pro-Hitler kulak. The question of Latvian independence did not have the same unifying power. One of the better-off peasants had talked of bringing Ulmanis back, but all stressed the need for good relations with the Russians. A government with the status of a British Dominion, a Soviet government with sufficient autonomy to pursue an agricultural policy based on co-operation rather than collectivisation, might have united all but the most hard line pro-German elements. However, listening to the views of the rural population, even when transmitted by military intelligence, was not a feature of Stalin's totalitarianism.

The first tasks faced by the new district administration were to implement the twin programmes of harvest collection and land reform. At first the harvest, always emotionally referred to as the need to feed the heroic Red Army, seemed to have priority. At its first meeting on 10 August 1944 the Daugavpils district committee started identifying collection points for agricultural deliveries,[84] and in the same spirit *Latgal'skaya Pravda* announced in mid-August that getting in the harvest was 'the most important task'.[85] However, Kalnbērziņš told the 5th Plenum on 25–26 August that it would be wrong to put the harvest before land reform. The land reform had to be implemented right away to ensure the political support of 'the working peasantry'. To ensure such support, the communists proposed a more radical land reform than that introduced in the first year of Soviet rule. The definition of a kulak, the category whose land would be expropriated, would no longer be those who owned 30 hectares, but anyone owning 20–30 hectares, depending on the quality of the land. At the same time, any peasant household accused of giving active support to the Germans would have its land holding reduced to 5–7 hectares. These changes would supposedly produce a larger state land fund than in 1940 that would enable 70 per cent of peasants to benefit either from the allocation of additional land, in the case of peasants with small holdings, or from the establishment of completely new farms, for those with no land at all.[86] The details of the land reform were published in *Latgal'skaya Pravda* on 11 September.

The land reform made perfect sense in terms of the Marxist-Leninist theory of class struggle in the countryside, but took no account of political reality, in particular the need to persuade those 'better off' peasants, who the military intelligence report had shown were sympathetic to Russia, that they had nothing in common with pro-German 'kulaks'. Broadening the definition of a kulak lumped together the 'better off' and the rich peasants, thus counting as one the potentially pro-Russian and the probably pro-German. It also did nothing to dispel the belief that, as in the Soviet Union in the 1930s, the assault on the kulak was merely the precursor to collectivisation. Nor did the land reform recognise that the difference in wealth between those owning under 20 hectares and those owning over 20 hectares was nominal in a society where all peasants were struggling to make a living. There were poor peasants who had had their land confiscated by the Germans and now wanted it back. Thus the 5th Plenum on 25–26 August heard the Abrene district-party secretary Aleksandr Nikonov, soon to be transferred to Daugavpils district, explain how local peasant demands for the return of their land were being met by the temporary expedient of allocating them abandoned plots of land.[87] There was, however, no popular pressure for the land reform to go beyond this.

Although Kalnbērziņš had criticised district-party secretaries for putting the harvest before land reform,[88] the reality was that the Central Committee monitored harvest deliveries at every meeting and issued repeated criticism of those districts which were falling behind. As early as 5 September Ilūkste and Daugavpils districts were being criticised for letting the harvest collection drift and not confronting those peasants unwilling to deliver grain;[89] ten days later deliveries in Ilūkste were said to be running at only 21 per cent of the planned target in the face of outright sabotage from some well-off farmers.[90] Two weeks later, at the start of October, Jēkabpils district was linked to Ilūkste as an area where the harvest was particularly poor,[91] and by mid-October Jēkabpils had been singled out as the worst area for grain deliveries; its district secretary Milda Birkenfelde was singled out for special criticism.[92] The situation improved in Daugavpils district only when, as the new district secretary Nikonov reported shortly after his appointment, seven 'kulaks' were brought before show trials.[93]

Show trials were not the only repressive measure used at this time. There was also the hunt for German collaborators. In mid-October, it was reported that the 'destroyer battalions' set up by the security services in Daugavpils and Ilūkste districts and recruited from local volunteers 'had become a group of armed men who carried out illegal arrests, searches and robberies'. This development was put down to the unwillingness of the district-party secretaries to become involved in security matters, leaving it instead to the local security apparatus. The result was that in Krāslava, Līvāni, Dagda and Asūne parishes of Daugavpils district, and the Mērdzene and Šķaune parishes of neighbouring Ludza district, the destroyer battalions had become a source of unrest rather than security.[94]

District-party secretaries had to use repression to obtain grain, while at the same time appearing as fairy godmother in handing out land to the poor. It was an impossible combination and, not surprisingly, the result was that few peasants trusted them. Implementing the land reform proved a nightmare and on 4 October Kalnbērziņš had to concede that the land reform therefore was going extremely slowly and that, at best, the harvest targets were being 50 per cent met.[95] At the end of October *Latgal'skaya Pravda* could no longer hide its concern at the slow pace of progress with the land reform. The article 'It must not slow down' praised Skaista as one of the few parishes which had made real progress implementing the reform, and criticised Līvāni where little progress had been made. However, even in Skaiste all that had happened was that the land taken away by the Nazis was restored; the new element to the reform was not embarked on.[96] Peasants were willing to accept the reversal of the Nazi reforms, but not to accept the new definition of the kulak, nor the punitive expropriation of those who had, allegedly, helped the Germans.

Many party secretaries in other districts were unwilling to force the issue, and for this they were criticised when the 6th Plenum was held on 16–18 November 1944. Kalnbērziņš, who had just returned from Moscow where the performance of the Latvian communists was severely criticised, was dismissive of those local activists who could not find a landless peasant who wanted the land taken from the kulak. He attacked those who tried to negotiate with kulaks and who apparently believed the kulak could peace-fully grow towards socialism. Milda Birkenfelde was singled out for special blame; in her district, it was said, there was no sabotage from the kulaks. How, Kalnbērziņš asked, was it possible to explain the situation when Soviet power was giving land to both the landless and those with little land, yet those who had thirsted for this land and dreamt all their lives of becoming independent farmers were now in many places refusing to take the land, and often would not even ask for the land? It could only be explained as the result of fascist propaganda and terror, the work of Hitlerite agents, of Latvian nationalists and all sorts of anti-Soviet elements, as well as our poor propaganda and agitation work, the weakness of Soviet power in the localities and the party organisations in the country-side, our indecisive struggle with the enemies of the Latvian people and the agents of Hitlerite Germany.[97] Kalnbērziņš was quite incapable of thinking outside the Marxist-Leninist paradigm. For him, the land reform had to be failing because of the action of enemy forces. That the land reform was ill judged, and that peasants preferred not to seize the land of their neigh-bours was beyond his comprehension. He could not appreciate the distinction between the better-off peasant and what Birkenfelde made clear were the real kulaks, those who refused to hand over their harvest and whose sons were still in the Latvian Legion fighting the Red Army. She had organised show trials for such peasants and they had been sentenced to five years in prison.[98]

Latgal'skaya Pravda tried to put a positive gloss on things, reporting at the end of November that 161 new farms had been established.[99] However, when the Daugavpils district party discussed the situation on 2 December it became clear that these 161 farms had only had restored to them the land taken by the Germans, the revised land reform had not been implemented. As the report candidly admitted, the problem was that soviet power lacked authority in the parishes, and that local land commissions were unwilling to challenge the better-off peasantry by embarking on that part of the reform which involved expropriating the newly redefined kulaks and German collaborators. Transferring this land was proceeding slowly and in sum the situation was 'extremely unsatisfactory'.[100] The situation was no better in neighbouring Rēzekne. There the expropriation of kulak land and the land of German collaborators had been purely token. Where progress had been made, it was simply to restore the 1940–1 allocations.[101]

The Daugavpils district committee discussed the situation again on 18 December. According to Zandmans's report the situation was worst in Rudzāti, Nīcgale and Aglona. Again, it became clear that the problematic areas were the decision to take land from those owning above 20 hectares and the decision to take land from German collaborators; the latter was going 'especially slowly'. As to the new farms, they often comprised only ten hectares, when there was sufficient land to make them 15 hectares, and the documentation concerning title deeds, not to mention proper fencing of the new properties, was slow in coming.[102] Titov, the Daugavpils security chief, told the meeting of opposition from 'well-off high-ups' in the villages and called for peasant meetings to be held in every village before 5 January 1945 to explain the law once again.[103]

On 23 January 1945 the Central Committee passed a resolution critical of Daugavpils district committee,[104] as a result of which the district committee addressed the land reform with new vigour. The party had set the start of February as the target for the implementation of the land reform, and work on it continued throughout January. *Latgal'skaya Pravda* stressed that where land commissions had been reformed and new more determined people appointed, real progress had been made; in Nīcgale, Preiļi and Līksna such a change of personnel had made a dramatic impact, the paper stressed. Events in Preiļi were a good example of how a land commission had failed to address the issue of collaboration. It refused to touch the land of '*aizsargs*' and simply took control of the nine farms whose owners had fled to Germany.[105] On Sunday 4 February 1945 the district party organised an agricultural conference attended by 1,000 people in the People's House, as Unity House had been renamed for the second time. Attended not only by local leaders like Zandmans and Luriņš, the key address was given by the Second Secretary of the Central Committee Ivan Lebedev: he called for the soviet apparatus in the parishes and villages to be strengthened, and stressed that the land reform had to be completed by 15 February. His message was short and to the point: soviet power 'is not here temporarily but forever'.[106]

It was, however, only on 27 March that enough progress had been made for the district committee to review the land reform and its implementation. Some 854 new farms had been established and in all 3,816 farms had received additional land; 1,061 hectares were still to be allocated, mostly in Rudzāti and Aizkalne. However, allocating land was one thing, establishing viable and efficient farms on the land was something far more complex. The main problem was the poor state of the newly established farms. Of the 854 new farms only 401 were fully equipped: of the rest 58 simply comprised a house; 76 only had one barn; 319 had no farm building at all; 190 had no horses; and 161 had no agricultural equipment.[107] Thus only half the new farms seemed viable, and, as things turned out, much land was still to be allocated. In May the district party was informed that land allocations had still not been completely finalised,[108] and mistakes in land allocation had resulted in the sacking of the chairman of the Biķernieki parish soviet; as well as being slow in issuing title deeds, he had expropriated the land of two Russian peasants on the grounds that they had collaborated with the Germans, only for an investigation to reveal that this was not the case, forcing him to return the land.[109] On 28 June, Nikonov reported that 40 acts of land transfer were still outstanding in Aizkalne, 22 in Dagda, 26 in Kapiņi and 80 in Preiļi.[110]

Thus the land reform was still not completed when the district party began its spring sowing campaign. On 21 April the People's House hosted a conference of village activists, who were addressed by Nikonov. He explained how machine-tractor stations and horse-hiring bases would again be established to help those with little farming equipment; there were 4,000 horseless farms, including 23 per cent of those newly established under the land reform. Nikonov expressed concern that most of the horse-hiring bases had only eight or nine horses, and that the tractors at the Preiļi machine-tractor station had yet to leave the yard, but he expressed confidence that the sowing would get done.[111] At the start of July *Latgal'skaya Pravda* published decrees on the compulsory deliveries of grain, hay, potatoes, milk, meat, wool and eggs;[112] all hope that the Bolsheviks might pursue a different policy than in 1940–1 had proved vain.

It could be asked why the party pressed ahead with a land reform designed to antagonise the 'better off' peasantry, the group which the military intelligence interviews had revealed to be potentially sympathetic to future collaboration with Russia. District-party secretaries like Birkenfelde were clearly unenthusiastic about this change, preferring to define a kulak as a farmer who actively opposed the Soviet regime by refusing to deliver the harvest or supporting those fighting in the Latvian Legion. However, the terms of the land reform could not be challenged because, as Kalnbērziņš told delegates to an emergency party meeting on 6 November 1944, the land reform was 'the personal initiative of Comrade Stalin'.[113]

Ideological re-education

The communists' message as the Red Army entered Latgale was brutally clear and offered little hope of compromise. In its first issue of 25 July 1944, two days before the capture of Daugavpils, *Latgal'skaya Pravda* carried a front-page article by Kalnbērziņš, 'Latvia was and will be Soviet'; to reinforce the point the paper carried a portrait of Stalin. The first task of both the city and district party organisations was to help organise mobilisation into the Red Army as Latvia's new army. This began within days of the Red Army's arrival; by 5 August, scarcely a fortnight after the German retreat, the Central Committee was already discussing the poor work of the Ludza and Rēzekne party and soviet organisations in organising the mobilisation of recruits[114] and calling on its Military Commissar and the head of the military department of the Central Committee to address the problem.[115]

The propaganda task of the returning communists was to stress both the brutality of the Nazi regime and the legitimacy of the Soviet regime which had preceded it. The first task was easier than the second. In order to inspire a new love of the 'soviet' various means were used. *Latgal'skaya Pravda* carried an article by Faifish Fridman which enumerated the names of some of those from the Daugavpils region who had fought in the Latvian Division.[116] Early in September the party organised a 'meeting between young people and the partisans', which was addressed by, among others, Rafael Blum, a Jew who had been commissar of the 2nd Partisan Detachment and who had attacked the Daugavpils–Rēzekne railway line more than once.[117] In October 1944 *Latgal'skaya Pravda* uncovered the story of Milentii Nikiforov, who had been inspired by Moscow radio to establish one of the first partisan groups in early spring 1942. The paper's version of the Nikiforov story concentrated as much on the Nazis' punishment burning of the farm near Višķi, where his associate Luka Alekseev lived, as on Nikiforov's success in killing a policeman. The same issue of the paper told the story of another early partisan, who operated near Rēzekne towards the end of 1942.[118] The underlying message was clear: good Latvian citizens had fought alongside the Red Army, and it was the duty of every Latvian now to do the same.

The other tactic used to win support for the communist cause was to remind the population of Daugavpils of the atrocities committed during the Nazi occupation. The first description of the horrors of the Nazi years was given in *Latgal'skaya Pravda* in late August by A. Sosnovskii, who had once been a gym teacher at the Daugavpils Polish School. Sosnovskii's account concentrated on the educational world he knew and the fate of his Polish School in particular. The Nazis had closed the school for 18 months, and then prevented it having a junior class or any senior classes. However, schools in general suffered, according to Sosnovskii, operating for only six months each year. He then recalled the buses used to transport Russians to forced labour in Germany and the shooting of the patients in the psychiatric hospital. Finally he recalled the way the rich had been able to pay bribes to avoid mobilisation into the Latvian Legion.[119] Sosnovskii's account was completely accurate.

On 31 August the Daugavpils city committee had established its own extraordinary commission to investigate Nazi atrocities and subsequently the press began to describe the full horror of what had occurred. Iosif Šteiman was made secretary of the extraordinary commission and Sosnovskii served on it as a token non-communist member.[120] By 24 October the commission had received 2,500 submissions,[121] ample material for the press reports which began to appear. On 7 September *Latgal'skaya Pravda* recounted how, in the course of the three-year occupation, 1,140 of the 1,640 inhabitants of Preiļi had been killed. This was followed on 8 October with the first instalment of a regular column entitled 'We will not forget, nor will we forgive'. This first instalment put the number of Nazi victims at an exaggerated 150,000, and retold the story of the forced recruitment for labour service in Germany.

On 1 November 1944 'We will not forget, nor will we forgive' told of the first Jewish massacre in the Railwaymen's Garden, reminding readers that this had taken place 'almost in the centre of the town'. However, the purpose of these accounts was to win sympathy for the Soviet system, not give a full picture of what had happened. The victims of Nazism were to be portrayed as, first and foremost, communists and activists. The press report, therefore, began by mentioning the relatively few communists and Red Army men shot at this site, before adding 'but in the main it was peaceful inhabitants, old men, even children, and the greatest part Jews' who were shot in groups of five at this spot, before the killings moved to Mežciems.[122] Excavations at Mežciems began on 26 November and were covered in gruesome detail by *Latgal'skaya Pravda*. The paper then reported the visit to the site just as the excavations started by Aleksandrov and Breidis, accompanied by a representative of the Russian Orthodox Church and an officer from the large number of German POWs detained in the city. The main focus of the visit, in accordance with the propaganda line, was the mass grave of Red Army POWs, although those present did also view the pits 'full of old men, women and children'. The report did not mention the fact that these were Jews.[123] For the communist authorities, it was important to highlight the Nazi assault on innocent Soviet citizens without dwelling on the fact that they were killed on racial grounds, or, indeed, that they had not been Soviet citizens very long.

It was easy to show the brutality of the Nazi regime, but it was far harder to show the legitimacy of the Soviet regime the Nazis had overthrown. In one article, published in *Latgal'skaya Pravda* on 3 October 1944, a half-hearted attempt was made to counter Nazi reports of Bolshevik atrocities in 1941. The paper suggested that the exhumation of bodies near Daugavpils prison was part of an elaborate charade. The Nazis had arrested communists, tortured and killed them, and then put their bodies on display as victims of 'the Reds'. At the time of the fifth anniversary of the establishment of Soviet power in June 1945, *Latgal'skaya Pravda* produced a pseudo-constitutional justification for the events of five years earlier. It was pointed out, quite speciously, that Ulmanis had invited the Red Army into Latvia, that this had sparked off revolutionary demonstrations: 'the plutocracy did not dare, in the presence of the Red Army, to take bloody vengeance on the rising workers and the Ulmanis government was forced to resign.' This article, and others published later in July, then gave great stress to Oškalns and the other partisan leaders who had fought to restore Soviet power in Latvia. One or two partisan operations were described in detail, especially those of the local partisan leader Ivan Muzykantik. The partisan war gave greater legitimacy to the cause of the Latvian communists than association with the Red Army.[124]

Reconstruction

Actions traditionally speak louder than words, and the new authorities realised that success in reconstructing Daugavpils itself would win more converts than any propaganda campaign. Not only had Daugavpils been consistently bombed by the Red Air Force during spring 1944, but, as the German Army retreated, it blew up those buildings or structures considered to have military significance. The railway network, the railway stations, the power station, the water tower and the bridges were all in ruins; on top of this, two-thirds of the factories were damaged, 42 in all, and the post and telegraph office was destroyed. The press reported 1,752 houses completely destroyed and 965 damaged, while Iosif Šteiman, the member of the 11-member soviet operative group responsible for allocating living space, considered that 65 per cent of homes were damaged.[125] When the former German field commandant for Daugavpils, Hans Kyupper, was put on trial in Riga in January 1946, he agreed that he had drawn up a plan for the destruction of military objects including the power station, the water tower, the bridges, the rolling-stock repair works, the railway depot and the People's House; factory managers had also been instructed to destroy their plants as they saw fit. Kyupper did not accept the prosecution charge that he had ordered the destruction of the whole town.[126]

Figure 4 Picking through the war damage

The combined damage to the city was extensive. The operative group found chaos when it arrived on 27 July. There were dead horses everywhere, buildings were still on fire and roads were blocked with fallen telegraph poles. Starting work on the 28th, despite continuing shelling from the Grīva side of the river, sappers cleared away the mines and the operative group assessed the damage. It had no supplies of its own, and was forced to beg food from the military. Food supplies remained difficult, for although there was some grain in the city, it could not be milled. Gradually, however, workers drifted back and there were soon a thousand railway workers laying track.[127] The astonishing thing was, as city soviet chairman Breidis later confessed, 'we did not expect to meet such destruction; we had no plans for reconstruction; we began work with empty hands'.[128]

Progress with reconstruction was first discussed at a meeting of the Daugavpils city party organisation on 8 September, intimated the previous day in *Latgal'skaya Pravda* by the headline 'Let's restore the city more quickly'.[129] The team in charge of restoring the railways reported how it found no tracks and no buildings; yet within a month its members had restored 50 per cent of the track network and trains were moving again, although water for steam generation remained a problem. The team in charge of the city's health care reported it had arrived to find no water, no bath houses and no doctors; they had toured the remnants of the city to beg for beds and other supplies and by September polyclinics and hospitals were in place and a surgical unit was planned. Overall the meeting heard that the first stage of the restoration of the water supply was complete; that 25 factories were operating, if not at full capacity; that flour mills and milk plants were back in production; that two temporary crossings of the Dvina were in place; and, most important of all, the population was beginning to return. The meeting resolved to restore light by 15 September and supply water to the whole of the city by October.[130]

These targets were wishful thinking and progress remained painfully slow. At the start of September some parts of the city had electricity restored,[131] but it was only at the end of November that Breidis could report that electricity was 'basically restored', and, even once restored, restrictions on its use had to be imposed.[132] On 11 October the Daugavpils city committee discussed, as it would do repeatedly over the next two years, why so little progress was being made in restoring flats. Breidis was called on to identify which flats could realistically be repaired in the current financial quarter.[133] Meeting in mid-October 1944, just before its move to Riga, the Central Committee resolved that progress on the reconstruction of Daugavpils was 'completely unsatisfactory',[134] and when the city committee again discussed the situation on 30 November, Kalnbērziņš attended. This meeting noted that there was still no plan for flat construction and that the water supply continued to be a major problem. It also noted that, although the railway network was operating, average track speeds were only 16.7 kph not the planned 28 kph. However, the meeting's major decision was to order the construction of a road bridge across the Dvina to be completed by March 1945. For this to happen, it would be necessary to clear away the debris from the damaged bridge, for it was feared that if the damaged structures were not removed from the river quickly, they would freeze in place during the winter and then restrict the river's flow when the ice melted, causing flooding.

At this meeting Kalnbērziņš criticised the Red Army and its political workers for not doing enough to support the reconstruction of the city.[135] Perhaps spurred on by such criticism, the Red Army took on the task of constructing the new road bridge. Work began behind schedule, in January rather than December, and this hampered the task of removing the collapsed metal structures.[136] However, the bridge was completed within March, if not by March, for its completion was welcomed by the Central Committee on 22 March[137] and reported in *Latgal'skaya Pravda* on 25 March. The official opening was reported on the 28th. Kalnbērziņš joined Aleksandrov and Breidis to open it officially and among the others present was Luriņš, as chairman of the district soviet and the secretary of the neighbouring Ilūkste district committee. Although the opening of the bridge was a major improvement to life in Daugavpils, the presence of Kalnbērziņš at the opening ceremony focused Riga's attention on the lack of progress in other areas of reconstruction. On 15 March 1945 the Central Committee called for the reconstruction of the rolling-stock repair works.[138] Two days later the city committee itself decided that progress on the restoration of the city was quite unsatisfactory since only 28.5 per cent of the credits made available from the centre for this purpose had been utilised.[139]

However, little was done to improve the situation and, as a result, on 11 June 1945 the Central Committee passed a resolution criticising the work of the Daugavpils city committee. In particular, the Central Committee stressed that progress with restoration work remained unsatisfactory: its investigations revealed that in 1944, instead of the planned 125,000 square metres of restored living space, only 78,253 square metres were restored; the picture was even worse in the first quarter of 1945, when only 1,710 square metres of the planned 10,000 square metres had been restored.[140] The Central Committee argued that the fruits of these political failings were now being harvested. Because of its passivity the city committee had not even discussed a workers' proposal that workers should donate 100 hours of labour per year for the restoration of the city. What was more, the city committee had distanced itself from the work to repair the rolling-stock repair works, despite the resolution of 15 March. All this reflected a deeper failing to take an interest in the life of the community. There was insufficient food to meet ration cards; bath-houses operated irregularly because of a lack of fuel; general sanitation was poor; and there were no organised games for children on holiday from school. On top of that party cells remained inactive, and nothing had been done about the party's membership.[141] The Central Committee's resolution concluded with the demand that the city soviet establish a new construction combine on the basis of two existing enterprises.[142]

On 13 June 1945 Aleksandrov was the target of a personal attack at the 8th Central Committee Plenum by its Second Secretary Lebedev. He accused Aleksandrov of not getting out and about to meet the rank and file, and of not seeing the importance of studying Marxism-Leninism; in sum his approach was bureaucratic. Aleksandrov had not choice but to eat humble pie.[143] The city committee discussed the Central Committee's damning resolution on 18 June. This meeting was reported quite frankly in the press. It noted in particular that the voluntary labour 'Sundays' planned for 20 and 27 May had simply not taken place.[144] At the meeting Breidis protested that he was being attacked unfairly: his soviet executive had been given little practical help and the city committee had even poached some of its best personnel; Iosif Šteiman, who had originally been attached to the soviet operative group, had been quickly diverted to taking on the post of secretary to the extraordinary commission, and then moved to head the party's political education office.[145] For his part Šteiman gave voice to those critical of Aleksandrov's bureaucratic approach; being a communist meant studying communist theory as well as shouting about the needs of the front, he said. The meeting ended with many promises about what would and should happen, including the commitment, a year after the German retreat, to remove once and for all the piles of rubble which still marred the city.[146]

Figure 5 The challenge of post-war reconstruction

The intervention by the Central Committee prompted a flurry of activity. Press coverage of the 100 hours programme intensified,[147] and on 6 July Lebedev again visited the city[148] and called for a determined effort to address the question of electric power.[149] On 27 July Aleksandrov made a pompous speech on the anniversary of the city's liberation. He announced that a new era of reconstruction was under way, boasting that 55 factories were back in operation; in his view the only major task still left was the reconstruction of the water tower.[150] The reality was that even the supply of electricity remained erratic, something which was partly due to the delay in reconstructing the power station chimney,[151] and partly due to an explosion in the generator. Initially Soviet engineers had repaired the electricity generator blown up by the Germans and with this improvised system had succeeded in generating about half the city's pre-war electricity needs. However, in an attempt to boost supply further, another generator had been acquired and this had suffered an explosion soon after its installation.[152] In mid-September a press campaign was launched to 'preserve every kilowatt of electricity'.[153]

In these circumstances Aleksandrov could not have been surprised when he was sacked on 14 August 1945 and replaced by another Moscow appointee, Vasilii Feoktistov.[154] Feoktistov immediately reallocated the contract to rebuild the power station chimney.[155] His style was scarcely less bureaucratic than that of his predecessor, but he established a close relationship with second secretary of the Central Committee Lebedev and this did something to improve supplies from Riga.[156] Although on 22 September the city committee concluded that the 100 hours campaign had again been reduced to a formality, while scarcely 20 per cent of the allocated construction funds had been spent because there were still no dedicated construction brigades or supply bases,[157] under Feoktistov progress was made. By mid-October a new rail link connected the railway goods depot with the power station, meaning fuel no longer had to be transported from the depot to the power station by lorry,[158] and by mid-November a replacement generator had arrived,[159] although it had still not been installed by the end of December, which meant that erratic supplies to industry continued.[160] Indeed, hitches with the new generator meant that, as late as May 1946, factories were receiving only half their needs and the population at large about a third of its needs.[161] It was not until October 1946, when reconstruction work on the water tower was finally completed, that anything like an uninterrupted supply of water could be guaranteed.[162] Nevertheless, *Latgal'skaya Pravda*'s claim on 1 December 1945 that Daugavpils had moved from reconstruction to redevelopment was not entirely spurious.

Daily life

Daily life in Daugavpils during the first year of restored Soviet rule was miserable. German marks were exchanged for roubles at the start of

September 1944. Unlike the way the Germans had tolerated the joint circulation of roubles and marks for an extended period, this change was carried out over night, something which caused some complaints.[163] However, initially money was not much of an issue; apart from bread there was nothing to buy. For the first three months of the new regime there were not even such basics as buckwheat and soap. This caused some complaints, for the city committee was told on 30 November 1944 that the appalling supply situation 'was creating all sorts of unnecessary conversations'.[164] The situation did improve a bit in early 1945. On 4 March it was reported that four public bath-houses were operating and the city's department store was again open for business.[165] At the start of 1945 the press wrote of 36 shops in the city and two hospitals.[166] The communists always claimed education was a priority and were determined that the ten schools[167] they established should start the school year on 15 September, a month earlier than under German rule. This ambitious target slipped to 1 October.[168]

As goods came into the shops, so black-market swindles developed. The first of these were discovered at the end of December 1944,[169] and in mid-March 1945 *Latgal'skaya Pravda* exposed a great scandal involving wide-scale under-the-counter sales.[170] At the end of May the director of the main dairy was sacked because production was under a third of that planned and much of the milk produced was found to be off; those families living illegally within the dairy buildings were removed at the same time.[171] Outside Daugavpils supplies were even worse: in May 1945 in Līksna, Višķi and Biķernieki shop deliveries were only 20 per cent of those planned, meaning the ration system had 'completely collapsed'.[172] Things were not that much better as summer turned to autumn. In August the families that had squatted in the buildings of the Polish School over the summer holidays were ordered to leave.[173] In the same month a shop assistant was expelled from the party for being involved in under the counter trading;[174] and in September the continuing shortage of shoes was debated at the first full-party meeting called by Feoktistov.[175] In October and November *Latgal'skaya Pravda* developed a campaign about the poor quality of bread and the length of the bread queues.[176]

In a major reversal of policy it was announced on 10 December 1944 that the Teachers' Institute was being re-established in Daugavpils. In 1940 the communists had closed the Daugavpils Teachers' Institute and transferred both staff and students to Rēzekne. The staff and students from what now became the former Rēzekne Teachers' Institute were to be relocated to Daugavpils and reorganised into three faculties, with parallel two-year teacher-training courses taught in Latvian and Russian. At the time of its formation it was predicted that the institute would become a centre for Latgale cultural life.[177] Over the years this would indeed be the case, but the institute scarcely functioned in 1944–5; the shortage of glass meant that its building had paper, not glass, in the windows.[178] However, over summer 1945 it recruited for a normal intake for September,[179] and in mid-January

1946 its premises were extended;[180] in February 1946 it was announced that the institute would be upgraded into a Pedagogical Institute, with four years of study.[181] Nevertheless rumours persisted among the staff that they might yet all be moved back to Rēzekne.[182]

The restoration of that great cultural edifice the People's House stretched well into 1946. On 11 October 1944 the party resolved to have a special 'Sunday' of voluntary work to clear away the collapsed sections of the building.[183] By the end of November the concert hall had been restored and the decision was taken to restore its shop, 16 of its hotel rooms and the whole of the third floor.[184] On 3 December it was the target of another 'Sunday',[185] but in January 1945 progress slowed when burst pipes damaged some of the restoration work already done.[186] Progress in 1945 was piecemeal, and a meeting in January 1946 heard that, while many parts of the building were nearing completion, little had been fully restored. The meeting resolved that work on the hotel should be completed by mid-February, as should work on the Turkish baths and the swimming pool; the theatre would be ready in August and the whole building by October 1946. Much of the labour for this phase of the project would be carried out by German POWs, the meeting was informed,[187] and it was perhaps as a result of this use of forced labour that in August 1946 it was reported that work on restoring the theatre had been unsatisfactory.[188] Nevertheless, the continuing repair work did not prevent the concert hall being used as a venue for political and cultural events from November 1944 onwards.

7 The nationalist partisan war

Back in spring 1944 the leaders of the Soviet partisans fighting the German and Latvian security forces had expressed concern that, near Rēzekne and Daugavpils, armed groups of nationalist partisans were in the process of formation. By the end of 1944 operations by these nationalist partisans were beginning to disrupt the work of the Soviet authorities. At first the party leadership tried to play down the extent of this unrest, but during the winter of 1944–5 there were several incidents which could not be passed over in silence. The authorities' first response was a propaganda campaign linking the nationalist partisans to German collaborators, but this had little effect; and so in April 1945 the party met to reassess the security situation. This meeting brought to an end nine months of tension between district party secretaries and the security forces, and evolved a twin-track policy for confronting the nationalist partisans. First, the brunt of the so-called 'anti-bandit' struggle would be borne by locally led 'destroyer battalions', whose activities would be jointly co-ordinated by the party and the security services. Second, propaganda efforts would concentrate on encouraging defections by the nationalist partisans, making it important to portray them as misguided rather than malign.

Even as the party introduced its coping strategy, the situation got dramatically worse. In Abrene, Rēzekne, Ludza and Ilūkste the nationalist partisan movement was growing, and in Daugavpils district places as far afield as Asūne and Rudzāti were effectively in 'bandit' hands. When the Daugavpils district committee met on 18 June 1945 there were signs of panic. Yet the international situation was beginning to undermine the cause of the nationalist partisans. Both Britain's public stance, and the work of its intelligence agents, encouraged the notion that the future of Latvia would be decided as party of an overall post-war settlement. This led the nationalist partisans to think they had everything to play for, until events at the Potsdam Conference made clear that the future of the Baltic States was not really on the Allied agenda. During autumn 1945 the policy of encouraging surrender seemed to be working. The biggest partisan group, the United Defenders of the Fatherland (Partisans of Latvia), was gradually undermined by defections, which reached a peak when the group's leader abandoned the forest.

These defections seemed to reflect tension within the nationalist partisan movement concerning the nature of the democratic state they claimed to be fighting for.

At the same time as the Daugavpils authorities were persuading some nationalist partisans to leave the forest, they were providing more recruits for the movement by the brutal way they enforced the policy of compulsory agricultural deliveries. When show trials did not work, it was decided that the time had come to cease being 'liberal with the kulaks'. Force was to be used, and in the area surrounding the small town of Preiļi this degenerated into a reign of terror. Later investigation revealed that it was local officials who had set the tome for such actions. Similarly, the action of local security officials called into question the government's whole strategy of developing a policy of surrender among the nationalist partisans. The arrest of partisans who had already surrendered under the terms of the government's amnesty contradicted the essence of the tactic, ensuring that the nationalist partisan movement would revive in 1946.

Early actions

The first groups of nationalist partisans were formed spontaneously as the Red Army arrived. Preiļi had been the scene of particular brutality against the Jews in 1941, and those Latvians linked to the terror there had reportedly taken to the forests as the Red Army arrived, where they were joined by some of those who had fought in police units or with the Latvian Legion. Fearing retribution, some Latvians were reported to have spent up to 1,000 Reichsmarks buying pistols from the retreating Germans. Groups such as these spread rumours that the Red Army would not be in the country for long. Either the Germans would hold a line further west on the Dvina, or the English and Swedes would arrive. Troops belonging to Soviet military intelligence were the first to be sent to confront such groups.[1] During September 1944 mobilisation into the Red Army swelled the ranks of these forest dwellers; desertions from the Red Army were often mass in character, with whole families following the men in to the forests.[2]

Optimism that the activities of the nationalist partisans would be quickly curbed was soon dented. Addressing the 6th Central Committee Plenum on 16–18 November 1944 Kalnbērziņš played down the issue. He noted two bands operating near Daugavpils, one led by a former policeman, but put their membership at only six and ten respectively; he mentioned four other groups operating further afield than Daugavpils, but stressed that none was bigger than twenty strong.[3] Events tended to belie this. On 29 November at Rudzāti, on the road between Līvāni and Preiļi, the local komsomol secretary was killed; this followed an incident nearby earlier in the month when three youths had been shot at and one killed.[4] In the light of this attack the district committee discussed a report on the need to improve the work of the Daugavpils destroyer battalion, commanded by Police Major Griekis. The report was compiled jointly by the Daugavpils security chief Titov and Ivan Myzykantik, now a district-party instructor but better known as a partisan commander in 1943–4.[5]

By the end of November 1944 the party was far less sanguine than Kalnbērziņš had been in the middle of the month. A report showed that Ilūkste and Abrene were the worst-affected areas, followed next by Daugavpils and then Ludza. These groups were small (the largest involved twenty) and lightly armed – some had light machine-guns; almost universally they were said to be led by former policemen.[6] By mid-December another report showed that 34 bandit groups had been formed since the arrival of the Red Army, with a total membership of 346: of these, 21 groups had been liquidated, involving the detention or arrest of 222 people, which left 13 groups still active, with a membership of 124; two-thirds of the incidents were concentrated in Abrene, Ilūkste and Daugavpils districts.[7] Early actions included setting light to a Russian school and torching grain collection points. However, from the start, the nationalist partisans attacked not only the symbols of the new regime but its personnel; a grenade attack on the farm of a Soviet sympathiser on 6 November 1944 resulted in the death of an eight-year-old child.[8]

As the authorities pushed ahead with the land reform in December 1944 and January 1945, some particularly nasty incidents occurred. Between 10 and 14 December 1944 there were two violent attacks on Soviet activists near Rēzekne; the activists were killed, but in both cases their wives were injured and in one case the 12- year-old daughter of one of the families was also killed. Then, on 20 December, in Aizkalne, in Daugavpils district, the sister of Luriņš, the chairman of the district soviet, was attacked: grenades were thrown into her house; a man died on the spot and Luriņš' sister later died of her wounds in hospital.[9] These three incidents made up the majority of the five actions accounted for in December as a whole; then in the first half of January 1945 there were a further 23 incidents.[10] In one of these, on 13 February 1945, the nationalist partisans succeeded in freeing from captivity some of their fellows held by the security forces after an earlier clash.[11] What alarmed the Soviet authorities most when such incidents were surveyed in February 1945 was that the nationalist partisans nearly always escaped; in all but a couple of the 26 incidents surveyed from September 1944 to January 1945 no arrests were made.[12] On top of that the situation seemed to be deteriorating, as the nationalist partisans undertook more ambitious actions. On the night of 6–7 February 1945, at Mērdzene, just north of Ludza, Donat Bazatskii led thirty men in an attack which involved the death of the local party organiser and the wrecking of the soviet buildings; although Bazatskii himself was one of the seven to die in the raid.[13] At the end of February one nationalist partisan group was reported as being 'seventy strong'.[14]

As part of the struggle against the nationalist partisans, the Soviet press was keen to link their activities to those of the *aizsargs* and the German collaborators. On 5 January 1945 *Latgal'skaya Pravda* carried an editorial on 'bourgeois nationalists' which stressed that it was not only Germans but Latvians too who had been involved in the massacres of Jews, communists and POWs. These '*aizsargs*', the editorial stressed, 'acting on the orders of their Hitlerite hosts, mercilessly killed not only Russians and Jews, but also Latvians themselves'. From January to May 1945 the theme of communist propaganda was that 'bourgeois nationalists' were directly involved in Nazi atrocities. Sometimes this was done in free-standing stories: on 6 January 1945 *Latgal'skaya Pravda* carried an article entitled 'Traitors' which told the story of two former *aizsargs* who had joined the police as soon as the German Army arrived and had then become involved in deporting Russian youngsters to Germany. However, more often the column 'We will never forget, nor will we forgive' was used to underscore Latvian involvement in the atrocities. Thus on 14 January the paper noted that a former Latvian Army officer who volunteered to become police chief in Aglona had been actively involved in the killings there, along with the seven former *aizsargs* he had recruited. A week later the paper stressed the involvement of the Latvian police in Līvāni in killing 'six hundred innocent people', and told how four former *aizsargs* had taken part in killings which took place not far away near Vārkava.[15] On 17 March the paper identified a Russian police chief responsible for killings which took place in Robežnieki, and on 13 April named seven Latvians responsible for the horrific killings in Preiļi. An eye-witness account by a survivor from the execution pits in Līvāni gave added veracity to these accounts,[16] as did the trial in Aglona on 13 May 1945 of a former policeman Butkevich on charges of complicity in the Aglona killings.[17]

As well as stressing the involvement of Latvian nationalist in the Nazi massacres, the press regularly returned to the deportations of Russians for forced labour in Germany. On 15 March 1945 *Latgal'skaya Pravda* reported how the village elder in Naujene had co-operated in selecting seventy people for deportation, and had been praised for his actions by Budže. The same story stressed the brutality of '*aizsarg* Budže' himself: he constantly abused the deportees, the article suggested, threatening them with the choice between death and hard labour; reportedly he ordered the hanging of one youngster who tried to escape. On 27 April the paper made essentially the same charge against the police chief in Krāslava: he had been involved in the deportation of 244 people from Krāslava and surrounding localities to Germany. While the charge against the Krāslava police chief and other officials could have been accurate, that made against Budže was unconvincing, since he had supported those parish elders who complained about the deportation of innocent Russians at this time.

These reports may have had an impact on public attitudes towards the nationalist partisans, but they did nothing to stop their activity. Just how daring the nationalist partisans could be became clear late in February 1945 when two Russian incomer officials were assassinated in the heart of

Daugavpils. Zoya Petrovich, the head of the agitation and propaganda department of the city committee, and Fedor Koshkin, brought in as a factory director, were walking back from a meeting in Daugavpils fortress and had almost reached the firemen's tower on the edge of the park when they were shot. The assassins then ran across the park and clambered up onto the flood embankment by the river Dvina and jumped onto a waiting lorry to make good their escape.[18] The funeral of Petrovich and Koshkin was reported on 24 February, together with an editorial which called for 'higher vigilance'.[19]

This assassination certainly had an impact. On 17 March a certain Junior Lieutenant Bodrak, then teaching at the Daugavpils Railway Technical College, was accompanying a group of recruits from Daugavpils by train, when he left his carriage to chat to fellow passengers. While the unsupervised recruits set off on a rampage of petty theft, Bodrak made a grandiloquent speech about how, in Daugavpils you walked along the street never knowing from what side of the road people would shoot at you next. Warming to his theme, he recalled how, when his unit had arrived in the area, local peasants had refused to feed them. In his view, both the parishes of Aglona and Biķernieki were run by anti-Soviet elements. The solution, he said, was to bomb every house in Latvia, since every house included at least one *aizsarg*; he would do it himself, he declaimed, but injury had forced him out of the air force.[20]

Bodrak exaggerated, but there were clear signs of unease in Daugavpils in early spring 1945. The local security services convinced themselves in March 1945 that a group of German parachutists had landed in the area and were seeking to set up a sabotage unit. Supposedly they intended to exploit the fact that the railway network was still largely administered by the same personnel who had run it during the German occupation.[21] This was simply paranoia, but a week later, a nationalist underground group was discovered in a local secondary school. The party resolved to try and defeat what it termed banditry 'before the spring, for it will be more complicated in the summer when they are based exclusively in the forests'.[22] With the police tied up in operations against nationalist partisans, ordinary crime grew apace. On 6 April it was decided that Daugavpils should have both a city as well as a district security department to cope with the rising incidents of hooliganism and murder.[23]

Planning a strategy

The party took stock of the situation at the start of April. From the very beginning there had been tension between the party district secretaries and the security services, in particular the People's Commissariat for Internal Affairs (NKVD). By December 1944 the NKVD had drawn up a list of 23,324 collaborators – policemen, *aizsargs* and town and parish elders – who needed to be arrested. These lists had been compiled on the basis of partisan reports, the debriefing of POWs and defectors, and a close reading of the German occupation press; as a result, many names were misspelled, or spelled in a variety of ways, which could easily result in misidentification. Of those on the list, 60 per cent had retreated with the Germans, leaving a target of 9,478 who had stayed behind; just over half of those who had stayed behind had been captured by December, leaving 4,564 still on the run.[24] As the NKVD worked methodically towards its target, it frequently trod on the toes of district-party secretaries. As early as the 5th Central Committee Plenum on 25–26 August this issue came up. The Ludza district secretary summed it up like this: 'you make enquiries and discover that during the occupation a certain citizen was linked to the partisans and seemed to be soviet in outlook; you allocate that citizen a job in the soviet administration, and a short time later the security organs arrive and discover that your 'Soviet man' is a German spy.'[25] Milda Birkenfelde echoed the point, stressing that finding reliable local cadres was already difficult enough; in her view the security organs needed to be more positive in their approach.[26] At the 6th Central Committee Plenum on 16–18 November 1944 the Valka district secretary, the former partisan leader Fricis Bergs, made a similar point: you tried to bring in the harvest with only 56 threshing machines for 22 parishes and suddenly the threshing-machine operator is arrested; 'perhaps he needed to be arrested, but the party committee and soviet needed to be warned in advance, so that a replacement operator could be found', he said.[27]

The Ilūkste district secretary was even less prepared to take the guidance of the security forces on the question of who was, and who was not, a security threat. In February 1945 he demanded to be provided with the evidence on which arrests were being made. When this was refused, he accused the security forces of arresting people according to control lists as in 1941, and therefore of arresting people for 'betraying the motherland' who were in fact innocent. Maintaining that arrests could not be carried out as they had been 'in 1937–8', he argued for a policy of the fewer arrests the better. He also challenged the basis for some of the charges that were made. He told the local prosecutor that 'if we were here, in occupied territory, we would have done the same thing in order to save ourselves'; in this context he was especially incensed by the arrest of a local komsomol activist, accused of betraying his komsomol organisation to the Germans.[28] He was also annoyed at the arrest in January 1945 of the man he had groomed to become chairman of the Ilūkste soviet on the charge that he had collaborated with the Gestapo in Ukraine.[29] Not surprisingly party leader Kalnbērziņš was quick to condemn all 'chatter about mistakes made in 1937–8'.[30]

Such incidents made party secretaries unwilling to become involved in security matters, and as the campaign by the nationalist partisans got under way, most party secretaries preferred to see the anti-partisan struggle as a purely security issue. Party organisations were happy to keep their distance and continued to stay on the sidelines until April 1945. The initial method of struggle against these nationalist 'bandits' ignored local activists completely and centred on staging comparatively large-scale military operations to clear the forests. This policy proved quite ineffective.[31] And so on 2 April 1945 a meeting was held to address the issue of tension between the district parties and the security services and to evolve a strategy whereby the two would work close together. Kalnbērziņš told the district-party secretaries that, henceforth, the local party had to be more actively involved in the struggle against the nationalist partisans, because, more often than not, the security services were unable to speak Latvian, did not know where best to concentrate their forces and were uncertain of the people and of the terrain. The security forces had not always recognised this failing, he explained, and there had been occasions when good local advice had been ignored by security officers who thought they knew better. The way forward was to make the most of local knowledge and develop the destroyer battalions as genuinely local, and genuinely responsible, front-line troops in the counter-insurgency campaign.[32]

This April meeting also agreed that the boosting of the destroyer battalions should be accompanied with an intensified political struggle against the nationalist partisans. Earlier, at the end of March 1945, the party had approached the Catholic Church hierarchy about calling on the nationalist partisans to leave the forests around Ludza, but the bishops had insisted this call should be accompanied by the issuing of an amnesty.[33] Kalnbērziņš was not yet ready to call an amnesty, at least not as a blanket policy, but he did urge the party to work with the families of nationalist partisans, offering alternately the carrot and the stick. The families of nationalist partisans should be told no harm would come to those who surrendered; but equally they should be informed that if they did not encourage their menfolk to surrender, then they could be arrested as 'bandit helpers'. When this process worked, and the nationalist partisans did leave the forest, Kalnbērziņš insisted that they should not be arrested; the promise given should be kept, for 'our organs must not appear to be deceitful', he said.[34]

Meeting on 16 April 1945 the Central Committee resolved to push ahead with the strategy of developing the destroyer battalions by turning them into a well-armed and mobile force, as well as by trying to involve in them more of those who had benefited from the Soviet regime or had relevant experience, like the former Soviet partisans.[35] Six weeks later the Central Committee took this idea one step further and decided, on 28 May, to form a special 'anti-bandit detachment' linked to the Central Committee's military department. This would be made up from one hundred former partisans and led by Laiviņš and Oškalns. The plan was that it would by highly mobile, with five lorries, three cars and two motor cycles, and armed with four rocket launchers, 85 machine guns and 15 pistols.[36] Next, to ensure proper co-ordination between the NKVD and the party, the Central Committee decided on 8 June 1945 to set up a special staff to help the

NKVD administer the destroyer battalions; a week later it instructed every party district to establish a similar staff, so that the local party secretary, the local soviet chairman, the local representative of the NKVD and the local destroyer battalion commander all met regularly and took on board that the destroyer battalions were in the front line in the 'anti-bandit' struggle. When the programme was complete, every parish would have destroyer battalion units of 20–50 men and every village units from 5–15.[37]

As to encouraging the nationalist partisans to surrender, the other aspect of this dual approach, a sharp distinction was drawn between leaders and led. The meeting of 2 April had heard Moscow's representative take precisely this line: many nationalist partisans, he argued, were simply people who had accepted 'German propaganda about Siberia'. They could not be treated in the same was as 'bandit leaders'.[38] As part of the programme of working with 'bandit' families, the Central Committee drafted a document which was to be discussed by all those with family members in the forests. This made clear that Latvians had been right 'to overthrow the plutocrats' and join the Soviet Union in 1940; nothing would change that. Rumours about the imminent arrival of the English and the Swedes were nonsense, as was the notion that the Latvians were to be exiled to Siberia. Such rumours were the work 'of those responsible for the shootings at Mežciems' and other execution sites in Latvia. However, most nationalist partisans were not such people but draft dodgers, rank-and- file members of the Latvian Legion or ordinary policemen and *aizsargs*, none of whom needed to fear the authorities. Having separated the leaders from the led, the document called on all rank-and-file nationalist partisans to leave the forests and resume their everyday life; they would be left in peace. However, the Central Committee made clear that families were also to be reminded verbally that this document represented a final warning; if the 'bandits' did not respond by putting down their arms, they would be considered traitors and those family members who helped them strictly punished.[39] The logic of this approach was that the press would no longer portray the nationalist partisans as malign, but simply as misguided.

The summer war

As the party was evolving its strategy for confronting the nationalist partisans, the situation on the ground was deteriorating. At the end of May things were worst in Abrene district, well to the north of Daugavpils. There 30 per cent of the village soviets were said to be out of operation because of nationalist partisan activity; every day there was an attack of some kind and the poorly armed destroyer battalions were unable to cope.[40] In addition, rumours abounded of an attack on the district town, Viļaka, and many junior soviet personnel were too terrified to work since they were unarmed and all the roads leading from the town were controlled by 'bandits'; this meant that for several days the post could not get through.[41] The situation in Rēzekne was said to be improving, after a number of assaults on village soviets early in May. Here the authorities not only worked with the families of nationalist partisans but, in the worst-affected areas, arrested those families when they did not co-operate. As a result, over one hundred nationalist partisans had been persuaded to surrender.[42]

As to Ludza, the situation there was mixed. It was serious in the three-quarters of the district with a Latvian population, but the authorities still felt things were under control, and in August a significant group of nationalist partisans did indeed leave the forests voluntarily, in spite of some heavy-handed behaviour by the destroyer battalions.[43] In Ilūkste district, just across the Dvina from Daugavpils, the situation was dire. In June 1945 and the first ten days of July 32 soviet activists were killed and 15 injured: normal soviet administration was paralysed in ten parishes; 15 milk points were inoperative, as were two horse hiring bases; two village soviets had been wrecked, and five were no longer working because their members had been terrorised; and three shops and one parish soviet building had been destroyed. There were six nationalist partisan groups operating, about 500 men in all, and they were better armed than the destroyer battalions charged with confronting them. The failure to arrest and isolate those families which most overtly helped the partisans made the authorities appear powerless.[44]

The situation in Daugavpils district in May 1945 did not inspire confidence. An NKVD report dated 22 May noted that the incidence of 'bandit' activity had 'increased sharply' with several incidents of killings and burnings. The victims were members of the destroyer battalions and village activists such as village soviet chairmen or party organisers; one named victim was Livdāns, a Latvian but the communist organiser in Aglona. However, it was Asūne and Rudzāti, at either extreme of Daugavpils district, where the situation was worst. In Asūne ten horses had been stolen from the horse-hiring base and the local destroyer battalions had not been able to respond. The report on this incident called for Major Griekis, the commander of the Daugavpils destroyer battalion, to be sacked and painted a grim picture of the 'anti-bandit' struggle. The destroyer battalion fighters in Daugavpils district were poorly armed, they still did not have machine-guns, and did not understand the politics of their mission; although each battalion had a deputy commander supposedly responsible for political education, no such education took place. The battalion needed to be strengthened to the point where it had 50 to 70 members in each parish, while all party and soviet activists needed to be provided with hand-guns. Little work was being done to win over the families of the nationalist partisans, since there was no newspaper in the Latgale language and *Latgal'skaya Pravda* never discussed the campaign of voluntary surrender.[45]

Other reports confirmed this picture: in May the Asūne machine-tractor station was relocated to Indra where it was less likely to be attacked,[46] and at the same time it was reported that the post of parish soviet chairman in Preiļi was vacant[47] as a result of the incumbent going over to the nationalist partisans.[48] District-party secretary Nikonov tried to put a positive gloss on a difficult situation when he addressed the 8th Central Committee Plenum on 13 June 1945: well-targeted military operations linked to propaganda work were bringing results and would ultimately bring success, he stressed. However, for this to happen throughout the district, the destroyer battalions needed better arms and propagandists needed literature in Latgalean. In Asūne, an area which he said was particularly badly affected by banditry, people were beginning to report nationalist partisan activity, and the nationalist partisans themselves were beginning to surrender.[49]

However, when the district committee met a few days later on 18 June it was to hear how the party organiser for Vārkava parish, A. I. Avgutsevich, and a colleague from the organisation which oversaw compulsory agricultural deliveries, had been killed while cycling from Vārkava to a local village soviet in order to hold a meeting with peasants; they were killed by a machine-gun. The meeting put this latest incident into the context of other incidents near Vārkava, Līvāni, Kalupe, Rudzāti and Nīcgale, incidents which included the destruction of telephone lines. The district committee recognised that in these areas the nationalist partisans controlled certain forests and appeared openly on certain roads. At the same time the destroyer battalions had proved unable to capitalise on the recent destruction of a nationalist partisan group near Asūne and simply sat around 'waiting for banditry to resume'. The committee therefore resolved to establish 'under the direct control of the district staff for the struggle against banditry' a 'destroyer battalion of special designation' to be made up from former partisans, former Red Army men, the best of the destroyer battalion volunteers and the komosmol.

This unit was to be headed by the former partisan commander Savitskii and its members would be chosen by a special commission comprising Savitskii, Avdyukevich, cadre secretary of the district committee who also had a partisan background, and commander Pipo, who had replaced Griekis as the man in charge of the Daugavpils destroyer battalion. The district committee circulated a list of former partisans whom it hoped to incorporate into the unit, and made clear that those who volunteered to join it would have special rights; they would continue to be paid by their existing employers, who were obliged to hold their jobs open for them until the unit had completed its task. As a sign of the unit's significance, it was assigned a lorry to ensure its mobility.[50] Among the five former partisans transferred from the city party to the district party for a two-month spell of fighting 'bandits' was komsomol first secretary Shkrabo, who had fought with the Soviet partisans from 1943.[51] Later in the year another former leading partisan would be brought into active struggle against the 'bandits'; Muzykantik was moved from being a cadre instructor within the district party to deputy commander for political work of the destroyer battalion.[52]

There were moments in summer 1945 when the situation seemed to be slipping out of control. At the start of July, Nikonov criticised his comrades in the city committee for not offering more support at a time when the district needed all the help it could in the struggle against 'banditry'.[53] When the district committee held a general meeting on 28 June to discuss the situation, there were some acrimonious exchanges. The party organiser for Nīcgale took the occasion to criticise the support given by the NKVD. He described an incident near Nīcgale, where, in a clash with nationalist partisans, a local party activist was wounded. When the NKVD was asked to send a car to take the wounded man to hospital, the NKVD refused, to the fury of the local activists and their comrades in the destroyer battalion. However, the party organiser for Nīcgale had hardly sat down after making this statement before he was accused of cowardice. Lyudmilla Bogdanovich, the district komosmol secretary, took great glee in telling delegates that when she had been in Nīcgale, the same party organiser had sent her, a young woman, on political work into the most dangerous villages, while he fled to the safety of Daugavpils. However, she too attacked the NKVD, for it had also refused to accompany her on her mission.

As the meeting went on, more tales of nationalist partisan activity were rehearsed. The head of the railway administration told how he had sent fifty men to the forests to cut wood and only three had returned. The Preiļi party organiser, Ivan Ivanov, reminded those at the meeting that his parish soviet chairman had gone over to the bandits and complained that his destroyer battalion was supplied with broken rifles and the wrong ammunition; cigarettes and porridge were also in short supply. Ivanov rejected the talk of cowardice which was still being bandied about, but said he would refuse to fight the 'bandits' unless help and support were provided. The representative of the city committee at this meeting was scarcely exaggerating when he stated: 'it has to be said, that in the parishes one can feel confusion, a fear of banditism.' This notion was dismissed out of hand by the local NKVD chief Titov. He stressed that while there was no reason to relax, there was equally no need to panic. He conceded that in places like Asūne apparently innocent people worked by day and turned to 'banditry' by night, but what the panicky party organisers did not realise was that the political agenda of the bandits was disintegrating. 'In their propaganda the bandits place great hopes on the issue of Poland and their expectation that the Polish question will not be resolved, thus giving rise to a new war and nonsense of this sort. Their hopes are now dashed.'[54]

The nationalist partisan agenda

Titov was premature in making this judgement, but ultimately his perceptions were not misplaced. What were the ambitions of the nationalist partisans? While the Second World War was still under way, the nationalist partisans issued propaganda that could easily be dismissed as pro-German. In April 1945 issue number four of *The Sword*, one of the two illegal papers circulating at this time, called for the 'national army', fighting in Kurzeme, to be preserved. This was a reference to the Latvian Legion, still fighting alongside the German Army until the surrender in early May. The 'holy task of our green partisans', the paper stressed, was to help that army. Conceding that in 1905 the Latvians had once been attracted to the ideas of socialism, the lesson of 1940–1 made clear that socialism was a disaster, the paper asserted. The Soviet militiamen and *Chekists* should be resisted because Soviet rule 'will not last long; everything will be decided by the summer'. The *Sword* made no mention of the western allies.[55]

However, the height of the nationalist partisan campaign came not while the Second World War was still under way and the Latvian Legion was fighting side by side with the German Army, but once the war was over, in late May, June and July. It was predicated not on any idea of German victory, or that the Latvian Legion might have a role to play in Latvia's future, but on the expectation that, as the peace settlement was negotiated, the western allies would take up Latvia's cause. In Ilūkste district nationalist partisans were spreading rumours in July that, because of its war debts to America and Britain, the Soviet Union would be forced to surrender the Baltic States to the western allies, who then intended to restore their independence.[56] It was quite logical to expect that, when the map of Europe was redrafted, borders would be restored to their 1939 positions rather than those of 1940. It was precisely this suggestion that the Soviet authorities sought to rubbish in their counter-propaganda. It had been a theme of the document drafted at the end of May for discussion with the families of nationalist partisans, and it became the theme of the summer's press campaign. Thus at the start of June an editorial in *Latgal'skaya Pravda* noted. 'They are trying to terrorise the population in some parishes of our district... spreading rumours of how the English and the Swedes support their bandit activity, and that Soviet power will exile the Latvians to Siberia.'[57]

The claim of nationalist partisans to be acting in the interests of the British was not entirely without foundation. There was no support from on high. Although Churchill had not been party to Roosevelt's nod and a wink to Stalin at the Tehran Conference about the future of the Baltic States, he had come to a similar conclusion. On 16 January 1944 he wrote to the British Foreign Secretary explaining that a combination of the 'deep-seated changes which have taken place in the character of the Russian state and government' and the fact that the Red Army would soon occupy the Baltic States had changed his feelings on this matter. Two days later he circulated a memo to his entire War Cabinet explaining that his views on the Baltic States had changed and suggesting it was time to discuss their future. A draft minute of the discussion held on 20 January summarised the rather shoddy compromise which was reached. The British public stance would remain what it had been since 1941: formal and public recognition that the Baltic States were part of the Soviet Union could only be agreed as part of the overall peace settlement with Germany and the other Axis powers.

However, in private 'we could assure Stalin that we had no intention of disputing the Soviet claims, but explain our difficulties and warn him in advance of our intention to go on saying that these territorial matters were all for final settlement at the Peace Conference'.[58] Initially, the British government had even assumed that, once a peace settlement was reached, it would both recognise the 1940 Soviet borders and recognise the government of Soviet Latvia as an autonomous administration. However, it dropped the latter idea after a British diplomat toured Riga in October 1945 and concluded that all talk of Latvian autonomy was a sham.[59]

This deliberately ambiguous position allowed other sections of the British establishment to suggest to Latvia's nationalist partisans that, at least until a peace treaty with Germany were signed, there was everything to play for. In August 1943 several Latvian political activists, with links going back to the days of the parliamentary republic, established in Riga the so-called Latvian National Council which committed a future independent Latvia to the principles of the Atlantic Charter. The council sent representatives to Sweden, where late in 1943 they made contact with a British intelligence officer and, for a while, radio contact between Sweden and Riga was established. These contacts were built on the basis of personal contacts and networks which had been developed during the inter-war years, when the British government had an intelligence-gathering centre in Riga which monitored developments in the Soviet Union and which inevitably had close contacts with the Latvian Foreign Ministry.

British intelligence showed no great haste in communicating the political agenda of the Latvian National Council to London – it was only received by the Foreign Office in June 1944[60] – but it did see the espionage potential offered by the Baltic States for running intelligence operations against the Soviet Union. This became a real issue in February 1945 when the British Government decided that spying on its war-time Soviet ally should resume. The espionage network thus established was quickly penetrated by the Soviet security service, for the first agent sent to Latvia during autumn 1945 was intercepted and from spring 1946 British intelligence was dealing not with genuine nationalist partisans but with Soviet double agents. However, it would be another year before the Soviets moved from monitoring these contacts to counteracting them, and in summer 1945 the rather tenuous links between the nationalist partisans and the British were genuine enough.[61] By December 1945 the nationalist partisans fighting in the forests around the Dvina were in contact with people who were in touch through intermediaries with British agents. On 7 December 1945 the ruling body of the biggest partisan organisation in Latgale 'examined closely the reports received from the English secret services'.[62]

To counter such moves the communist authorities constantly stressed that the international situation was actually calm. In the first half of August 1945 the party organised meetings of both the city and district party organisations to discuss what had been agreed at the Potsdam

Conference between Stalin, Attlee and Truman.[63] Responding towards the end of August to nationalist partisan incidents near Vārkava and Kalupe, *Latgal'skaya Pravda* stressed 'relations between the USSR and England have never been stronger or firmer than now' and any assertion to the contrary was a silly rumour.[64] At the beginning of the summer, and towards its end, *Latgal'skaya Pravda* made the position absolutely clear. It wrote towards the end of May: 'These Judases have not yet abandoned the notion of Latvian 'independence'. They stoop to the very lowest level to turn back the clock of history. The Latvian people decided its own fate. It joined the great Soviet family of nations as an equal member, and there is no force on earth that can change this. Soviet power has not been established in Latvia temporarily, but for ever; such is the will of the Latvian people.'[65] Towards the end of August it made precisely the same point. 'Soviet power in Latvia was established by the will of the Latvian people themselves, established for ever. There will never be a return to bourgeois Latvia!'[66]

The United Defenders of the Fatherland

The biggest nationalist partisan organisation in the Daugavpils area, the one which 'examined closely the reports received from the English secret service' in December 1945, was the United Defenders of the Fatherland (Partisans of Latvia). This was the key development of the spring and early summer, after Germany's defeat: the scattered groups of nationalist partisan bands linked together into large-scale organisations. The United Defenders of the Fatherland (Partisans of Latvia) co-ordinated activity in most of eastern Latvia, not only in Latgale proper, but in Ilūkste and Madona districts as well. The authorities became aware of the extent of its operations after chance arrests in August and September 1945. Its base was near Līvāni and the meeting which adopted its statutes was held in July in the Russian Marsh near Jersika, ironically the same place which served as the base in 1942 for Nikiforov and one of the first Soviet partisan groups to be formed near Daugavpils. The United Defenders of the Fatherland (Partisans of Latvia) was led by the former Roman Catholic deacon of Vanagi, Antons Juhnēvičs; he headed the ruling presidium, whose secretary was Jānis Zelčāns, the author of the founding statutes.[67] Other members of the presidium, formally established on 24–26 August 1945, were Kārlis Blūms, Juris Rudzas and Arvids Puids.[68] By this time meetings were being held in the forest near Vārkava, where further meetings were held on 29 August and 27 September.[69] In September 1945 the United Defenders of the Fatherland (Partisans of Latvia) brought together the various nationalist partisan groups operating in the area and designated them its 2nd Division at a meeting held near Jersika.[70] The chief of staff of the 2nd Division was Zelčāns and its adjutant Puids;[71] the commander of the 2nd Division was Blūms.[71]

The 2nd Division was just part of the complex structure envisioned by the organisation's statutes, which borrowed much from the structure of the inter-war Latvian Army.[72] Thus on 17 November 1945 Soviet military intelligence reported the arrest of 'bandits' belonging to the 1st, 2nd and 3rd companies of the 3rd battalion of the 5th partisan regiment of the 2nd Latgale partisan division.[73] However, the United Defenders of the Fatherland (Partisans of Latvia) were not in fact as strong as this rather grandiose structure suggested. The NKVD managed to dislocate its activities quite successfully. In late summer and autumn 1945 the Soviet authorities tried to perfect their strategy of encouraging nationalist partisans to surrender by penetrating the 'bandit' groups. One initiative taken at the end of August 1945 was to establish small intelligence-gathering units to prepare the ground for the twin strategy of liquidation and surrender. Seven such units, numbering three to four members each, were established in Daugavpils district in Līvāni, Nīcgale, Preiļi, Krāslava, Asūne, Ezernieķi and Silajāņi. This was a pilot, which, if successful, would be followed elsewhere in the country.[74] It did seem to succeed.

By September 1945 the authorities had decided that individual approaches to bandits and individual offers of amnesty were not having the desired effect. A general amnesty would be offered instead. On 22 August *Latgal'skaya Pravda* appealed to those rank-and-file legionaries, rank-and-file *aizsargs* and rank-and-file policemen who had joined the bandits, along with the deserters from the Red Army, to join their many comrades who were already leaving the forest. Those who surrendered would not be repressed, the paper stressed. To make the promise of an amnesty absolutely clear, on 12 September 1945 the national Communist Party daily *Cīņa* published a statement by the head of the NKVD promising that all those bandits who legalised themselves and surrendered their weapons would face no punishment.[75] This was repeated in *Latgal'skaya Pravda* on 16 September.

There then followed a whole string of press reports about nationalist partisans who had decided to surrender. On 19 September a former nationalist partisan from Preiļi wrote how he had been 'deceived' by his 'bandit' comrades and had left the forest. His call was echoed by another Preiļi nationalist partisan Francis Pastors, who had been living rough for over a year.[76] On 23 September in Asūne 18 nationalist partisans surrendered and appealed to others to do the same;[77] on 18 October an appeal to 'leave the forest' was made by 15 former nationalist partisans from Kalupe;[78] and on 30 October a similar appeal 'to those still hiding' was made by 39 former nationalist partisans from Rudzāti.[79] When necessary, important party leaders were prepared to be associated with such surrenders. Thus on 17 September 97 nationalist partisans from Krāslava surrendered in person to district-party secretary Nikonov.[80] These occasions were carefully stage-managed, with all those who surrendered making similar statements of contrition. Nevertheless, they appear to have had an impact.

By the end of October other successes in the 'anti-bandit' struggle could be reported. A report written on 5 October 1945 noted 281 recent surrenders nationwide,[81] and at the end of October the surrender of the 'bandit leader' Antons Zutis was given great coverage in *Cīņa* when he agreed to publish a letter explaining the reasons for his move.[82] Zutis had been based near Ludza. Under Ulmanis he had been an *aizsarg*, but although hostile to the establishment of Soviet power in 1940 he had not actively opposed it. When the Germans came in 1941 he put himself forward to work in his local parish administration. Fearing he would be arrested by the Red Army in summer 1944 he had fled to the forest. There he had been joined by others and established a band of nationalist partisans which began to operate in the spring. He had first argued that the Germans would return, then that the western democracies would intervene, but he came to realise by the autumn that he had fooled himself; he surrendered on 24 October, calling on others to do the same.[83]

It would be wrong to exaggerate the degree of Soviet success at this time. When both the city and district parties reviewed the struggle against the nationalist partisans during the autumn, it was agreed that the situation was still difficult. It was worst in Asūne, where the parish soviet had been attacked and where, in nearby Dagda, the former director of the agricultural college had been actively recruiting anti-Soviet forces.[84] However 30 nationalist partisans from Asūne had been persuaded to surrender,[85] and by the end of the year a further 127 were reported to have given themselves up. All the village soviets in Asūne parish were also said to be in operation again by the end of the year,[86] although for the best part of the year three village soviets had simply not operated.[87] The other black spot continued to be Preiļi 'where for an extended period a number of village soviets did not operate'.[88]

Nationalist partisans were surrendering rather than being militarily defeated, for the picture concerning the destroyer battalions in Daugavpils district was mixed: the Kalupe battalion was the best, but in Asūne, Robežnieki and Indra the battalions had collapsed, while there was reason to believe that the Līvāni battalion had been penetrated by the nationalist partisans, and the same was true in nearby Rudzāti. This 'infection' of Soviet cadres was widespread. In Kalupe a former policeman and the brother of an active nationalist partisan was working in the local horse-hiring base, even though the Preiļi machine-tractor station, which oversaw the work of the Kalupe horse-hiring base, was aware of the man's police past.[89] The chairman of the Dviete parish soviet in Ilūkste district, A. Krapāns, was an active supporter of the nationalist partisans and had helped to hide them and protect their farms and cattle since October 1944. He had connived at an attack on the parish soviet offices and his son, who worked for the local agricultural co-operative, had let them plunder its shop. Near Rēzekne several parish soviets were also reported to be 'widely infected' by nationalist elements, some of whom were in touch with 'bandits'.[90]

Yet the surrender policy advanced by the authorities did make progress. Between September and December 1945 some key surrenders had a dramatic impact on the United Defenders of the Fatherland (Partisans of Latvia). An important moment came in early November when counter-intelligence officers working for the Red Army's Latvian Division managed to persuade 14 members of the group to surrender, including a certain Stanislavs Lācis. On 7 November Sergeant Fokt of the Latvian Division made contact with the 14 and gathered them together at the farm owned by Lācis near the village of Turki in Līvāni parish; they brought with them six rifles, two grenades and 60 rounds of ammunition, and gave details of where their heavy machine-gun was hidden. This surrender was an important step in the dismantling of the United Defenders of the Fatherland (Partisans of Latvia), for among those involved was Arvīds Puids, adjutant of the 2nd Division, and evidence gained after his interrogation enabled the security forces from Daugavpils to make further arrests. By 1 January 1946 a total of 68 people were in detention, 22 of them alleged 'bandits' and 46 alleged 'bandit supporters', those who had been providing the nationalist partisans with supplies and information.[91] These surrenders forced significant changes on how the United Defenders of the Fatherland (Partisans of Latvia) operated. On 11 November the 2nd Division was asked to take control of the regiments operating in Ilūkste and Jēkabpils as well as Daugavpils.[92] On 1 December the presidium was forced to meet some distance from Preiļi and even further from Daugavpils, in Meirāni, south-west of Lubāna.[93] More surrenders soon followed. An NKVD officer made contact with Stanislavs Urbāns, the Ilūkste regimental commander.[94] He agreed to call on his men to surrender and 100 men left the forest with him on 19 December.[95]

Without a doubt the most significant surrender was that of Juhnēvičs himself. When the presidium of the United Defenders of the Fatherland (Partisans of Latvia) met on 11 November it noted that Juhnēvičs had either disappeared or gone into hiding; in fact he had already begun preliminary contacts with the national leadership of the NKVD.[96] After a meeting between Juhnēvičs and the commissar for internal affairs himself, held on the Līvāni to Līksna road on 10 January 1946, Juhnēvičs agreed to surrender to the Daugavpils NKVD.[97] He then issued a public statement on 1 February 1945 to the effect that he had left the forest and called on all those who had been members of the United Defenders of the Fatherland (Partisans of Latvia) to do the same. He confessed that he had actively supported the Germans, had gone underground in January 1945 and from 24 August had played an active role in the United Defenders of the Fatherland (Partisans of Latvia), serving as its chairman until 5 October. He then called on his former fellow commanders to recognise that, with his surrender, the organisation had been closed down. He reassured them that he was at liberty and had resumed his pastoral work for the Catholic Church.[98]

Collapse then followed. At the end of February 1946 it was reported that the 5th Rēzekne Regiment of the Union for the Defence of the Fatherland (Partisans of Latvia), its staff and its units, which owed allegiance to the 2nd Daugavpils Division, had been wound up: 15 had been killed; 23 arrested and 79 legalised themselves. Among those arrested was Jānis Mateisons, known as 'Dadzis', who had served with the German police in Daugavpils.[99] However, the commander in the Rēzekne area, Stanislavs Strods, escaped.[100] Shortly afterwards Blūms, the commander of the 2nd Divisions, and the commanders of the Daugavpils and Jēkabpils regiments, were killed. As the historian of the national partisan movement, Heinrihs Strods, has noted, the nationalist partisans were destroyed as a centralised organisation before the first half of 1946.[101]

Why was it that Juhnēvičs surrendered? The Soviet military-intelligence report of August 1944 had noted the distinction between pro-German 'kulak' farmers and the 'better off' farmers, who were potentially more friendly to Russia. The impact of the land reform had been to push these groups together, and the defeat of Germany, coupled with the apparent British support for an independent Latvia, had cemented this alliance. The accepted aim of the United Defenders of the Fatherland (Partisans of Latvia) was to restore Latvia's parliamentary republic with the help of western democracies, a programme around which both elements could unite.[102] Soviet propaganda always liked to portray the nationalist partisans as being led by those 'who had been at Mežciems', but Juhnēvičs was a deacon of the Catholic Church. Yet did tension remain between those with a more pro-German orientation and those with a clearly western one? Although the United Defenders of the Fatherland (Partisans of Latvia) were committed to parliamentary government, the statutes adopted on 5 October reflected a certain ambiguity. Their main demand was for a nationally independent Latvia and they repeatedly invoked God, the fatherland and the long struggle against the 'Red Dragon of Bolshevism' since the foundation of the Latvian Republic in November 1918. However, when comparing the Hitler and Stalin regimes, the statutes characterised the Hitler regime as human and the current Stalinist regime as that of a red monster reducing people to slavery.[103] Hyperbolic criticism of Stalin was one thing, but could those who had lived through the Holocaust in such places as Daugavpils, Preiļi or Ludza really be satisfied with the assessment that Hitler's regime was human? Did this not imply a brutal understanding of the idea 'Latvia for the Latvians'? Hitler had killed the Latvian Jews and deported the Latvian Russians, but been humane to the Latvians themselves. Could good Catholics endorse such a policy?

Juhnēvičs made clear in his public statement of 1 February 1945 that he had been involved in the United Defenders of the Fatherland (Partisans of Latvia) since 24 August, implying he was not at the July meeting that had adopted the statutes. He was, however, present on 5 October when the statutes were debated,[104] and it was at this same meeting that he considered his role as president came to an end.[105] Was he uncomfortable with the more pro-German elements in his movement? The nationalist partisans continued to refer to themselves as 'green' partisans, rather than the cumbersome United Defenders of the Fatherland (Partisans of Latvia); but this was the term used by the partisans who published the pro-German *Sword* broadsheet, and green was the colour of the armbands worn by the Latvian auxiliary police. One Soviet report, compiled early in 1946 but referring to the events of the autumn, described some of the Līvāni partisans as loyal to Celmiņš, the former Pērkonkrusts leader,[106] who was at this time busily trying to shed his past and establish good relations with the British.[107] Was this too much for Juhnēvičs, who simply wanted to revive the inter-war democratic tradition of Catholic representation from Latgale within parliament? The contradictions within the programme of the nationalist partisans were picked up by the press. *Latgal'skaya Pravda* continued to write about 'Gestapo agents trying to restore bourgeois Latvia',[108] but could also adopt a less hysterical tone: it tried to convince those of its opponents campaigning for a 'democratic republic' that this was unnecessary, since the Soviet Union already was a democratic state.[109]

Terror in the countryside

Just as the war-time partisans had sought to disrupt agricultural deliveries for the German authorities, so the nationalist partisans sought to disrupt the state programme of compulsory agricultural deliveries introduced by the soviet administration. In the first part of the summer, the main problem was milk. At the end of May 1945 the district committee discussed the half-year plan for milk deliveries and calculated that it would only be met by 15 per cent; what was particularly worrying was the dramatic decline that had taken place during May itself. The worst areas were Rudzāti to the north and then stretching to the east Biķernieki, Aglona, Asūne, Auleja, Kapiņi, Krāslava, Robežnieki and Skaista. In an effort to improve matters the chairman of the Biķernieki parish soviet was sacked, as was the party organiser in Skaista; there, in the first quarter of the year, the milk-delivery target had been met by only 1 per cent.[110] When the district committee held its general meeting on 28 June, Nikonov confirmed that milk deliveries were still only at 15 per cent of the target.[111]

The grain harvest could not be allowed to fail in the same way, although the war against the nationalist partisans made bringing in the harvest extremely difficult.[112] In August the press was used to denounce kulaks like M. Birzaks from Līvāni; he had divided his 50-hectare farm between his two brothers in order to reduce his liabilities, even though it was discovered that all three lived in the same house.[113] In the past show trials had proved an effective means of bringing pressure to bear on the peasantry and on 18 September the military tribunal in Indra staged the show trial of a certain Juzef Stivriņš. He owned 20 hectares, had one son who had joined the nationalist partisans and another who had fled to Germany, and he refused point blank to make deliveries or pay the fine for the deliveries he had failed to make the previous autumn. He was sentenced to five years imprisonment. The other accused, Pavel Vasilevskii, was fined and given a two-year suspended sentence because he had started to co-operate with the authorities and make deliveries.[114] However, despite these measures, when the district committee debated the harvest on 1 October it concluded that the situation was desperate since only 58 per cent of the planned harvest had been collected and the weather was beginning to worsen. The NKVD chief Titov was called on to mount a guard at every grain collection point and each leading party official was allocated their own parish to oversee. The district party reported a week later that the harvest in Višķi was only 45 per cent collected.[115]

More drastic action was called for. By the start of November *Latgal'skaya Pravda* was writing about the dangers of 'being liberal with the kulaks'. In Izvalta it had been discovered that two kulaks were giving only a fraction of what they owed: Augusts Janiņš owned 22 hectares of land and should have delivered 832 kilograms, but in fact had delivered only 200; the other kulak, Jānis Tukāns, was supposed to have delivered 750 kilograms, but had provided only 90. These kulaks had been treated liberally and only issued with a warning; the message of *Latgal'skaya Pravda* was that such liberalism should stop.[116] However, where liberalism was abandoned in the desperate struggle to meet impossible harvest targets, some of the methods used to bring in the harvest could only make 'banditry' more likely.

In fact, there had been very few displays of liberalism, especially in Preiļi. There, from August to October 1945, there was what can only be described as a reign of terror. The local party organiser Ivan Ivanov, who had joined the party during 1945, the non-party chairman of the Preiļi soviet Stanislavs Ancveirs and his non-party deputy Jānis Pasters were given the task of bringing in the harvest. At the end of August they were told that their target had not been met and they were not being interventionist enough, so the Daugavpils district committee sent them two helpers, A. Karnačs, a party member since 1939, and Lt. Edgars Strazdiņš, from the political department of the Red Army's Latvian Division. They were joined by Mikhail Baklitskii, head of the Preili parish branch of the NKVD. Throughout September, when Karnačs and Strazdiņš were still in Preiļi, and throughout October, when they had moved on, illegal methods were used by this group to extract grain from the peasantry. They acted without warning, and without discrimination, seizing grain not only from kulaks but from the families of poor peasants, and the families of those who had fought in the Red Army or had supported the Soviet partisans. Family members would be illegally detained until deliveries were made, or, more frequently, their passports or other crucial documents would be confiscated until deliveries were made; then they were made to queue up to have their documents returned. When it came to seizing cattle, Baklitskii would bring along the NKVD destroyer battalion and Strazdiņš four soldiers from the Latvian Division; their men would then feed off the confiscated pigs. None of the rules concerning documenting confiscated property were followed.

In one incident these officials encountered nationalist partisans near a farm owned by a Latvian. Three of the 'bandits' were killed in an exchange of fire, after which the officials confiscated the cattle and burned down the farm, even though there was no evidence to link the Latvian farmer to the nationalist partisans. In another incident Baklitskii ordered that a certain Jānis Rubāns be executed for possessing an illegal rifle. These two incidents were aimed at Latvians, but the details of the charges later brought against the officials make clear that in general these abuses were directed as much at the Russian as the Latvian population; those families affected with members serving in the Red Army were mostly Russian. There was an attempt to end this reign of terror. In mid-September the Daugavpils procurator warned Ivanov that what was happening was illegal, but Ivanov called a meeting of local activists and told them that the procurator's office was simply interfering and the campaign should continue with renewed vigour. The most extraordinary aspect of all this was that this was not the work of Russian incomers. Ivanov was a local Preiļi man, who had retreated with Red Army in 1941; Ancveirs came from Nīcgale and in the 1930s had been an *aizsarg*; Karnačs was of Polish extraction and came from Ilūkste district; and Pasters was another Preiļi man. Strazdiņš was an outsider in that he came from Riga, but only Baklitskii was an incomer having been born in Altai in Siberia.[117] Neighbour was again assaulting neighbour, but in the name of class struggle rather than racial purity.

This reign of terror came to light in mid-December[118] and was discussed by the district committee on 18 and 19 January 1946;[119] it was then debated by the Central Committee in Riga on 29 January 1946 in the presence of those ultimately responsible, district-party secretary Nikonov and district NKVD chief Titov. The Central Committee issued a party warning to Nikonov and criticised Titov for failing to undertake sufficient political work with his men. In an understatement, Kalbērziņš stressed that these were the very sorts of actions which drove people away from supporting the Soviet regime. Titov explained that the level of political education among his locally recruited men was low and that he had not been in a position to oversee such things since his main focus had been the 'anti-bandit' struggle: 'over the whole summer I was not at home for more than a week – the whole time I was in the forest and the marshes, and my attention was not focused on the state of my organisation.' (How many of the Latvian-language classes he missed from 9–10 on a Monday morning he did not say.) Nikonov's defence was weakened by Strazdiņš's assertion that Nikonov had told him: 'if the kulaks resort to sabotage, set things on fire, take no account of anything.'[120] On 21 February 1946 *Latgal'skaya Pravda* reported the punishments handed down by the Military Tribunal on 18 February. Baklitskii was sentenced to six years imprisonment; Anceirs to three years; Ivanov to 18 months; and Strazdiņš to one year. Karnačs and Pasters were both given a six months suspended sentence.

Although these incidents in Preiļi were the worst and most sustained examples of illegal activity by the security services, they were not unique. In June the chairman of the Aizkalne parish soviet Pirushko confiscated a horse for his own use.[121] In August a drunk NKVD officer in Aglona carried out an illegal search of a woman's house and beat her up, while in Kapiņi a member of the destroyer battalion shot a woman in the foot when she protested that her house was being searched illegally.[122] In November the chairman of a village soviet near Viški raped a woman because a deserter was found in her house, while in Rudzāti a local destroyer battalion commander, sent to arrest bandits, simply shot the first person he came across. In Vārkava the chairman of the parish soviet and a representative of the district-party committee killed a Latvian peasant when he refused to make any deliveries; apart from being drunk, their excuse was that the peasant had a son who was a 'bandit'. In Līksna the local party organiser was accused of keeping for his own use the animals and other property seized from nationalist partisans.[123] In December an officer of the Līvāni NKVD got drunk and, while checking how many cows were owned by the peasant Kazimirs Daukšte, insulted his daughter, shot in to the air, confiscated a cow and then shot Daukšte in the back.[124] Finally, throughout December Indra suffered at the hands of an NKVD officer who simply ran amuck. His assaults during interrogations were directed not only at potential enemies, but at colleagues like a representative of the district committee and a member of the pre-war underground. He encouraged the men from his destroyer battalion to strip-search female suspects, and he attempted to rape the daughter of a destroyer battalion volunteer.[125]

Incidents such as these could only encourage support for the nationalist partisans at a time when the authorities were trying to encourage voluntary surrender. However, the surrender policy itself was dealt a severe blow by the actions of the Daugavpils NKVD. Information gathered during the interrogation of Arvīds Puids, adjutant of the 2nd Division of the United Defenders of the Fatherland (Partisans of Latvia), had led to the arrest by 1 January 1946 of 68 people, 22 national partisans and 46 of their supporters. The charges on which these people had been detained began to unravel as preparations were made to bring the case to trial. In the immediate aftermath of the arrests, 26 of the alleged 'bandit supporters' were quietly released without charge. Then it became clear that four of the 'bandits' accused of raiding a shop in Jēkabpils would have to be cleared because, although they had indeed intended to raid the shop, they had not in fact done so since they fled the scene when disturbed by a guard. In May 1946 the Military Prosecutor returned the whole case to the NKVD, insisting that more work needed to be done if there was any chance of it standing up in court. Charges against a further seven of the 'bandits' were then dropped, and two of these men later successfully claimed that their gold watches had been stolen during their interrogation.

As the case progressively unravelled, it became clear that the whole affair had started with the arrest of several nationalist partisans who had actually surrendered. As noted above, back on 7 November 1945 Sergeant Fokt of the Red Army's Latvian Division had persuaded several leading members of the 2nd Division of the United Defenders of the Fatherland (Partisans of Latvia) to surrender at the Lācis farm, near Turki in Līvāni parish, bringing their weapons with them. On 8 November Senior Lieutenant Bondarenko of the Līvāni NKVD surrounded the farm and arrested these legalised bandits. Sergeant Fokt was detained for a while, but later released.[126] This embarrassing revelation wrecked the case completely. Almost a year after the event, those nationalist partisans who had surrendered to Fokt were finally released from detention; indeed, only 14 of the 68 people arrested in the follow-up investigation were successfully prosecuted.[127]

Nor was this the only case of those nationalist partisans who surrendered being kept in detention. At the end of 1945 the NKVD was horrified to find that several groups of 'legalised bandits', on being released after NKVD processing, were promptly re-arrested by the Commissariat for Military Affairs, presumably for alleged draft dodging, and deported to filtration camps outside Latvia. Those still *en route* to the filtration camps were returned, but it was too late for those who had already arrived. The authorities took belated action against other violators of the surrender policy; in April 1946 a security officer who killed two nationalist partisans after they had surrendered was sentenced to seven years imprisonment.[128] As Kalnbērziņš noted, such incidents made a nonsense of the amnesty policy.[129] The damage was done. In summer 1946 a nationalist partisan operating near Madona wrote to the prime minister of the Latvian Soviet Government Vilis Lācis explaining 'at first people believed that we would not be punished, but we were bitterly disappointed'. He asked that a genuine amnesty be granted so that his group could surrender.[130] It is not therefore surprising that operations by nationalist partisans should resume in spring 1946.

8 Stalinist Daugavpils

In February 1946 elections to the USSR Supreme Soviet were held in Daugavpils city and district, which gave the local party the opportunity to assess its position. Although it accepted it had little genuine support, it was pleased that the campaign had thrown up a reasonable core of activists, that some of these activists were people new to politics and, in the district at least, that several of these activists were Latvian by ethnicity. However, Stalin had called these elections for reasons of greater significance than the state of the Daugavpils party organisation. Their real purpose was to give Stalin a mandate for his policy of post-war reconstruction through the same system of five-year plans that had so characterised the Soviet Union in the 1930s. For Daugavpils this meant contributing to the greater national design, but it also meant Daugavpils would benefit from the planning system. Post-war reconstruction through Soviet planning brought Daugavpils a tram network.

The construction of the Daugavpils tram network, despite the sham popular enthusiasm which surrounded it, was a success story, one of the few successes in a city where corruption and shortages were the order of the day. It acted as a symbol of the future, when all were only to well aware of the misery of the day-to-day life which surrounded them. At a time when the party found it difficult to deliver the basics of beer and skittles socialism, the tram eased the practicalities of daily life. The symbol of the tram as a beacon of socialism stood in stark contrast to the free-market rough and tumble of Daugavpils peasant market where most citizens still obtained the essentials of life. The tram represented the Soviet achievements of the 1930s under Stalinist socialist planning, while the peasant market was some bygone relic of the pre-Stalin 1920s when peasants had still got rich under the New Economic Policy. It was equally symbolic that, with the tram completed, the party should turn to plans for the collectivisation of agriculture and the end of the peasant market.

Talk of collectivisation was only made possible by the gradual subsiding of rural unrest. By May 1946 there were clear signs that nationalist partisans were again very active, and by mid-July the Daugavpils district party was expressing real concern, prompting an unpleasant row with the local security chief. But events in July which took place further afield dealt the nationalist partisan movement a death blow from which it scarcely recovered. A visiting British delegation to Riga made clear that the British government accepted Latvia's incorporation into the Soviet Union, while events at the Paris Peace Conference, called to discuss the fate of Germany's allies, confirmed that the future of the Baltic States was well and truly off the international agenda. Thereafter the nationalist partisan movement subsided as government forces became increasingly successful in all but isolated pockets of nationalist strength. The success of the 'anti-bandit' struggle made it easier in the summer and autumn of 1946 to collect the milk deliveries and bring in the harvest. By and large, this was done through the use of the courts, rather than arbitrary violence. Although some incidents occurred, there was no repeat of the events in Preiļi of 1945. Pressure from Moscow to bring in the harvest was more intense than the previous year, because of the danger of famine elsewhere in the Soviet Union, but there was no resort to mass terror. Yet, in those areas 'infected with banditry' harvest deliveries remained problematic.

Although the nationalist partisans were defeated, nationalist ideas were not. Various underground nationalist groups were found to be operating in schools in the Daugavpils area, and the party had soon decided that the teaching profession was politically unreliable and needed to be replaced. This was difficult to achieve, but by 1947 the majority of Daugavpils teachers had been trained within the Soviet system. Purging the teaching profession was part of a broader project to create a new Soviet intelligentsia. This involved removing dubious elements from the party and fostering the growth of the komsomol, particularly its Latvian membership. Young Latvians were joining the komosmol, but they tended to come from poorly educated sections of that community. So at the end of 1946 the party turned its attention to strengthening communist ideas among the Latvian students at Daugavpils Teachers' Institute in the confident expectation that the coming generation could be won over to their cause.

The Supreme Soviet elections

In October 1945 the Central Committee was informed that elections to the USSR Supreme Soviet would be held in the New Year. At one of a series of meetings held between 16 and 20 November 1945 the Central Committee endorsed the membership of the electoral commission for the Daugavpils division, and then on 30 November deputed one of its members to offer help and guidance.[1] The first big surprise of the election campaign came when it was revealed that the population of Daugavpils was far greater than the communist authorities had expected. On 1 January it stood at 43,000, of whom 26,700 were registered as electors; when the campaign had begun at the start of December the population was estimated at 30–33,000, with an electorate of only 13,700. And the city continued to grow; between 20

January and 10 February a further 2,400 people had arrived in the city.[2] This inevitably meant that some of the preparatory work for the election was poor. Several polling stations were only properly established at the last moment, and the final electoral register was only compiled on 5 February and polling was due to take place on the 10th.[3]

There were to be three candidates. Two were locals, the current deputies Luriņš and Smagars, who were nominated to the Soviet of Nationalities, while for the Soviet of the Union Lebedev, the Central Committee Second Secretary who had intervened to dismiss Aleksandrov, was nominated. Jān Smagars was born in Līksna parish in 1906 and, after a short spell as an agricultural labourer in Ilūkste district, moved to Daugavpils in 1923 to work in the rolling-stock repair works. In 1940 he was the first Stakhanovite in the city, and was elected to the USSR Supreme Soviet. During the German occupation he was evacuated to Murom, where he worked in a factory, joining the party in 1942 and attending a party training school in June 1944. He then returned to the rolling-stock repair works as director. Antons Luriņš was born in Vārkava parish in 1911 into a peasant family. He was unable to complete his secondary education, but later took casual jobs and studied in the evening at the commercial college. This got him a job as a bank courier, but by 1932 he was heavily involved in the underground work of the Communist Party. Arrested in 1932, he was later released for lack of evidence in 1933 and then called into the army. After six more years as a casual labourer he joined the party in 1940 and was made chairman of the Daugavpils district soviet, a post he resumed in 1944 having spent the German occupation years in the Soviet towns of Gorky and Tashkent. Ivan Lebedev was born in Samara province, Russia, in 1907 and at the age of 14 started work in one of the shipbuilding yards on the river Volga. Aged only 15, he fought with the Red Army in operations against anti-Bolshevik peasant insurgents, who in 1921–2 took control of large areas of the Volga river basin; this was a strangely relevant background for 'bandit ridden' Latgale. He later worked on the riverboats, became a komsomol secretary and a party secretary, studied at the Saratov Economics Institute, and became a deputy to the Russian Federation Soviet in 1938 and was appointed Third Secretary of the Stalingrad Oblast. In 1941 he organised the evacuation of Kursk, before working in the Far East from 1942–4.[4]

The elections were an important opportunity for the communist authorities to gauge what support they had among the population and identify where the most dangerous opposition lay. In 1940 the party had been able to call on at least a partial memory of communist campaigning in the late 1920s, as well as a widespread hostility to the Ulmanis regime. After this popular mood had evaporated, they had been able to resort to a sort of beer and skittles approach to socialism, relying on the prejudices of the backward working class, even though this meant tolerating a degree of great Russian chauvinism. Only when the system had failed to deliver beer, under the strain of Stalin's preparations for war, had there been reports of serious working-lass unrest. In 1944 things were different. As Kalnbērziņš told party secretaries on 6 November 1944, 'this is not 1940'.[5]

Given the approach adopted, it was not surprising that the overall standard of propaganda was low. While propaganda posters were adequately displayed in Daugavpils city, in the districts it often just piled up on the floor.[6] The Central Committee was horrified to learn that the chairman of the Rēzekne soviet had told electors that 'in England there is only one theatre and only the lords attend it'.[7] In Daugavpils agitators were unaware that a conference of Allied foreign ministers had taken place in Moscow in December 1945.[8] Yet there were some successes in mobilising the population. During the election campaign in Daugavpils a mass meeting at the rolling-stock repair works was attended by 2,150 people; according to a report sent to Moscow from Riga such a mass meeting had never before taken place in Soviet Latvia.[9] On election day itself a team of over 500 activists was formed to 'knock up' and ensure people had voted.[10] Every effort was made to stress the 'Latvianness' of these elections. At the first big rally held in the People's House in early January, the prominent speakers all had Latvian names.[11] Indeed, the local party became engaged in an arcane row with the electoral commission in order to be allowed to refer to Smagars in the press as Jānis rather than Ivan, the name which had been entered on the candidates' register.[12] On 31 January the chairman of the electoral division reminded party members that all the ballot papers and other official material would be printed only in Latvian, 'which will undoubtedly complicate our work'. Activists were also reminded of the fact that many church-goers would insist on visiting church before voting.[13]

A month before the poll, on 10 January 1946, the leading communists in Daugavpils district were called on to carry out security checks on all election candidates and, more particularly, electoral officials. To help in this task military intelligence operatives were seconded from the army units based in the city.[14] They discovered a catalogue of fairly minor problems. In Līvāni parish the soviet chairman, a certain Staris, turned out to have links with the nationalist partisans, having been trusted by the German police during the war years. One chairman of a village soviet in the same parish was a former *aizsarg* who was also linked to the 'bandits'. In Rēzekne district soviet the man appointed to head the communal trade department had once been a deputy to the inter-war parliament, as well as being an active *aizsarg*.[15] A similar investigation across the Dvina in Ilūkste revealed that a woman candidate had a slightly cloudy past; although when the Red Army arrived in 1944 she was indeed landless as she claimed, from 1934–8 she had been married to a wealthy peasant, and had only become a landless labourer after her divorce. However, since the woman had volunteered as a nurse for the Red Army, this selective amnesia was forgiven.[16]

Not that this security operation was able to frustrate all 'bourgeois nationalist' activity in the run up to the elections. In Daugavpils polling station no. 6 a portrait of Stalin was defaced, as was a painting of a Red

Army man. A portrait of Stalin was also defaced in the Grīva polling station. In one Daugavpils district 'former bandits' managed to get themselves elected to the electoral commission.[17] In Asūne, where the bandit problem had been particularly acute throughout the year, the authorities were pleased that only a small five-strong group called the 'Grey Horse' had shown any activity during the election period.[18] On the other hand, leaflets were discovered on the streets of Daugavpils on 10–11 January 1946, written in Latvian, which called on people not to vote, and explained that it had been agreed at the Potsdam Conference that, if less than 90 per cent of the electorate voted for the communist candidates, then Latvian independence would be restored. To increase the likelihood of such an outcome, the authors of the leaflets threatened to shoot those who voted communist, to burn down polling stations and to hang the members of the destroyer battalions who guarded them. The leaflet was signed by the 'commander of the 18th region of green partisans'.[19]

On election day itself there were few incidents. In the city 10 per cent of the voters were queuing as the polls opened; 27 per cent had voted by 8 a.m. and 75 per cent by midday; voting was effectively over by 6 p.m.[20] Daugavpils district had taken careful precautions and most polling stations were guarded by soldiers from the local garrison.[21] Reflecting on the elections in Daugavpils city and the surrounding districts, a Central Committee representative felt they had gone better than expected. The divorce between party activists and the people was so great, the report stated, that the party was uncertain of people's real attitudes and had overestimated the importance of 'alien elements'.[22] In both city and district, there had been some success in mobilising the population at large. The city committee reckoned that about 1,000 people took an active part in the electoral campaign as agitators; 315 of these were in the party, 313 in the komosmol, while the rest were recruited during the campaign itself, a reservoir of future party activists.[23] In Daugavpils district 4,000 people were reported to have taken part in electoral work, and during the election campaign the komsomol had grown from 848 to 1,050 members. The fact that most of the new recruits were Latvians was felt worthy of special comment.[24] Indeed, a post-election report singled out Daugavpils district for special praise. In terms of area and territory, it was one of the biggest and most difficult districts to manage, and there was a very great 'bandit' presence; yet Nikonov and Avdyukevich had organised things especially well, the report said.[25]

It was on the eve of the poll that Stalin made clear the true purpose of the elections. In his speech to his electors, he stated clearly that the lesson of the Second World War was the system he had constructed in the 1930s worked. Doubters had scoffed at rapid industrialisation through five-year plans and the collectivisation of agriculture, but victory in the war had proved them wrong. Stalinism in its 1930s variety would be the basis for post-war reconstruction. Stalin's 9 February speech was a body blow for those who shared the widespread belief at the time that the post-war Soviet

Union would be a more democratic state that its pre-war incarnation. There were many in the Soviet Union who hoped that the horrors of the 1930s were a thing of the past, an aberration in socialism caused by the need to industrialise at great speed against the backdrop of the growing fascist threat which had now been removed. Such people hoped that post-war recovery in the peaceful climate established by the nations united in victory would allow the more humanistic elements of socialism to come to the fore. Such attitudes were noticeable among members of the Latvian Division and those who volunteered from it to lead the Soviet partisans.[26] Any such notion that the post- war Soviet Union might be different, that autonomy for the Soviet Republics might be real and evolve towards something like 'Dominion' status, was firmly rejected by Stalin in his speech.

The impact of Stalin's speech was immediate. After the elections, the new Supreme Soviet adopted the fourth five-year plan and from then on the propaganda offensive was aimed at successful plan fulfilment, and the role of Daugavpils in this process. Latvia was very clearly part of the greater Soviet economy and linked to Stalin's policy objective of the most rapid possible recovery through self-reliance. At the 11th Central Committee Plenum of 11–12 April 1946 the planning chief for Latvia reminded delegates that the decision to industrialise Latvia within three to four years, which had been taken back in 1940, was still in force and remained the party's prime objective. Rapid Stalinist industrialisation was the order of the day,[27] and the introduction of Soviet-style planning to Daugavpils was epitomised by the decision to build a tram network for the city. News of this project began to leak out almost as soon as the elections were over, although the formal press announcement was delayed until 20 April.[28]

Living in Stalinist Daugavpils

Latgal'skaya Pravda reported on 24 February 1946 that Feoktistov had told the city committee a few days previously that Riga had endorsed a development plan for Daugavpils over the next two decades, a plan which included the construction of a tram network. At the 10th Central Committee Plenum on 25–26 February 1946, called to discuss the fourth five-year plan and its impact on Latvia, Feoktistov put forward a shopping list of demands, which included both new bus routes and the request for a tram network. His plea was that the Central Committee should 'make Soviet Daugavpils the centre of Soviet Latgale', and he insisted when the rival claim of Rēzekne to this status was mentioned by delegates from the floor of the meeting: 'the city of Daugavpils was and will remain the centre of Latgale'.[29] The matter of the tram rested there for a while, but, after the personal intervention of Lebedev,[30] the Central Committee resolved on 26 March 1946 to construct a tram network in Daugavpils;[31] the Daugavpils city committee was told that work would commence on 3 June.[32]

The proposal for a tram network went ahead, not simply because a public-transport system was desperately needed, but because it was seen as a practical way of showing the superiority of socialism over capitalism. The idea of bringing trams to Daugavpils had first been discussed before the First World War. Back in 1906 the press had written of the need to construct a tram network, and, in 1910, a company had even been formed for this purpose. In 1912 quite detailed plans for a four-line network were elaborated and discussed first with an American firm and then with a Petersburg company. However, in November 1913 Daugavpils city council turned down the proposal.[33] During the inter-war years talks were again held between the city fathers and both Swedish and British firms about building a tram network, but nothing came of them,[34] although in December 1931 a second company was established.[35] Now, the tram network would be built according to the classic Stalinist formula of administrative chaos and sham popular enthusiasm.

The population were informed on 21 May 1946 that all able-bodied citizens would be expected to volunteer 32 of their annual 100 hours of voluntary labour to the tram project;[36] to this end a mass meeting was held in the People's House on 23 May.[37] Work began a week behind schedule, on 11 June not 3 June,[38] and, after an initial burst of activity, ceased completely. On 12 July the supply of rails suddenly dried up and work stopped, resumed for two days, and then stopped again.[39] By mid-August the city committee was extremely concerned: the project was supposed to be completed within 75 days, but after 50 days the planned network was not even half complete; despite clear instructions to start building work at both ends of the line, this had not happened. On 9 September the city committee decided to give each of its members, including Feoktistov, responsibility for a certain section of track.[40] A new deadline was set, 1 November, and the press went into overdrive with stories and pictures of happy workers devoting themselves to tram construction. The end of September saw a special tram 'Sunday' and a special 'schoolchildren's day';[41] on 13 October it was reported that one thousand volunteers had joined in the construction work.[42] The 1 November deadline was not met, but the first tram was manoeuvred onto the track only a few days late.[43] The official opening merged with the celebrations of the October Revolution on 7 November: Lebedev cut a ribbon and was ceremoniously issued with ticket number 1,[44] while *Latgal'skaya Pravda* issued pictures of the event for three days running.[45]

Building the tram was certainly an achievement, more important as a symbol than as a means of transport. It showed that Soviet Daugavpils had a future as an industrial city, that, when the party turned its mind to something, it was able to deliver. The tram was a physical symbol of the better life to come. But that better life was still some way off. The tram network was the only public-transport system available. It was reported in March 1946 that six buses were being repaired in Riga and would soon arrive in

Daugavpils to start serving the suburbs.[46] In December 1946 an outraged citizen wrote to the editor of *Latgal'skaya Pravda* demanding to know what had happened about these buses, for they had never materialised. An investigation by the paper discovered the truth; the buses were ready for service, but there was no petrol to run them.[47] Day to day life in Soviet Daugavpils was certainly not easy, as those workers in one factory who went unpaid for both April and May could testify.[48]

However, the rigours of the Stalinist system could be eased by corruption. In February 1946 it was discovered that many of the goods confiscated by officials during searches were being sold at a second-hand shop.[49] In May 1946 the former head of the city soviet's trade department was sentenced to ten years' imprisonment for the numerous corrupt practices he had engaged in.[50] In August 1946, when the city committee discussed the question of supplies, it heard that bribe-taking in the allocation of flats was widespread; it also tried to think of ways of addressing the fact that 'very many goods' simply never entered the shops, but found their way immediately to the black market.[51] On 11 October the city committee faced the moral dilemma of what to do with a party member who had paid a bribe in order to obtain a flat.[52] On 13 November 1946 the Daugavpils procurator heard the case of the chairman of the local fish producers' co-operative who was accused of abusing the fish ration and supplying friends and contacts under the counter.[53] The authorities tried to explain away some of these failings by pointing to some of the inappropriate people being employed in the retail sector. A party investigation in November 1946 revealed that the trade department still employed such people as the daughter of an Orthodox priest, a former merchant from the Ulmanis era and someone who had worked for the Germans in the ghetto.[54]

Nor were the authorities always squeaky clean themselves. After the Supreme Soviet election it was discovered that there was even a blemish on the record of Smagars. In 1944 he had been loaned some seed by the state to use on his allotment. He turned out not to have green fingers, the allotment produced nothing, and he was either unable or unwilling to repay the loan. On 23 September 1946 he informed the party that he would do so at once.[55] Party officials were more seriously tainted. In December 1946 it was discovered that leading party officials were quietly reallocating to other purposes money which was intended to be offered as loans to poor peasants for their basic agricultural needs; in Aglona the party organiser had used this money to buy a suit and in Aizkalne the party organiser had used it to equip his own house.[56] Another case was less clear-cut. In October the director of the bread combine was expelled from the party for mis-selling flour and hiding the fact that he owned farm animals. Earlier, in March, he had criticised the work of the NKVD, saying that factory workers would not stay behind for meetings after their shift because there were too many hooligans around, whom the police seemed unable to deal with. He was restored to party membership in December 1946 when the charges against him were shown to be a pack of lies. It is hard to avoid the conclusion that the NKVD had set up his expulsion in revenge for his criticism of its failings.[57]

There were even question marks over the probity of Feoktistov, who according to those in the higher party echelons at the time, would go into shops and commandeer anything he wanted.[58] However, this was more to do with leadership style than corruption. Feoktistov was a little Stalin. He was divorced from the people and encouraged a leadership cult, as a critical report later acknowledged; the phrase 'Vasilii Ilych has ordered' was often heard.[59] While first secretary he could do almost anything he pleased. He routinely stitched up the agenda of meetings so as to prevent criticism being heard,[60] and he also deliberately used money allocated for one purpose for another quite different purpose. This was not for personal gain, but for his vision of the well-being of the city. To the irritation of Riga he deliberately overspent his budget.[61]

Alongside the corruption went the shortages. In March a report had confirmed that complaints about the poor quality of bread were justified.[62] In June 1946 a survey of the city's 62 shops and kiosks revealed that not even the ration provisions could be met.[63] In mid-June *Latgal'skaya Pravda* printed an article 'Where to buy lemonade', which described its correspondent's hunt for a restaurant able to serve him with a glass of refreshing lemonade.[64] With the shops and even restaurants empty, real trade took place in the market. Daugavpils market was a law unto itself. Three days a week two or even three thousand peasants would enter the city and trade. There were no controls. This was tolerated by the authorities, since people had to live. It was only in June 1946 that Feoktistov suggested the time might have come to regulate the market when he told the district committee, the plenary session of which he had been invited to address, that something would have to be done. He proposed a joint initiative by the city and district committees, but put forward no specific proposals.[65]

From a Soviet perspective, the Daugavpils peasant market represented the past, just as the Daugavpils tram system represented the future. Beer and skittles socialism required the two to operate side by side in order to overcome such crises as the shortage of lemonade. But such co-existence, such tolerance of a 'mini-NEP' within the boundaries of a Soviet city, could not last indefinitely. Just as the Latvian communists had steadily extended their control of trade in 1941, preparing the way for the collectivisation of agriculture, so getting to grips with the Daugavpils peasant market was linked to the first moves taken towards the post-war collectivisation of agriculture. At the last meeting of the city committee in 1946 Feoktistov explained the radical way forward that had been decided. He broke the news that the collectivisation of agriculture would shortly begin; already the first moves had been taken in Viški.[66] The future of Soviet Daugavpils was becoming clear.

Rural unrest subsides

Collectivising Latvian agriculture would have been tantamount to suicide were it not for the fact that rural unrest had dramatically subsided in the course of 1946. There were still people willing to fight against the notion of a Soviet Daugavpils and a Soviet Latgale. The war against the nationalist partisans was not over in 1946 but it was far less intense, although the 'destroyer battalion of special designation' formed by the district party, which had been set up initially for a two-month period was still active in March 1946.[67] On 26 April 1946 the district committee heard that in Robežnieki two village soviets were not working because of 'bandit' activity and that the situation in nearby Asūne was still tense: when a district official visited to help organise a meeting with peasants he had travelled three kilometres out of town, called a meeting and then suddenly cancelled it when told that 'bandits' were about to attack; it turned out later that these 'bandits' had not existed.[68] However, Daugavpils was not one of the areas to report national partisan unrest in May, although both neighbouring Jēkabpils[69] and Rēzekne reported renewed activity that month.[70] In June, both these districts were concerned at the ease with which the nationalist partisans seemed to operate. A report from Rēzekne issued in June made clear that in the last two months there had been 27 victims of attacks by nationalist partisans, with only five 'bandits' killed in return.[71] In Susēja parish, Ilūkste district, the local party organiser confessed in June that he was in contact with nationalist partisans and even went drinking with them.[72]

By June, Daugavpils district was feeling the recovery in the nationalist partisan movement. Early in the month *Latgal'skaya Pravda* reported that in Naujene, Višķi and Līksna there had been a number of unexplained fires which could have been started deliberately.[73] Such incidents were not confined to the region close to Daugavpils. When the district party held a plenary session on 7 June, the new party organiser for Robežnieki described how he had just taken over after the parish soviet building had been burnt down by nationalist partisans.[74] The traditional mid-summer's night holiday of Līgo was marked by nationalist partisan activity,[75] and shortly afterwards, on 24 June, nationalist partisans staged an open, but small-scale attack on a village near Preiļi. This action was unsuccessful. The local four-member destroyer battalion first held off the nationalist partisans and then pinned them down long enough for reinforcements to arrive; two 'bandits' were killed and their rifle and machine-gun recovered. One member of the destroyer battalion later died of his wounds in Preiļi hospital.[76]

As elsewhere in the country, part of the reason for the successful revival of nationalist partisan operations over the summer was the poor state of the destroyer battalions. On 11 June the party discussed the low level of political awareness among the destroyer battalions operating in Preiļi, Krāslava, Nīcgale and Naujene. The same meeting tried to resolve a dispute which had arisen between the NKVD chief Titov and one of the destroyer battalion commanders. This dispute concerned the deployment of the few lorries under the control of the destroyer battalions; it was suggested that these lorries were being used on personal rather than professional missions. The meeting also discussed the difficulties involved in finding suitably experienced soldiers to staff the officer corps.[77]

When the Central Committee held its 12th Plenum on 18–19 July 1946 one of the items discussed was 'the situation in the Daugavpils district'. The meeting was not specifically called to discuss the 'bandit' situation, but to assess how the local party had responded to the scandal of the illegal arrests in Preiļi which started with the detention of Arvīds Puids. Reviewing the situation relating to the nationalist partisans, Nikonov gave a measured assessment of the situation. 'Banditry' had been a real problem in 1945, he conceded, but was less of a problem now. A combination of active military operations and widespread propaganda work had persuaded not one but many groups to legalise.[78] He did not add, but could have, that at the end of June the authorities had captured Andrejs Upenieks, the most recent commander of the 5th Daugavpils regiment of the United Defenders of the Fatherland (Partisans of Latvia).[79]

When the district committee discussed the situation at a plenary meeting held on 31 July, Titov gave a fairly relaxed assessment of the situation. In Asūne part of the problem, he said, was that party organisers allowed themselves to be scared by the 'bandits', the majority of whom could be persuaded to abandon their struggle if properly approached; panicking, cancelling meetings, crying out that you were under attack did not help, he suggested. However, he did admit to some problems of the security services' own making; thus in Robežnieki the destroyer battalion had refused to turn out for duty because it was not being properly fed. The party organiser from Asūne responded to Titov's criticism in kind. He stressed that Titov's men threw their weight around, and refused to allow party officials to carry guns: of course people felt afraid, he said, going unarmed into such an area. He then added pointedly that the only meeting that had been cancelled was a gathering of kulaks for which permission had not been granted. The party organiser concluded by stating that the root cause of the problem was that the district party still did not recognise the very Latvian nature of the Asūne parish. The final resolution adopted by the district committee at this meeting had little choice but to note the continuing existence of the 'bourgeois nationalist underground'.[80]

When he reported to the Central Committee Plenum early in July, Nikonov stated that the propaganda issued by the nationalist partisans once again concentrated on the likelihood of war between America and Great Britain, on the one hand, and the Soviet Union, on the other; various dates were even given for the start of this conflict. In this context a large amount of space was devoted by the nationalist partisans to the forthcoming Paris Peace Conference, so much in fact that Nikonov later organised a series of party meetings to discuss the speech made by Molotov at the opening session.[81] It was entirely logical for the nationalist partisans to focus on the Paris Peace Conference in this way. Britain had always stated in public that the borders of Latvia and the other Baltic States would be agreed as part of the final post-war settlement. The conference in Paris was called to discuss the fate of Germany's allies, rather than Germany itself, but it was anticipated that the conference would pave the way for a further conference to discuss the future of Germany. Just in case the issue of the Baltic States did come up, Stalin included the foreign ministers of all three Baltic States in his delegation to Paris.

On the eve of the July Central Committee Plenum *Latgal'skaya Pravda* published an article which was to have enormous significance in the struggle against the nationalist partisans. Completely out of the blue, a delegation from the Anglo-Soviet Society was given permission to visit Riga. Officials learnt of the visit only on 11 July, and from the 13th to 17th were responsible for ushering around the city nine British visitors, some of whom were determined to ask awkward questions about the state's policy towards religious tolerance. Put up in the best hotels, with five cars and a bus at their disposal, they were treated like visiting royalty; one poor woman who met the delegation on a Riga street thought it was a group of British diplomats come to negotiate Latvia's independence. In fact, the delegation was made up of trade unionists and radical journalists broadly sympathetic to the communist cause.[82] The most prominent member of the group was the Labour MP Julius Silvermann and, before leaving Latvia, he issued a long press statement which was widely reported and ended thus: 'thoughts of a new war over Latvia are nonsense … most Englishmen and a significant majority in the English parliament willingly recognise as final and correct the adhesion of the Baltic States to the Soviet Union.'[83]

Silvermann's statement was borne out by the fact that, as the Paris Peace Conference got down to work on 29 July, the fate of the Baltic States was ignored. To capitalise on this, the Latvian authorities decided to repeat the offer of an amnesty to the nationalist partisans. On 22 August 1946 *Latgal'skaya Pravda* published an appeal 'To everyone hiding in the forest', signed by the local NKVD chief Titov and Supreme Soviet deputy Luriņš. It underlined the reality of the international situation. In Paris 21 allied and united nations had come together to restructure the world, making a nonsense of the expectation that there would be a war between the Soviet Union and its allies. The appeal then quoted in full the last part of Silvermann's statement, where he stressed that the British parliament recognised the incorporation of the Baltic States into the Soviet Union. Having outlined the futility of further struggle, the appeal asserted that the amnesty offered on 12 September 1945 was still in force. Bending the truth more than a little, the appeal claimed that 'no vengeance was exacted' on those who had accepted the terms of the amnesty; they now 'lived peaceably in their homes'. Of course, the appeal ended with a repeat of the previous year's warning: those who did not respond and leave the forests would be pursued 'as traitors and enemies of the people'.

To reinforce that threat, the authorities staged a trial of Asūne nationalist partisans who had been captured a year earlier. In the first half of September 1946 a military tribunal in Daugavpils heard how two men who had volunteered to fight alongside the Germans, Aleksandr Narushevich and Osip Dubrovskii, had hidden when the Red Army returned and then, in April 1945, had gathered around them a group of 15 deserters. This became the core of a band, which prevented peasants delivering produce to the state and terrorised representatives of the soviet administration, twice killing their victims; a school was wrecked on 1 May and a milk-collection point on 24 June, but their most daring raid was their last when on 26 June 1945 they attacked the Asūne soviet building. During this raid Narushevich was wounded and captured and thereafter the group gradually disintegrated. The military tribunal sentenced Narushevich and Dubroviskii to death and other members of the band to terms of imprisonment, but two of their accomplices, the brothers Pavels and Stanislavs Pinks, were freed on the grounds that they had been forced to join the group.[84]

Asūne remained the worst-affected area. On 27 August, a special 35–strong operative group that had been formed in Asūne over the summer engaged the local nationalist partisan leader Stanislavs Ludziņš and gunned him down.[85] Yet unrest carried on well into the autumn. On 10 November the district committee discussed the 'bandit situation' in Asūne.[86] In the course of a week, two serious incidents had occurred. On 29 October a village soviet had been attacked and the local party instructor and party organiser captured. Then, on 8 November, bandits murdered the family of a member of the destroyer battalion who had been killed in an earlier action. The district committee resolved on decisive action. It would send in a team of 15 men to help out and ensure that the local destroyer battalions were properly armed and trained; every village was to establish its own destroyer battalion units from local people, and telephone connections were to be extended.[87] This response was effective. On 13 December the operational group discovered a well-hidden bunker: three bandits were killed in the operation and a further two arrested; their weapons, three rifles, two pistols and two light machine-guns, were confiscated.[88]

Over the summer of 1946 there were other successes in the districts surrounding Daugavpils. The 'Special Group against Banditry', established by the Central Committee and headed by the former partisan leaders Oškalns and Laiviņš, had been operating in an ark to the north of Daugavpils, based first at Lubāna, then Madona and then Odziena, north of Pļaviņas, and then back via Madona to Cesvaine; a sub-group moved further east to operate near Abrene. These activities were successful both in capturing nationalist partisan groups and in persuading their members to leave the forests. At the end of August, the 'Special Group against Banditry' moved into Jēkakabpils district where, after several false starts, it succeeded in capturing the nationalist partisan leader 'Black Peter' on 2 October 1946; he was operating to the west of Jēkabpils near Sece. At the end of October the group reported a successful action near Viesite and then moved into Daugavpils district and reported a successful operation near Līvāni on 25 October.[89] By the end of the year the situation was also reported to be improving in Rēzekne.[90] There, on 3–4 August an operation had been mounted against the last remnants of the United Defenders of the Fatherland (Partisans of Latvia): Stanislavs Strods, appointed back on 11 November 1945 as commander of the 6th Rēzekne regiment was taken prisoner.[91]

Where nationalist partisan activity continued in Daugavpils district, it was firmly put down to failings within the security services rather than the strength of the nationalist partisans. A report considered by the Daugavpils district party on 17 October made clear that recently four parish security chiefs had been expelled from the party for drunkenness, and that this had inevitably had an impact on military preparedness.[92] In Preiļi the morale of the destroyer battalions was said to have fallen because the local party had distanced itself from security work.[93] Increased partisan activity in Skaista, Izvalta and Robežnieki parishes was put down to the half-hearted attempts to confront the partisans; not even weapon stores had been properly guarded, with the result that weapons had been disappearing.[94] Yet such incidents were isolated. Unlike in 1945, by the end of 1946 nationalist partisan activity was confined to just one area, Asūne. And there were signs, despite the brutal killings there, that those nationalist partisans who were still active were no longer as gratuitously violent as they had once been. On the night of the 22–23 October two 'bandits' near Indra broke into the house of a member of the local destroyer battalion to steal his weapons; having seized both gun and grenades they left, forgetting their earlier threat to kill not only the member of the destroyer battalion but his wife and child as well.[95]

Bringing in the harvest

In the relatively calmer climate of summer and autumn 1946, the authorities tried to collect the compulsory deliveries and bring in the harvest through the use of the courts rather than brute terror. However, recourse to the courts did not always work. When the district committee met on 21 May to consider milk deliveries, it painted a dismal picture and blamed kulak sabotage; overall, only 11.4 per cent of the target had been reached, and in areas like Dagda it was as little as 4 per cent.[96] Earlier investigations had revealed how a farmer like Ivan Barovik, from near Kalupe, had simply hidden his cows to prove he could not deliver milk,[97] and the Kalupe soviet chairman reported to a district plenary meeting in June that if you travelled around the country-side it was not difficult to find many other hidden cows. Some village soviet chairmen even connived in issuing certificates exempting peasants from milk deliveries.[98] So the Kalupe soviet chairman tried to bring one of the non-delivering kulaks to court. The accused was a former *aizsarg* whose son was fighting with the nationalist partisans, so to the communist authorities the case seemed open and shut. However, the court, on examining the evidence, did not think there were sufficient grounds to prosecute.[99]

Things went even more badly awry in Preiļi on 6 July. There a show trial was actually staged and a certain Brutis accused of hiding two cows and making no milk deliveries; but once again the judge found the accused not guilty for lack of evidence. The two hundred 'of the worst non-deliverers' brought to the court to be taught a lesson must have shared a wry chuckle on their way home. The district party called for the judge concerned to be sacked, but the damage was done.[100] Other court cases did succeed. A successful prosecution was launched in Naujene against a peasant who delivered watered-down milk,[101] and two 'saboteurs', one a Latvian and one a Russian, were successfully fined in Aglona on 4 July for making no milk deliveries.[102] By the end of June, milk deliveries had crept towards 40 per cent of the target; but a candid report noted that 70 per cent of farmers were 'only formal deliverers'. Kulaks might take a lead, but they were by no means the only farmers resisting the compulsory delivery programme.[103]

In some ways the autumn campaign to bring in the grain harvest was more determined in 1946 than it had been in 1945. The reason was no longer so much the troubles caused by 'banditry' as the general economic crisis faced by the Soviet Union as a whole. In 1946 famine threatened, and Latvia could not be excluded from the campaign to collect as much grain as possible from those parts of the Soviet Union where the harvest was good. In Daugavpils district things were as difficult as anywhere else in the country. On 20 September there were eight trials under way of kulaks accused of not delivering the harvest, a number equalled by only one other district.[104] And yet, at an emergency meeting on 21 October the Latvian party leadership and its Moscow minders singled out Daugavpils for special criticism. Lebedev accused Daugavpils activists of 'simply sitting in restaurants'; every leading member needed to be given a specific task to strengthen village soviets, he said. Moscow's representative said of Daugavpils: 'Comrade Nikonov, your district is the worst, return to it and to do not come back until things are sorted.'[105] All party members were called on to become involved in the campaign, and those who did not faced immediate disciplinary action. On 24 October 1946 Prokopii Eliseev, a party member since 1932 and the Daugavpils district procurator since March 1946 was given a party warning because he refused to go to Dagda on 13 October to talk to peasants about the importance of making grain deliveries.[106]

Figures published at the end of October made clear where the problem lay: in Nīcgale, Višķi and Līksna, parishes relatively close to Daugavpils, grain deliveries stood at 67 per cent, 65 per cent and 64 per cent respectively; in 'bandit ridden' Asūne deliveries were only 30 per cent and only 40 per cent in nearby Dagda; in Preiļi, the site of such unrest a year earlier, deliveries were scarcely any better at 42 per cent.[107] A report dated 17 October 1946 revealed that of the 80 families of nationalist partisans who had surrendered in Vārkava parish, only 20 had made harvest deliveries. In Asūne, of the 154 farms only 37 had started to deliver.[108] In Preiļi it was discovered that one of the village soviet chairmen, a certain Miezītis, had helped two of his fellow Latvians carry out a purely fictitious division of their land in order to reduce their delivery targets.[109] In Līvāni the parish soviet was accused of adopting a conciliatory line by trying to negotiate with the non-deliverers rather than confronting them.[110]

On 1 November 1946 the Latvian State Prosecutor wrote in *Latgal'skaya Pravda* that it was time 'to abandon rotten liberalism and strengthen the struggle against kulak sabotage'. A year earlier, this had been the signal for the sort of terror unleashed by the security services in Preiļi. In 1946, however, there were far fewer violations of socialist legality by the security services. One of the worst such violations concerned milk deliveries and predated the campaign against 'rotten liberalism'. In April 1946 the soviet chairman in Višķi was accused of arresting a peasant on his way to market and confiscating his milk.[111] Three months later he had ordered the chairman of a village soviet near Višķi to detain five peasants for failing to deliver milk and had sentenced two of them to forced labour, digging a memorial grave for Red Army soldiers.[112] There were other incidents later in the year. In August the security services in Krāslava illegally detained two Latvian men for a fortnight,[113] while in November 1946 three members of the Daugavpils district operational group, used to such effect in Asūne, were involved in burgling a peasant household.[114] However, there was nothing on the scale of 1945.

Indeed, when the Rēzenke district secretary, inspired by the *Latgal'skaya Pravda* editorial, resorted to 'campaign methods' to 'break kulak sabotage', he was immediately called to account by the procurator. An agreement reached on 1 July 1946 between the Central Committee and the Procurator's Office stated that party secretaries could not tell court officials what to do, but the Rēzekne district secretary simply ignored this. Without seeking the agreement of the procurator's office, he had 'bullied' local court officials into accompanying his men to the villages, and, when they refused to organise trials, accused them of 'lacking political determination'; one court official was even arrested by the destroyer battalion for refusing to obey the instruction of the Rēzekne district secretary.[115] However, instead of being praised for his actions, this 'abandonment of rotten liberalism' marked the end of the Rēzekne district secretary's career.

The party was also prepared to take firm action against those in the security services who continued to manifest Great Russian chauvinist attitudes. In an extraordinary outburst in June 1946 a member of the Daugavpils security services beat up a Latvian telephone engineer and assaulted the secretary of the komsomol branch in the telephone exchange, ripping off his komsomol badge and shouting that Latvians did not have the right to serve in the komsomol; when asked to explain his behaviour, he told his superior that 'he hated Latvians'; he was sacked and expelled from the party.[116] In September 1946 the district party also ended the party and police career of the NKVD chief in Aglona. He had shot deserters soon after his appointment in April 1946; he had then got repeatedly drunk; he had done black-market deals with thieves; but the final straw came on 7 August when he told two members of his destroyer battalion that the day would very soon come when everyone of Latvian nationality would be arrested.[117]

Destroying the old intelligentsia

The defeat of the nationalist partisans did not mean the defeat of nationalist ideas. Investigations continued to reveal 'bandit' sympathisers in positions of authority. When the district committee held a plenary session on 3 April 1946 it was asserted that in Izvalta the local party organiser was still allowing a former *aizsarg*, who had helped in the deportations to Germany, to be chairman of a village soviet. The situation was rather similar in a village of Viški parish; there the soviet chairman was a former German-appointed elder, but he was so respected by all the villagers and was such an excellent organiser that and no one locally thought that his position was compromised. The same meeting heard that in Rudzāti parish, one of the local agricultural co-operatives was composed entirely of legalised bandits.[118]

In the middle of August there was a nationalist incident at Viški Horticultural College. At the graduation ceremony one of the women students made a nationalist speech, and investigations revealed that she was part of a nationalist group formed in the college during the course of the year. Further inquiries suggested a degree of protection for those with nationalist views on the part of the college authorities. The college director had known of these activities and done nothing about them: worse, he had allowed the college to become a haven for those associated with the German-occupation regime; despite warnings from the district committee, he continued to have on his staff two people who had served as village elders during the Nazi years. Support for the komsomol at the college was purely token; only seven of the 114 students were members. What particularly alarmed the district committee when it discussed this affair was the final throw-away sentence of the investigative report. This stated that the situation was similar in many of the district's schools, especially those in Aglona, Dagda, Krāslava, Preiļi and Vārkava.[119]

This was not the first time such a conclusion had been reached about the world of education. A security review undertaken at the end of 1945 had made clear that the most active supporters of the nationalist partisans were rural schoolteachers. One teacher's home was said to have become a regular 'haunt of bandits'. One school director, a former captain in the *aizsargs*, was assumed to be in cahoots with the bandits. In several schools portraits of

Ulmanis had suddenly appeared.[120] Soon the security services were seeing signs of political unreliability wherever they looked. In September 1945 the NKVD enquired into the supposedly suspicious background of the director of the non-graduating secondary school in Kapiņi. He had once been an *aizsarg* and this original sin was thought to explain why, although he had been arrested by the German security police and sent to a POW camp in Pskov, he had later been chosen to act as a camp supervisor.[121] Nor was the situation that much better in Daugavpils. In April 1946 the security forces there uncovered a nationalist group working within the 1st Latvian Secondary School. Organised by a teacher, but made up primarily from older pupils, it had established links with the nationalist partisans and had been trying to supply them with arms, as well as spreading its own propaganda.[122] A contemporaneous report into the Daugavpils Teachers' Institute showed the underlying national tension there. Of the 128 students, 36 were in the komosmol, but only four of these komsomol members were Latvians. Relations between the two ethnic groups were described as unhealthy. When students gave presentations or took part in plays and concerts, the language issue kept coming up: Latvian students would shout out 'we do not understand' when presentations were given in Russian, whereas Russian students would shout 'enough of that' when presentations were given in Latvian. The decision of Russian lecturers to ban a display made by some of the Latvian students had made matters worse.[123]

The party had always had its concerns about the reliability of the teaching profession, but was not at first in a secure enough position to act. A report of 1 December 1944 stated that some teachers had had to be dismissed for political unreliability and replaced by people drafted in from the Red Army or who had been deployed from other parts of the Soviet Union.[124] Another attempt to get to grips with the situation took place over summer 1945: the city committee's cadre department carried out a survey of all those with teaching qualifications who were not working as teachers and sought to deploy them locally;[125] a start was made at reintroducing the 'leader' system of 1940–1, the party cell in the city soviet administration being given the task of guiding the work of the 1st Latvian secondary school;[126] teachers were encouraged to attend courses held in Daugavpils and Krāslava; and a general teachers' conference was held in Daugavpils on 21–22 August.[127]

More drastic measures had to await the academic year 1945–6, the year when the socialist reconstruction of Soviet Daugavpils began. The authorities carried out a purge at the end of 1945, which removed the directors of the 1st Russian secondary school, the 2nd Russian non-graduating secondary school and the Polish secondary school.[128] The impact of the purge on the Polish secondary school showed how far things had changed in the course of a year. A security investigation revealed that the history teacher taught not just the Soviet Constitution but comparative constitutions; she also taught world history rather than the history of the peoples of the USSR. The slogans hung around the school made no mention of the party, but were generally progressive: 'we are building a new life, a new culture' was one example. Ultimate blame for this state of affairs was put on the school's director Sosnovskii. The NKVD thought it was suspicious that Sosnovskii had once been an officer in the Russian Imperial Army and that during the German occupation he had engaged in private trade, specialising in goods brought in from Germany. The fact that, given his age, there was no other army than the Imperial Army in which he could have served, and the fact that the Germans had closed down the Polish school depriving him of any job other than trading, was not considered worthy of note.[129] Sosnovskii was also criticised for allowed the majority of his staff to accompany the children to mass. Looking for a scapegoat, the party also criticised the man who taught history at the school part time, one of its own leading members Iosif Šteiman. Šteiman was rebuked for failing to respond to the 'obvious signals' that all was not well in the Polish School, and for failing to inform the city committee secretary of these developments.[130]

For the likes of Feoktistov, brought up in the Soviet Union and experiencing two decades of atheist propaganda, it might have seemed strange that Polish children went to mass with their teachers, but to Šteiman such behaviour must have seemed simply unremarkable. The affair also put Šteiman in a slightly awkward position personally. In the first months after the restoration of Soviet power in Daugavpils, it was Sosnovskii who had come forward to publicly welcome the new order. Writing in *Latgal'skaya Pravda* in August 1944 he had described the closure of his school by the Germans, the deportation of many members of the Russian population and the massacre of psychiatric patients. On the strength of this he had been appointed the token non-party member of the extraordinary commission to investigate Nazi atrocities of which Šteiman was the secretary.[131] The two men were not close, but had inevitably met from time to time.[132] Sosnovskii's dismissal showed that, whatever had been the case in autumn 1944, opposition to the Nazis coupled with a vague sympathy for the Soviet cause was no longer enough. Active commitment to the communist cause was expected of teachers.

Clearly some educationalists were sympathetic to the Sosnovskiis of this world and thought this purge had achieved enough; the press wrote about 'our fantastic teachers' when reporting the Daugavpils city teachers' conference of 8–9 January 1946.[133] However, the new director of the Polish secondary school, Zdislav Filipeckii, who also headed the party committee in the Daugavpils department of education, was determined to orchestrate further purges of those considered politically unreliable. He told a city committee meeting on 20 February 1946 that the 1st Latvian secondary school, recently praised for its high level of komsomol activity, needed a new director, and that in three or four of the city's schools a whole string of teachers needed to be replaced. Up to that month, from a total of 298 teachers in the city's ten schools, 58 had been sacked; at the same time 96 teachers demobilised from the Red Army had been found jobs.[134] However, as Filipeckii explained in August 1946, bringing in teachers from the Soviet Union might improve ideological reliability, but it was not a cure all; many of those recruited in 1945–6 left when it became clear that the city authorities were unable to allocate them a flat.[135]

The purge of teachers continued into the academic year 1946–7. When a teachers' conference was held at the end of August 1946, the press expressed concern that very few Latvian teachers had taken part in the courses offered to those wishing to improve their qualifications. There was a perfectly good reason for this. The courses on offer all revolved around the Sovietisation of the education system, and the majority of Latvian teachers, who had trained either in independent Latvia or in Imperial Russia, saw no need to update their qualifications according to the Soviet model.[136] In October 1946 the city committee decided that the current academic year was the occasion to take decisive action and solve once and for all the continuing problem posed by the 'many teachers who had worked during the period of bourgeois Latvia'; their presence, it was stated, made 'our teaching cadres far from satisfactory'.[137] By 1947 the change was indeed dramatic. If in 1945 18 per cent of teachers had been trained in the Soviet Union and 68 per cent trained in Imperial Russia, independent Latvia or abroad, by 1947 57.3 per cent had been trained in the Soviet Union and only 42.7 per cent in Imperial Russia, independent Latvia or abroad.[138]

Creating a new intelligentsia

Although the purge of the pre-war intelligentsia affected teachers above all, they were not the only people affected. Once the course towards a Soviet Daugavpils had been set, veterans of the party's underground generation could also appear a liability. This was not a universal phenomenon, because on 22 November 1946 Mikhail Yukhno was brought back into the city administration and made second secretary of the city committee in the place of the Russian incomer who had not lived up to expectations,[139] but during 1946 some important figures among what remained of the underground and partisan generations found themselves out of sympathy with the party leadership. As early as the elections of February 1946 an investigation was carried out into the Jēkabpils region and Milda Birkenfelde, the district secretary, was severely criticised: she was charged with unilaterally changing decisions arrived at after a vote within the local party committee, and of appointing her relatives both to the district committee and to parish committees; the report recommended that she be dismissed. It also considered it highly suspicious that the nationalist partisans had sent every other local party leader threatening letters, but had not sent one to her.[140] No action was taken at this stage, but the security authorities continued to collect negative information about her. In October 1946 Moscow's representative in Latvia said that he had been informed that Birkenfelde's husband had acquired one farm and his relatives another; in all, her family had control of three farms. Although investigations were still under way, Moscow's representative felt there were clear grounds for her being sacked and even expelled from the party.[141]

The true reason for the party's hostility to Birkenfelde was not her accumulated wealth and influence, which she shared with Feoktistov and other local leaders, but her outspoken criticism of incoming Russian cadres and her 'soft' line on the kulaks. At the 12th Central Committee Plenum in June 1946 she had accused Russian incomers of having no appreciation of the class situation in Latvia and treating all Latvians the same, as real or potential enemies.[142] Her policy of bringing gradual pressure to bear on the kulaks, rather than resorting to open confrontation with them, contradicted the official line that only where the kulak was confronted would grain deliveries improve.[143] Her policy of pressure rather than confrontation was shared by several other district-party leaders, who were all accused of nationalism at this time. In his report on the year 1946, Moscow's representative noted that three national party leaders had been expelled for 'bourgeois nationalism' and four district-party secretaries disciplined; Birkenfelde was amongst those disciplined.[144]

In April 1946 the veteran of the underground and partisan period Dominiks Kaupužs fell foul of the authorities. He had been made deputy-editor of the Latgale-language paper *Latgolas Taisneiba* and on 22–23 April decided to visit that part of Abrene district which Latvia had been forced to cede to Russia at the end of the war. There, the Latgale peasants were being forced to join collective farms, and, petitioned by an angry mob, Kaupužs undertook to raise their concerns with the authorities. Instead of urging them to accept their fate and join the collectives, he collected details of the injustices done to the peasants and promised to organise a meeting to discuss their complaints further. The crux of the matter was that the peasants wanted to return to Latvian administration. Kaupužs and an accomplice were detained by the NKVD before any such meeting could be held, and were returned to Latvia.[145] This episode did not immediately end Kaupužs's career, for on 10 December 1946 he was made editor of *Latgolas Taisneiba*.[146] However, shortly afterwards he was edged out of the limelight, his style of popular activism being out of tune with the times.

The party bureaucracy feared those who had even the most transient contact with old Latvia. The party had few enough Latvian members and might have been thought to have welcomed a certain P. Purmals into its ranks. Purmals came from Līvāni, had evacuated to the Soviet Union in 1941 and fought with the Latvian Division; he joined the party in 1943, becoming the party organiser for Līvāni in July 1945. But then it was discovered that, back in 1923, he had worked as a guard on the Latvian–Soviet border and for two years in the mid-1920s had been an *aizsarg*; he was at once expelled from the party.[147] It was not the only sins of the past which could not be forgiven, but the sins of the fathers. Ligija Švirksts, daughter of the last mayor of 'bourgeois' Daugavpils, was one of the first students to start a course at the Teachers' Institute. When there was a security clamp-down, she wrote in her autobiography that her father had been evacuated in July 1941, not deported in June 1941; if it had not been for some powerful local lobbying she would have been expelled from the Institute. As it was, she graduated and spent her life teaching in a rural school, an exception that perhaps proved the rule.[148]

At the same time as writing off Latvia's inter-war intelligentsia, the party set about constructing a new loyal intelligentsia. Nationally the komsomol was growing far more quickly than the party itself. Between 1 January 1945 and 1 April 1946 it rose from 2,552 members to 19,135.[149] The Central Committee noted this trend; when the 11th Central Committee Plenum met on 11–12 April 1946 the first item on the agenda was the fourth five-year plan, but the second item was the komsomol.[150] By October 1946 the komsomol had risen in membership to 23,739. Here was a basis on which to build support for the regime, even though some komsomol groups were described as 'riddled with nationalism'. The most striking thing about komsomol members was their lack of education; 70 per cent of those who joined in 1945–6 had not completed their secondary education and of the 837 leading cadres, only eight had higher education and only 155 full secondary education.[151] Right from the start, however, there had been a determined effort to 'Latvianise' the komsomol, and this had paid off. When cadres were reviewed in April 1945 and Latvians were shown to make up only half the city and district party apparatuses throughout Latvia, the komsomol apparatus was 74 per cent Latvian.[152]

As to Daugavpils district, the komsomol had grown from 848 to 1050 early in 1946, and most of the new recruits had been Latvians;[153] by April 1946 there were 1,130 komsomol members in 106 cells. Even in troubled Preiļi the komsomol had grown from 20 to 102.[154] The city komsomol organisation was not quite such a success story, by 1 November 1945 it had 808 members. The komsomol was strongest among white-collar workers, but had appreciable representation among manual workers as well. Thus 45 per cent of young administrative workers in the city were komsomol members, as were one in four of the industrial workforce; indeed, during March 1946 the komsomol cell at the steam depot doubled in size.[155] The quality of the membership might not be all that was wanted – less than half the members were committed enough to attend meetings regularly[156] and at best half the members took part in Marxism-Leninism study sessions[157] – but it was a base of sorts on which to start constructing a new, Soviet, Latvian intelli-gentsia. That process could be severely hampered if the failure of the komsomol to recruit students continued. In the Teachers' Institute and various colleges only 13 per cent of the students were in the komsomol.[158]

If there really was going to be a new Latvian intelligentsia committed to socialism on which the party could rely, communist ideas had to be popu-larised amongst the students at the Teachers' Institute. It was to address this

issue that the party decided to transfer Iosif Šteiman, the head of its political education office, to a lecturing post in the Teachers' Institute. Šteiman, a
full party member since 9 February 1945,[159] had been taking his political
education work seriously. He organised party schools, bringing on the
partisan generation[160] and constantly campaigning to make the party
bureaucrats take seriously the study of Marxism-Leninism as a liberating
ideology;[161] in June 1945 he organised a day conference on Marxism and the
national question,[162] and in November 1946 he gave a lecture in Latvian on
'Marx's Dialectical Method'.[163] Attendance at these schools and study
sessions suggested that many party members were loath to take ideological
work seriously, and raised the possibility that Šteiman might like to put his
energies to more rewarding work. On 11 October 1946, a meeting of the city
committee discussed what to do about the lack of a lecturer in Marxism-
Leninism at the Teachers' Institute who knew Latvian.[164] Not long
afterwards, Šteiman was approached by the Ministry of Education and
offered the job.[165] Thus it was that the task of moulding a new Latvian
Soviet intelligentsia for Latgale was entrusted to one of the youngest
survivors of the inter-war intelligentsia, the volleyball player of 1936 with
which this story began.

Conclusion

Experiencing class war and race war

Although as late as March 1947 some Latvians had expected that the fate of their country would be discussed by British Foreign Minister Ernest Bevin when he visited Moscow to take part in a further conference of allied foreign ministers,[1] they were to be disappointed; the topic was never raised. By summer and autumn 1947 the Cold War was well under way and Europe was clearly divided into two hostile camps. The Marshall Plan was announced in July, the Cominform was set up in September, and by February 1948 Czechoslovakia and Hungary were firmly in Stalin's grip. All talk of renewed independence for the Baltic States had long been forgotten. In this new international climate Stalin had a free hand in Latvia. When, at the end of 1946, Feoktistov had suggested the collectivisation of agriculture was the order of the day, he had rather jumped the gun. Despite some rather lacklustre experiments, the collectivisation campaign did not really get off the ground until the end of 1947.[2] It was accelerated in 1948, prompting resistance from the peasantry and a revival of the nationalist partisan movement. Stalin's response, as it had been to peasant resistance to collectivisation in every part of the Soviet Union, was to deport his kulak opponents to Siberia. In March 1949 some 50,000 Latvians were exiled.

These deportations coincided with the move from industrial recovery after the Second World War to industrial expansion. With so many Latvians exiled, industrial expansion could not draw on rural Latvian labour, but instead attracted migrants from elsewhere in the Soviet Union. By the mid-1950s there were so many migrants that the ethnic integrity of Latvia seemed under question. This situation prompted the formation of a short-lived 'national communist' movement in Latvia. Nikonov, the one-time Daugavpils district-party secretary, played a prominent part in this movement and was disciplined with all the other leaders when it was defeated in July 1959. Although not an active participant in the national communist movement, Kalnbērziņš was also dismissed at this time. The failure of the national communist movement meant that the process of in-migration continued. It was particularly acute in Daugavpils, situated as it is so near the borders with Russia and Belorussia. By 1995 58 per cent of the population of Daugavpils was Russian, and with the inclusion of Belorussians and Ukrainians, that figure rose to 69.5 per cent. Just under 15 per cent of the population was Latvian, roughly the same as the Russian population in 1925.[3]

Some comparisons

The opening of this study made clear that 'this book will have failed if all the reader gains is an understanding of the dramas faced by a small town in a country of which we know little'. The challenge was to see if a detailed case study could say something of interest about the nature of the two totalitarianisms which dominated the twentieth century. Case studies of non-Russian areas of the wartime Soviet Union are in their infancy. Alexander Dallin's *Odessa, 1941–44: A Case Study of Soviet Territory under Foreign Rule* was the first, published originally in 1957 and subsequently re-issued in 1998. This ground-breaking work established some of the broad parameters for the response of a local population to occupation and liberation, but the fact that this area was administered by the Romanians rather than the Nazis meant that generalisations were hard to make. Dallin established that 'if, at the start, many residents of [what the Romanians christened] "Transnistria" seemed to be prepared to adapt to the new system, two years later, under conditions of war weariness, Romanian rule was widely perceived as futile, unjust, or antiquated, while an upsurge of patriotism and wishful thinking led more people to think of the Red Army as the People-under-Arms, bearers of a new message'.[4]

Romanian rule, for all its unpleasantness, was never as terrible as Nazi rule. Those living under Romanian occupation retained an ironic attitude towards their rulers, but were well aware that their material conditions continued to be on a par with the inter-war years, and that privatisation of the economy had ushered in for them a new version of NEP; they were thus substantially better off than those living in German- controlled areas. With no forced labour deportations and no de-industrialisation policies, the local economy remained vibrant, while cultural life thrived, if with a Romanian tinge. Without labour deportations, the partisan movement found it difficult to get off the ground, especially as, after an initial period of persecution, former communist activists were simply required to report regularly to the police. And yet there were some similarities with the situation in Daugavpils. It was the blowing up of the former NKVD building in Odessa by a Soviet agent which was given as the excuse to launch the assault on the Jews. The Romanian fascists found fellow anti-Semites among the liberated population, who helped in that assault; eventually the Jewish population of Odessa was reduced from an estimated 60,000 at the start of the occupation to 54 in 1943. In another parallel the Romanian authorities were only interested if developing a 'bourgeois' culture in their newly acquired territory. Thus they spent a great deal of money re-establishing the university, but had no interest in general primary education. Here the Romanians were, if anything, worse than their counterparts in Latgale, abolishing compulsory education and introducing fees for state schools.[5]

Dallin based his study largely on German documentation seized at the end of the war and interviews with survivors of the Romanian administration who fled westwards. Only the Gorbachev era and the subsequent collapse of the Soviet Union made possible detailed local studies based on Soviet archives. Amir Weiner's *Making Sense of War: The Second World War and the Fate of the Bolshevik Revolution* was published in 2001 and looks at the area around Vinnytsia in Ukraine.[6] Vinnytsia is situated in the western Ukraine, but not so far west that it was one of the regions incorporated into the Soviet Union under the Nazi–Soviet Pact. Many parallels can be drawn between its experience of the Second World War and that of Daugavpils, but the fact that its inhabitants had been a constituent part of the Soviet Union since its formation means that a fundamental difference remains.

While there was no direct parallel with the Soviet deportations of June 1941, the inhabitants of Vinnytsia were well aware of Stalin's terror of 1937–8; at its height mass executions took place in the surrounding countryside. These killings were made use of by the Nazis. When they arrived, Ukrainian nationalists encouraged their members to join the new police force and were happy to issue anti-Semitic proclamations, in line with their well-established anti-Semitic tradition. However, as in Daugavpils, it took the arrival of a Nazi Einsatzgruppe for the liquidation of the Jews to begin. The local population had to be incited to take an active role and the discovery of Stalin's mass graves greatly helped that process. As in Daugavpils so in Vinnytsia, the Germans made sure the local militia took an active part in the killings. In another parallel, the Ukrainian nationalists brought forth by the German administration were as hostile to the Russians as they were to the Jews; the Germans on the other hand were prepared to establish a *modus vivendi* with local Russians.

The partisan experience was also similar. In Vinnytsia partisans noted that that the attitude of the local population towards them became more sympathetic in spring 1943, and that by summer 1943 the impact of German propaganda about the terror was beginning to wane. Even more so than in Latvia, the Vinnytsia Soviet partisans had come into contact during the war with nationalist partisans, sometimes coming to military agreements with them. As in Latgale, the partisans had a significantly lower proportion of Ukrainians in their membership than Russians. As ruthless as any other partisans when it came to executing German-appointed elders, the Vinnytsia partisans found that, with the re-establishment of Soviet power, they were first used to help combat the nationalist partisan movement and then sidelined by politicians who believed that simply surviving the Nazi occupation was a sign of political unreliability. As tension developed between the partisan veterans and the party hierarchy, this spilled over into resentment against Russian incomers; early in 1947 a plot was discovered to oust the Russian first secretary. All these events had their echoes in Daugavpils and there were also parallels in the assessment of the Holocaust. The main propaganda tool in Vinnytsia was the newspaper column 'We cannot forgive,

nor can we forget' and by the end of the war, if not earlier, all specific references to the suffering of the Jews had ceased as 'the Holocaust was
incorporated into the epic suffering of the entire Soviet population'.[7]

However there were differences between the war years in Vinnytsia and the
war years in Latgale and these concerned two related areas, land reform and
the nationalist partisans. The Nazi agrarian reform in Latgale was real; in
Vinnytsia it suited the Germans to keep collective farms, only tinkering with
their administration and changing their name. This was partly because the
collective farms were an easy way of ensuring grain deliveries, but also
because by 1941 soviet power had made significant inroads into village life.
This was not the case in Latgale. Soviet support in the countryside around
Daugavpils was minimal and collective farms were feared by all. This difference was linked to the other major difference between Vinnytsia and
Daugavpils, the authorities' response to the nationalist partisans. In Vinnytsia
the newly re-established Soviet authorities faced a powerful nationalist
partisan movement, often better armed than their own destroyer battalions.
As in Latgale, ideological support for this movement came from rural
schoolteachers. However, this confrontation was bloodier than those which
took place around Daugavpils. What Weiner describes is a fight to the death,
with most nationalist partisans dying on the battlefield in a war with no prisoners. That is not the whole story in Latgale, where the carrot and stick
approach of amnesty and surrender became so important. In Vinnytsia many
of the nationalist partisans were outsiders, from the formerly independent
parts of western Ukraine. In Daugavpils the nationalist partisans did not
come from outside, they were local. If they had a base it was a social base,
not a regional one; they came from 'kulakdom'. As the Soviet authorities
found, too brutal a destruction could, and did, breed further resistance. So in
Latgale the nationalist partisans had to be isolated and weakened, the leaders
separated from the led, an important softening-up process before the final
social solution to the problem, collectivisation and deportation. Essentially,
both these differences between Vinnytsia and Daugavpils stemmed from the
fact that Latvia had been an independent state until June 1940.[8]

Quiescent paternalism

A case study of wartime Daugavpils, then, quite understandably reveals
elements quite unlike the experience of other parts of the non-Russian Soviet
Union under German occupation. What else does it show? While everyone in
Daugavpils and the surrounding region experienced class war and race war
between 1940 and 1946, only a tiny minority actively participated in those
wars. The active participants were those among Latvia's ethnic minorities
who felt discriminated against by the Ulmanis regime; those with friends or
relatives deported by the communists in June 1941 who rallied to the Nazi
cause; and those with friends and relatives victimised by the Nazis who made
the decision to resist. Even many of those who actively participated in the

fighting were not as ideologically committed as their leaders. Only 5 per cent of Soviet partisans were members of the Communist Party; in Vinnytsia the equivalent figure was 7 per cent.[9] On the other side of the ideological divide only 20 per cent of those mobilised into the Latvian Legion in Latgale in February 1944 reported for duty, and the numbers avoiding conscription with false medical papers caused a public scandal. As to the nationalist partisans, despite communist propaganda to the contrary, only some of the nationalist partisans were former members of the Latvian police force hell-bent on cleansing Latvia of Jews and Russians; the majority, as the surrender policy suggested, were low-level officials of the collaborationist regime and those unwilling to serve in the Red Army.

In March 1944 the Daugavpils administration produced in its budget an appendix which showed how *Daugavas vēstnesis*, the mouthpiece of the Daugavpils Gebietskommissar, was funded. Apart from a small income from advertising (18,180 Reichsmarks), the remaining income of 285,710 Reichsmarks came from sales. However, of those sales only 5,700 copies were bought daily in the kiosks, the vast bulk of the income accruing from 9,000 yearly subscriptions taken out by institutions.[10] This was not a large circulation for a paper which was distributed throughout Latgale; the population of Daugavpils never fell below 24,000. Communist newspapers were no more popular. In December 1940 the circulation of *Latgolas Taisneiba* was only 4,700, forcing the party to provide a subsidy of 10,000 roubles.[11] On 26 February 1946 the editor of *Latgolas Taisneiba* told the Daugavpils district committee that he was only getting two or three letters a day from readers, a situation which he suggested meant that the paper was far from successful.[12] Most inhabitants of Daugavpils and the surrounding region during these years were passive, allowing others to act in their name. Had the parliamentary system continued in Latvia, those living on the banks of the Dvina would have continued to support and vote for moderate socialist and Christian parties as they had done in the past. However, the choice of a multi-party parliamentary democracy was not open to Latgale after 1946. By then Latvia was well and truly within the Soviet orbit and political activity remained the concern of a self-selecting minority.

The Latgale experience of life in the Soviet Union was a bitter one, but even back in 1947, Soviet administration could offer certain advantages over the Nazi administration that preceded it. Throughout the period of this study, the citizens of Daugavpils endured shortages and hardship in organising their daily lives. Life was miserable under both regimes, but within that context of misery there were symbols of a different approach which said something about the priorities of the two totalitarianisms. Health care and education were priorities for the communists, they were not for the fascists. For the first six months of Nazi rule there was no soap. As the authorities conceded, this was one of the major causes of the typhus outbreak, an outbreak made more likely, as Schwung conceded in a report to Riga, by the mass graves of the executed Jews and communists which caused an additional health hazard.

Soap was in short supply in the first six months after the return of the Red Army in July 1944, but one of the priorities of the Daugavpils communists was the reconstruction of public baths, and this was one of the few reconstruction targets they met. On their arrival in Daugavpils, the Nazis had two priorities for the hospital service during autumn 1941: sterilisation and euthanasia. When Soviet power was restored in 1944, the first health priority was to restore a network of polyclinics and hospitals; beds were begged, borrowed and stolen to create a basic health-care structure from scratch in six weeks.

Even at the time, pro-Soviet commentators were keen to compare the Soviet educational provision of 1945 and 1946 with that of the Nazis. In 1940–1 the Soviet authorities had done much to establish Russian schools and Jewish schools, reflecting their 'internationalist' agenda. When the Germans came their initial response was to close the schools for the national minorities, reopening them again only when this became politically opportune and consistent with the policy of inter-ethnic self-administration for the national minorities. However, the types of school offered by the two totalitarianisms was not the most striking difference in approach; that related to the start of the school year. Under the Nazis the start of the school year was put back to mid-October in order to allow children to take part in the harvest. *Latgal'skaya Pravda* reported on 1 September 1944 that in the last year of Nazi rule the schools operated for only 34 days. Such things did not happen in the first years after the Soviet reoccupation. The school year began a month late on 1 October in 1944, and then always on 1 September. Understandably, Soviet propagandists sought to show this difference as symbolic: the Nazis put work before schooling, and the communists schooling before work.

Comparative terror

In terms of comparative terror, Daugavpils suffered more under German fascism than Soviet communism and this must have had a subliminal effect on people's attitudes to the regimes. There was no Soviet equivalent to the 20,000 Jews killed by the Nazis in the Latgale region, 13,000 of them in Daugavpils. Those Jews were killed as part of a war on 'Jewish-Bolshevism'. This meant almost certain death to communists. Any communist official unable to flee in 1941, any communist resistance worker during the Nazi occupation and any captured partisan was executed. The fate of the ghetto resident Fridman, mistaken for the Daugavpils second secretary Faifish Fridman, showed how casually alleged communists could be killed. When the Red Army returned to Latvia in 1944, the new Soviet authorities did not deal so ruthlessly with representatives of the regime they had overthrown. True, the Soviet security service had its target of collaborators to capture, but the vast majority of these were exiled rather than shot. As to captured nationalist partisans, some were quietly shot, others were executed after being put on trial, and yet other leaders died within Stalin's gulag system; but most, the led rather than the leaders, were exiled. Some exiles wrote of deportation as a form of living death, but it was certainly less final than death itself.

Both regimes exiled their perceived enemies in pre-emptive actions. In 1941 Stalin deported just over a thousand representatives of the old regime from Daugavpils city and district. In May 1942 and August 1943 the Nazis deported 11,500 people from the Latgale region, mostly Russian Old Believers suspected of sympathising with the partisans. German fascism again proved the more horrific, despite direct comparison being complicated by the different sizes of district and region.[13] It was not only that the communists deported fewer people than the fascists, but that the methods they used were less random. The methods by which the fascists and communists carried out their deportation differed considerably. Both were arbitrary in that there was no pretence at establishing the guilt or innocence of those deported, and no sense in which all those in comparable situations would be deported or left untouched; yet there was more method in the soviet deportations.

In June 1941 Stalin had established nine clear and verifiable categories of those to be deported. National target figures were issued, but it was then up to locally based commissions to find sufficient local victims to meet that target. Sometimes the categories had to be stretched in order to reach the target, sometimes the target was smaller than the number of people in the category, but by and large the victims matched the categories required. Nazi deportations were far more random. In May 1942 the deportation was scarcely planned at all. It grew out of the failure of the civilian authorities to recruit enough volunteers for work in Germany. The security authorities announced that they could do better, and although they were supposed to build on the work of parish elders who had been struggling to rustle up volunteers, the involvement of local elders was cursory. The security authorities decided unilaterally to abandon the voluntary principle espoused by Schwung and target the perceived enemies of the new regime, the Poles and in particular the Russian Old Believers. As arrests took place there was little attempt to distinguish between Old Believer and Orthodox Russians, but then in Daugavpils, in the last desperate effort to reach the target, all guiding principles were abandoned and arrests were carried out completely at random, seizing Latvians as well as Russians.

Few lessons had been learnt by the time of the next deportation wave in August 1943. This action was more carefully planned and had a clear target, those believed to be sympathetic to the Soviet partisans. Over summer 1943 attempts were made to draw up detailed lists by involving local parish elders in identifying 'partisan sympathisers'; commissions were established comprising representatives of the German authorities, Latvian administrators and the minority communities. However, the police became impatient with such procedures and decided to press ahead, arresting people according to their own lists. Just as in May 1942 when Schwung had found himself working to get detained Latvians released, so in August 1943 Riecken found himself calming down parish elders incensed that the wrong people had been arrested and smoothing the ruffled feathers of the recently formed Russian National Committee, since most of those targeted were again Russian Old Believers. The different approaches of fascism and communism were noticed at once by Shaike Iwensky, shortly after his detention in Daugavpils prison: 'we had been in prison for nine days; no documents had been checked, none requested, none issued to us. I was surprised that we had experienced none of the expected bureaucratic procedures.'[14]

Structural incoherence versus structural cohesion

The deportations of May 1942 and August 1943 also brought out clearly the structural incoherence of German fascism. Unless recourse could be made to Hitler himself, there was no way of co-ordinating the policies of the different institutions of government. In Daugavpils the policy pursued by the security services was quite at odds with that being pursued by the Gebietskommissar. Schwung did not want violent anti-Semites or right-wing army officers as his city and district elders, but former activists from the Christian peasant parties. He first sung the praises of Latgale's Russian population in November 1941 when he asserted that they were as racially and politically aware as the Latvians. He had already begun to have doubts about the activities of the Latvian intelligentsia in March 1942, expressing the view that they were deliberately trying to turn the Germans against the Russians; he rejected the automatic assumption that the Russians were infected with Bolshevism. Yet this was precisely the principle on which the security police worked. The May deportations were targeted against the Russians, and to a lesser extent the Poles, because a whole series of security reports, as well as the incidents at Audriņi and elsewhere, suggested the Old Believer Russians were politically unreliable. The result was a botched deportation which, as Schwung noted himself, was a propaganda gift to the Bolsheviks.

The same security obsession about the political reliability of the Russian population governed the Winter Magic campaign in February 1943, the worst atrocities of which took place outside Latvia although the Latvian authorities had to pick up the pieces by dealing with the one thousand orphaned Russian children. The *Sommerreise* assault on partisan sympathisers in August 1943 was also targeted on the Russians. By summer 1943 it was clear that another wave of anti-Russian deportations would seriously disrupt the work done by Riecken in establishing self-administration for Latgale's minority communities. By spring 1943 Riecken had spent much time wooing the Russian population, bringing forward Russian representatives and using the privatisation of the economy to win over Russian entrepreneurs. Budže had appealed to the Russian and Latvian communities to work together, and the press had acknowledged Russian victims of Stalin's deportations. The formation of Russian Security Battalions was a clear sign that not all Russians were enemies. It was in order to protect these achievements that Riecken expended a great deal of energy on involving parish elders in the process of identifying those destined for deportation. Yet when *Sommerreise* began the security services paid only token attention to the local lists, ignoring most of Riecken's work and alienating those local officials who had come forward to work with the German administration.

After the disaster of *Sommerreise*, Riecken expressed his despair at the way the security services had disregarded both his office and that of the self-administration; his authority had been completely undermined, he wrote to his superior in Riga, Generalkommissar Drechsler. Drechsler was equally despondent; he noted at the same time that he too had absolutely no influence when it came to security matters. Reichskommissar Lohse, Drechsler's superior, was equally despairing at the damage done by the whole affair. He wrote and urged Drechsler to warn him in advance if the security services were ever planning something similar in Latvia, so that he could raise the matter with the highest police authorities and thus hopefully prevent it. Yet Lohse's representative had already promised Riecken earlier in the year that there would be no repeat of the May 1942 action, a promise that turned out to be mere wishful thinking. Between them, Schwung and especially Riecken invested enormous energy in trying to establish a working relationship with all the ethnic communities of Latgale, and that work was vitiated overnight by the security services, whose actions simply provided additional recruits for the Soviet partisans.

This picture of the structural incoherence of the fascist regime was not mirrored by that of the Soviet communists. There were, of course, serious tensions between district Communist Party secretaries and the security services, but such tensions were successfully resolved. For the first few months after the return of the Red Army in July 1944, while collaborators were being sought everywhere, relations between party secretaries and the NKVD were frequently tense. Faced with an enormous shortage of personnel, it was deeply upsetting for party secretaries to discover that the person they had selected as soviet chairperson stood accused of collaboration. On occasion incidents like this boiled over into accusations that the security services were behaving as they had in 1937–8 or 1941, operating according to predetermined target figures. Although this was not in fact the case, there was a strong element of hearsay in the way the lists were compiled and inevitably this meant the detention of innocent people. Yet the tension between the party secretaries and the NKVD was resolved by the intervention of the Central Committee. In April 1945, when it was clear the nationalist partisans were going to prove a considerable challenge, the Central Committee instigated a meeting between party secretaries and security chiefs and thrashed out an agreed policy. It then oversaw the implementation of that policy, which ensured that at every level the party secretaries, the local soviet chairman and the local security commander were brought into a close working relationship.

Of course this did not always work. The harvest had to be got in, and this involved putting pressure on the peasants. Where, as in the case of Preiļi in autumn 1945, pressure turned to terror, the policy of using force to bring in the harvest could end up encouraging the formation of nationalist partisan bands, just as Nazi deportations of partisan sympathisers created yet more partisans. Equally, poor liaison between the party and the NKVD could continue, despite the best efforts of the Central Committee. When the Līvāni NKVD arrested Arvīds Puids after he had already surrendered, the whole of the government's surrender policy was thrown into confusion. Yet there were mechanisms through which these incidents could be resolved. Both the Preiļi and Līvāni affairs were investigated by the Central Committee, and those concerned were disciplined as necessary. Nor were the mistakes repeated: in 1946 the policy of 'ending liberalism towards the kulaks' did not result in terror; there was no repeat of 1945 in the way the errors of May 1942 were repeated in August 1943. Feoktistov and Nikonov worked under the constant supervision of Riga in a way that Riecken would clearly have envied.

The existence of such rational channels for the resolution of inter-institutional tension not only meant less chaotic government, it also meant more rational policies. The Soviet authorities had a dual strategy for dealing with the nationalist partisans, military confrontation and the encouragement of surrender. The Nazis had no equivalent for the surrender policy. It is true that a couple of articles in *Dvinskii vestnik* talked of the possibility of surrender, one claiming to be written by a Soviet partisan who had 'seen the light' and had settled back into a normal life, but the reality was that Soviet partisans were shot on capture after a brief interrogation. By contrast the Soviet strategy of surrender had a whole series of high-profile successes, and where it was obviously violated, as in Līvāni and by the actions of the Military Commissariat, counter-measures were taken. The surrender policy was a tactic, not a principle. It got nationalist partisans out of the forest and disarmed them. All former partisans were marked men thereafter and could be, and were, arrested later on other charges. But while the policy was in operation, the party leadership was determined to defend its credibility, since it avoided unnecessary bloodshed.

Hitler and Stalin's hegemony

Most Latvian communists and Latvian fascists believed that when they joined their respective organisations, they were joining movements of European and even world- wide significance which were working for a better future. It was the inspiration of such ideals that enabled them to abandon conventional morality and take part in acts of barbarism. Communists accepted Stalin's wisdom in deporting the representatives of old Latvia, while fascists adapted to the grisly task of killing Jews. They performed these tasks because they believed that Latvia would play an important role in the world they were creating. This study has shown clearly that such beliefs were naïve in the extreme. Daugavpils communists found themselves working to Stalin's agenda which was seriously at variance with Latvia's perceived needs, while the Daugavpils fascists found that neither Hitler nor his representatives in Daugavpils had much sympathy with their type of racism. National communists and national fascists were equally subjected to the wills of Stalin and Hitler.

There was little evidence of any form of 'national communism' in the first year of Soviet rule, 1940–1. Communists were essentially swept along by events, and because they considered incorporation into the Soviet Union as a self-evident blessing, they were not overly worried about how it was done. Although Soviet Latvians were sent in to help, like Treimans the first secretary of the Daugavpils city committee, appointments such as these fuelled little resentment. The picture was very different in 1944. Then there were far more 'incomers', far more of them were Russian rather than Latvian and they were deeply resented by some party members. This was especially true of those who had worked to establish the partisan movement and who had a different outlook to those who had spent the war on Soviet territory. Their experience of Nazi occupation made them far more sensitive to the realities of Latvia in 1944–5, and their dispute with the Central Committee about where to locate partisan headquarters had emboldened them to challenge directives. Milda Birkenfelde spoke for many when she told the first Central Committee plenum after the re-establishment of Soviet power that the only way forward was to find local cadres and trust them; nothing would be achieved if the party relied solely on those cadres brought in from the Soviet Union.

Former partisan leaders were aware of the same truth that Soviet military intelligence had unearthed immediately prior to the return of the Red Army. There were a number of rich peasants who had benefited from German rule and had been associated with the administration of old Latvia; such people would always be hostile to the Soviet Union. However, there were plenty of 'better off' peasants who were more open-minded and ready to collaborate with the Russians if approached in the right way. District-party secretaries like Milda Birkenfelde tried to limit their assaults on the kulaks to just these pro-German elements. At the same time they campaigned against the excessive deployment of incoming Russians; but on both issues they were going against the clear wishes of Stalin. It was Stalin who insisted that the land reform introduced in Latvia in 1944 should be more divisive than that of 1940 and should target the better-off peasant as well as the kulak, and it was Stalin's representatives in Latvia who were the most vociferous in highlighting the alleged kulak danger and were the most determined to suggest that Birkenfelde represented some form of nationalist deviation. As to the use of Russians to establish Soviet rule, one of the most striking differences between 1940 and 1944 was Russian dominance of the security services. In 1940 Latvian communists had entered the security services and incoming Russians had been deployed to other duties, but in 1944 Latvian *Chekists* were the exception rather than the rule. Stalin was taking no chances and was determined to stamp out even the mildest suggestion that Latvia could follow a path different to that taken by the rest of the Soviet Union by abandoning the prescribed path of land reform followed by collectivisation.

If national communism of former partisan leaders failed, so too did national fascism. Although it had been members of the Pērkonkrusts party and its sympathisers who had rushed forward to help the Nazis implement their genocide in 1941, they had very soon fallen out of favour. The arrest of Blūzmanis and his subsequent sidelining was an extreme example of a common trend. The Pērkonkrusts party was banned under the 20 September 1941 legislation outlawing political associations, and the energies of its members were redirected into the good works of encouraging volunteers to fight on the Eastern Front and supporting the families of such volunteers through the People's Aid organisation. Any pretensions towards political power were squashed. This happened on a national level, with Hitler's consistent refusal to allow Latvia any sort of independence, and also on a local level, where the most vociferous collaborators constantly found their ambitions being thwarted. Schwung found his most loyal collaborator to be Budže, a politician from Latvia's parliamentary past, rather than those who had rushed forward to execute the Jews.

Those who continued to argue that the Latvian people had a special role in the New Europe soon came under criticism, as witnessed by Schwung's complaints that he was constantly being pushed towards a Latvian 'national chauvinist' agenda. Hitler's view of the Latvians was that they were racially beneath the Germans and ultimately had no future. The Latvian fascists considered themselves not only superior to the Jews, but superior to the Slavs as well. Such views could not be reconciled. Schwung found his Slav population on a par with the Latvians, if not in some ways better. On these grounds he tired of what he called the Latvian collaborators' attempt to get him to do their dirty work for them and deport the Russians from Latgale. Riecken's attitude was the same. After efforts lasting for more than a year, he finally established a system of self-administration for the Belorussian and Russian communities in November 1943. He therefore did not welcome the immediate complaints from what he described as typical national chauvinists that bringing Russians into the self-administration and making them elders simply played into the hands of the partisans. Administering a multi-ethnic self-administration and creating an ethnic Latvian state were completely different ventures. Both Schwung and Riecken must have regretted shunting Blūzmanis and his associates into police work, where they reinforced the anti-Russian prejudices of the German security police.

Nation and class

Although Soviet communism proved the more rational, dynamic and there-fore longer-lasting of the two totalitarianisms, its ideology completely failed to inspire. Ironically the concept of the nation, which stood at the heart of fascism, the form of totalitarianism doomed to self-destruction, proved a far stronger motivating force than the concept of class. The language of 1940–6 was by and large the language of nationalism – it pervaded and even perverted all discussion of class. With the Communist Party being domi-nated by members of Latvia's Russian and Jewish minorities, it was not difficult for the party's opponents to portray it as 'anti-Latvian'. In 1940–1 the communists feared their new regime would be seen as part of a Russian take-over, and that is not only how many Latvians experienced it but how many Russians experienced it as well; the notion 'now its our turn' was not far below the surface as Russians and Jews replaced Latvians as the city's administrators, albeit acting in the name of the working class. It was the same in 1941–2, when many Latvians who came forward to help the Germans had family members among the deported and were keen to settle scores with the former 'Russian regime'. To General Dankers, the multi-ethnic composition of the Latvian Soviet Government in Exile deprived it of the right to speak in the name of the Latvian people. Then in 1944, Russian dominance of the security services made it almost impossible to counter the impression that the Russians were taking over, despite Latvian-language classes for leading officials and the determined efforts to 'Latvianise' the 1946 elections. The party spoke the language of class, the people spoke the language of nation.

One of the most powerful myths of the period under consideration was the notion, encouraged by the Nazis, that the Soviet deportations of 1941 were aimed at the annihilation of the Latvians as a people. When coupled with the suggestions that the deportations were part of a broader 'Jewish-Bolshevik' campaign, the Nazis had a powerful tool with which to unleash the genocide of neighbour against neighbour. Guilt for that act then haunted some of those involved, reviving the idea that the Latvians were destined for destruction. As early as 1943 there were rumours that the Latvians might be shot in revenge for the Jews, and in 1945 Soviet security agents regularly monitored the popular view that 'we will be sent to Siberia soon'.[15] Those Soviet representatives who tried to persuade nationalist partisans to surrender constantly noted how their minds had been infected by 'nationalist poison'. The 1941 deportation myth was so powerful because it was in essence true. It was not the Latvians as a people who were deported, but their inter-war leadership, and for many people the two were interchangeable.

Class never had the same motivating power as national survival, even if there were occasions when it too could mobilise. Although the communists' plans for collectivisation scarcely got off the ground in 1941, the fear of collective farms was ever present. Communists were supposed to counter that fear of collectivisation by encouraging peasants to divide along class lines and attack the rich kulaks. Stalin's land reform of 1944 was based on this proposition. The rhetoric of class war was on the lips of the party and NKVD leaders in Preiļi during their reign of terror in autumn 1945. Fired up with talk of 'ending liberalism towards the kulak' these local men encouraged assaults on those amongst whom they had grown up. But there was a crucial difference between those inspired by class in Preiļi and those inspired by the survival of the Latvian people. The language of class remained the prerogative of party activists and never spilled over into the population at large. The language of the threatened annihilation of the Latvian people was fed by the steady progress of in-migration in the later Soviet period. It fuelled the debates of the national communists in 1959, those men and women who embodied the new Soviet intelligentsia formed in the late 1940s. It even survived the death of communism.

Soviet modernisation

Introducing his study of Vinnytsia, Amir Weiner wrote:

> The soviet ethos was ingrained in the politics that shaped the modern era where states sought the transformation of societies with the help of scientific models and a myriad of institutions charged with managing all social spheres. The soviets co-opted or juxtaposed their ideology and practices to this phenomenon.[16]

Understanding this is to understand how two generations of Latvians accepted Soviet rule and even participated in it. Ukrainian nationalism stressed that a sovereign Ukraine would be a peasant state.[17] It was the same for Latvian nationalists.

In the Nazi scheme of things Latgale was destined to lose what industry it had and concentrate on agriculture. The children who passed through Latgale schools would end up agricultural labourers, so there was no harm in them gaining harvest experience. Despite some grumbling from Schwung, the closure of the local textile industry was accepted as inevitable, while the problem of rural underemployment would be addressed by encouraging migration to areas of labour shortage. The only industries to survive would be the small-scale manufacturing and service sector covered by the privatisation process. These Nazi ambitions did not contradict the nostrums of the Latvian fascists. In summer 1942 one of the Pērkonkrusts leaders, Adolfs Šilde, wrote in *Daugavas vēstnesis* criticising the inter-war Social Democrats for wanting to industrialise Latvia, and arguing that Latvians were first and foremost peasants.[18] That was precisely what both German and Latvian fascists wanted them to stay. Of course, it was not only the inter-war Social Democrats who had wanted to industrialise Latgale, but the communists as well. Their industrialisation programme had been drafted in 1941 and was re-issued as soon as they returned to power, symbolised in Daugavpils by the tram project, brought to a successful conclusion in November 1946. Although this remained the only tangible result of the post-war five-year plan for some time, it did announce to the population that communism brought new prospects. The tram equalled modernity.

If for communists this quest for modernity was an integral part of their colossal project of building a new socialist world and ultimately a communist society, disposing of myriad enemies on the way, for many more it was the continuation of something cut short by Ulmanis in 1934 with the introduction of the cult of the peasant. The career of Aleksei Bartkevich offers just one example. A Belorussian, who studied in Prague and settled in Daugavpils when he married, was dismissed as a schoolteacher for his social democrat views in 1934. After a spell in prison, he found work as an auxiliary in the psychiatric hospital until, in 1940, he was asked to help run the education department, becoming its *de facto* leader. He was arrested by the Germans in 1941, but survived the war and in 1944 was made director of the 1st Latvian secondary school, only to be sacked in Filipeckii's purge. Later he found work in a local college, heading a department and protecting teachers who openly expressed their religious beliefs or were considered unreliable; for a while he protected the daughter of last mayor of Daugavpils in this way.[19] This was a journey that communists could never comprehend, centred on unrestricted access to the benefits of education and science, but it enabled Bartkevich to link the anti-fascist struggles of his youth to the potentials and possibilities of the Soviet system. He was not alone: others could choose modernity according to their personal world-view, without engaging with the official ideology.

To take another example. A little farm girl from a Polish family, Helena Krukowska, missed a year's schooling because the Germans closed the Polish school. She then struggled with her studies when the Red Army came, because she could only attend a Russian school. The demands of the farm meant she left school to tend the animals. Later she married, moved into the city, attended evening classes at a local college and ended up the director of a shop, while continuing to adhere to and practise her deeply held Catholic faith. Marxism-Leninism was the modernising ideology *par excellence*, and the journey from farm girl to shop director was a parable that helped people to rationalise, and for some even to justify, the Soviet experience.

Soviet Daugavpils offered prospects to its young people. Communism encouraged a road out of the village, fascism did not, which was why there was a slow but sure rise in the number of Latvians who joined the komsomol. The Germans kept open the Rēzekne Teachers' Institute, but only opened it to Russian students in autumn 1943.[20] The communists had a mission for young people. They wanted to revive the long buried revolutionary tradition of 1917 when Latvians had stood at the forefront of the world revolution; Kalnbērziņš was told as much when he visited Moscow in

November 1944.[21] By 1945 the communists accepted that this would be a grandiose project. It would mean getting rid of the inter-war intelligentsia completely and starting again from scratch. The party would have to eliminate much of the existing teaching profession and train a new intelligentsia. For those not destined for the dustbin of history, real prospects were opening up. The Teachers' Institute, re-established in Daugavpils, would be expanded into a Pedagogical Institute, and there would be opportunities for the brightest and the best of Latgale. The party, in the jovial guise of Iosif Šteiman, would help students match their personal ambitions to the official nostrums of Marxism-Leninism, but the ambitions of those students would be real enough.

Notes

1 Introducing bourgeois Daugavpils

1 I. Šteiman, *Vremya i lyudi* (Latgale Cultural Centre: Rēzekne, 2001), p. 26.
2 S. Iwens, *How Dark the Heavens: 1400 Days in the Grip of Nazi Terror* (Shengold Publishers: New York, 1990), p. 101.
3 I am fully aware that it is conventional in contemporary Latvian historiography to talk of the nationalist partisans fighting a war against the Soviet occupation which lasted until 1956. However, although fighting did continue until 1956, its scale after 1946 was greatly reduced. It seems to me important to distinguish between 1945–6, when there was large-scale fighting and an albeit inaccurate expectation that the future of Latvia would be resolved in the peace discussions concerning Germany and its allies, and the revival of more piecemeal violence from 1947–8 as peasant farmers tried to resist the collectivisation campaign.
4 G. Roberts, *The Unholy Alliance* (Indiana University Press: Bloomington, 1989), pp. 136–9.
5 A. Ezergailis, *The Holocaust in Latvia, 1941–44: The Missing Center* (Historical Institute of Latvia: Riga, 1996), p. 61. The figure for Latvians comes from *Daugavas vēstnesis* [hereafter DV] 24.7.1943. Although this source is potentially unreliable, the other figures coincide with those given by Ezergailis, suggesting a common source in the census. Z. Yakub, *Daugavpils v proshhlom* (AKA: Daugavpils, 1998), p. 99, gives the figure for Latvians as 34 per cent, but in this book all percentages have been rounded up. Yakub gives the 18 per cent figure.
6 This summary is taken from Yakub, *Daugavpils.*
7 S. Kuznetsov, 'Domu Edinstva segodnya 65 let', *Seichas* 19.12.02.
8 I. Šteiman and S. Kuznetsov, *Nezavisimaya Latvia, 1918–40* (SI: Riga, 1996), p. 178.
9 J. Billington, *The Icon and the Axe* (Weidenfield and Nicolson: London, 1966), pp. 121–62.
10 DV 24.7.43.
11 S. Kuznetsov and I. Saleniece, 'Nationality Policy, Education and the Russian Question in Latvia' in C. Williams and T. Sfikas (eds) *Ethnicity and Nationalism in Russia, the CIS and the Baltic States* (Ashgate: Aldershot, 1999), p. 249.
12 J. Šteimanis (I. Šteiman), *History of the Latvian Jews* (East European Monographs: Boulder, 2002), pp. 47–52.
13 M. Laserson, 'The Jews in the Latvian Parliament', in M. Bobe *et al.* (eds) *The Jews in Latvia* (Association of Latvian and Estonian Jews in Israel: Tel Aviv, 1971), p. 108.
14 Kuznetsov and Saleniece, 'Nationality Policy', pp. 247–52.
15 B. Press, *The Murder of the Jews in Latvia, 1941–45* (Northwestern University Press: Evanston, 2000), pp. 25–9.

16 These points are taken from I. Šteiman *et al.*, *Daugavpils v proshlym i nastoy-ashchem* (Riga, 1959), p. 17; and his *Vremya i lyudi*, p. 14, p. 28.

17 Šteiman and Kuznetsov, *Nezavismaya Latviya*, p. 172.

18 Bobe *et al.*, *The Jews in Latvia*, p. 122.

19 Šteimanis, *History of the Latvian Jews*, p. 51.

20 Šteiman *et al.*, *Daugavpils v proshlym*, pp.12–44.

21 This history of the Latvian communists in the 1930s is discussed more fully in G. Swain, 'Wreckage or Recovery: A Tale of Two Parties' in M. Worley (ed.) *In Search of Revolution* (I. B. Tauris: London, 2004), pp. 129–51.

22 This summary is taken from various accounts given in the memoir collection, Institut Istorii Partii pri TsK KPL, *Kommunisty Latgalii v gody podpolya, 1920–40* (Riga, 1960). For Fridman taking over from Yukhno, see Šteiman *Vremya i lyudi*, p. 48, and for the conference of the League of Working Youth, see his *Politicheskaya aktivnost' mass* (Riga, 1979), p. 59. Yukhno refers to his difficulties, explaining the popular-front strategy in Latvian State Archives [here-after LVA] fond 101, opis'2, delo 34, [hereafter given as 101.2.34], p. 17.

23 See, for example, M Yukhno's speech to the 8 December 1940 Meeting of the Daugavpils city party organisation (LVA 101.2.34, p.16) where he thanked the Red Army for their liberation; the idea that Latvia experienced a revolution in 1940 was a Soviet myth first propounded under Khrushchev which then became the orthodoxy of the 1960s and 1970s.

24 LVA 101.2.34, p. 17

25 *Kommunisty Latgalii*, pp. 327–8.

26 These views come from an unpublished paper by I. Saleniece, 'Sovetskie voiny glazami zhitelei Latvii: 40–e gg. XX veka (po istochnikam ustnoi istorii', part of an oral-history project started by Daugavpils University in 2002. Some of the Red Army men were unaware of the political ramifications of their mission. When a well-dressed Jew thanked a poorly clad Red Army man for putting an end to his suffering, the Red Army commented, in a bemused but sarcastic way, that he could see that the well-dressed Jew had really suffered. This comment, by a Russian observer, underlines that there was no great affinity between Russians and Jews, despite their shared minority status.

27 I. Šteiman, 'Daugavpils, 1940–50' (unpublished manuscript kindly made avail-able to me by Professor Šteiman; a shorter and edited version of this manuscript was published as *Vremya i lyudi*).

28 D. Levin, 'The Jews and the Sovietisation of Latvia, 1940–41', *Soviet Jewish Affairs* Vol. 5, No. 1, 1975, p. 40.

29 Šteiman, 'Daugavpils', pp. 16–17; the same author put the figure at 600 in his *Taktika KPL v sotsialisticheskoi revolyutsii 1941g.* (Riga, 1977), pp. 61–2.

30 *Kommunisty Latgalii*, p. 327.

31 *Latgalskaya Pravda* [hereafter LP] 3.7.40.

32 LP 29.6.40.

33 Levin 'Jews', p. 40.

34 LP 26.6.40.

35 *Kommunisty Latgalii*, p. 247.

36 A report of the Police Director noted on 19 June the buoyant mood of the communists and their attempts to contact the Red Army; see *Politika okkupat-sionnykh vlastei v Latvii, 1939–91: Sbornik dokumentov* (Nordik: Riga, 1999), p. 83.

37 *Lat. Rep. Ministru Kabineta sežu: protokoli* (Zinatne: Riga, 1991), pp. 30–1. For their positions in Latgale, see Šteiman 'Daugavpils', p. 19.

38 A. Drizulis (ed), *Sociālistiskās revolūcijas uzvara Latvijā 1940. gadā* (Latvian Academy of Sciences: Riga, 1963), document 88. For the size of the crowd, see Šteiman, 'Daugavpils', p. 20.

2 Daugavpils during the terrible year

1 *Politika okkupatsionykh vlastei v Latvii, 1939–91: Sbornik dokumentov* (Nordik: Riga, 1999), p. 85.
2 I. Šteiman, *Politicheskaya aktivnost' mass* (Riga, 1979), p. 116.
3 A. Drīzulis (ed.), *Sociālistiskās revolūcijas uzvara Latvijā 1940. gadā* (Latvian Academy of Sciences: Riga, 1963), document 143. For the death of the militia member, see Šteiman, 'Daugavpils', p. 21.
4 Drīzulis, *Sociālistiskās*, document 130.
5 Drīzulis, *Sociālistiskās*, documents 114 and 130.
6 LP 28.6.40.
7 LP 26.6.40.
8 I. Šteiman, *Taktika KPL v sotsialisticheskoi revolyutsii 1941g.* (Riga, 1977), p. 144.
9 LP 26.6.40
10 LP 28.6.40
11 LP 28.6.40.
12 LP 9.7.40.
13 LVA 101.2.34, p. 18.
14 LP 29.6.40.
15 Drizulis, *Sociālistiskās*, document 220.
16 Drizulis, *Sociālistiskās*, document 165.
17 LP 8.7.40.
18 LP 26.6.40.
19 LP 8.7.40.
20 LP 11.7.40.
21 LP 10.7.40.
22 Drizulis, *Sociālistiskās*, document 165.
23 'Ocherki po istorii KPL' in Kommunist Sovetskoi Latvii No. 5, 1965, p. 45.
24 Drizul, *Sociālistiskās*, document 231; E. A. Zhagar, 'Nekotorye voprosy klassovoi bor'by v LSSR nakanune Otechestvennoi Voiny, 1941–5 gg.' in A. A. Druzul, *V dni voiny* (Latvian Academy of Sciences: Riga, 1964), p. 33.
25 Drizulis, *Sociālistiskās*, document 17.
26 LP 12.7.40.
27 Šteiman, *Politicheskaya*, pp. 132, 140.
28 Šteiman, 'Daugavpils', p. 26.
29 Drizulis, *Sociālistiskās*, document 357.
30 LP 16.7.40.
31 Drizulis, *Sociālistiskās*, documents 367 and 608.
32 LVA 101.2.34, p. 18
33 Šteiman, *Politicheskaya*, p. 40.
34 Drizulis, *Sociālistiskās,* document 382.
35 Drizulis, *Sociālistiskās*, document 635.
36 LP 7.8.40.
37 LP 16.8.40.
38 LP 22.8.40 (11.9.40 has pictures of the formation).
39 LVA 101.2.35, p. 17.
40 LP 1.9.40.
41 LP 8.8.40.
42 LP 22.8.40.
43 LVA 101.2.34, p. 16.
44 LVA 101.2.54, p. 20.
45 LP 23 and 29.7.40.
46 LVA 101.2.34, p. 18.
47 LP 24.7.40.

48 Drizulis, *Sociālistiskās*, document 612.
49 LP 30.7.40.
50 LP 2.8.40.
51 LP 21.8.40.
52 LP 31.7.40.
53 LP 3.8.40.
54 LVA 101.2.34, p. 19.
55 LP 3.10.40.
56 LP 11.10.40.
57 LP 18.10.40.
58 LP 22.10.40.
59 LP 17.11.40.
60 LVA 103.1.2, p. 1.
61 LVA 103.1.6, pp. 1, 3.
62 Levin, 'Jews', pp. 46, 51.
63 LP 29.11.40.
64 LP 30.11.40, p. 11.
65 LP 1.12.40: of course, this is not an exact science. Establishing ethnicity against names can only ever be a rough estimate; but the pre-eminence of ethnic Russians seems clear.
66 LVA 103.1.1, p. 1.
67 LVA 101.2.34 p. 4.
68 LVA 101.2.35, pp. 2, 12, 30.
69 LP 17.12.40.
70 LP 3.1.41.
71 LP 3.1.41.
72 LP 22.12.40.
73 LP 14.1.41.
74 LVA 101.2.54, pp. 3–4.
75 LVA 101.2.34, pp. 23, 27.
76 LP 3.7.40.
77 LP 11.8.40.
78 LP 6.9.40.
79 LP 22.9.40.
80 LP 28.9.40.
81 LP 29.3.41.
82 LP 10.4.41.
83 LP 9.8.40.
84 LP 14.9.40.
85 LP 26.9.40.
86 LP 5.10.40.
87 LP 9.10.40.
88 LP 1.10.40.
89 LP 12 and 26.9.40.
90 LP 21.9.40.
91 LP 31.10.40.
92 LP 13.2.41.
93 LVA 101.2.35, p. 38.
94 LVA 101.2.38a, p. 3.
95 LP 1 and 7.9.40: work on the Jewish school was delayed because for the next two weeks at least the building of the Daugavpils Teachers' Institute was being 'temporarily' occupied by the Red Army; see J. Riekstiņš (ed.) *Izpostītā zeme* (ROTA: Riga, 1995), p. 12.
96 Šteiman 'Daugavpils', p. 69.

97 LP 19.9.40.
98 LP 18.10.40.
99 LP 24.11.40.
100 LP 23 and 24.11.40.
101 LP 3.11.40.
102 LP 29.11.40.
103 For example, LP 4.1.41.
104 LP 24.1.41.
105 LVA 101.2.34, p. 4.
106 LP 5 and 8.1.41.
107 LP 24.1.41.
108 LP 15.2.41.
109 LVA 101.2.54, p. 44.
110 LVA 101.2.38a, p. 15.
111 LP 11.4.41.
112 LP 18.4.41.
113 LP 4.5.41.
114 LP 11.5.41.
115 LVA 101.238a, pp. 21, 31–2.
116 LVA 103.1.6, pp. 9–14.
117 LVA 101.2.34, pp. 30–1.
118 LVA 101.2.38a, p. 7.
119 LP 6.3.41.
120 LP 9.4.41.
121 LP 9.3.41.
122 LP 11.5.41.
123 LVA 101.2.34, p. 5.
124 LP 7.3.41.
125 LP 25.3.41.
126 LVA 101.1.40, p. 28.
127 LP 15.4.41.
128 LP 20.4.41.
129 LP 18.4.41.
130 LP 22.4.41.
131 LP 9.5.41.
132 LVA 101.2.35, p. 28.
133 'Ocherki', *Komunist Sovestskoi Latvii* No. 9, 1973, p. 33.
134 LVA 103.1.4, p. 6.
135 LVA 101.2.467, pp. 1–88.
136 LVA 101.1.48, pp. 16–23.
137 LP 19.4.41.
138 LP 23.4 and 5.4.41.
139 LP 17.5.41.
140 LP 8.5.41.
141 LP 11.5.41.
142 LP 14.5.41.
143 LP 15.5.41.
144 LP 20.5.41.
145 LP 22.5.41.
146 LP 21.5.41.
147 LP 4.6.41.
148 LP 19.4.41.
149 LP 17.5.41.
150 LP 8.8.40.

151 LP 16.8.40.
152 LVA 101.2.452, p. 37.
153 LVA 116.1.1, p. 47.
154 LP 21.3.41.
155 LVA 101.2.445, p. 17.
156 LP 17.4.41.
157 LP 20.4.41.
158 LVA 116.1.1, p. 104.
159 LP 29.4.41.
160 LP 11.5.41.
161 LVA 101.2.452, p. 37.
162 LP 22.5.41.
163 LP 25.5.41.
164 LP 31.5.41.
165 LP 16.6.41.
166 'Ocherki', *Kommunist Sovetskoi Latvii*, No. 7, 1973, p. 40.
167 LP 23.6.41.
168 LVA 101.2.445, p. 16.
169 LVA 101.2.445, pp. 48–60; 101.2.452, pp. 1, 28.
170 *Istoricheskii arkhiv* No. 4, 1998, p. 29.
171 B. Spridzāns, 'Tā sākās Latvijas iedzīvotāju masveida represijas', *Represēto saraksts: 1941*, no. 1, Riga, 1995, and Latvijas Vēsturnieku Komisijas Raksti (6 sējums) *1941. gada 14. jūnija deportācija: Noziegums prēt cilvēci* (Latvijas Vēstures Institūta Apgāda: Riga, 2002), pp. 40, 78. Politika, pp. 167–8.
172 J. Riekstiņš, 'Staļinisko represiju aizsākums Latvijā', *Latvijas Vēsture*, no. 1, 1991.
173 Public Record Office [hereafter PRO] FO 371/29267, p. 153.
174 Institute of Philosophy and Sociology, University of Latvia, *Oral Sources of Latvia: History, Culture and Society through Life Stories* (Riga, 2003), p. 95.
175 *1941 gada 14 jūnija: deportācija* 79 and LVA 101.1.31, p. 1.
176 Spridzāns, 'Tā sākās Latvijas iedzīvotāju masveida represijas', pp. 35–52.
177 LVA 101.1.31, p. 39.
178 It is implicit from the documents available for 1941 that the local commissions were responding to national targets. I am grateful to Anu Mai Köll, who has studied the 1949 deportations, for confirmation that this system operated as described.
179 LVA 101.1.31, p. 19.
180 Šteiman, *Vremya i lyudi*, pp. 53–5.
181 Šteiman, *History*, p. 122.
182 Šteiman, 'Daugavpils', p. 83; Spridzāns 'Tā sākās Latvijas iedzīvotāju masveida represijas', p. 2.
183 Spridzāns, 'Tā sākās Latvijas iedzīvotāju masveida represijas', p. 2. (The arithmetical inconsistency is in the original, presumably because there were five people whose nationality was not recorded.)
184 Šteiman, 'Daugavpils', p. 80.
185 *Politika*, p. 147.
186 LP 24.1.40.
187 J. Ciganovs, 'The Resistance Movement against the Soviet Regime in Latvia between 1940–41' in A. Anušauskas (ed.) *The Anti-Soviet Resistance in the Baltic States* (Du Ka: Vilnius, 2000), p. 123.
188 LVA 103.1.4, p. 3.
189 LVA 103.1.2, p. 18.
190 LP 8.5.41.
191 LP 14.6.41.

192 LVA 101.2.445, p. 20.
193 LVA 103.1.2, p. 26.
194 LVA 101.5.1, p. 15.
195 Šteiman 'Daugavpils', p. 57.
196 LP 1.12.40.
197 LP 8 and 10.12.40.
198 LVA 101.2.54, p. 1.
199 LVA 116.1.1, p. 1.
200 LVA 101.2.54, pp. 8–16.
201 LVA 116.1.1, p. 14.
202 LVA 101.2.34, p. 9.
203 LVA 101.2.34, p. 16.
204 LVA 116.1.1, p. 124; by employment these were 14 workers, 11 peasants, two employees and four handicraftsmen.
205 LVA 103.1.2, p. 26.
206 LVA 116.1.1, p. 93.
207 LP 29.6.40.
208 LP 5 and 8.9.40.
209 LVA 101.2.34, p. 9.
210 Šteiman 'Daugavpils', pp. 37–51. The archives show clearly how, after Treimans's appointment, the record keeping of the Daugavpils party became much more structured.
211 Levin 'Jews', p. 49.
212 LVA 101.2.54, p. 30, pp. 53–4; for Kaupužs's expulsion, see Šteiman, 'Daugavpils', p. 66. Although the party was happier with the content of the paper after Kaupužs's departure, its circulation of only 4,700 demanded a monthly subsidy of 10,000 roubles.
213 LVA 101.2.35, p. 150.

3 Genocide

1 Interview between Dmitrijs Olehnovičs and Zalman Yakub, 3.11.99.
2 *Daugavas vēstnesis* [herafter DV] 1.7.42.
3 DV 1.7.42.
4 I. G. Kapitanov *Vozmezdie* t. II (Riga, 1980), p. 89.
5 Šteiman, 'Daugavpils', p. 85.
6 Šteiman, 'Daugavpils', p. 87.
7 LVA 101.5.1, pp. 15–16.
8 LVA 101.1.52, p. 132.
9 Iwens, *How Dark*, p. 22.
10 Interview between Dmitrijs Olehnovičs and Zalman Yakub, 3.11.99. Yakub dates the evacuation to 27 June, but that would appear to be a mistake.
11 Iwens, *How Dark*, p. 22.
12 Interview between Dmitrijs Olehnovičs and Zalman Yakub, 3.11.99: Yakub's father was one of those who refused to flee on these grounds. For the appointment of a Jewish mayor, see Šteimanis, *History*, p. 136.
13 M. Altshuler, 'Escape and Evacuation of Soviet Jews at the Time of the Nazi invasion' in L. Dobroszycki and J. Gurock (eds) *The Holocaust in the Soviet Union* (M. E. Sharpe: New York, 1993), pp 78–90.
14 Kapitanov, *Vozmezdie* t. II, p. 12.
15 Šteiman, 'Daugavpils', p. 86.
16 LVA 101.5.6, p. 20.
17 Kapitanov, *Vozmedie*, t. II, p. 12.

18 Iwens, *How Dark*, p. 25.
19 *Seichas*, 25.7.02.
20 LVA 101.5.6, p. 20.
21 I. G. Kapitanov, *Vozmedie* t. I, (Riga, 1977), p. 61.
22 Quoted in Ezergailis, *Holocaust*, p. 272.
23 State Archive of the Russian Federation [hereafter GARF] 7021.148.206, p. 2.
24 *Daugavpils latviešu avīze* [hereafter DLA] 6.8.41.
25 DV 1.7.42.
26 Iwens, *How Dark* p. 23.
27 DV 31.5.42. This report gave rather different statistics for damage to Daugavpils, stating that 1,490 houses had been destroyed along with 921 administrative buildings.
28 Ezergailis, *Holocaust*, p. 272.
29 Iwens, *How Dark*, p. 23.
30 LVA 101.5.6, p. 20.
31 S. Shpungin, 'Do i posle pobega', Testimony from the Yad Vashem Memorial, Israel, 2001, p. 1.
32 Kapitanov, *Vozmezdie* t. II, p. 25.
33 DLA 19.7.41.
34 Kapitanov, *Vozmezdie* t. II, p. 25.
35 DLA 1.8.41.
36 DLA 17.8.41.
37 DLA 16.8.41.
38 DLA 18.7.41.
39 Latvian State History Archive [hereafter LVVA] R-70.5.4, p. 186.
40 DLA 6.8.41; I have taken this to be a reference to the Vārkava not far from Preiļi, rather than that in the Ilūkste district near Bebrene.
41 DLA 12.8.41.
42 DV 6.2.42.
43 LVA 302.1.29, p. 31.
44 Ezergailis, *Holocaust*, p, 273.
45 DV 1.7.42 Ehrlinger suggests in the report cited by Ezergailis above, that both the police and the civil administration were formally established on 3 July.
46 Ezergailis, *Holocaust*, p, 273.
47 Personal information from Iosif Šteiman; this is alluded to in his *Vremya i lyudi*, p. 26.
48 DLA 15,17,19.7.41.
49 DLA 19.7.41.
50 Shpungin, 'Do i posle pobega', p. 1.
51 DLA 24.7.41.
52 DV 9.1.42.
53 Iwens, *How Dark* p. 25.
54 Iwens, *How Dark* p. 25.
55 GARF 7021.93.22, p. 100.
56 LVA 101.5.6, p. 20. Fridman dates the instructions to gather in the town square as 28 June; but Sunday 29th as recorded by Iwens seems more likely.
57 Shpungin, 'Do i posle pobega', p. 1.
58 I. Rochko, 'Zhertvy, spasennye i spasiteli' in B. Volkovich *et al.* (eds) *Kholokost v Latgalii* (V Prints: Daugavpils, 2003), p. 86.
59 LVA 101.5.6, p. 20.
60 Shpungin recalls how, although others suffered, at this time his family was allowed to move in with his grandmother since their own house had been bombed; see 'Do i posle pobega', p. 2.
61 Ezergailis, *Holocaust*, p. 273.

62 Iwens, *How Dark*, pp. 25–9.
63 Ezergailis, *Holocaust*, p. 274.
64 See Stahlecker's report of 31 January 1942 in GARF 7021.148.206, p. 22.
65 Ezergailis, *Holocaust*, p. 272.
66 GARF 7021.148.206, p. 3.
67 Iwens, *How Dark*, pp. 31–6, 104. In her account, Fridman gives the same outline of events, but the time-scale is shorter. Thus she has the male Jews working for only three days as forced labourers before the executions began 'on the fourth day'. Once again, the Iwens account seems the more precise. Fridman talks about difficulties in getting food and trading in cigarettes, which suggests a longer time-scale than three days. Later her account inexplicably jumps backwards from 16 July to 14 July.
68 Ezergailis, *Holocaust*, pp. 273–5; since this figure was more than the number of Jews detained in the prison, and some Jews survived the prison massacre, reports of two other execution actions at this time, one near Stropi cemetery and one at Mežciems, are likely to be true.
69 Ezergailis, *Holocaust*, p. 273.
70 LVA 101.5.6, p. 22: here it is possible to reconcile the Iwens and Fridman accounts, since Iwens has the prison filling up with a new batch of Jews on 10 July.
71 Ezergailis, *Holocaust*, p. 276.
72 Iwens, *How Dark*, p. 42; LVA 101.5.6, p. 22. It is quite likely, since POWs were reported to be in the prison at this time, that some of the victims were POWs. At the rather battered memorial in the Railwaymen's Garden today, the only group to be commemorated are Red Army POWs. Some of those listed by Fridman as executed at this time included non-Jewish school directors who were executed as pro-Soviet elements.
73 LVA 101.5.6, p. 24.
74 Rochko, 'Zhertvy', p. 89.
75 LVA 101.5.6, p. 24.
76 Iwens, *How Dark,* p. 44.
77 LVA 101.5.6, p. 25.
78 Iwens, *How Dark*, p. 48.
79 LVA 101.5.6, p. 25.
80 LVA 101.5.6, p. 25 and Iwens, *How Dark*, p. 49. Again, there is some confusion of dates in these two testimonies. Here I have accepted Fridman's account that the first transfer to the non-existent camp took place on 29 July, the day she was transferred from prison to the ghetto, a date she was likely to recall; however, it should be noted that Iwens recalls only one incident, when non-Daugavpils Jews were told they were being transferred to a new camp. The third survivor to write an account, Shpungin, confirms that his grandmother went to her death believing she was being moved to a less crowded camp. For the inclusion of Višķi on this list, see LP 12.4.45.
81 DLA 15.7.41.
82 Rochko, 'Zhertvy', p. 86.
83 DLA24.7.41.
84 I. Šteiman, 'Nekotorye aspekty istoriografii kholokost v Latgalii' in Volkovich, *Kholokost*, p. 11.
85 Iwens, *How Dark*, pp. 51–5; LVA 101.5.6, p. 25. Again, there is a slight discrepancy in these two accounts; Fridman recalls only the 18–19 August action. Iwens recalls 'a fine steady rain' on 6 August, while Fridman remembers 'the pouring rain' on 19 August.
86 GARF 7021.93.22, p. 102.
87 GARF 7021.93.22, p. 80.

88   GARF 7021.93.22, p. 68.
89   Rochko, 'Zhertvy', p. 93.
90   GARF 7021.93.22, p. 15.
91   GARF 7021.93.22, p. 72.
92   Rochko, 'Zhertvy', pp. 99, 122, 132.
93   Ezergailis, *Holocaust*, pp. 225, 271. LP 13.3.45, citing the work of the Extraordinary Commission. LP reported on 7.9.44 that in the three years of the German occupation, 1,140 of Preiļi's inhabitants had been tortured and killed.
94   Rochko, 'Zhertvy', pp. 109, 122.
95   Rochko, 'Zhertvy', p. 104.
96   A. Shneer, 'Gibel' evreev Ludzy' in Volkovich, *Kholokost*, pp. 33–45.
97   Rochko, 'Zhertvy', pp. 122, 135.
98   GARF 7021.93.10, pp. 2–36.
99   LVVA R-69.1a.20, p. 7.
100 Iwens, *How Dark,* pp. 36, 104.
101 Ezergailis, *Holocaust*, p. 277.
102 Shpungin, 'Do i posle pobega', p. 3.
103 *Inprecor*, no. 56, 1933.
104 A. Kasekamp, *The Radical Right in Interwar Estonia* (Macmillan: Basingstoke, 2000), p. 142.
105 Kasekamp, *Radical Right*, p. 143.
106 Kasekamp, *RadicalRight*, p. 152.
107 Kasekamp, *Radical Right*, p. 149.
108 Kasekamp, *Radical Right*, p.149.
109 Ezergailis, *Holocaust*, p. 48.
110 Kasekamp, *Radical Right*, p. 152 and note 76, p. 194.
111 LVA 101.2.467, p. 19; personal information from I. Steiman.
112 PRO FO 371.47062 (no page numbers).
113 Kasekamp, *Radical Right*, p. 147.
114 Kasekamp, *Radical Right*, p. 150.
115 DLA 25.9.41.
116 L. Mai, 'Pērkonrusts bez maski, ili fenomen Pērkonkrustov i ego sovremennye apologety' in *Kniga spasitelei* t. III, (Mezhdunarodnoe obshchestvo istorii getto i genotsida Evreev, Jurmala: Riga, 2002), pp. 65–6. Mai tells the story of F. Rikards, who moved from being a Pērkonkrusts member at university, to become a 'flaming soviet activist', and finally the head of the Gestapo. The career of Štāls is rather similar, and even Arājs is rumoured to have applied to join the Communist Party. For those who had disguised their true views for so long, it was presumably invigorating to be able to act freely.
117 Ezergailis, *Holocaust*, p. 177.
118 Ezergailis, *Holocaust*, p. 157.
119 Rochko, 'Zhertvy', p. 89.
120 GARF 7021.93.22, p. 72.
121 GARF 7021.93.22, p. 9.
122 GARF 7021.93.22, p. 70.
123 GARF 7021.93.22, p. 70.
124 GARF 7021.93.22, p. 72.
125 GARF 7021.93.22, p. 15.
126 GARF 7021.93.22, p. 9.
127 GARF 7021.93.22, p. 81.
128 GARF 7021.93.22, p. 9.
129 GARF 7021.93.22, p. 14.
130 GARF 7021.93.22, p. 9.
131 GARF 7021.93.22, p. 87.

132 Ezergailis, *Holocaust*, p. 303 (note 18).
133 GARF 7021.93.22, p. 9.
134 The practice of leaving the graves open overnight seems to have been abandoned because of dogs and wild animals seizing body parts; see 101.5.6, p. 23.
135 LVA 101.5.6, p. 68.
136 GARF 7021.93.22, p. 77.
137 GARF 7021.93.22, p. 69.
138 GARF 7021.93.22, p. 72.
139 GARF 7021.93.22, p. 14.
140 GARF 7021.93.22, pp. 9, 68, 83.
141 GARF 7021.93.22, p. 71.
142 GARF 7021.93.22, p. 70.
143 GARF 7021.93.22, p. 86.
144 Bundesarchiv [hereafter BA] R92/483, pp 1, 18–19. The page numbers in this file are not consecutive. Schwung writes June, rather than July, but this is clearly a slip.
145 DLA 30&31.7.41.
146 DLA 26.7.41.
147 DLA 25.7.41.
148 DLA 17.7.41.
149 DLA 3.8.41.
150 DLA 30.7.41.
151 DLA 1.8.41.
152 DLA 29.7.41.
153 DLA 13.8.41.
154 DV 1.7.42.
155 DLA 10.8.41.
156 DLA 22&24.8.41.
157 DLA 25.7.41.
158 DLA 27.7.41.
159 DLA 1.8.41.
160 DLA 12.8.41.
161 DLA 7.8.41.
162 DLA 9.8.41.
163 DLA 7.8.41.
164 DLA 16&20.8.41.
165 DLA 16&20.8.41.
166 DLA 9.8.41; there are reports of the campaign in DLA for 3, 5, 7, 8, 9, 12 and 15 August.
167 DLA 16.8.41.
168 The ban had to be reissued with the threat of death: DLA 20.8.41.
169 DLA 20.8.41.
170 DLA 7.9.41.
171 DLA 23.8.41.
172 DLA 24.8.41.
173 GARF 7021.93.20, p. 4; 7021.93.19, p. 14.
174 DV 2.10.41.
175 Šteiman, *Daugavpils v proshlom*, p. 73.
176 BA R92/1124. Report of the Arbeitsverwaltung for 17.10.41 (no page numbers).
177 GARF 7021.93.3695, p. 2.
178 DLA 6.9.41.
179 DV 12.7.42.
180 *Dvinskii vestnik* [hereafter DB] 24.12.43.

181 DV 19.10.41.
182 DV 27.11.41.
183 DLA 19.7.41.
184 DLA 20.8.41.
185 Kasekamp, *Radical Right*, p. 153.
186 J. Silabriedis *et al.*, *'Politiskie bēgļi' bez maskas* (Riga, 1963), p. 98; Ezergailis (p. 47) states that the activity of the Pērkonkrusts was banned in mid-August, and cites information received from Šilde found in the Koblenz archives. The military authorities could have begun to clamp down on them before the civilian authorities were fully established.
187 GARF 7021.93.3695, p. 31.
188 DV 8.10, 5.11.41.
189 DV 23.11.41.
190 DLA 12.8.41.
191 DLA 22.9.41.
192 DLA 26.9.41.
193 DLA 11.9.41.
194 DV 4, 9, 10.10.41.
195 DV 10, 16, 25, 28.10.41.
196 DLA 2.9.41.
197 DLA 16, 17&.9.41.
198 DLA 7.9.41.
199 DLA 12.9.41.
200 DLA 11.9.41.
201 DV 1, 14, 17.10.41.
202 I. Trunk, *Judenrat* (Macmillan: London, 1972), p. 27.
203 Šteiman, *History*, pp. 136–8.
204 Ezergailis, *Holocaust*, p. 278.
205 Iwens, *How Dark*, p.60.
206 LVA 101.5.6, p. 27.
207 DV 12.10.41.
208 GARF 7021.93.22, p. 80.
209 GARF 7021.93.22, p. 6.
210 GARF 7021.93.22, p. 26 .
211 GARF 7021.93.22, p. 49.
212 Shpungin, 'Do i posle pobega', p. 3.
213 BA R92/1124 Arbeitswerwaltung Report, 7.8.41 (no page numbers).
214 DLA 26.7.41.
215 DLA 3, 9&13.8.41.
216 DLA 7.9.41.
217 DLA 14, 16, 17&18.9.41.
218 Ezergailis, *Holocaust*, p. 273.
219 LVA 101.5.6, p. 22–3.
220 DV 16–19.11.41.
221 Ezergailis, *Holocaust*, p. 279. (Ezergailis implies he is not present on p. 184.)
222 Iwens, *How Dark*, p. 65,
223 LVA 101.5.6, p. 26.
224 LVA 101.5.6, p. 23.
225 Shpungin, 'Do i posle pobega', p. 3.
226 LVA 101.5.6, p. 25.
227 GARF 7021.93.3695, p. 36.
228 Ezergailis, *Holocaust*, p. 279.
229 Iwens, *How Dark*, p. 70.
230 Ezergailis, *Holocaust*, p. 279.

231 Iwens, *How Dark*, p. 70.
232 GARF 7021.148.206, p. 3.
233 GARF 7021.93.3695, p. 37.
234 LVA 101.5.6, p. 25.
235 BA R70 Sowjetunion/20, pp. 45, 126.
236 BA R/198, p. 52.
237 BA R91/Dünaburg/9 (no page numbers); R92/732, pp. 1–6.
238 LVA 101.5.6, p. 24.
239 Iwens, *How Dark*, pp. 18–20.
240 Iwens *How Dark*, p. 65.
241 Iwens, *How Dark*, pp. 55, 73.
242 Shpungin, 'Do i posle pobega', p. 4; he gives the date in an article he wrote as S. I. Shpungin in LP 27.7.46.
243 Šteiman, *History*, pp. 140–1.
244 Rochko, 'Zhertvy', pp. 109, 136, 139.
245 DV 4.10.41.
246 DV 17.10.41.
247 DV 5.11.41.
248 GARF 7021.93.22, p. 13.

4 Dünaburg under Schwung

1 LVA 101.4.6, p. 84.
2 LVA 302.1.33, p. 2. Other reports give slightly different figures for these early operations; see, for example, 101.4.6, p. 94.
3 LVVA R-70.5.37, p. 27.
4 M. Afremovich, I. Steiman, *Pavel Leibch* (Riga, 1974), pp. 102–22.
5 BA R70 Sowjetunion/20, p. 107. The originals of these documents are in the LVVA, but I consulted them in Berlin.
6 BA R70 Sowjetunion/20, p. 104.
7 Quoted in Ezergailis, *Holocaust*, p. 281.
8 LSSR Archive Directrate, *My obvinyaem* (Riga, 1967), pp. 138–9.
9 *My*, pp. 140, 142; see also BA R70 Sowjetunion/20, pp. 50–1.
10 *Rēzeknes zinas* [hereafter RZ] 7.1.42.
11 *My*, pp. 141–2; BAR70 Sowjetunion/20, pp. 50–1 gives the date of the executions in the market square as 4 January 1942.
12 *My*, p. 144, citing DV 7.1.42.
13 BA R70 Sowjetunion/20, p. 53.
14 BA R70 Sowjetunion/20, pp 46–7, 96, 113.
15 LVVA R-70.5.38, p. 133.
16 LVVA R-69.1a.17, p. 44.
17 *My*, p. 142.
18 DV 16.1.42.
19 DB 28.3.42.
20 DV 14.5.42, DB 23.5.42.
21 BA R70 Sowjetunion/20, p. 48.
22 DV 29.11.41.
23 Iwens, *How Dark*, p. 78.
24 Iwens, *How Dark*, pp.74–5.
25 GARF 7021.93.20, p.6.
26 GARF 7021.93.19, p. 8; 7021.93.19, p. 30.
27 GARF 7021.93.19, p. 33.
28 RZ 6.12.41.
29 DV 10,13,14.1.42.

30 DV 15.2.42.
31 DV 8.3.42.
32 LVVA R-69.1a.18, p.6.
33 DV 7.2.42.
34 DV 15&17.2.42.
35 DV 27.1.42.
36 DB 7.2.42.
37 DV 10.2.42
38 DV 3.2.42.
39 DV 12.2.42.
40 DV 4.2.42.
41 For example, DV for 6,7&8,2.42.
42 For example DV 12&24.3.42, & 11.4.42.
43 DV 7.2.42.
44 DB 14.3.42.
45 DV 4.2.42.
46 DV 10.2.42.
47 LVVA R-69.1a.18, p. 6.
48 LVVA R-69.1a.18, p. 170.
49 GARF 7021.93.3695.122.
50 GARF 7021.93.3695.124.
51 DV 15.5.42.
52 RZ 21.1.42.
53 DV 25.2.42; see also RZ 28.2.42 and DB 7.3.42.
54 LVVA R-69.1a.18, p. 6.
55 DV 11.2.42.
56 LVA 101.3.1, pp. 1–2.
57 A. A. Drizul' (ed.) *Bor'ba latyshkogo naroda v gody Velikoi Otechestvennoi Voiny, 1941–5* (Latvian Academy of Sciences: Riga, 1970), p. 399.
58 LVA 101.4.2, p. 8.
59 LVA 101.3.1, p. 11.
60 LVA 101.4.5, p. 7.
61 LVVA R-69.1a.18, p 15.
62 LVVA R-69.1a.18.p. 3.
63 LVVA R-69.1a.18, p. 168.
64 LVVA R-69.1a.18, p. 173.
65 LVVA R-82.1.20, p. 1.
66 Kapitanov *Vozmezdie*, t. I, pp. 38–43; 302.5.13, p. 1. For Lazdovskii's involvement in the workers' militia, see Kapitanov, *Vozmezdie* t. II, p. 12.
67 DV 29.3.42; the paper gives the date as 27 not 26 March.
68 LVA 302.5.13, p. 1.
69 Kapitanov *Vozmezdie* t. I, pp. 12–31.
70 LVVA R-70.5.37, p. 107.
71 LVA 302.1.29, p. 48.
72 LVA 101.5.6, p. 9.
73 DV25.10.41.
74 DV 14.2 42.
75 A. Silgailis *Latvian Legion* (James Benner Publishing: New York, 1986), p. 13; Silgailis states that the first troops went to the front at the end of November, but press reports put it as early December; see RZ 17.12.41.
76 DV 6.2.42.
77 DV 13.2.42; this was 24–148 roubles per day plus three meals a day; however, volunteers were to provide their own clothes, cutlery, plates, etc. RZ 18.2.42 gave the allowance as 2.40 marks to 14.80 marks per day, with an extra 1 mark front

allowance. Monthly income, with no outgoings on food, could range from approximately 100–475 marks, when the average income was 180 marks.

78 DV 24&25.2.42.
79 DV 18.2.42.
80 DV 28.2.42.
81 For example, DV 5.3.42.
82 RZ 7.3.42.
83 DV 11.3.42.
84 LVVA R-69.1a.18, p. 183.
85 For the first letters from volunteers, see DV 18.3.42.
86 DV 12.4.42.
87 LVVA R-84.1.2, p. 1. A later report by the security police put the date of the application as 18.12.41; see R-69.1a.8, p. 99.
88 LVVA R-69.1a.8, p. 99.
89 DV 6.3.42.
90 LVVA R-69.1a.8, p. 99.
91 LVVA R-69.1a.18, p. 17.
92 LVVA R-69.1a.17, p. 430.
93 LVVA R-69.1a.18, p. 3.
94 LVVA R-69.1a.18, p. 5.
95 DV 4.2.42.
96 DV 21.4.42.
97 BA R92/198, p. 4.
98 BA R92/483, p. 1.
99 BA R92/483, p. 11.
100 BA R92/483, p. 3.
101 LVVA R-69.1a.18, p. 276.
102 LVVA R-70.5.37, p. 136.
103 BA R70 Sowjetunion/20, p. 46.
104 DLA 22.7.41.
105 DLA 31.7.41.
106 DLA 17.8.41.
107 DV 5.2.42.
108 DB 7.2.42.
109 DV 24.1.42.
110 RZ 21.2.42.
111 RZ 30.5.42.
112 RZ 28.3.42.
113 Shpungin, 'Do i posle pobega', p. 6.
114 Ezergailis, *Holocaust*, p. 279.
115 LP 12.4.45, reporting the testimony of S. I. Shpungin.
116 Iwens, *How Dark*, p. 96. That they were taken first to the prison, and only later to Mežciems, is confirmed by the testimony of a certain Mr Gordon, imprisoned at that time for his past activities on a factory committee; see LP 3.2.46.
117 LVVA R-70.5.37, p. 114.
118 Ezergailis, *Holocaust*, p. 271.
119 LVVA R-69.1a.42, p. 274.
120 LVVA R-60.1a.18, p. 490.
121 DV 8,13,15,29.1.42.
122 For example, DB 14.3.42.
123 DV 24.3.42.
124 LVVA R-69.1a.18, p. 4.
125 LVVA R-69.1a.18, p. 169.
126 DV 17.5.42.

127 DV 20.5.42.
128 LVVA R-69.1a.18, p. 274.
129 LVVA R-69.1a.18, p. 274.
130 LVVA R-69.1a.18, p. 490.
131 LVVA R-82.1.1, p. 34.
132 V. Samsons, *Partizanskoe dvizhenie v severnoi Latvii v gody Velikoi Otechestvennoi voiny* (Riga, 1951), p. 38.
133 GARF 7021.93.3695, p. 122.
134 GARF 7021.93.3695, p. 124.
135 LVVA R-69.1a.18, p. 274.
136 This account is compiled from LVVA R-82.1.1, p. 34; Samsons *Partizanskoe*, pp. 42–3; and LVVA R-69.1a.18, p. 274.
137 RZ 27.5.42.
138 LVVA R-69.1a.18, p. 274.
139 LVVA R-69.1a.18, p. 490.
140 Samsons, *Partizanskoe*, p. 38.
141 LVVA R-82.1.1, p. 20.
142 LVVA R-82.1.1, pp. 40–3.
143 LVVA R-82.1.1, p. 20. Some of this report is reproduced in *My*, p. 237.
144 DV 4.6.42.
145 LVVA R-82.1.1, pp 40–3.
146 GARF 7021.93.3695, p. 125.
147 LVVA R-69.1a.18, p. 490. That the 42,000 workers were for Kurland is made clear in R-82.1.1, p. 20.
148 LVVA R-70.5.37, p. 119.
149 Samsons *Partizanskoe dvizhenie*, p. 45.
150 LVVA R-69.1a.18, p. 492; R-70.5.37, p. 121.
151 LVVA R-69.1a.18, p. 275.
152 LVVA R-70.5.37, p. 57.
153 LVVA R-69.1a.18, p. 559.
154 LVVA R-70.5.37, p. 133.
155 LVA 101.4.1, p. 24; 101.4.6, p. 61.
156 The story of the 'For a Soviet Latvia' Regiment is given by two of its survivors; see A. Rashkevits, *Zapiski partizana* (Riga, 1963) and V. Samsons, *No Lovates līdz Zilupei* (Riga, 1987). Contemporary reports are in LVA 302.1.33, pp. 44–52. Rashkevits and Samsons see this 'raid' rather like the British see the evacuation at Dunkirk in 1940, a heroic failure from which the kernels of future victory were salvaged.
157 LVVA R-70.5.37, p. 74.
158 LVA 101.4.6, p. 78.
159 LVA 101.4.6.100.
160 LVA 301.1.29, pp. 1–3.
161 LVA 101.4.6, p. 85.
162 J. Dzintars, *Neredzamā fronte* (Riga, 1970), p. 94.
163 LVA 302.5.13, p. 1.
164 Samsons, *No Lovates*, pp. 183–90.
165 LVVA R-69.1a.18, pp. 9, 79.
166 GARF 7021.93.3695, p. 128.
167 DV10.5.42.
168 DV 28.4.42.
169 DV 24.7.42.
170 DV3.7.42.
171 DV 16.6.42.
172 DV 12.8.42.

173 DV 29.8.42.
174 GARF 7021.93.3695, p. 128.
175 DV 1.1.42.
176 DV 8.8.42.
177 Iwens, *How Dark*, pp. 106, 118.
178 DB 3.10.42.
179 GARF 7021.93.3695, p. 128.
180 DV 25.10.42.
181 DV 11.4.42.
182 DV 16.4.42
183 DV 3.5.42. There had been less assertive appeals in a similar vein on 26.3.42 and 8.4.42.
184 DV12.5.42.
185 DV 13.5.42.
186 DV 9&19.6.42.
187 DV 16.6.42.
188 DV 29.5.42.
189 DV 13.2.42.
190 DV 24.6.42 & DB 4.7.42.
191 DV 22.7.42.
192 DV 23.8.42.
193 DV27.8.42.
194 DV 12.9.42.
195 DV 12.7.42, 1.8.42.
196 DV5.8.42.
197 DV 18.8.42.
198 DV22.8.42.
199 DB 29.8.42.
200 DV11.10.42.
201 BA R91/Dünaburg/7.
202 DV 12.2.42.
203 DV 8.3.42.
204 DV 11.3.42.
205 LVVA R-69.6.10, p. 2.
206 DV 5.3.42.
207 DV 30.4.42.
208 DV 1.4.42.
209 DV 12.4.42.
210 DV 24.4.42.
211 For example, DV20.10.42.
212 DV 22&24.10.42.
213 DV 7&8.5.42.
214 DV21.5.42.
215 DV 3.6.42.
216 DV13.6.42.
217 DV 16.6.42.
218 DV 3.7.42.
219 DV 30.7.42.
220 LVVA R-69.6.3, pp. 72–4.
221 LVVA R-69.1a.18, p. 485.
222 LVVA R-69.1a.18, p. 561.
223 DV 16.7.42.
224 LVVA R-69.1a.18, p. 561–2.
225 DV 17.7.42.

226 BA R92/ 198, p. 52 (no consistent page numbering).
227 BA R92/483, p. 3 (no consistent page numbering).
228 BA R92/ 377 (no page numbers).
229 BA R92/ 10359 (no consistent page numbering).
230 BA R92/ 483, p. 12.
231 BA R92/ 10359 (no consistent page numbering).
232 BA R92/ 10359 (no consistent page numbering).
233 BA R92/ 377 (no page numbers).
234 T. Puisāns, *Latviešu Katoli Kanadā* (Latvian Catholic Cultural Centre: Toronto, 1984), p. 94.
235 DV 25.10.42.
236 DV 18.10.42.
237 DV 13.10.42.
238 BA R92/483, p. 34.
239 DV 17.10.42.
240 DV 14.10.42.
241 DB 12.9.42.
242 DV 19.5.42.
243 LP 3.2.46.
244 DV 23.6.42.
245 DB 4.7.42.
246 DB 19.9.42.
247 DB 29.8.42.
248 DB 17.10.42.
249 DV 9.9.42.
250 DV 9.10.42.
251 DV 4.10.42.
252 LVVA R-69.1a.18, p. 170.
253 Iwens, *How Dark*, pp. 113–14.

5 Dünaburg under Riecken

 1 LVA 101.4.2, p. 20.
 2 LVA 101.3.1, p. 46.
 3 LVA 302.1.29, p. 39.
 4 Samsons, *No Lovates*, p. 193, 222.
 5 LVVA R-82.1.2, p. 3.
 6 LVA 302.1.44, p. 1.
 7 LVVA R-82.1.2, p. 1.
 8 V. Samsons, 'Sovmestnye deistviya Vitebskikh, Kalininskikh i Latviiskikh partisan v boyakh protiv gitlerovskikh karatel'nykh ekspeditsii v nachale 1943 g.' in A. A. Drizul' (ed.) *V dni voiny* (Latvian Academy of Sciences: Riga, 1964), p. 145; BA R92/1022 (no page numbers).
 9 LVA 302.1.29, p. 1.
10 LVA 302.1.44, p. 2.
11 LVVA R-97.1.6, pp. 1–2.
12 LVA 302.1.44, p. 2.
13 BA R92/1022 (no page numbers).
14 LVVA R-82.1.39, p. 181.
15 LVA 302.1.29, p. 3.
16 BA 92/424 (no page numbers).
17 BA R92/9, pp. 11–13.
18 BA R92/9, p. 14.
19 BA R92/888, p. 1.

20 LVVA R-82.1.39, p. 180.
21 LVVA R-70.5.4, 176.
22 LVA 302.1.44, p. 2.
23 LVA 101.5.5, p. 40.
24 LVA 302.1.29, p. 15; Dzintars, *Nerezamā fronte*, p. 129.
25 'Ocherki', *Kommunist Sovetskoi Latvii*, 11, 1973, p. 47; LVA 101.3.2, p. 1.
26 Kapitanov, *Vozmezdie*, t. I, p. 43.
27 LVVA R-82.1.39, p. 5.
28 LVVA R-82.1.39, p. 198.
29 Dzintars, *Neredzamā*, pp. 95, 125.
30 Iwens, *How Dark*, pp. 119–25.
31 Shpungin, 'Do i posle pobega', p. 6. Shpungin dates this to the end of the summer, but Iwens (*How Dark*, p.130) has it as June and is largely accurate in his dates.
32 Iwens, *How Dark*, pp. 130–8.
33 Kapitanov, *Vozmezdie*, t. I, pp. 114–16.
34 Dzintars, *Neredzamā*, p. 123.
35 Kapitonov, *Vozmezdie*, t. I, pp. 43–5.
36 Dzintars, *Neredzamā*, pp. 124–5.
37 M. Smirnov, 'Latviiskie zheleznodorozhniki v bor'be protiv nemetsko-fashist-skikh zakhvatchikov na territorii Latvii' in *V Dni Voiny*, p. 203.
38 Dzintars, *Naredzamā*, p. 126. This account is weak on precise dates, but circumstantial evidence suggests this happens in the autumn.
39 Silgailis, *Legion*, pp. 19–20.
40 *Politika*, p. 186.
41 *My*, p. 268. Silgailis says conscription started on 26 February; see *Legion*, p. 22.
42 Silgailis, *Legion*, p. 23.
43 LVVA R-70.5.4, pp. 173, 181.
44 LVVA R-70.5.4, pp. 183–6.
45 LVVA R-82–1–39, p. 137.
46 LVVA R-84.1.9, p. 1.
47 DV 28.3.43.
48 DV 6.4.43.
49 DV 29.4.43.
50 DV 30.4.43.
51 DV 8.10.43.
52 DV 14.10.43.
53 DV 27.10.43.
54 DV 3.11.43.
55 DV 30.10.43.
56 DB 29.5.43.
57 DB 5&19.12.42.
58 DB 9.1.43.
59 LVVA R-82–1–39, pp. 47–9.
60 DB 20.2.43.
61 DB 6.3.43.
62 DV 7.4.43.
63 DB 6.3.43.
64 DV 10.4.43.
65 LVVA R-82–1–39, p. 138.
66 DV 7&8.7.43.
67 DB 1.1.44.
68 DB 30.1.43.
69 DB 20.3.43.

70 DB 27.3.43.
71 LVA 101.6.11, p. 141.
72 H. Fireside, *The Icon and the Swastika: the Russian Orthodox Church under Nazi and Soviet Control* (Harvard University Press: Cambridge, MA, 1971), p. 138.
73 DB 29.5.43.
74 For example, DB 16.6.43.
75 LVA 101.6.11, p. 141.
76 DB 14.8.43.
77 DB 21.8.43.
78 DB 28.8& 11.9.43.
79 DB 29.9.43.
80 LVA 101.6.11, p. 141.
81 V. P. Samsons, *Druzhba narodov pobedila: sovmestnye deistvie krasnykh partisan i sovetskikh razvedchikov v 'Kurlandskom kotle' v 1944–5 gg.* (Riga, 1980) note, p. 120.
82 LVA 101.6.11, p. 141.
83 LVA 101.6.11, p. 3.
84 DB 26.3.44.
85 DB 24.4.43.
86 LVVA R-69–6–10, pp. 5–19.
87 DB 29.5.43.
88 DB 13.2.43.
89 DB 12.6.43.
90 DB 3.7.43.
91 DB 21.7.43.
92 DB 20.2.44.
93 LVVA R-69–6–37, pp. 10–13.
94 DV 16.7.43.
95 BA R92/433 (no page numbers); DV 28.8.43.
96 BA R92/705 (no page numbers).
97 DV 8.9.43.
98 BA R92/732, pp. 1–6, p. 26.
99 DB 27.3.43.
100 DB10.4.43.
101 DV 31.7.43.
102 LVVA R-69.1a.7, pp. 8, 17, 18, 22.
103 BA R92/888 (no page number).
104 LVVAR-69–6–37, pp. 5–9.
105 LVVA R-69–1a-7, p. 54.
106 LVVA R-70.3.86, pp. 7–13, 70.
107 LVVA R-69–1a-7, p. 61.
108 LVVA R-69–1a-7, pp. 136, 146.
109 DB 26.5.44.
110 LVVA R-69.1a.16, p. 118.
111 Shpungin, 'Do i posle pobega', pp. 8–13.
112 Iwens, *How Dark*, pp.165–206.
113 DV 8.4.43.
114 DV 21.8.43.
115 DV 12& 21.10.43.
116 DV 12.9.43.
117 DV 24.9.43.
118 DV 26.8.43.
119 DV 9,12&27.8.43.

120 DV 9&16.10.43.
121 DV 6.8.43.
122 DV 27.8.43.
123 LVA 101.6.11, p. 129.
124 DV 19.9.43.
125 DV 16.8.43.
126 DV 17.9.43.
127 DV 8.4.43.
128 DV 8.8.43.
129 DV 27.8.43.
130 DV 9.9.43.
131 DV 19.9.43.
132 DV 24.9.43.
133 DV 8.7.43.
134 DV 30.7.43.
135 DV 1.9.43.
136 DV 19.9.43.
137 DV 5&6.10.43.
138 DB 13.10.43.
139 LVVA R-70.5.36, p. 11 *et seq.*
140 LVA 101.5.5, p. 53 *et.seq.*
141 *Na pravyi boi, na smertnyi boi: sbornik vospominanii i dokumentov* (Riga, 1968), vol. I, p. 368.
142 V. Samsons, *K vesne* (Riga, 1989), p. 37.
143 LVA 101.5.6, p. 151.
144 Samsons, *K vesne*, pp. 44–50; 302.1.29, p. 44; *Na pravyi*, p. 378.
145 Samsons, *K vesne*, pp. 97–100.
146 LVA 302.1.44, p. 3.
147 LVA 302.1.87, p. 1.
148 LVA 302.1.44, p. 26.
149 Laiviņš stated that 30 men were transferred to Ezernieks in summer 1943; see LVA 302.1.34, p. 12. Ezernieks had suffered some desertions, but was reported to have 18 men with him in August 1942 when contacted by an intelligence agent; see LVA 101.4.6, p. 99. Samsons says he never had less than 20 men; see his *Partizanskoe dvizhenie*, p. 76.
150 LVA 101.5.5, p. 125.
151 LVA 101.5.5, p. 106.
152 LVA 101.6.11, p. 132.
153 V. Samsons, 'Vācu drosības policijas un SD "Latgales Akcijas"', *Latvijas Zinātņu. Akadēmijas Vēstis*, 1990, no. 12, p. 109.
154 *My*, p. 150.
155 BA R92/8, p. 6.
156 BA R92/8, p. 8.
157 Samsons *K vesne* pp. 83–90; V Samsons 'Vācu', pp. 110–12; LSSR *My*, p. 154.
158 V. Samsons 'Vācu', p.113.
159 LVVA R92/8, p. 22.
160 LVVA R92/8, pp. 1–5.
161 LVVA R92/8, pp. 23–36.
162 LVA 101.6.11, pp. 139–41.
163 Samsons, 'Vacu', p. 113.
164 BA R92/8, p. 26.
165 BA R92/8, p. 113–14.
166 BA R92/8, p. 50.
167 BA R92/4, p. 5.

168 LVA 101.6.11, p. 137.
169 DV 1.8.43.
170 DV 26.10.43.
171 LB10.11.43.
172 LB 9.2.44.
173 LB 15.6.44.
174 DV.13.10.43.
175 DV 16.10.43.
176 DV 16.11.43.
177 LVVA R-69.1a.8, p. 99.
178 LVVA R-70.5.4, p. 173.
179 DV 17.9.43.
180 DV 3&4.7.43.
181 DV 6.7.43.
182 DV 4.4.43.
183 DV 12.8.43.
184 DV 1.10.43.
185 *Latgolas Bolss* [hereafter LB] 3.10.43.
186 LB 6.6.43.
187 LB 3.10.43.
188 LVVA R-69.6.10, p. 23.
189 DV 23.10.43; DB 30.10.43; LB 3.11.43.
190 LVVA R-69.6.10, pp.26–8.
191 DV 28.11.43.
192 DV 30.11.43.
193 DB 26.1.44.
194 LVVA R-69.1a.29, p. 194.
195 LVVA R-69.1a.29, p. 196.
196 LVVA R-69.1a.29, p. 199.
197 LVA 301.1.29, pp. 26–8.
198 LVA 301.1.29, pp. 7–12.
199 LVA 301.1.29, pp. 26–8.
200 Samsons *K vesne*, pp. 107–8.
201 LVA 101.5.5. p. 83.
202 LVA 301.1.29, pp. 7–12.
203 Samsons, *K vesne*, pp. 108–9.
204 *Na pravyi*, p. 422.
205 Samsons, *K vesne*, pp. 112, 202.
206 LVA 302.1.29, p. 50.
207 BA R92/1022 (no page numbers).
208 BA R92/1022 (no page numbers).
209 LVVA R-69.1a.8, pp. 103, 110.
210 LVVA R-82.1.25, p. 12; 101.5.5, p. 122; ironically, Stromberg was suspected of having 'gone native' in 1941 by being too sympathetic to the local population; see BA R92/373 (no page numbers).
211 LVVA R-82.1.15, pp. 1–3.
212 LVVA R-82.1.15, p. 3.
213 LVVA R92/12, p. 322, p. 383.
214 LVA 101.6.11, p. 145.
215 LVA 101.5.5.106.
216 LVA 302.1.35, p. 2.
217 LVA 101.5.7, p. 35.
218 LVA 101.5.8, p. 56.
219 LVVA R-69.1a.8, p. 113.

220 LVVA R-82.1.14, p. 67.
221 *Na pravyi*, p. 422.
222 Samsons, *Partizanskoe dvizhenie*, p.168. It is interesting that Samsons only refers to these talks in his book published in 1951.
223 LVA 301.1.29, p. 23.
224 LVA 301.1.29, p. 46.
225 LVA 301.1.29, p. 46.
226 *Na pravyi*, p. 422.
227 Letter from Mr Gunārs Spodris of Bristol.
228 K. Sainsbury, *The Turning Point* (Oxford University Press: Oxford, 1985), p. 274.
229 *Pravda* 14.12.43.
230 DB 10.11.43.
231 DV 13, 14 &17.11.43.
232 DB 24.11.43.
233 DV 20.11.43.
234 DB 19&24.11.43.
235 DV 23.10.43; DB 30.10.43; LB 3.11.43.
236 DB 8.3.44.
237 LB 9.2.44.

6 Re-establishing Soviet Daugavpils

1 DB 3.11.43.
2 LB 9.2.44.
3 DV 3.3.44.
4 Dzintars, *Neredzamā*, p. 147.
5 DB 9.6.44.
6 V. Samsons, 'Latvijas valstiskuma idejā laikagriezos. Pēc vācu okupācijas laika dokumentiem, 1942–3 g.' *Latvijas PSR Zināņu Akadēmijas Vēstis*, 1990, no. 4, p. 15, citing the work of H. Biezais.
7 LVA 101.6.11, pp.12, 37.
8 LVA 101.6.11, p. 5.
9 LVA 101.6.11, p. 82.
10 LVA 302.1.29.30.
11 LVVA R92/468, p. 1, p. 5.
12 Samsons, *K vesne*, p. 172.
13 Samsons, *K vesne*, p. 203.
14 'Ocherki' 12, 1973, p. 42; Akademiya Nauk LSSR, *Istoriya LSSR* (Latvian Academy of Sciences: Riga, 1958), p. 564.
15 LVVA R-69.1a.29, p. 469.
16 LVVA 101.6.11, p. 208; H. Strods, in his *Latvijas nacionālo partizānu karš, 1944–56* (Preses Nams: Riga, 1996), p. 62, incorrectly dates this as May; however, he has spotted that the totals do not add up and that the grand total is 5,871 not 6,071 as given in the document.
17 Iwens, *How Dark*, p. 155.
18 Samsons, *Vesne*, p. 97.
19 Kapitanov, *Vozmezdie*, t, I, p. 131.
20 GARF 7021.93.19, p. 210.
21 Kononov was accused of war crimes in 1998 and the case went backwards and forwards to the Latvian Supreme Court until in 2003 it was decided that, since the villagers had been issued with arms by the Germans for self-defence, they were not civilian victims pure and simple. The charge was then reduced from war

crimes to banditry, on which a statute of limitations applies. I am grateful to Matthew Kott for summarising this tortuous affair for me.

22 DB 25.2.44.
23 LB 29.3.44; DB 5.4.44.
24 LB 12.4.44.
25 BA R92/1124 (no page number).
26 LB 3.5.44; DB 5.5.44.
27 DB 21.5.44.
28 BA R92/10042, pp. 1–8.
29 DB 13.2.44.
30 DB 26.5.44.
31 LB 11,12&17.7.44.
32 LVVA R-69.1a.29, pp. 432, 440, 443.
33 LVA 101.1.52, p. 132.
34 A. A. Drizul (ed.), *Bor'ba latyshkogo naroda v gody Velikoi Otechestvennoi Voiny, 1941–5 gg.* (Latvian Academy of Sciences: Riga, 1970), pp. 171–3; 217; 604–7.
35 Šteiman, 'Daugavpils, 1940–50', p. 118.
36 LVA 101.5.1, p. 18.
37 LVA 101.3.8, p. 7.
38 LVA 101.3.9, pp. 11, 14, 29, 42.
39 A. Udris, 'Podgotovka sovetsko-partiinykh rabotnikov LSSR i ikh deyatel'nost' v operativnykh gruppakh na osvobozhdenoi ot gitlerovskikh okkupantov territorii respubliki, 1944–45 gg.', in *Izvestiya akademii nauk LSSR*, no. 12, 1966, p. 27.
40 *Seichas*, 25.7.02.
41 Šteiman, 'Daugavpils', p. 136.
42 LVA 101.3.10, p. 15.
43 LVA 101.6.11, p. 194.
44 GARF 7021.93.3736, p. 16.
45 Šteiman, 'Daugavpils', p. 136; Drizul', 'Bor'ba', p. 740.
46 LVA 103.2.2, p. 1.
47 LVA 101.3.10, p. 15.
48 Šteiman, 'Daugavpils', pp. 137–43. Fridman attended the city committee meeting on 31 August 1944, but then his name disappears; see LVA 103.2.2, p. 3.
49 LVA 103.2.5, p. 17.
50 LVA 103.2.5, pp. 54, 71.
51 LVA 103.4.1, p. 15.
52 Šteiman, *Lyudi i vremya*, p. 67.
53 LP 25.7.44.
54 LVA 116.2.2, pp. 1, 4.
55 LVA 101.7.11, p. 18.
56 LVA 101.3.5, p. 35.
57 LVA 101.3.7, pp. 14, 115–17.
58 LVA 101.3.13, p.64.
59 LVA 101.7.4, pp. 104, 183–7, 216–7; 101.7.13, p. 76.
60 LVA 101.7.14, p. 92.
61 LVA 116.2.2, p. 228.
62 LVA 101.7.14, p. 161.
63 LVA 101.9.6, p. 153.
64 LVA 116.2.2, pp. 76–80.
65 LVA 103.2.5, p. 58.
66 LVA 116.2.2, p. 139.
67 LVA 116.2.2, p. 165.
68 LP 29.5.45.
69 LVA 116.2.1, p. 19.

70 LP 1.7.45.
71 LP 14.9.45.
72 LP 6.9.45.
73 LVA 103.2.5, p. 115.
74 LVA 103.2.5, p. 115.
75 Strods, *Partizānu karš,* p. 356.
76 LVA 101.7.18, pp. 5–6.
77 LVA 101.7.6, p. 259.
78 I. Saleniece, 'Sovetskie voiny glazami zhitelei Latvii: 40–e gg. XX veka (po istochnikam ustnoi istorii)', unpublished conference paper, Daugavpils University, 2002.
79 LVA 101.6.8, pp. 2, 9.
80 Saleniece, 'Sovetskie voiny'.
81 LVA 101.6.21, pp. 16–20.
82 Russian State Archive for Social and Political Research [hereafter RGASPI] 600.1.3, p. 33.
83 LVA 101.6.8, p. 26.
84 LVA 116.2.2, p. 1.
85 LP 17.8.44.
86 LVA 101.3.5, pp. 14–18.
87 LVA 101.3.5, pp. 33, 53, 97.
88 LVA 101.3.5, p. 14.
89 LVA 101.3.10, p. 57.
90 LVA 101.3.10, p. 77.
91 LVA 101.3.11, p. 9.
92 LVA 101.3.11, p. 75.
93 J. Riekstiņš (ed.), *Represijas Latvijasl laukos, 1944–49* (Latvijas Valsts Arhīvs: Riga, 2000), p. 18. There is a possible error here. In November 1944 Nikonov was still district secretary for Abrene, not Daugavpils. It is therefore possible that these trials took place in Abrene. I have not had the opportunity to double-check this against the archival reference LVA 101.3.7, p. 43.
94 LVA 101.3.11, p. 100.
95 LVA 101.6.1, p. 12.
96 LP 24.10.44.
97 LVA 101.3.7, p. 11.
98 LVA 101.3.7, p. 30.
99 LP 26.11.44.
100 LVA 116.2.1, p. 2.
101 LVA 101.3.13, p. 35.
102 LVA 116.2.1, p. 8.
103 LP 22.12.44.
104 LVA 116.2.2, p. 85.
105 LP 4&5.1.45.
106 LP 7.2.45.
107 LVA 116.2.2, p. 121.
108 LP 29.5.45.
109 LVA 116.2.2, p. 174.
110 LP 1.7.45.
111 LP 24.4.45.
112 LP 3&4.7.45.
113 LVA 101.7.44, pp. 21–7. The date of this meeting is not given, but can be inferred from a pencil note in the margin of LVA 101.3.12, p. 80.
114 LVA 101.3.10, p. 6.
115 LVA 101.3.15a, p. 1.

116 LP 25.7.44.
117 LP 7.9.44.
118 LP 3.10.44.
119 LP 26.8.44.
120 LVA 103.2.2, p. 3.
121 LP 24.10.44.
122 LP 1.11.44. The memorial which still stands in the Railwaymen's Garden makes no specific mention of the Jewish victims.
123 LP 30.11.44, 10.12.44 & 22.12.44. Although the date for the start of the excavations is given as 26 November on 30.11.44, in the account of 22.12.44 it is stated that the visit took place on 24 November.
124 LP 14, 21, 24.7.45.
125 LP 27.7.45; and Šteiman *Daugavpils v proshlom*, p. 87.
126 LP 4.2.46.
127 LP 31.1.45.
128 LVA 103.2.1, pp. 1–2.
129 LP 7.9.44.
130 LVA 103.2.1, pp.1–2.
131 LP 27.9.44.
132 LP 14.1.45.
133 LVA 103.2.2, p. 23.
134 LVA 101.3.11, p. 90.
135 LVA 103.2.1, p. 7.
136 LVA 103.2.2, p. 106.
137 LVA 101.7.10, p 136.
138 LVA 101.7.10, p. 128.
139 LVA 103.2.2, p. 129.
140 LVA 101.7.13, p. 44.
141 LVA 101.7.13, p. 44.
142 LVA 101.7.13, p. 45.
143 LVA 101.7.4, pp. 34, 57, 72, 101.
144 LP 20&2,2.6.45.
145 LVA 103.2.5, p. 70. This appointment was confirmed by Riga on 1 July 1945 some time after he actually took on the job.
146 LVA 103.2.1, pp. 41–50.
147 LP 3&4.7.45.
148 LVA 103.2.1, p. 57.
149 LP 10.7.45.
150 LP 27.7.45.
151 LVA 103.2.21, p. 63.
152 LP 18.10.45.
153 LP 16.9.45.
154 LVA 103.2.21, p. 62.
155 LVA 103.2.21, p. 63.
156 Šteiman, *Vremya i lyudi*, p. 66, and his 'Daugavpils', p. 169.
157 LVA 103.2.21, p. 118.
158 LP 18.10.45.
159 LP 16.11.45.
160 LVA 103.2.20, p. 3; 103.4.2, p. 1.
161 LVA 103.4.5, p. 12.
162 There is a picture of the nearly completed water tower in LP 16.10.46; the inability of the authorities to provide the population with a timetable for when they might receive water during the day was discussed at the city party conference on 1–2 December 1945; LVA 103.2.20, p. 3.

163 LVA 103.2.1, p. 2.
164 LVA 103.2.1, p. 4.
165 LVA 103.2.1, p. 19.
166 LP 31.1.45.
167 LP 31.1.45.
168 LP 1&11.9.44.
169 LVA 103.2.2, p. 71.
170 LP 14.3.45.
171 LVA 103.2.2, p. 176.
172 LVA 116.2.2, p. 181.
173 LVA 103.2.21, p. 57.
174 LVA 103.2.21, p. 66.
175 LVA 103.2.1, p. 65.
176 LP 9.10.45; 19.11.45.
177 LP 10, 17.12.44, 12, 21.1.45.
178 LVA 103.2.1, p. 7.
179 LP 8.6.45, 19.7.45.
180 LVA 101.9.12, p. 40.
181 LVA 116.5.2, p. 2.
182 LVA 103.4.2, p. 158; 103.2.22, p. 70.
183 LVA 103.2.2, p. 23.
184 LVA 103.2.1, p. 7.
185 LP 5.12.44.
186 LVA 103.2.2, p. 100.
187 LVA 103.4.2, p. 67.
188 LVA 103.4.4, p. 49.

7 The nationalist partisan war

 1 LVA 101.6.21, pp. 20–1.
 2 LVA 101.6.21, pp. 24, 28.
 3 LVA101.3.7, p. 18.
 4 LVA 116.2.2, p. 43.
 5 LVA116.2.2, p. 32. Muzykantik's career was summarised when he joined the party on 25 December 1944; see LVA 116.2.2, p. 53; Titov came from the Russian town Murom where other Latvian exiles had spent the war years; see LVA 103.2.5, p. 93.
 6 LVA 101.6.21, pp. 49–53. Often the leaders are referred to as *aizsargs*; but by the end of the war this term was being used to describe anyone with a past in the security forces, whether or not they were linked to the real pre-war *aizsarg* organisation.
 7 LVA 101.6.21, p. 58.
 8 RGASPI 600.1.4, p. 17; another report describes the death of an 11-year-old son and the wounding of the man's wife and elder son; see LVA 101.3.15a, p. 10.
 9 LVA 101.3.15a, p. 10.
10 LVA 101.8.18, p. 3.
11 LVA 101.8.18, p. 9.
12 RGASPI 600.1.4, p. 17.
13 RGASPI 600.1.4, p. 5.
14 LVA 101.8.18, p. 11.
15 LP 21.1.45. A report on 2.3.45 gave more details about Vārkava. The surnames of those accused of these crimes is given in the paper, but it has proved impossible to establish whether they existed, let alone whether they were responsible.

16 LP 15.4.45. The survivor was named as S. Goldov who had escaped by simply running away from the execution pit, reaching the cover of the forest, and living on the fringes of society for the rest of the war.

17 LP 20.5.45.

18 Šteiman, 'Daugavpils', p. 172.

19 LP 28.2.45.

20 LVA 101.7.11, p. 19; 101.8.9, pp. 58–60.

21 LVA 103.2.1, p. 24.

22 LVA 116.2.1, p. 10.

23 LVA 103.2.2, p. 144.

24 LVA 101.6.21, pp. 56–8.

25 LVA 101.3.5, p. 13.

26 LVA 101.3.5, pp. 13, 35.

27 LVA 101.3.7, p. 75.

28 LVA 101.8.19, pp 8–9. This incident is also touched on in Strods, *Partizānu karš*, p. 127.

29 LVA 101.8.38, p. 16. The case was complicated by the fact that the Ilūkste secretary, Matužs, initially tried to win the prosecutor bringing the case to his side by flirting with her; when she refused to join his campaign against the security forces, he turned against her and started spreading gossip about her sex life, prompting her to issue a formal complaint.

30 LVA 101.7.3, p. 14.

31 LVA 101.7.31a, p. 8.

32 LVA 101.7.44, p. 3. This meeting is briefly referred to in Strods, *Partizānu karš*, p. 249.

33 H. Strods, 'The Roman Catholic Church of Latvia and the Resistance Movement, 1944–1990' in A Anušauskas (ed.) *The Anti-Soviet Resistance in the Baltic States* (Du Ka: Vilnius, 2000), p. 178.

34 LVA 101.7.44, p. 5.

35 LVA 101.7.31a, p. 8. On 5 May 1945 Kalnbērziņš wrote to Moscow requesting extra financial support for the destroyer battalions, LVA 101.8.18. p. 32.

36 LVA 101.7.31a, p. 12.

37 LVA 101.7.31a, p. 23.

38 LVA 101.7.44, p. 8.

39 LVA 101.8.18, pp. 40–4.

40 LVA 101.8.18, p. 55.

41 RGASPI 600.1.4, pp.60, 101.

42 LVA 101.8.18, p. 49.

43 RGASPI 600.1.4, p. 105; 101.8.18, p. 146.

44 LVA 101.8.18, pp. 90–3; 101.9.69, pp. 88–9.

45 LVA 101.8.63a, p. 27; there is another copy of this report in LVA 116.2.2, p. 152.

46 LVA 116.2.2, p. 163.

47 LVA 116.2.1, p. 18.

48 LVA 116.2.1, p. 25.

49 LVA 101.7.4, p. 115.

50 LVA 116.2.2, p. 200.

51 LVA 103.2.5, p. 78.

52 LVA 116.2.3, p. 72.

53 LVA 103.2.1, p. 52.

54 LVA 116.2.1, pp. 25–8.

55 LVA 101.8.18, pp. 18–19.

56 LVA 101.8.18, p. 90.

57 LP 3.6.45.

58 PRO FO371 43052, pp. 3, 6–9.

59 PRO FO371 47061 (no page numbers).
60 PRO FO371 43052, p. 90.
61 T. Bower, *The Red Web* (Aurum Press: London, 1989), pp. 30–79.
62 Strods, *Partizānu karš*, p. 302. As Professor Strods comments, there is no way of knowing whether this was genuine material or material planted by the NKVD, who were by then already in contact with Juhnēvičs. That the partisans wanted to believe they were in touch with the British clarifies their political orientation.
63 LP 9.8.45.
64 LP 22.8.45.
65 LP 20.5.45.
66 LP 22.8.45.
67 Strods, *Partizānu karš*, p. 186.
68 LVA 101.9.73, p. 73.
69 Strods, *Partizānu karš*, p. 189.
70 Strods, *Partizānu karš*, p. 204.
71 Strods, *Partizānu karš*, p. 192.
72 Strods, *Partizānu karš*, p. 195.
73 RGASPI 600.1.4, p. 150.
74 Strods, *Partizānu karš*, p. 285.
75 LVA 101.9.69, p. 104.
76 LP 19.9.45.
77 LP 27.9.45; all 18 were named, five had Slavonic names.
78 LP 18.10.45; all had Latvian names.
79 LP 30.10.45; ten names were given and all were Latvian.
80 LP 22.9.45; of the 16 names given, 15 were Latvian.
81 LVA 101.8.18, p. 177.
82 LVA 101.8.18, p. 188.
83 The letter was published in LP 29.11.45.
84 LVA 103.2.20, p. 4.
85 LVA 116.2.1, p. 37.
86 LVA 101.8.63a, p. 33.
87 LVA 116.5.2, p. 3.
88 LVA 103.2.20, p. 4.
89 LVA 116.2.1, p. 37.
90 LVA 101.7.17, pp. 46, 127.
91 LVA 101.9.73, p. 73.
92 Strods, *Partizānu karš*, p. 195.
93 Strods, *Partizānu karš*, p. 193.
94 Strods, *Partizānu karš*, p. 207.
95 Strods, *Partizānu karš*, pp. 236–7.
96 Strods, *Partizānu karš*, p. 302.
97 Strods, *Partizānu karš*, p. 237.
98 LP 13.2.46. He was arrested later in 1946 and executed in Riga prison; see Strods, 'The Roman Catholic Church', p. 177.
99 LVA 101.9.69, p. 23.
100 Strods, *Partizānu karš*, p. 206.
101 Strods, *Partizānu karš*, p. 415.
102 LVA 101.9.73, p. 73.
103 Strods, *Partizānu karš*, pp. 192–3.
104 Strods, *Partizānu karš*, pp. 192–3.
105 LP 13.2.46.
106 LVA 101.9.2, p. 20.
107 PRO FO 371 47062 (no page numbers).
108 LP 22.8.45.

109 LP 19.9.45.
110 LVA 116.2.2, pp. 172, 180.
111 LP 1.7.45.
112 LVA 101.7.19, p. 44.
113 LP 31.8.45.
114 LP 20.9.45.
115 LVA 116.2.3, pp. 34–6, 42.
116 LP 1.11.45.
117 LVA 101.9.72, pp. 1–21. These events are briefly summarised in Strods, *Partizānu karš*, p. 133.
118 LVA 101.8.20, p. 339.
119 LVA 116.5.4, p. 22.
120 LVA 101.9.35a, pp. 8–10, 136–40.
121 LP 1.7.45.
122 LVA 116.2.2, p. 265.
123 LVA 116.2.2, p. 73.
124 D. Kļaviņa, *Represijas Latvijas laukos, 1944–9* (Latvijas Valsts Arhīvs: Riga, 2000), p. 183. The same incident is referred to in LVA 101.9.69, p. 8.
125 LVA 116.5.4, p. 3.
126 LVA 101.9.73, pp. 73.
127 LVA 101.9.73, p. 176.
128 LVA 101.9.72, p. 92.
129 LVA 101.9.61. p. 1.
130 LVA 101.9.69, pp. 97–100.

8 Stalinist Daugavpils

 1 LVA 101.7.18, pp. 39, 187.
 2 LVA 101.9.2, pp. 122–3, 126.
 3 LVA 101.9.55, p. 92.
 4 LP 11&13.1.46.
 5 LVA 101.7.44, p. 26. The date of this meeting is not given in this document, but can be inferred from a pencil note in the margin of LVA 101.3.12, p. 80.
 6 LVA 101.9.55, p. 88.
 7 LVA 101.9.55, p. 13.
 8 LVA 101.9.55, p. 88.
 9 LVA 101.9.55, p. 9.
10 LVA 103.4.2, p. 60.
11 LP 10.1.46.
12 LVA 103.4.2, p. 55. Despite being criticised for calling Smagars Jānis rather than Ivan, the paper continued to do so as any survey of the paper at this time will reveal.
13 LVA 103.3.3, p. 2.
14 LVA 101.9.110a, p. 40.
15 LVA 101.9.2, pp. 20–1.
16 LVA 101.9.55, pp. 27–8.
17 LVA 101.9.55, pp. 85–6, 92.
18 LVA 116.5.2, p. 3.
19 LVA 101.9.55, p. 26.
20 LVA 101.9.2, p. 123.
21 LVA 101.9.55, p. 93.
22 LVA 101.9.55, p. 101.
23 LVA 103.4.2, p. 93.
24 LVA 101.9.2, p. 52.
25 LVA 101.9.55, p. 93.

26 The prevalence of such views among Latvian intellectual circles is asserted by Bernhard Press in his *The Murder of the Jews in Latvia, 1941–45* (Northwestern University Press: Evanston, 2000), p. 194. That such feelings were common among members of the Latvian Division is clear from a personal letter to me from Iosif Šteiman on 7 August 2000; the extension to volunteers for the partisan movement comes from a study of the career paths of former partisans, who soon drifted away from the party altogether or become involved in the various national communist groups resistant to Moscow's line.
27 LVA 101.9.4, p. 26.
28 LP 20.4.46.
29 LVA 101.9.2, p, 131.
30 LVA 101.9.6, p. 198.
31 LVA 101.9.14, p. 54.
32 LVA 103.4.5, p. 50.
33 Z Yakub, *Daugavpils v proshlom* (A.K.A: Daugavpils, 1998), p. 161.
34 Šteiman, *Daugavpils v proshlom*, p. 100.
35 Yakub, *Daugavpils*, p. 165.
36 LP 21.5.46.
37 LP 26.5.46.
38 LP 16.6.46.
39 LP 11.9.46.
40 LVA 103.4.5, pp. 157, 197.
41 LP 27&29.9.46.
42 LP 16.10.46.
43 LP 5.11.46.
44 LP 7.11.46.
45 15,17&19.11.46.
46 LP 13.3.46.
47 LP 3.12.46.
48 LVA 101.9.73, p. 9.
49 LP 27.2.46.
50 LP 9.5.46.
51 LVA 103.4.4, pp. 50, 59.
52 LVA 103.4.1, p. 62.
53 LVA 101.9.73, p. 197.
54 LVA 103.4.6, p. 72.
55 LVA 103.4.6, p. 11.
56 LVA 116.5.7, p. 7.
57 LVA 103.4.1, p. 3; 103.4.6, pp. 53, 114.
58 Šteiman, *Vremya i lyudi*, p. 66.
59 LVA 101.9.55, p. 93.
60 LVA 103.4.1, pp. 33–9.
61 LVA 101.9.17, pp. 23, 86–7.
62 LVA 103.4.4, p. 25.
63 LVA 103.4.5, p. 111.
64 LP 14.6.46.
65 LVA 116.5.3, p. 45.
66 LVA 103.4.4, p. 77.
67 LVA 116.5.4, p. 56.
68 LVA 116.5.2, pp. 14, 18.
69 LVA 101.9.35a, p. 21.
70 LVA 101.9.69, p. 58.
71 LVA 101.9.69, p. 77.
72 LVA 101.9.69, p. 63.

73 LP 5.6.46.
74 LVA 116.5.3, p. 28.
75 LVA 101.9.69, p. 84. This short report refers to an attached detailed account, which has not been preserved in the archives. This incident is summarised in Strods, *Partizānu karš*, p. 155.
76 LVA 116.5.4, p. 221.
77 LVA 101.9.110a, p. 40.
78 LVA 101.9.6, p. 171.
79 Strods, *Partizānu karš*, p. 420.
80 LVA 116.5.3, pp. 45–8.
81 LVA 101.9.6, p. 172.
82 RGASPI 600.1.15, pp. 119–21, 143–6; LVA 101.9.54, pp. 64–75.
83 LP 24.7.46.
84 LP 11.9.46.
85 Strods, *Partizānu karš*, p. 355.
86 LVA 116.5.5, p. 134.
87 LVA 101.9.110a, p. 49.
88 LVA 101.10.75, p. 3.
89 LVA 101.9.69, pp. 159–62. The activities of this unit are summarised in Strods, *Partizānu karš*, p. 299.
90 LVA 101.9.69, p. 115.
91 Strods, *Partizānu karš*, pp. 200, 420.
92 LVA 101.9.110a, p. 47.
93 LVA 101.10.75, p. 3.
94 LVA 101.9.110a, p. 47.
95 LVA 116.5.5, p. 181.
96 LVA 116.5.4, p. 163.
97 LVA 116.5.3, p. 10.
98 LVA 116.5.3, p. 31.
99 LVA 116.5.3, p. 31.
100 LVA 116.5.4, p. 235.
101 LP 26.6.46.
102 LP 7.7.46.
103 LVA 116.5.4, p. 217.
104 LVA 101.9.73, p. 116.
105 RGASPI 600.1.11, pp. 11, 27.
106 LVA 101.9.110a, p. 47.
107 LP 25.10.46.
108 LVA 101.9.110a, p. 47.
109 LP 13.10.46.
110 LP 23.10.46.
111 LVA 116.5.3, p. 10.
112 LVA 116.5.4, p. 236; 116.5.5, p. 8.
113 LVA 116.5.5, p. 59.
114 LVA 101.10.75, p. 8.
115 LVA 101.9.73, p. 183.
116 LVA 103.4.5, p. 113.
117 LVA 116.5.5, p. 88.
118 LVA 116.5.3, pp. 6, 12.
119 LVA 116.5.5, p. 72; for reasons which remain mysterious, on 3 September 1946 *Latgal'skaya Pravda* published a picture of some of the horticultural students tending their flowers.
120 LVA 116.2.1, p. 37.
121 LVA 101.8.2, pp. 116–17.

122 LVA 103.4.4, p. 36.
123 LVA 103.2.22, pp. 69–70.
124 LVA 103.2.5, p.18.
125 LVA 103.2.5, p. 78.
126 LP 10.8.45.
127 LP 27.8.45.
128 LVA 103.2.5, p. 125.
129 LVA 101.8.2, pp. 116–17.
130 LVA 103.4.2, p. 25.
131 LP 26.8.44; LVA 103.2.2, p. 3.
132 Letter from Iosif Šteiman, 10.7.2003.
133 LP 13.1.46.
134 LVA 103.4.4, p. 16.
135 LVA 103.4.4, p. 49.
136 LP 25.8.46.
137 LVA 103.4.1, p. 63.
138 I. Saleniece, 'Teachers as the Object and Subject of Sovietization in Latvia: Daugavpils 1944–53' in O. Mertelsmann (ed.) *The Sovietization of the Baltic States, 1940–1956* (Tartu: Kleio, 2003), pp. 201–5.
139 LVA 103.4.1, p. 78.
140 LVA 101.9.55, pp, 96–7.
141 RGASPI 600.1.11, p. 27.
142 LVA 101.9.6, p. 217.
143 RGASPI 600.1.11, p. 16.
144 RGASPI 600.1.23, p. 2.
145 RGASPI 600.1.13, p. 59.
146 LVA116.5.5, p. 181.
147 LVA 116.5.4, p. 76.
148 Šteiman, 'Daugavpils', p. 207.
149 RGASPI 600.1.12, p. 65.
150 LVA 101.9.4, p. 1.
151 RGASPI 600.1.12, p. 155.
152 LVA 101.8.2, p. 59.
153 LVA 101.9.2, p. 52.
154 LP 18.4.46.
155 LVA 103.4.4, p. 35.
156 LP 11.9.46.
157 LVA 103.4.4, p. 35.
158 LVA 103.2.22, pp. 43–6;103.2.5, p. 125.
159 LVA 103.2.2, p. 117. His membership was endorsed by the city committee on 26.2.45.
160 L P 24.10.44 & 16.11.44.
161 LP 4.1.45 & 9.5.45.
162 LP 6.7.45.
163 LP 13.11.46.
164 LVA 103.4.1, p. 60.
165 Letter from Iosif Šteiman, 10.7.2003.

Conclusion

1 FO 371/56753 (no page numbers).
2 The delay in collectivisation is the theme of G. Swain, 'Deciding to Collectivise Latvian Agriculture' *Europe–Asia Studies*, vol. 55, no. 1, 2003.

3 Saleniece and Kuznetsov, 'Nationality Policy, Education and the Russian Question in Latvia', pp. 248, 259. Russians were 17 per cent of the population of Daugavpils in 1925.

4 Alexander Dallin, *Odessa, 1941–44: A Case Study of Soviet Territory under Foreign Rule* (Centre for Romanian Studies: London, 1998), p. 11.

5 Dallin, *Odessa*. Here I am essentially summarising the whole book, but see pp. 92, 93, 105, 114, 124, 145, 165, 175, 179 and 231. The fate of the Jews is discussed on pp. 206–9; there Dallin suggests that about two-thirds of Odessa's 175,000 Jewish residents at the start of the war escaped to the east, hence my figure of 60,000 as the Romanians took over.

6 Amir Weiner, *Making Sense of War: The Second World War and the Fate of the Bolshevik Revolution* (Princeton University Press: Princeton, 2001).

7 Weiner, *Making Sense*. This is essentially a brief summary of a long book. See pp. 60, 67, 70, 73, 79, 111, 114, 156–8, 170, 178, 246, 260 and 276. The quoted passage is p. 209.

8 Weiner *Making Sense*, pp. 172–6, pp. 305–7.

9 This figure is calculated from statistics given in *Kommunisticheskaya Partiya Latvii v tsifrakh* (Riga, 1972), p. 40. For Vinnytsia, see Weiner, *Making Sense*, p. 156.

10 BA R92/705 appendix 15.

11 LVA 101.2.54, p. 54.

12 LVA 116.54, p. 43.

13 I am aware that some might retort, what about the 50,000 victims of Latvian collectivisation in 1949? An educated guess would put the figure deported from Daugavpils district at this time at 3,500–4,000, bringing the total closer to the Nazis' figure, although still lower. My reason for discounting the victims of 1949 is because this was not a pre-emptive move to cope with a military danger, but an integral part of one of Stalin's social policies.

14 Iwens, *How Dark*, p. 30.

15 For 1943, see LVA 101.5.6, p. 154; for 1945, see RGASPI 600.1.3, p. 33.

16 Weiner, *Making Sense*, p. 7.

17 Weiner, *Making Sense*, p. 298.

18 DV 26.7.42.

19 Šteiman, *Vremya i lyudi*, pp. 19–21.

20 DV 16.7.43.

21 Kalnbērziņš's visit to Moscow is discussed in G. Swain, '"Cleaning up Soviet Latvia": the Bureau for Latvia (Latburo)' in O. Mertelsmann (ed.) *The Sovietization of the Baltic States, 1940–5* (Tartu: Kleio, 2003), pp. 64–6.

Bibliographical note

This book is based primarily on archival documents and the contemporary press. In the Latvian State Archives in Riga the *fonds* consulted were the voluminous 101, the Central Committee of the Latvian Communist Party; 103, the Daugavpils City Committee of the Communist Party; 116, the Daugavpils District Committee of the Communist Party; and 301 and 302, material relating to the Soviet partisan movement. In the Latvian State Historical Archive in Riga the main *fonds* consulted were R-69, R-70, R-82 and R-84, all relating to the German occupation of Latvia. In the Bundesarchiv in Berlin, files relating to the German occupation of Latvia were consulted, in particular R70 Sowjetunion, R91/ Dünaburg, and the extensive R92. In the Russian State Archive for Social and Political Research in Moscow the *fond* consulted was 600, the Latvian Bureau of the Central Committee of the All-Union Communist Party (Bolsheviks). In the Public Record Office in London the documents consulted were some of the FO 371 files relating to Latvia, 29267, 43052, 47045, 47061, 47062 and 65753. In the State Archive of the Russian Federation in Moscow Dmitrijs Olehnovičs consulted parts of *fond* 7021, in particular *opis'* 93, the records of the Extraordinary Commission Investigating Nazi Barbarity in the Occupied Soviet Union.

The newspapers consulted were: *Latgal'skaya Pravda*, 1940–1 and 1944–6; *Daugavpils latviešu avīze*, 1941; *Daugavas vēstnesis*, 1941–4; *Dvinskii vestnik*, 1942–4; *Latgolas Bolss*, 1943–4; and *Rēzeknes ziņas*, 1941–4.

The following secondary works, published document collections and memoirs have been cited more than once:

A. Anušauskas (ed.), *The Anti-Soviet Resistance in the Baltic States* (Du Ka: Vilnius, 2000).

J. Dzintars, *Neredzamā fronte* (Riga, 1970).

A. Ezergailis, *The Holocaust in Latvia, 1941–44: The Missing Center* (Historical Institute of Latvia: Riga, 1996).

S. Iwens, *How Dark the Heavens: 1400 Days in the Grip of Nazi Terror* (Shengold Publishers: New York, 1990).

I. G. Kapitanov, *Vozmedie* t. I (Riga, 1977).

I. G. Kapitanov, *Vozmezdie* t. II (Riga, 1980).

Latvijas Vēsturnieku Komisijas Raksti (6 sējums), *1941. gada 14. jūnija deportācija: Noziegums prēt cilvēci* (Latvijas Véstures Institūta Apgāda: Riga, 2002).

LSSR Archive Directorate, *My obvinyaem* (Riga, 1967).

Na pravyi boi, na smertnyi boi: sbornik vospominanii i dokumentov (Riga, 1968).

I. Rochko, 'Zhertvy, spasennye i spasiteli' in B. Volkovich *et al.* (eds) *Kholokost v Latgalii* (V Prints: Daugavpils, 2003).

V. Samsons, *No Lovates līdz Zilupei* (Riga, 1987).

V. Samsons, *Partizanskoe dvizhenie v severnoi Latvii v gody Velikoi Otechestvennoi voiny* (Riga, 1951).

V. Samsons, *Druzhba narodov pobedila: sovmestnye deistvie krasnykh partisan i sovet-skikh razvedchikov v 'Kurlandskom kotle' b 1944–5 gg.* (Riga, 1980).

V. Samsons, *K vesne* (Riga, 1989).

V. Samsons, 'Vācu drošības policijas un SD 'Latgales Akcijas'' *Latvijas Zinātņu. Akadēmijas Véstis*, 1990, no. 12.

A. Silgailis, *Latvian Legion* (New York: James Benner Publishing, 1986).

B. Spridzāns, 'Tā sākās Latvijas iedzīvotāju masveida represijas', *Represēto saraksts: 1941*, no. 1, Riga, 1995.

I. Šteiman, *Vremya i lyudi* (Latgale Cultural Centre: Rézekne, 2001).

I. Šteiman *et al.*, *Daugavpils v proshlom i nastoyashchem* (Riga, 1959).

J. Šteimanis (I. Šteiman), *History of the Latvian Jews* (East European Monographs: Boulder, 2002).

H. Strods, *Latvijas nacionālo partizānu karš, 1944–56* (Preses Nams: Riga, 1996).

Z. Yakub, *Daugavpils v proshlom* (AKA: Daugavpils, 1998).

Two unpublished memoirs have also been cited more than once:

S. Shpungin, 'Do i posle pobega', Testimony from the Yad Vashem Memorial, Israel, 2001.

I. Šteiman, 'Daugavpils, 1940–50'.

Index